Microsoft SharePoint 2013: Designing and Architecting Solutions

Shannon Bray
Miguel Wood
Patrick Curran

D1537713

ISBN: 978-0-7356-7168-3

Third Printing: August 2015

Printed and bound in the United States of America.

Microsoft Press books are available through booksellers and distributors worldwide. If you need support related to this book, email Microsoft Press Book Support at *mspinput@microsoft.com*. Please tell us what you think of this book at *http://www.microsoft.com/learning/booksurvey*.

Microsoft and the trademarks listed at *http://www.microsoft.com/about/legal/en/us/IntellectualProperty/Trademarks/EN-US.aspx* are trademarks of the Microsoft group of companies. All other marks are property of their respective owners.

The example companies, organizations, products, domain names, email addresses, logos, people, places, and events depicted herein are fictitious. No association with any real company, organization, product, domain name, email address, logo, person, place, or event is intended or should be inferred.

This book expresses the author's views and opinions. The information contained in this book is provided without any express, statutory, or implied warranties. Neither the authors, Microsoft Corporation, nor its resellers, or distributors will be held liable for any damages caused or alleged to be caused either directly or indirectly by this book.

Acquisitions and Developmental Editor: Kenyon Brown

Production Editor: Christopher Hearse

Editorial Production: S4Carlisle Publishing Services

Technical Reviewer: Chris Givens

Indexer: Bob Pfahler, Potomac Indexing, LLC

Cover Composition: Ellie Volckhausen

Illustrator: S4Carlisle Publishing Services

Contents at a glance

Contents

Chapter 3   Gathering requirements   61

PART II   DESIGN CONSIDERATIONS FOR MICROSOFT SHAREPOINT 2013

Chapter 4   Understanding the service application model   91

What do you think of this book? We want to hear from you!

Microsoft is interested in hearing your feedback so we can continually improve our
books and learning resources for you. To participate in a brief online survey, please visit:

microsoft.com/learning/booksurvey

What do you think of this book? We want to hear from you!

Microsoft is interested in hearing your feedback so we can continually improve our
books and learning resources for you. To participate in a brief online survey, please visit:

microsoft.com/learning/booksurvey

PART III   CONCEPTS FOR INFRASTRUCTURE RELIABILITY

Chapter 9   Maintaining and monitoring Microsoft SharePoint   297

Chapter 10 Planning your business continuity strategy   339

Chapter 11   Validating your architecture   375

Introduction

Welcome to *Microsoft SharePoint 2013: Designing and Architecting Solutions*. The purpose of this book is to help Microsoft SharePoint professionals understand the Microsoft SharePoint 2013 architecture and give them the tools they need to be successful in planning, designing, building, and validating infrastructure architectures. As with previous versions of SharePoint, SharePoint 2013 contains many features with which you will be familiar. Some features have not changed at all; others will have changed, but at a high level, and will provide similar functionality that will not be new to you. However, there are new components that you will need time to understand fully before you can decide how they will benefit you and your organization.

With this version of SharePoint, Microsoft focuses on various implementations whether they exist on premises, in the cloud, or a combination of the two. With the focus now on social collaboration and the ability to share content in a variety of ways, how you build your implementation will define how users can share, organize, discover, build, and manage ideas and content in a SharePoint environment.

The following descriptions define these concepts further:

- **Share**   You can share your content and information, spreading it socially, spreading it online, and spreading it easily across multiple places and devices where you might need to interconnect, whether it is on premises, mobile, tablet, in a cloud, or at a client site.

- **Organize**   This is how you structure and categorize the information, whether it is project, team, or information held in documents using Microsoft Office 2013 applications, such as Microsoft Outlook or Microsoft Project, and syncing your content in SharePoint to your desktop with Microsoft SkyDrive Pro.

- **Discover**   This concept includes connecting people across your organization, the discovery of insights and answers through the use of business intelligence, and finding what you're looking for by using enterprise Search. In this version of SharePoint, Microsoft has invested a great deal of effort into the integration of enterprise Search.

- **Build**   SharePoint 2013 has undergone major changes to the application model for how to build applications that are hosted on systems that are maintained by organizations, on premises, or when the systems are maintained outside the control of an organization, in the cloud; how to publish these applications internally through a corporate catalog; and how to publish them outside an organization, as well as sharing them across on-premises farms and cloud-based farms through a public store. The new application mode also makes it possible for applications to be shared within Microsoft Office applications using the new Windows 8 interface computers, laptops, Ultrabooks, tablets, and Windows Phone. These are now introduced to the Office 2013 applications.

- **Manage**   SharePoint 2013 provides better support for managing SharePoint as a platform. It can be run in the cloud with Microsoft Office 365. It contains new archiving, eDiscovery, and case management capabilities that include SharePoint 2013, Microsoft Exchange Server 2013, and Microsoft Lync 2013.

You can find more details about Office 365 at office365.microsoft.com.

Microsoft still aims for SharePoint to be a self-service product; that is, a product that provides users with the ability to complete their tasks with no-code solutions by using the browser and Office applications.

SharePoint 2013 consists of two products: Microsoft SharePoint Foundation 2013 and Microsoft SharePoint Server 2013. The exposure of two sets of functionality still exists and is implemented using standard and enterprise client access licenses with a new licensing model. There is no longer a separate Microsoft FAST Search Server for SharePoint. You will find much of the functionality that was included in that product now incorporated as part of SharePoint 2013. Another change is that Office Web Apps (OWA) is a separate product and should be installed on servers on which SharePoint is not installed. Also, if your organization is a heavy user of SharePoint to automate business processes, there are changes that allow you to distribute the workflow business logic onto servers where SharePoint is not installed. How you design your solutions will weigh heavily on the architecture and design strategies that are applied during the planning phases. Because planning is an important aspect, this book also shares with you how SharePoint has changed, what questions you need to ask to be successful in designing the architecture, how service applications work, and much more.

Who this book is for

Although this book offers insight into many of the new features of SharePoint 2013, it is not designed for the typical user or business user. This book is best suited for SharePoint professionals who plan on designing, planning, or implementing architectures that support organizations ranging from the small to large enterprise farms. This book will help you understand how SharePoint works at its core and will provide everything from how SharePoint is structured to how to take your SharePoint 2010 environment and upgrade it to SharePoint 2013. Finally, one of the topics that has rarely been addressed is the validation of your infrastructures. This book will walk you through the concepts you need to not only build successful solutions, but to test them against a wide variety of workloads.

This book does not provide step-by-step instructions on how to install or complete tasks by using SharePoint 2013 or provide an in-depth coverage or analysis of the new functions. You can find those details in the following books:

- *Microsoft SharePoint 2013 Plain & Simple* by Johnathan Lightfoot, Michelle Lopez, and Scott Metker, which is aimed at users who are new to SharePoint.

- *Microsoft SharePoint 2013 Step by Step* by Olga Londer and Penelope Coventry, which is aimed at new and intermediate users.

- *Microsoft SharePoint 2013 Inside Out* by Darvish Shadravan, Penelope Coventry, Tom Resing, and Christine Wheeler, which is aimed at intermediate and advanced power users (who are also referred to as *citizen* or *consumer developers*). This book is also aimed at project managers, business analysts, and small business technicians.

- *Microsoft SharePoint 2013 App Development* by Scot Hillier and Ted Pattison, which is aimed at professional developers.

Regardless of your role, we hope that this book helps you to understand how SharePoint works at its core and that you take away the importance of how planning and design can provide success in your new SharePoint 2013 environment.

Assumptions about you

This book is designed for readers who have experience with installing and administering SharePoint; it is assumed that the reader isn't brand new to the topic, and many of the topics in this book are considered either essential building blocks for a successful implementation or advanced topics. A book of this size cannot cover every feature; therefore, it is assumed that you have advanced familiarity with SharePoint already. The focus is on planning, designing, building, upgrading, and testing your SharePoint 2013 infrastructures.

Organization of this book

This book provides a high-level preview of the various new or changed features you might want to use in SharePoint 2013. This book is structured so that you, as an IT professional, understand the architectural changes before detailing features that the business might need you to install. This book is broken down into three distinct parts: "Planning for Microsoft SharePoint 2013," "Design considerations for Microsoft SharePoint 2013," and "Concepts for infrastructure reliability."

Chapter 1, "Understanding the Microsoft SharePoint 2013 architecture," discusses the core architecture components of SharePoint, including how the file system works and coexists with both v14 and v15 architectures and feature fallback behaviors. The chapter breaks down the core components of the SharePoint farm and the databases.

Chapter 2, "Introducing Windows PowerShell and SharePoint 2013 cmdlets," introduces the reader to what Windows PowerShell has to offer and explains how to use self-discovery to learn what you need to know to be successful.

Chapter 3, "Gathering requirements," discusses the importance of gathering requirements prior to implementation and how the requirements will affect design choices. The chapter highlights logical and physical architecture design so that you will have these critical concepts in mind while learning the specifics of SharePoint design concepts.

Chapter 4, "Understanding the service application model," goes into depth on the differences between services and service applications in SharePoint 2013, while highlighting design considerations for each. It will ensure that you understand how to properly plan and implement service applications that have supporting databases or support federated scenarios.

Chapter 5, "Designing for SharePoint storage requirements," identifies what storage options are available for SharePoint 2013 and why understanding storage requirements is important to the process. The chapter then discusses planning for Microsoft SQL Server 2008 R2, SQL Server 2012, and SQL Server Reporting Services.

Chapter 6, "Mapping authentication and authorization to requirements," goes into detail about the changes between SharePoint 2010 and SharePoint 2013 authentication models and then discusses options for each. The chapter provides a step-by-step process for configuring SharePoint to work with Windows, Forms-Based, and Federated authentication models. The chapter closes by going into detail about the changes in SharePoint authorization and highlights features that should be considered prior to the rollout.

Chapter 7, "Designing for platform security," highlights topics such as privileges, service and managed accounts, shell admin accounts, preventing and tracking installations, antivirus options, server communications, and other platform security topics to ensure that you understand how your decisions affect how SharePoint works.

Chapter 8, "Upgrading your SharePoint 2010 environment," discusses the new features of the SharePoint 2013 upgrade process and makes sure that you have a clear understanding of the options that are available. The chapter then goes into detail on preparing for and performing all aspects of the upgrade process. It closes by discussing troubleshooting techniques and common pitfalls and concerns.

Chapter 9, "Maintaining and monitoring Microsoft SharePoint," discusses monitoring and maintaining the environment to ensure that it keeps up with the changes in the organization. This chapter highlights timer jobs, SharePoint reports, and the ULS Viewer. It continues by giving you an understanding of the health analyzer and demonstrates how to implement custom rules. The chapter closes by discussing patching strategies.

Chapter 10, "Planning your business continuity strategy," discusses the importance of planning reliability. Prior to building the SharePoint farm, an organization should have a plan that focuses on how their decisions will affect their responses to critical issues. This chapter highlights planning an organization's SLAs, RPO, and RTO and discusses how to build a BCM plan that will satisfy those requirements.

Chapter 11, "Validating your architecture," discusses how to validate the design choices that have been implemented in the farm. It demonstrates how to create load tests that will test and validate your architecture to ensure that it holds up to the peak demands of your organization.

We hope that this book serves you well as you move forward with the new SharePoint 2013 platform.

Acknowledgments

One of the most challenging things one can do is choose to write a book and then complete it. Writing a book on a brand-new technology ups the bar a bit because the process often starts while the product is still in the early beta cycles. Screens and features change, and core pieces of functionality are either introduced late in the cycle or removed just before the release of the product. Knowing this, the authors of this book have tried to give you their best attempt at sharing the knowledge that they believe is critical when designing architectures. There are a number of folks on our team that helped bring this project to light, namely Kenyon Brown, Microsoft Press senior editor, who presented us with the opportunity to write this book. We would also like to thank our project editor, Kathryn Duggan, for her tireless efforts to make sure that we presented our thoughts in a clear and concise manner. Her job had to be difficult, and her efforts are truly appreciated. The final stages of the book process offer their own set of challenges. We would like to thank our production editor, Christopher Hearse, for putting the finishing touches on our chapters. Finally, we would like to thank our technical editor, Chris Givens, for his efforts to make sure that the information presented here is both clear and factual. Chris did a fantastic job and really helped the authoring team to present the book we all tried so desperately to produce.

Shannon Bray

Since this was my second book, I had envisioned that the process would have magically become easier, but as mentioned above, writing a book about SharePoint while it is still in beta is difficult, to say the least. I knew that I would need help bringing the best book possible to the market, and I chose my team very carefully. I would truly like to thank the efforts of Patrick Curran and Miguel Wood for helping me complete this book. We certainly found enough challenges to last a lifetime. I am also super pleased that my longtime friend, Chris Givens, agreed to join our project. I have known Chris for many years and always respected him as both author and trainer.

When you are writing a book in the beta stages, it is impossible to personally understand every aspect of the product. With the release of SharePoint 2013, there were many hidden components that I needed to dive into. Often, I found myself referring to the hard work of members of the Microsoft Certified Solution Master (MCSM) community and while it is impossible to name them all, I want to thank Spence Harbar and Wictor Wilén for their contributions to both the community and for allowing me to reference some of their work in this book. I would also like to thank the members and instructors of the MSCM beta rotation (U3); I was lucky to have spent two fantastic weeks with the best SharePoint folks on the planet.

Finally, I would be remiss if I didn't thank my beautiful family. I spent many more hours at the keyboard than I had expected, and it took time away from them. Without the support of my wife, Anna, and her ability to keep our two daughters (Eden and Kenna) wrangled in, I would not have been able to complete this project.

Patrick Curran

I am not usually one to mince words and spend a lot of time talking, so when Shannon Bray asked me to help write this book, I was a bit nervous about having to come up with content. Luckily, I was working with Shannon and Miguel, so when I did have questions, I was able to get excellent guidance for content. It was also fantastic working with Chris Givens because I really felt like I was writing the book for him. Having such a perfectionist as Chris for our technical editor, I did not want to disappoint and bore him with trivial SharePoint information. It was great to come up with things in this book that were both new to Shannon and Miguel (the MCSMs) and Chris, so I think that there is content in this book suitable for everyone.

I cannot express enough how grateful I am to Shannon Bray, who since day one at Planet Technologies has challenged me to continually learn more about SharePoint and become more involved with the SharePoint community. It has been a pleasure to work with him on this project, and also get to know him personally over the years. Thank you, Shannon, for everything.

I was lucky enough to meet Miguel Wood in Denver before he joined the Planet Technologies team, and I don't think I have ever met anyone who could usurp knowledge as well as Miguel. Every conversation I have with this man, I learn something new and simultaneously see that there is another level of knowledge that I have yet to obtain. I am lucky to have access to Miguel for guidance on a professional level, and a personal level, and really appreciate the guidance that he has given me over the years. Thank you, Miguel.

Having locked myself in my office for many nights to help get this book into your hands, I would like to thank my beautiful wife, Sandra, for having to manage our three lovely children in the evenings and a grumpy, sleep-deprived adult in the mornings. I must thank my father, Arthur, who has done nothing but encourage and support me through whatever wackiness I decide to pursue. And I want to mention my beautiful wee-ones, Liam, Mamie, and Michelle, who have been more understanding and patient than any children should have to be at the nightly disappearance of their father.

Miguel Wood

When I agreed to assist with writing this book, I had no idea of the challenge I was undertaking. I must first thank my coauthors for keeping me to task and for their much needed assistance in this endeavor. It is an honor to work with both Shannon and Patrick, not only on this book, but professionally as well. Also, I cannot fail to echo the previous acknowledgment of Chris Givens, our technical editor, and the entire Microsoft Press team in their undeserving patience with me and ensuring a quality product.

The knowledge and ability required to write a book like this requires the acknowledgment of many people, starting with my parents, for allowing me to indulge my technical addiction at such a young age. There is no doubt that I must also acknowledge, especially for this book, my fellow MCM R6 (#WUB) and MCSM Beta instructors and candidates for filling in my many gaps of the technical knowledge required to participate in authoring this book. Of course, I would also like to thank the numerous clients and friends who entrusted me to assist them in successfully meeting their visions and goals with the SharePoint platform.

During the entire book authoring process, personal life is near nonexistent, especially while maintaining a demanding work schedule. Therefore, I must thank my loving, supportive wife, Cara, and my sons for understanding and forgiving the extended time spent away from them, during not only this project but also my demanding work and travel schedule. Honestly, without their undying support, I could not have completed this book or be the person I am today.

Finally, I need to thank my closest friend and brother, Allen Capps, for always believing in me, even when I didn't; my in-laws, for their faith and personal investment in my profession; and, finally, my close friends in Time Machine for maintaining my minimal sanity and "enabling" Mike Honcho via live music, crazy antics, and the blue dolly.

Errata & Book Support

We've made every effort to ensure the accuracy of this book and its companion content. Any errors that have been reported since this book was published are listed on our Microsoft Press site:

http://aka.ms/SP2013DAS/errata

If you find an error that is not already listed, you can report it to us through the same page.

If you need additional support, email Microsoft Press Book Support at *mspinput@microsoft.com*.

Please note that product support for Microsoft software is not offered through the addresses above.

We want to hear from you

At Microsoft Press, your satisfaction is our top priority, and your feedback our most valuable asset. Please tell us what you think of this book at:

http://www.microsoft.com/learning/booksurvey

The survey is short, and we read every one of your comments and ideas. Thanks in advance for your input!

Stay in touch

Let's keep the conversation going! We're on Twitter: *http://twitter.com/MicrosoftPress*

Planning for Microsoft SharePoint 2013

## CHAPTER 1

Understanding the Microsoft SharePoint 2013 architecture

In this chapter, you will gain architecture knowledge as you:

- Explore the SharePoint farm components.

- Explore the file system and Feature Fallback behaviors.

- Examine the SharePoint databases.

First of all, welcome to Microsoft SharePoint 2013. For many of you, architecture and design may be new to you; for others, you are continuing your education. No matter which category you fall into, SharePoint 2013 has a rich set of features that affect how you, as architects, plan and design successful SharePoint implementations.

For those of you who spent a great deal of time learning SharePoint 2010, you will find SharePoint 2013 a welcoming friend. The product is similar enough that you will quickly become comfortable with it, but different enough that additional planning aspects must be considered.

In this chapter, you will be introduced to SharePoint 2013 from the inside out. You will start with the components that make up the SharePoint farm and then dig your way down into the file system. There are new features that allow SharePoint 2010 and 2013 components to work together, so for those of you with experience in previous versions, you will certainly find value learning about the Feature Fallback behavior. SharePoint has a number of ways to deploy solutions. This chapter will review the farm and sandbox solutions and give you an introduction to the new SharePoint application model. Finally, you will be introduced to the various databases and encounter some critical nuggets that will help you understand the SharePoint 2013 architecture.

Exploring the SharePoint farm components

Most SharePoint professionals, when they first learn of SharePoint, are introduced through the web browser; after all, it is a web application. But the deeper their understanding goes, the more complex the SharePoint platform seems to get. While on the surface it may look like a simple web interface, in reality the object hierarchy, file system, and databases quickly inform you of the massive beast that lies beneath the covers of those web components. If you are accustomed to talking about SharePoint infrastructures with technology folks who lack an understanding of how SharePoint works, then you may find yourself referencing the "farm," only to find out that the person on the other side of the conversation has no idea of what you are talking about. With that said, you will begin the SharePoint journey at its highest logical container: the farm.

The SharePoint farm hierarchy

The SharePoint farm, in its simplest terms, is a collection of SharePoint and Microsoft SQL Server roles that are bound by a single configuration database. A farm may consist of a single server that will have both a version of SQL Server and SharePoint, or it may have many SharePoint servers similar to what's shown in Figure 1-1.

Farm

When building the farm, the first component that gets created is the SharePoint Configuration and Admin Content Databases. You will learn more about these later in this chapter, but for now, it is important to note that these databases are created either while running the SharePoint Products Configuration Wizard or executing the *New-SPConfigurationDatabase* cmdlet; you will review the latter in the chapter dedicated to Windows PowerShell.

Prior to building the farm for SharePoint 2013, many things must be considered. Chapter 3, "Gathering requirements," discusses many of the issues that are common to a wide variety of SharePoint environments and will offer suggestions on how you, as the architect, can avoid them. Now turn your attention to the SharePoint web application, which is hosted in Internet Information Services (IIS), as this is the next major component of the farm.

Web applications

In order for a SharePoint farm to exist, it must contain at least one SharePoint web application. This web application, known as the SharePoint Central Administration, is created for you during the installation process either by using the SharePoint Products Configuration Wizard or executing the *New-SPCentralAdministration* cmdlet using Windows PowerShell. This web application, along with every other SharePoint web application, is hosted within IIS, as shown in Figure 1-2.

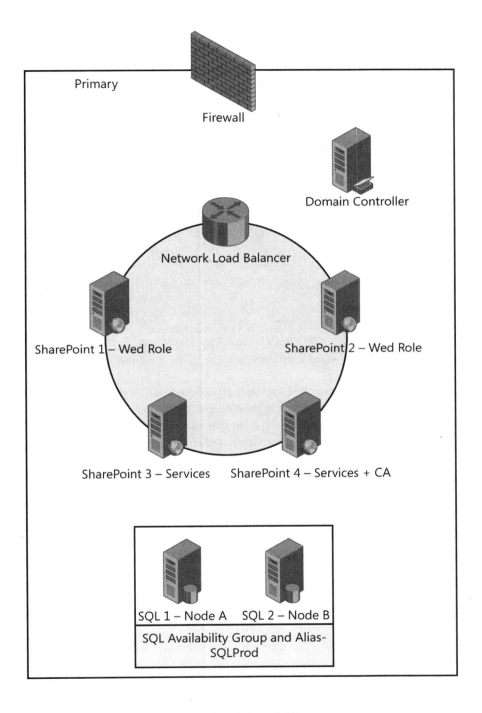

FIGURE 1-1 A SharePoint farm contains SharePoint and SQL servers.

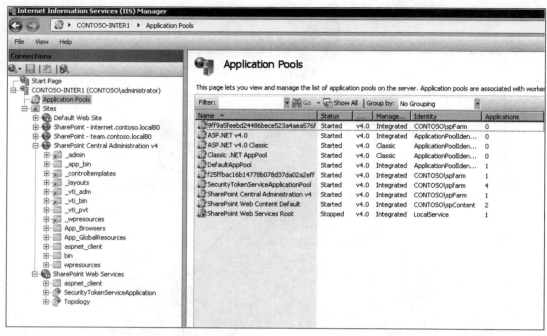

FIGURE 1-2 SharePoint web applications are hosted in IIS.

As a SharePoint professional, a basic understanding of IIS is helpful—if not required. For those of you who are familiar with SharePoint 2010, the biggest difference you will notice here is the use of the Microsoft .NET Framework 4.5. Later in this chapter, you will gain a deeper understanding of how HTTP requests are handled through IIS, but for now, you will continue with your survey of the web application component.

The SharePoint web application has several subcomponents that should be planned prior to the creation of the web application. These include the name of the IIS website, port, host header, location of the IIS files, whether or not to allow anonymous access, whether or not to use Secure Sockets Layer (SSL) authentication, the use of a default sign-in page, application pool, failover database server, search server, database name, and service application proxy group.

In SharePoint 2010, there was an option to select Classic or Claims mode authentication. In SharePoint 2013, this option has been removed from the GUI. This may give you the impression that Classic mode is no longer available. While Classic mode has been deprecated in the product, it is still fully supported. Web applications will not be required to be migrated to Claims mode since there are still some business cases that will require Classic mode authentication: Business Connectivity Services (BCS), in conjunction with Kerberos delegation.

When selecting a name for the IIS website, choose between using an existing IIS website or create a new one to serve the SharePoint Foundation application. If you select an existing IIS website, that website must exist on all servers in the farm and have the same name, or this action will not succeed.

The first web application that is created is generally defaulted to port 80. Once a web application is assigned to this port, the GUI will autogenerate a port number. You may reuse port numbers if the web application uses a unique host header. Additional planning may be required if several sites are going to use SSL on port 443.

A host header allows for the specification of friendly URLs. The URLs will be configured in Domain Name System (DNS) and will be directed to the servers hosting web requests; this can be either directly to a server or to a network load balancer (NLB) that will direct traffic. The use of host headers allows for web applications to occupy the same ports as other web applications. Without host headers, the URLs may need to contain port numbers and may not be as friendly to the user. Port 80 and port 443 are implicit and do not need to be specified in the URL.

It is important to understand that you are not limited to using a host header per web application; the use of host headers for SharePoint site collections offers a scalable way to offer vanity URLs for each site collection. This process is often used in hosting situations, but it has some benefits in environments unrelated to hosting as well. The use of host headers for a web application where the site collections are differentiated by path (such as *http://www.contoso.com/sites/team1* and *http://www.contoso.com/sites/team2*) are referred to as *path-based site collections*. The use of individual host headers for each site collection (such as *http://team1.contoso.com*) is referred to as *host header site collections*. While these two techniques can coexist, it requires additional web application zones. SharePoint web application host headers are intended only for path-based site collections; IIS will not respond to requests that have a different host name from that in the host header binding. You will continue your focus on site collection host header names later in this chapter.

When creating a new SharePoint web application, the GUI states:

> If you opt to create a new IIS website, it will be automatically created on all servers in the farm. If an IIS setting that you wish to change is not shown here, you can use this option to create the basic site, then update it using the standard IIS tools.

While this is true, it is generally not recommended to make changes using IIS. It is also worth noting that the verbiage may be a little misleading. SharePoint web applications will be created only on SharePoint servers that are running the Web Application SharePoint Service.

The anonymous access setting does not guarantee that visitors will have anonymous access to the site; it simply allows the content owners to decide if they would like to allow anonymous access to their content. If this setting is set to *false*, content owners will not have the option. The configuration of anonymous access is a two-part process.

Configuring your SharePoint web application to use SSL allows for the communication between the users and the web server to be encrypted. A certificate must be added on each server or offloaded to the load balancer (if it supports it) in order for the web application to be accessible. For more information, please see Chapter 6, "Mapping authentication and authorization to requirements."

 Note You cannot use the SSL protocol with a site that is hosted by Microsoft Office 365.

There are many options when configuring authentication for a SharePoint web application. Negotiate (Kerberos) is the recommended security configuration to use with Windows authentication, but it requires the use of Service Principal Names (SPNs); for more information, see Chapter 6. If Negotiate is selected and Kerberos is not configured correctly, the authentication will fall back to NTLM. For Kerberos, the application pool account needs to be Network Service or an account that has been configured by the domain administrator. NTLM authentication will work with any application pool account and with the default domain configuration.

 Note *NTLM* stands for Windows NT (New Technology) LAN (Local Area Network) Manager.

The Basic authentication method passes users' credentials over a network in an unencrypted form. If you select this option, ensure that SSL is enabled so that the credentials are encrypted over the network.

The ASP.NET membership and role provider are used to enable Forms-based authentication (FBA) for a SharePoint web application. The use of membership and role providers requires additional changes to be made to the *web.config* files of the SharePoint web application, Central Administration, and the Secure Token Service. For more information on this configuration, please refer to the Chapter.

Trusted Identity Provider authentication enables federated users to access a SharePoint web application. This authentication is claims token-based, and the user is redirected to a logon form for authentication, which is normally outside of the SharePoint farm. For more information on this configuration, please refer to Chapter 6.

The default sign-in page is available to Claims mode authentication SharePoint sites. While it is obvious that this feature allows for the customization of the logon page, there are some additional benefits that aren't so obvious. In SharePoint web applications that have multiple authentications available to them, by default, the users are prompted to select their authentication type. For many organizations, this is not a desired option. The use of a default logon page removes this option but still allows the web application to use multiple authentications. For more information, please refer to Chapter 6.

The public URL is the domain name for all sites that users will access in this SharePoint web application. This URL domain will be used in all links shown on pages within the web application. By default, it is set to the current server name and port unless a host header is specified for the site.

There are five zones that can be associated to a SharePoint web application: Default, Intranet, Internet, Extranet, and Custom. When creating or extending a SharePoint web application that uses a content database of another, you have the option to select a zone other than Default, which is already in use. This is not the case for a new SharePoint web application. You will learn about zones in more detail in Chapter 6.

An *application pool* is a grouping of URLs that is routed to one or more worker processes. In SharePoint, you have the opportunity to either use a unique application pool for each web application or share one among several pools. In general, application pools provide process boundaries that separate each worker process; therefore, a SharePoint web application in one application pool will not be affected by application problems in other application pools.

SharePoint 2010 introduced two distinct types of application pools, one for SharePoint web content applications, and another for SharePoint service applications. While it is technically possible to associate an application pool designed for SharePoint service applications to a web content application, it is not supported. Web content applications must be hosted by SharePoint web content application pools and vice versa.

Microsoft has soft limits around the number of application pools that should be used on a particular web server. If your design uses a distinct application pool for every SharePoint web content application and SharePoint service application, you will have more application pools than are technically supported without supplying more RAM to the minimum requirements. There are some design considerations to remember when determining how you plan your application pools. You will want to keep the total number of application pools under the recommended guideline, which is expected to stay at 20 application pools on a particular web server. As more testing is done, this guideline may change, so review these from time to time on Microsoft TechNet. Keep in mind that the more application pools you have, the more server resources will be dedicated to each web application. There may be business requirements that dictate if a SharePoint web application can share process boundaries with another. It is important to know that there are tradeoffs for either decision. In implementations that do not require process isolation, one approach is to use a common application pool for SharePoint web content applications and another for SharePoint service applications.

When creating a new application pool, you will need to specify a SharePoint Managed Account that will be used as the identity of the application pool. If the SharePoint Managed Account is not specified prior to entering the web application settings in the GUI, you will have the opportunity to create one at the time of adding the web application. This process will wipe out the settings you have entered and will need to be reviewed. You will learn about SharePoint Managed Account setting in more detail in Chapter 7, "Designing for platform security."

SharePoint 2013 supports SQL Server database mirroring that is native in the product. This feature was introduced in SharePoint 2010. Using the failover database server property, you can choose to associate a database with a specific failover server. While planning how you will implement high availability in SharePoint, keep in mind that database mirroring has been deprecated in SQL Server 2012. Chapter 10, "Planning your business continuity strategy," discusses the available options.

The database server will be prepopulated with the value that was used for creating the farm. The database server name should incorporate a SQL Server alias instead of referencing a database server directly by name. The use of SQL Server aliases will be discussed later in this chapter when the focus turns toward the databases.

When creating or managing SharePoint web content applications, you have the ability to choose the service applications that will be connected to the web application. A web application can be connected to the default set of service applications or to a custom set of service applications. You can change the set of service applications that a web application is connected to at any time by using the Configure Service Application Associations' page in Central Administration. Please review Chapter 4, "Understanding the service application model."

Databases

Every SharePoint web application requires a database in SQL Server to support it. This is true even of the SharePoint Central Administration. Along with the farm configuration database, a configuration content database is required. Content databases are the backbone of any SharePoint environment; therefore, you will find a section dedicated to SharePoint databases later in this chapter.

Site collections

Every functional SharePoint web application is required to have at least one site collection. The site collection is a logical container that has one or more SharePoint sites (known as *webs*) that serve content to the users. Understanding the site collection is critical in SharePoint. The idea here is to not cover everything pertaining to the SharePoint site collection, but there are some features that may require additional planning outside of the normal information architecture components. For those of you familiar with previous versions of SharePoint, you will find that the SharePoint site collection has some exciting new features.

SharePoint 2013 continues to support both path-based and host-named site collections. Path-based site collections share the same host name as other site collections inside the SharePoint web application. The following are examples of path-based site collections:

- *http://team.contoso.local/sites/blueteam*

- *http://team.contoso.local/sites/redteam*

Additional site collections are added to the SharePoint web application through the use of a managed path. The managed path in this example is *sites*. It is important to note that there are software boundary limits associated to the number of managed paths in a SharePoint web application. In the previous version, the limit was 20 managed paths per web application. As the product continues to be tested, this may change, so refer to TechNet from time to time to review the latest boundaries. Keep in mind that managed paths are cached on the individual web servers and require CPU resources to process incoming requests against the list of managed paths. The more managed paths you have defined, the more load on the web server for each request, because managed paths are cached on the servers and require CPU resources for processing incoming requests against the managed path list. Exceeding the supported boundary can cause poor performance and is not recommended.

Path-based site collections can be configured using Central Administration and support URLs that have implemented Alternate Access Mappings (AAMs). Depending on the configuration, path-based site collections can utilize any zone associated with AAM configurations.

Host-named site collections allow for the use of unique DNS names and provide a scalable solution to the use of managed paths as described previously. Unlike path-based site collections, host-named site collections cannot be created using Central Administration and must be done either through the SharePoint application programming interface (API) or Windows PowerShell. Here is an example of how to create a host-named site in Windows PowerShell using the *New-SPSite* cmdlet.

Create a host-named site collection using PowerShell

```
PS C:\> $wa = Get-SPWebApplication http://contoso-inter3
PS C:\> $site = New-SPSite -URL "http://blueteam.contoso.local" `
    -OwnerAlias "contoso\spAdmin" `
    -HostHeaderWebApplication $wa `
    -CompatibilityLevel 15
PS C:\>$site
Url                                           CompatibilityLevel
---                                           ------------------
http://blueteam.contoso.local                 15
```

You can select a SharePoint site collection template using this script, or if you would like the content owners to decide, leave it blank and they will be prompted to select one, as shown in Figure 1-3.

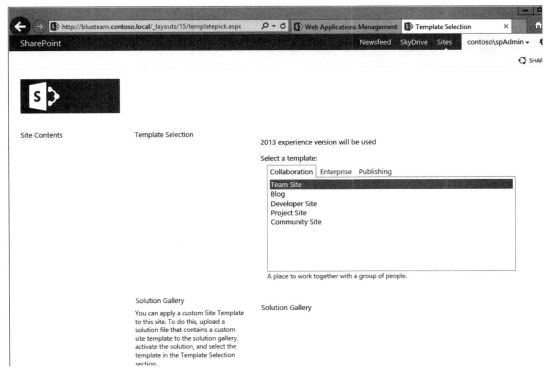

FIGURE 1-3 Creating a site collection without a template will allow a user visiting the site for the first time to select a template.

Host-named site collections take on the same protocol scheme as the public URL in the web application. Review the code listing and output shown previously. The SharePoint web application public URL is *http://contoso-inter3*. If HTTPS was required, the public URL would need to be available over SSL. Since there is only one DNS name associated with a host-named site collection, they will only utilize the Default zone and do not support AAM configurations.

The Self-Service Site Creation feature is enabled at the SharePoint web application level inside Central Administration and is turned off by default. This feature allows users to create site collections without the need of a SharePoint administrator. The new site collections will utilize a path-based site collection schema. Once turned on, users will need to know the URL to create a new site collection. The page location is /_layouts/15/scsignup.aspx, as shown in Figure 1-4. You will learn more about the SharePoint file locations and their syntaxes later in this chapter.

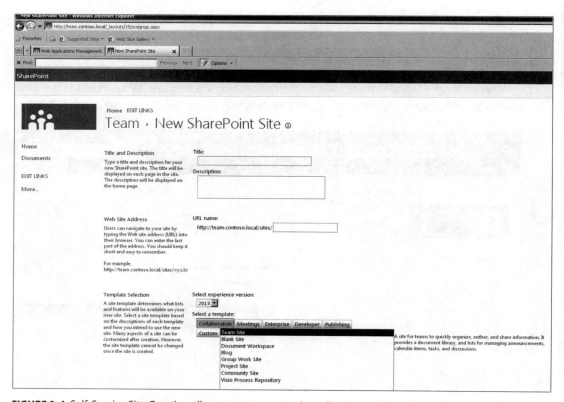

FIGURE 1-4 Self-Service Site Creation allows users to create site collections without farm administrators.

Quota templates can be used to restrict the size of the new site collections. They can warn the site collection administrator as they approach their max limit and then lock the site collection upon reaching the limit. It is highly recommended that quotas be used for all site collections.

Depending on the business requirements, the Self-Service Site Creation feature may offer some value, but it should not be turned on without proper planning. Make sure you review the latest software boundaries and have business processes in place to ensure that the number of site collections does not get out of hand.

Note Multi-tenancy requires that Self-Service Site Creation be enabled.

The SharePoint site collection is the highest level of security autonomy, with the single exception of user policy settings that can be configured to allow a particular domain account explicit access to the entire SharePoint web application. An example of this would be the Search Service Application, since it grants the crawling account full read access to all SharePoint web applications that it needs to crawl. While farm administrators have the ability to give themselves access, either through the user policies or to grant themselves site collection administrator rights, these permissions are not granted by default. Site collection administrators are responsible for granting users rights to the site collections they control. Rights may be given either to particular authentication provider groups (such as Active Directory (AD) security groups, FBA roles, and so on) or to a specific individual. Rights given in one site collection cannot be inherited by another. The site collection acts as a logical boundary and will restrict composite applications and sandbox solutions to stay within the confines of the site collection.

 Note Sandbox solutions are restricted within a site collection by default, but may be given extended rights by way of a full-trust proxy.

Users and groups created at the site-collection level are available to all sites within the site collection. While sites may be able to break inheritance and change the permission structure, the site collection administrator has complete control over the site collection.

The site-collection level now exposes new search service configurations. Some of the search features available to the site collection administrator are as follows:

- **Search settings** Allows the site collection administrator to specify a search center for the site collection. If configured, users will see a system message that will allow them to retry their search from the specified search center. The site collection administrator also has the ability to configure which pages the search queries should be sent to.

- **Result types** Allow the site collection administrator to customize how the content in the site collection will be returned. The result types can be matched to specific content and can be displayed using a specific template. The out-of-the-box result types cannot be modified; this is shown in Figure 1-5. They are reserved for the search service. Site collection administrators may make a copy of the original and make changes to it.

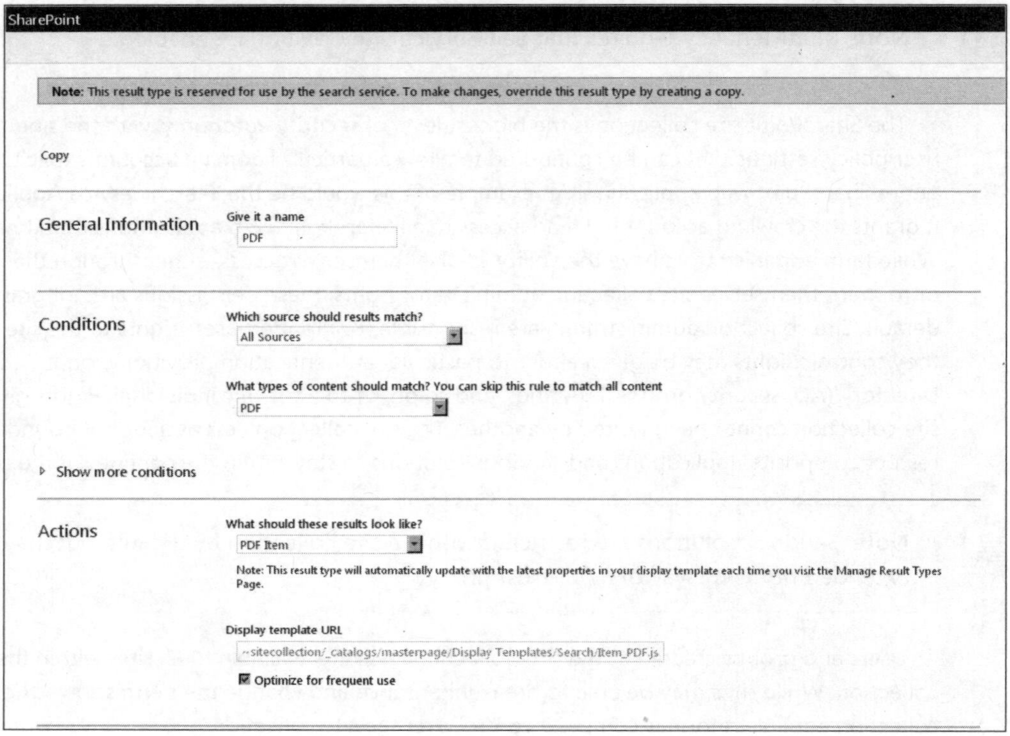

FIGURE 1-5 Some result types are reserved for the search service.

- **Search schema** Site collection administrators may use the search schema page to view, create, or modify managed properties and map crawled properties to managed properties. Crawled properties are automatically extracted from crawled content. You can use managed properties to restrict search results, and present the content of the properties in search results. Changes to properties will take effect after the next full crawl. Please note that the settings which can be adjusted depend on your current authorization level.

- **Search result sources** Site collection administrators can configure search federation. By using search federation, users can simultaneously search content in the search index of the search service, as well as in other sources, such as Internet search engines.

- **Import search configuration** Site collection administrators may import search configurations created as an *.xml* file from an export.

- **Export search configuration** Site collection administrators may use this option to create an *.xml* file that contains their custom search configurations. This file may be used to share configurations or act as a backup of the current configurations.

- **Search query rules** Site collection administrators can create query rules to promote important results, show blocks of additional results, and even fine-tune ranking.

SharePoint 2013 offers a set of features that allow for site collections to function with components in other site collections. The features listed here will be discussed throughout other chapters, but it is important to know that they exist.

- **Content deployment source feature**   Enables content deployment-specific checks on source site collection and enables setting up content deployment from the site collection to a target site collection.

- **Content type syndication hub**   Provisions a site to be an Enterprise Metadata hub site.

- **Cross-farm site permissions**   Use the cross-farm site permissions feature to allow internal SharePoint applications to access websites across farms.

- **Cross-site collection publishing**   Enables site collection to designate lists and document libraries as catalog sources for cross-site collection publishing.

HTML field security allows the site collection administrator to specify whether contributors can insert external *iFrames* in HTML fields on pages in a site. IFrames are commonly used on webpages to show dynamic content from other websites, like directions from a mapping site, or a video from a video site. By default, the following external domains are allowed:

- Youtube.com

- Youtube-nocookie.com

- Player.vimeo.com

- Bing.com

- Office.microsoft.com

- Skydrive.live.com

Sites (webs)

The site collection is composed of at least one top-level site, often referred to as a *web*. When users create a new site, they will be prompted to create a website URL that will be appended to the DNS name assigned to the site collection. For instance, if a user created a new site for a blog, the URL name could be *http://team.contoso.local/blog*. During the site creation process, the user also has the ability to select a site template, specify permissions, and make decisions on how the navigation will work for the site. The site templates that are available to the user are dependent on the features that have been activated at the site collection and site level. While these templates may be important to the information architecture of the site, they will not be discussed here. The important action to note here will be to monitor the number of websites in a given site collection to ensure that they stay within the specified boundaries. There are some added benefits of grouping like site templates together in databases, so this should be considered while planning the information architecture. The creation of sites is generally handled by users in the Information Worker role, and it is difficult to plan for how they will structure their sites. Incorporating a solid governance plan is recommended.

Note There is often a terminology conflict when referring to SharePoint site collections and SharePoint sites. This is largely due to the fact that the original programming objects used the term *site* for site collections and *web* for what is now called sites in the UI. Since the UI uses sites at this level, this same practice will be followed here to reduce confusion.

Site owners can give permission to access the site to the same users who have access to the parent site, or you can give permission to a unique set of users. This will be a recurring theme to the objects contained within the site. Creating a new permission structure that is different from the parent is referred to as *breaking inheritance*. You should encourage users to document the permission structures within their sites. This is important for a number of reasons. For one, it can be difficult to track document level permissions and be difficult to find a particular document if the wrong permissions are set on it. If the site owner is separate from the site collection administrator, they may choose to break inheritance solely for the purpose of having complete control over their site. If permissions are inherited, they will not be able to change user permissions on the new site unless they are site collection administrators.

Lists and libraries

As you dive deeper into the farm hierarchy, much of how the Information Workers choose to use SharePoint falls out of the hands of the SharePoint architect and into the hands of governance. A SharePoint environment can contain a single library that contains millions of documents or it may contain a large number of libraries that contain documents specific to business units. The choices here should be defined in the information architecture. There are some considerations that will need to be planned for and captured in the information architecture and governance plans. These include how to use lists and libraries, the supported security models, and how the new application infrastructure comes into play.

In truth, lists and libraries require planning. You invest a great deal of time and money building your SharePoint environments and you hope that the information architect works with the content owners to ensure that each list and library are well thought out. Here are a few questions that may help in this planning:

- What kind of document should live here?

- Who is responsible for it?

- How long should it be here?

- How many versions are needed?

- Is this the only copy of this document?

- Who has access to the library, folders, or documents?

- What business processes are ties to documents in this library?

Large lists   SharePoint 2013 supports the use of large lists. As in the previous version, a list (or library) can contain tens of millions of items. From a SQL Server scalability perspective, this isn't an issue. In the back end, all of these items are stored in a single table, so breaking lists into smaller units doesn't impact performance. What can impact performance is the number of items the users decide to bring back into a particular view. By default, SharePoint will bring back pages in chunks of 30, but this is a setting that can be easily overridden by the user. As the list view approaches 5,000, performance will degrade and could potentially impact server performance. SharePoint has incorporated list view thresholds that can be fine-tuned and prevent the users from putting excessive loads on the servers. You will examine these settings in Chapter 9, "Maintaining and monitoring Microsoft SharePoint."

Security   Similar to the security described for sites, lists can break inheritance from their parent. This allows for the ability to restrict users who have site access from a particular list or library. The governance plan should highlight how and when security can break inheritance, since it has the tendency to start causing confusion the lower the unique access rules go down.

Apps   You may have noticed that many of the features that existed in previous versions of SharePoint are now considered apps. The SharePoint App model offers a new paradigm for deploying customizations to SharePoint. SharePoint apps, including everything from lists and libraries, are the preferred way of extending the platform (see Figure 1-6). They are deployed from the Corporate Catalog or Office Marketplace and offer flexible and reusable options for any SharePoint deployment: On Premise, Hybrid, or SharePoint Online. This topic is discussed further later in this chapter.

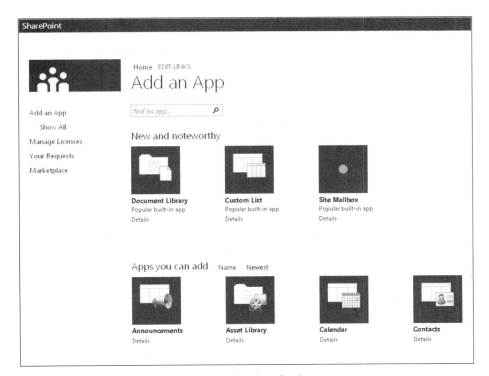

FIGURE 1-6 Lists and Libraries are now considered applications.

Folders

Over the years, folders in SharePoint have been associated with negative connotations. The truth is, folders are a critical component of the SharePoint information architecture and provide scalability to lists and libraries. The negative aspects have mainly stemmed from how people organize their documents in their network file systems. Often times, documents are thrown into any folder and when your information workers migrate content from their file system, they often bring the data in as is. Without a proper governance plan, this is simply moving a mess from one corner of the room to another.

The SharePoint view should be restricted to as few items as possible, while still adding business value. The performance hit is from the rendering of thousands of items. Folders allow for the organization of these items in much smaller units. The large list thresholds help to keep these designs from negatively impacting our infrastructure.

As with the SharePoint site and libraries, folders support unique permissions. For many organizations, this is a preferred method of dividing the permissions while still keeping documents in one library.

Folders have the ability to capitalize on library features like the *Column default value settings* feature, which allows for the automatic configuration of metadata based off of hierarchies inside the document library.

List items

The lists, libraries, and folders would have no value without the list item. Everything that is important to you inside your environment will probably fall within this category. List items can inherit permissions from the item, folder, list, and site, or have a unique permission assigned to them. While unique permissions at the item level aren't typically recommended, it is a nice feature when used in conjunction with automated workflows.

Examining the SharePoint file system

As discussed earlier, the SharePoint farm contains web applications that are made up of content databases and a number of files located on the SharePoint servers. In this section, you will examine where the various sets of files are located and understand how they work. You will start your survey of the files system by being introduced to the IIS hierarchy. Once you have a basic understanding of the IIS files, you will look at how the files located in the SharePoint root folder work with the system. SharePoint 2013 has introduced a new methodology that allows content from SharePoint 2010 to work within the 2013 implementation. You will examine how Feature Fallback behavior works, which will be valuable for those planning on either upgrading to 15 or looking to deploy customizations written for SharePoint 2010 into the 2013 environment.

Finally, you will take a look at how SharePoint customizations are deployed to the farm. It is important to understand how these files work, not only from the perspective of a deployment process, but also how the locations of the files determine how the solution works from a security perspective. For those of you who understand code access security (CAS) policies in SharePoint 2010, you will find that the trust model in SharePoint has changed.

IIS files

Each SharePoint server in the farm is required to have the IIS role configured; IIS is responsible for hosting the application pool and web applications (see Figure 1-7) and receives and responds to user requests. You will learn how IIS works from the HTTP request later in this chapter, but for now, you will examine where these files are located.

IIS, by default, stores the SharePoint web application files at *%SystemDrive%\inetpub\wwwroot\ wss\VirtualDirectories*. Each web application gets a unique folder that contains a series of files.

The file system and the database tables are fairly static throughout the life of the SharePoint environment. While SharePoint patches may change the contents within these structures, they are essentially the same as they were when the product was installed. As you add new lists and libraries to SharePoint, new files and database tables are not created.

From the IIS perspective, the file structure is pretty simple. Each web application gets both a unique set of files for that specific web application and a group of common files that are used by the entire SharePoint farm. Examine Figure 1-7. You will note that the team.contoso.local web application has a series of folders associated with it. Notice that some of the folders have blue arrows associated with them.

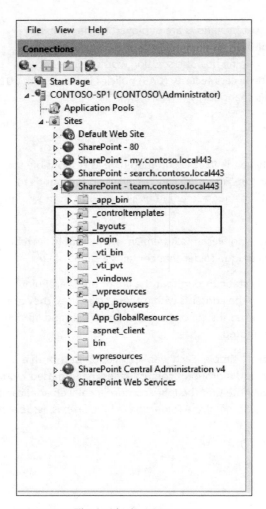

FIGURE 1-7 Files inside the IIS structure.

The top-level folders that do not have the blue arrow associated with them are local to the IIS web application and are unique. These folders (and files) are shown in the file system view in Figure 1-8. Any changes made to files in this location will affect only a single web application. If you have incorporated extended web applications, you will need to change the files in both sources. This is a common mistake when making changes to the *web.config* file.

_app_bin	5/12/2012 6:01 PM	File folder	
_vti_pvt	5/12/2012 6:01 PM	File folder	
App_Browsers	5/12/2012 6:01 PM	File folder	
App_GlobalResources	5/12/2012 6:01 PM	File folder	
bin	5/12/2012 6:01 PM	File folder	
wpresources	5/12/2012 6:01 PM	File folder	
global.asax	5/12/2012 6:01 PM	ASAX File	1 KB
web.config	5/12/2012 6:01 PM	CONFIG File	149 KB

FIGURE 1-8 Files inside the IIS web application.

_app_bin

Inside the _app_bin folder is a series of *Microsoft.Office* and *Microsoft.SharePoint* dynamic-link library (DLL) files that support the individual web applications. In addition to the *.dll* files, you will find *.sitemap* files. The SharePoint web content application will have a *layouts.sitemap* file. Central Administration is supported by *layouts.sitemap* and *admin.sitemap*.

_vti_pvt

The *vti* naming convention is left behind from the old FrontPage days. The original creator of FrontPage was Vermeer Technologies Incorporated; since SharePoint Designer's roots originated with FrontPage, these extensions are still used today. The _vti_pvt contains three files by default: *Buildversion.cnf*, *services.cnf*, and *service.cnf*.

App_Browers

SharePoint populates this folder with three files by default: *compat.browser, compat.crawler .browser,* and *compat.moss.browser*. These files are used for SharePoint's mobile support and contain XML that helps browsers interpret SharePoint sites. As new mobile browsers are released, these files will need to be updated if they are to support SharePoint. Additionally, if you were to deploy a new mobile Web Part adapter, the *compat.browser* file would need to be deployed to each server in the farm. Hopefully, this would be done using a SharePoint package and the SharePoint timer service. To review the contents of these files, open them using Notepad.

App_GlobalResources

SharePoint is localized to work in a number of worldwide cultures; the files, located in the App_GlobalResources folder, are responsible for localization (*.resx*) and contain XML entries that specify objects and strings that map the right text to the object when the application is rendered.
An example is shown in Listing 1-1.

LISTING 1-1 Sample *.resx* entry

```
<data name="aclinv_AddressBook_TXT">
    <value>Address Book</value>
  </data>
```

Bin

The SharePoint web application Bin folder is used to store code files that can expand the functionality of SharePoint. This will be discussed later in the chapter as you learn about deploying solutions. As for this topic, custom development code files that are compiled as *.dll* files are typically deployed to either the Bin folder or the global assembly cache (GAC). Anything that is deployed to the GAC is fully trusted and has access to server resources; the bin relied on CAS policies. The policy was specified inside the *web.config* file on each server and one of the biggest changes along this topic from

SharePoint 2010 is that the default trust level of the SharePoint web application is now *Full* instead of *WSS_Minimal*. It is no longer supported to use CAS policies in SharePoint.

wpresources

Upon examining IIS, you may notice that there are two folders for Web Part resources: wpresources and _wpresources. As with the other files that begin with an underscore, the *_wpresources* are for globally deployed Web Parts, and their code files are located in the GAC. The local Web Part resource files for the specific web application would exist in the wpresources folder. By default, both locations contain *web.config* files that are used for their specific scopes. The local version contains a number of defined handlers, while the global resource *web.config* file does not.

global.asax

The *global.asax* file has been a part of the .NET Framework since version 1.0 and is intended for handling application-level events raised by ASP.NET applications or HttpModules. The *global.asax* file that is deployed with SharePoint 2013 is an optional file and does not contain anything other than its assembly location.

web.config

As with the *global.asax* file, the *web.config* file has been part of the .NET Framework from the beginning. This file, however, contains critical configuration information and becomes complicated when comparing a standard *web.config* file with that of SharePoint. While making changes to the *web.config* file may be required to deploy new features to SharePoint or configure authentication, it is highly recommended that these changes not be done manually. Furthermore, each change that does happen will have to be implemented on each server that is hosting that particular SharePoint web application. As features are added to SharePoint web application, a copy of the *web.config* file is automatically created containing the last configuration. Making incorrect changes in this file can disable your SharePoint web application.

SharePoint Root

The SharePoint Root folder contains all of the critical files that are used by the SharePoint infrastructure. The virtual IIS folders discussed previously live in various places within this location. You will see a brief description of each of these folders and then dive into more detail on the ones that you are more likely to care about. Pay close attention to the case in the names. If the folder contains all capital letters, in many cases, it has a virtual mapping to IIS for each SharePoint web application.

- **ADMISAPI** Contains a number of files that provide or support administration web services. This location is mapped to the IIS _vti_adm virtual folder.

- **BIN** Contains a number of *.dll* and *.exe* files that support SharePoint. Most notably, this location contains *OWSTIMER, PSCONFIG, SPMETAL, WSSTracing, WSSADMIN, VideoThumbnailer, SPWriter*, and *CsiSrvExe*.

- **Client**   Contains files for the support of Microsoft Online services.

- **CONFIG**   Contains configuration files that are needed for a wide variety of SharePoint operations, including mapping objects from SharePoint 2010 to SharePoint 2013 during the upgrade process.

- **HCCab**   Contains a series of *.cab* files that are broken down into the various languages installed on the system. These files are used in the SharePoint Help system.

- **Help**   Contains a compiled HTML file that opens up the SharePoint Help system.

- **ISAPI**   Contains a number of web service (*.asmx*), web service discovery pages (*.aspx*), and dynamic libraries (*.dll*) files that support web service operations for SharePoint. This location is mapped to the IIS virtual _vti_bin folder.

- **LOGS**   By default, this is the location (*%CommonProgramFiles%\Microsoft Shared\Web Server Extensions\15\LOGS*) of the Unified Logging System (ULS) logs that are configured in Central Administration. Depending on how the Diagnostic Log Settings are configured, this location may hold a wealth of information. Finding errors in this location may be difficult but is made easier by the implementation of the correlation token. You will learn about this in more detail in Chapter 9. These logs are used to populate the Usage and Health database as configured by the *Diagnostics Data Provider: Event Log* timer job.

- **Policy**   Contains a number of configuration and dynamic library files that are responsible for assembly redirection. SharePoint 2013 has support for both SharePoint 2007 and SharePoint 2010.

- **Resources**   Contains resources for localizing SharePoint 2013.

- **TEMPLATE**   Contains a number of folders that support various customizations, features, and core website files. Figure 1-9 shows the complete listing of folders. Descriptions of the most notable folders include the following:

  - **LCIDSts**   Contains the local ID files that are copied to the root of the website when the Team Site template is selected.

  - **ADMIN**   Contains master pages and templates for the Central Administration website and other core features like BDC, Content Deployment, Search, and the Secure Store service.

  - **CONTROLTEMPLATES**   Contains control templates that determine the layout of list item forms.

  - **DocumentTemplates**   Contains the *wkpstd.aspx* page that is used to create document libraries.

  - **FEATURES**   Contains the additional functionality and features that extend SharePoint.

  - **IMAGES**   Contains images that are shared by all of the SharePoint web applications on the server. This location is accessible by the _layouts/images virtual directory.

- **LAYOUTS**   Contains a wide variety of folders and files that are used for creating lists and site administration pages. This location is accessible by the _layouts virtual directory.

- **SiteTemplates**   Contains the files that are copied when various site templates are created. These templates include the Blog, Central Administration, Meeting Workspaces, Group Work Site, Team Site, Tenant Administration, and Wiki Site.

- **SQL**   Contains stored procedures for SQL Server.

- **THEMES**   Contains a number of folders and their supporting files that provide the themes in SharePoint.

- **WorkflowActivities**   Contains the *Microsoft.SharePoint.WorkflowServices.Activities.dll* file.

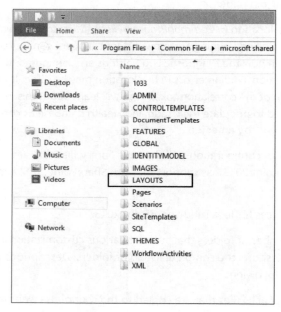

FIGURE 1-9 Files inside the SharePoint Root directory.

- **UserCode**   Contains the User Code Host Service, User Code Worker Process, and User Code Process Proxy applications that support the Sandbox Solution architecture.

- **WebClients**   Contains web client configurations for a number of SharePoint Service Applications and Services.

- **WebServices**   Contains the *web.config* files for the application root, Business Data Connectivity, Security Token, Subscription Settings, Application Management, PowerPoint Conversion, Secure Store, and Topology services.

Feature Fallback behavior

One of the new features of SharePoint 2013 is the Feature Fallback infrastructure. In SharePoint 2010, if you installed a SharePoint on a new server, you would see the 14 (SharePoint root) and wpresources folder. In SharePoint 2013, we see not only the current version (15) and the wpresources folder, but also a folder for the previous version (14). The hierarchy of this folder is shown in Figure 1-10.

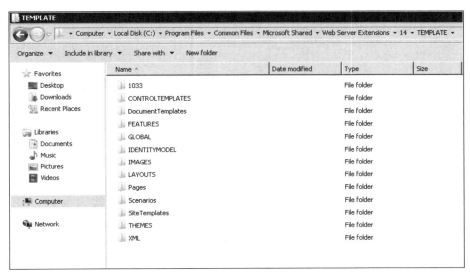

FIGURE 1-10 Files inside the SharePoint 14 directory for Feature Fallback.

In SharePoint 2010, custom code from previous versions could be deployed, but depending on how the code was upgraded, it may have needed .*dll* redirections. The Feature Fallback infrastructure goes well beyond the capabilities of SharePoint 2010 by providing a full backward-compatible folder structure. To test how it works, take a SharePoint deployment project (.*wsp*) from SharePoint 2010 and deploy it to the 2013 infrastructure. You will notice, as shown in Figure 1-11, that the deployment files are implemented into the 14 root structure and the feature works exactly the way it did in SharePoint 2010.

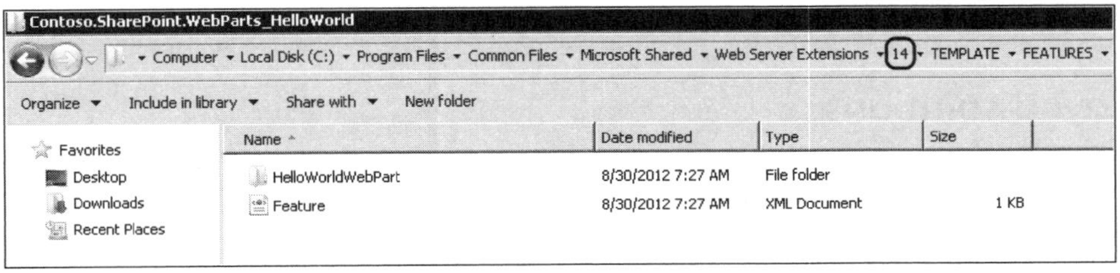

FIGURE 1-11 SharePoint 2010 features are deployed to the SharePoint 14 folder.

In addition to being able to support previous versions of deployed solutions, the infrastructure of SharePoint 2013 also fully supports branding and other customizations from SharePoint 2010. In fact, when selecting new site templates, you can elect to choose a template from SharePoint 2010, as shown in Figure 1-12. This is a fantastic feature that may help organizations that have invested a great deal of time and money into their corporate brand to make the move to SharePoint 2013 without the fear of losing their investment. This is different from what SharePoint 2010 offered with its Visual Upgrade. New sites that were created in SharePoint 2010 had to use new templates and it was unsupported to use Windows PowerShell to modify those sites to use the 2007 master pages.

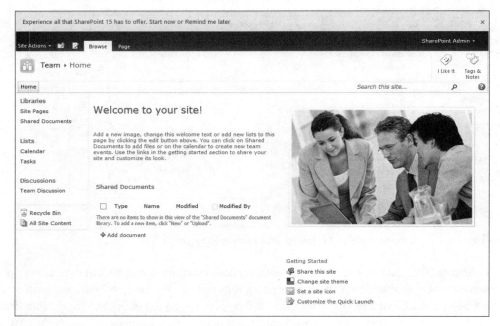

FIGURE 1-12 SharePoint 2013 fully supports the 2010 experience.

The SharePoint 2010 experience works through the entire site; you can, of course, upgrade to the SharePoint 2013 experience simply by clicking Start Now in the message bar across the top of the page, as shown in Figure 1-12.

Deployed solutions

The extensibility of SharePoint is one of its greatest product features; with the release of SharePoint 2013, the platform introduces yet another way to deploy solutions to your implementation: the SharePoint application model. The SharePoint application model joins farm and sandboxed solutions to help ensure that the information workers are getting the full power of what SharePoint has to offer. Previously, if an organization needed a particular solution, it may have been restricted to On Premise deployments. With the focus of bringing SharePoint to the cloud, Microsoft needed to reexamine how solutions would be deployed. In this section, you will see the highlights of farm solutions and sandboxed solutions, and then be introduced to the new SharePoint application model. Knowing how each of these types of solutions work may have implications about which SharePoint offering helps meet the business requirements you are trying to satisfy.

Farm solutions

Prior to SharePoint 2010, the only way to deploy customizations was by way of farm solutions. This model deployed fully trusted solutions to the file system of the server; therefore, if extending SharePoint was needed, a full understanding of the file system would certainly benefit SharePoint professionals. It is important to understand what type of solution is needed since some can still only be deployed as farm solutions. An example of these types of jobs would include timer jobs and other customizations that required server-side code. Farm solutions are restricted to On Premise deployments and deploy files to either the GAC (Windows Assembly) or the BIN folder of the SharePoint web application. Because of the global nature of this type of solution, a farm administrator would be required to deploy them.

Sandboxed solutions

As the SharePoint product matures and the needs of the organizations that use it change, other models were needed. With the release of SharePoint 2010, customizations were able to be deployed via sandboxed (or User Code) solutions. This model allowed for elements to deploy partially trusted code, meaning that the solutions only had access to certain resources. This helped isolate the code and offered resource throttling to ensure that a particular solution wouldn't have a negative impact on the entire SharePoint farm. Sandboxed solutions took the deployment responsibilities from the farm administrators and handed it to the site collection administrators or a user who had full control at the root of the site collection. The overall configuration was still in the hands of the farm administrators. They were responsible for ensuring that the User Code Service was running and that the load balancing, quotas, and resource points were configured. Sandboxed solutions (like Farm solutions) are packaged as *.wsp* files, and they contain any number of elements: features, site definitions, assemblies, and Web Parts. The *.wsp* package was then deployed to a solution gallery for the site collection, where it could be put in service by the site collection administrator.

Once activated, the sandboxed solution shows its available components in the same way as a farm solution. Requests for sandboxed solution elements are passed to the SharePoint User Code service (*SPUCHostService.exe*), which either starts a new sandbox worker process (*SPUCWorkerProcess.exe*) or uses an existing one. The worker process then loads the solution assembly into a new application domain. If the maximum number of application domains is reached, an existing one is released prior to creating a new one. Once the assembly has been loaded, it is free to execute the code. Some solutions that are ideal for the sandbox would include Web Parts, event receivers, feature receivers, SharePoint Designer workflow activities and Microsoft InfoPath business logic.

SharePoint App model

Sandbox solutions were definitely a step in the right direction. For organizations who had policies that restricted the deployment of farm solutions or used SharePoint Online, the partially trusted model offered options they wouldn't have with farm solutions.

Even with the flexibility offered by sandbox solutions, they still had limitations due to the nature of what they were designed to do. SharePoint 2013 and the growing implementations of SharePoint Online needed a new application deployment model. Enter the SharePoint App model.

The SharePoint App model offers a new paradigm of deploying customizations to SharePoint. SharePoint apps only support client-side code and offer a safer way to add customizations than farm solutions. Information workers can browse the SharePoint Platform Storefront or Corporate Marketplace and get the solutions they need. The app model has three different deployment models: SharePoint-Hosted App, Self-Hosted App, and Azure-Provisioned App. While the last two models don't impact the design of the architecture, they are included here for reference.

The SharePoint-Hosted App is basically a subweb of a site collection, and apps can only deploy web-scoped features. One of the built-in features of SharePoint apps is that information workers cannot manipulate them; this avoids accidental breaking of the apps using the browser or Microsoft SharePoint Designer.

The Self-Hosted App model allows organizations to provide solutions on any platform using any language that is supported on that platform. In this model, the developing organization is responsible for providing the hosting infrastructure, which allows for greater flexibility in exchange for greater responsibility.

The Azure-Provisioned App model allows the flexibility of building solutions without having the developing team or organization host the solution. These components are provisioned as needed in Windows Azure.

The SharePoint app is isolated and the features are not visible outside of the app. If site collection resources are needed, farm solutions would still be the only option. From a security perspective, SharePoint apps are restricted to the permissions of the user, so having the information worker gaining access to resources they are restricted to is not an issue. To gain an understanding of how the infrastructure can be configured to support the new SharePoint App model, see Chapter 4, "Understanding the Service Application model."

Examining the SharePoint databases

The SharePoint file system doesn't change as new site collections or sites are created. These components are created in new or existing databases. This means that the databases are considered the principal vehicles for service; see Chapter 10 for methodologies on protecting the SharePoint databases. The databases used in a specific environment are determined by the product, version, edition, and features that are running. Database size and the edition of SQL Server that should be used are determined by the capacity and feature requirements of the desired implementation.

In this section, you will review techniques for building the SharePoint environment using the SQL Server alias and encounter a brief overview of the databases that are the backbone of the SharePoint 2013 infrastructure.

SQL Server aliases

One might wonder why a book on the SharePoint 2013 architecture mentions SQL Server aliases. It is important to highlight them here because when reviewing a great number of SharePoint farms, this is one of the critical steps that is often neglected. Prior to the SharePoint 2010 June 2010 cumulative update, SQL Server aliases were required if the SharePoint implementation used named instances and provisioned the User Profile service. While this is not a limitation in the SharePoint 2013 infrastructure, it is still highly recommended that you use SQL Server aliases when addressing named instances. SQL Server aliases are essentially a variable that is configured on each SharePoint server that points to a particular SQL Server.

Type **cliconfg** into a cmd window or Windows PowerShell Mangement Shell. The SQL Server Client Network Utility will open, as shown in Figure 1-13.

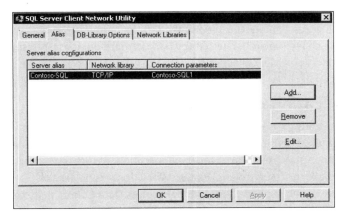

FIGURE 1-13 SQL Server aliases are recommended when configuring SharePoint.

Create a new TCP/IP server alias that points to the actual SQL Server named instance. In the event that you need to move data to another server, you simply need to modify the alias and move the data to the server you wish to use. If you fail to use aliases, there are many configuration settings that will need to be modified using Windows PowerShell.

SharePoint system databases

When you create the initial farm (either using the SharePoint Products and Configuration Wizard or Windows PowerShell), two databases are created: *SharePoint_Config* and *SharePoint_Content_Admin*. SharePoint web applications store their data in content databases.

- **SharePoint_Config**   Contains data about all SharePoint databases, all IIS web applications, trusted solutions, Web Part packages, site templates, and farm and web application settings specific to SharePoint, such as default quotas and blocked file types. It must be colocated with the Central Administration content database (*SharePoint_Content_Admin*) and only one database *SharePoint_Config* database is supported per farm. The *SharePoint_Config* database isn't expected to grow significantly, so it is considered to be a small database and can grow up to 1 GB.

- **SharePoint_Content_Admin**   Similar to the content databases created for SharePoint web applications, this database stores the actual data for the Central Administration web application. The *SharePoint_Content_Admin* database must be colocated with the *SharePoint_Config* database. Similar to the *SharePoint_Config* database, it is not expected to grow significantly, so it is considered to be a small database and can grow up to 1 GB.

- **WSS_Content**   Stores all site content, including files in document libraries, list data, Web Part properties, audit logs, apps for SharePoint, and user names and rights. All of the data for a specific site resides in one content database. Content databases can contain one or more site collections. The size of the content database will vary in size; while the databases are supported up to 4 terabytes, it is strongly recommended to keep them under 200 GB. The 4 terabyte size limits are for single-site repositories and archives with non-collaborative I/O and usage patterns such as Records Centers. It is recommended that administrators scale up databases that supports a site collection and scale out (by adding more databases) to support web applications that need additional site collections.

SharePoint service application databases

There are a number of service applications that rely on databases; these databases are created when the various service applications are provisioned. These services include User Profile service application, Search service application, App Management service application, Secure Store service application, Usage and Health Data Collection service application, Word Conversion service, Microsoft SharePoint Foundation Subscription service application, Business Data Connectivity service application, PerformancePoint Services service application, State service application, and Word Automation Services service application. Here is a breakdown of these services and their databases:

- **User Profile service**   Contains the following three databases:

  - **Profile**   Stores and manages users and some social information; the majority of the social information has been moved to the My Site of the user. The size of the database can range up to 1 terabyte in some instances and is considered to be medium to large and is read-heavy.

  - **Synchronization**   Stores configuration and staging data for use when profile data is being synchronized with directory services such as Active Directory. The size of the database is dependent on the number of users, groups, and the ratio of users to groups. The database can get quite large.

  - **Social Tagging**   Stores social tags and notes created by users along with their respective URLs. The size of the database is determined by the number of tags and ratings created and used and can span from small to extra large (over 1 terabyte).

- **SharePoint Search service**   Contains the following four databases:

- **Search Administration**   Hosts the Search application configuration and access control list (ACL) for the crawl component. The database may grow up to 100 GB.

- **Analytics Reporting**   Stores the results for the usage analysis reports and extracts information from the Link database when needed. The database can grow in excess of 100 GB and it is recommended using an additional *Analytics Reporting* database when the main database size becomes greater than 200 GB. During analytics updates, the database is write-heavy.

- **Crawl**   Stores the state of the crawled data and the crawl history. Additional crawl databases should be created for every 10 million items crawled. The database is read-heavy and should be hosted by SQL Server 2008 Enterprise edition or higher so that the Search service can take advantage of data compression.

- **Link**   Stores the information that is extracted by the content processing component and the click-through information. On sites with heavy traffic, the database should utilize separate spindles from other databases. Additional *Link* databases should be created for every 60 million documents crawled. The database grows on disk by 1 GB per 1 million documents fed and the click data grows linearly with query traffic (1 GB per million queries). An additional *Link* database should be added per 100 million expected queries per year. The database experiences heavy-writes during content processing.

- **App Management service application**   Stores the App licenses and permissions that are downloaded from the Global Marketplace. The database is write-heavy during Apps installation and license renewal.

- **Secure Store service application**   Stores and maps credentials such as account names and passwords. Microsoft recommends that the database be hosted on a separate database instance, with access limited to one administrator since it may contain sensitive data.

- **Usage and Health Data Collection service application**   Stores health monitoring and usage data temporarily, and also is used for reporting and diagnostics. The *Usage* database is the only SharePoint database that can be queried directly and have schema modified by either Microsoft or third-party applications. The database size varies based on the retention policy and actual traffic load. It is recommended that the *Usage* database be placed on a separate spindle, and it is extremely write-heavy and can grow in excess of 1 terabyte.

- **Word Conversion**   Stores information about pending and completed document conversations. The database is very small and is read-and-write-heavy once per conversion item.

- **Microsoft SharePoint Foundation Subscription Settings service application**   Stores features and settings information for hosted customers. This database is not created by default and must be created by using Windows PowerShell or SQL Server. The database is typically small, being less than 100 MB. The database is read-heavy.

- **Business Data Connectivity service application**   Stores external content type and related objects.

- **Project Server 2013**   Stores all the data for a single Project Web App–enabled site along with all project and portfolio management (PPM) data, time tracking and timesheet data, and aggregated SharePoint project site data. The database is typically read-heavy.

- **SQL Server PowerPivot service application**   Stores data refreshed schedules and PowerPivot usage data that is copied from the central usage data collection database. When in use, PowerPivot stores additional data in content databases and in the Central Administration content database. It requires SQL Server 2012 Analysis Service, Business Intelligence, or Enterprise edition.

- **Managed Metadata service**   Stores managed metadata and syndicated content types. The database is read-heavy.

- **PerformancePoint service application**   Stores temporary objects and persisted user comments and settings. The database is read-heavy.

- **State service application**   Stores temporary state information for InfoPath Forms Service, Exchange, the chart Web Part, and Visio Services. The database size depends on the usage of the feature but can grow in excess of 200 GB. The database is read-heavy.

- **Word Automation Services service application**   Stores information about pending and completed document conversions and is read-heavy.

- **Machine Translation Services service application**   Stores information about pending and completed batch document translations with file extensions that are enabled. The database is read-heavy.

- **App for SharePoint**   Stores information about apps for SharePoint and Access Apps. The databases are read-heavy.

Putting it all together

Up until this point, you have learned about the core components that make up a SharePoint farm and its subsequent web applications. To help understand how these components work together, this chapter will conclude by walking you through the SharePoint 2013 pipeline. To review, when you create a SharePoint web application, a new IIS web application is created that has a number of elements ranging from a content database to web application-specific files that include the *web.config* file. As you will learn in this section, config files are critical to how SharePoint responds to a particular user request. On a given SharePoint server, there are actually a number of config files, and each plays a distinct role in not only how SharePoint web applications work, but ASP.NET web applications in general. The configuration files operate in a narrowing scope from a high-level, server-wide configuration down to the specific details of each web application. The configuration file hierarchy starts with the *machine.config* file and ends with the *web.config* file within the IIS website. Remember that extending a SharePoint web application will create another IIS web application, so if the *web.config* file of one zone requires modification, the same may be true for the other IIS web application as well.

The various *web.config* files define a number of HTTP handlers and HTTP modules that map out the components that should be included in the HTTP pipeline. For the sake of this topic, this chapter will focus on the elements that are important to the SharePoint request. The modules that are listed in Figure 1-14 are at the end of the HTTP pipeline. These can be reviewed in greater detail by visiting IIS, selecting Modules | View Ordered List. Once there, examine the second column to see where the SharePoint *.dll* files enter the picture.

SPNativeRequestModule	C:\Program Files\Common Files\Microsoft Shared\Web Server Extensions\15\isapi\spnativerequestmodule.dll	Native	Local
SPRequestModule	Microsoft.SharePoint.ApplicationRuntime.SPRequestModule, Microsoft.SharePoint, Version=15.0.0.0, Culture=neutr...	Managed	Local
ScriptModule	System.Web.Handlers.ScriptModule, System.Web.Extensions, Version=4.0.0.0, Culture=neutral, PublicKeyToken=31...	Managed	Local
SharePoint14Module	C:\Program Files\Common Files\Microsoft Shared\Web Server Extensions\15\isapi\owssvr.dll	Native	Local
StateServiceModule	Microsoft.Office.Server.Administration.StateModule, Microsoft.Office.Server, Version=15.0.0.0, Culture=neutral, Pub...	Managed	Local
PublishingHttpModule	Microsoft.SharePoint.Publishing.PublishingHttpModule, Microsoft.SharePoint.Publishing, Version=15.0.0.0, Culture...	Managed	Local
DesignHttpModule	Microsoft.SharePoint.Publishing.Design.DesignHttpModule, Microsoft.SharePoint.Publishing, Version=15.0.0.0, Cult...	Managed	Local
FederatedAuthentication	Microsoft.SharePoint.IdentityModel.SPFederationAuthenticationModule, Microsoft.SharePoint.IdentityModel, Versi...	Managed	Local
SessionAuthentication	Microsoft.SharePoint.IdentityModel.SPSessionAuthenticationModule, Microsoft.SharePoint.IdentityModel, Version=...	Managed	Local
SPWindowsClaimsAuthentication	Microsoft.SharePoint.IdentityModel.SPWindowsClaimsAuthenticationHttpModule, Microsoft.SharePoint.IdentityM...	Managed	Local
SPApplicationAuthentication	Microsoft.SharePoint.IdentityModel.SPApplicationAuthenticationModule, Microsoft.SharePoint.IdentityModel, Versi...	Managed	Local

FIGURE 1-14 The SharePoint modules in IIS.

Web applications, like SharePoint, have the ability to modify the HTTP modules that will be processed within their *web.config* file. Upon examining the *web.config* file for Central Administration, take note that a number of modules have been removed: AnonymousIdentification, FileAuthorization, Profile, WebDAVModule and Session. A number of modules have also been added: SPNatvieRequest-Module, SPRequestModule, ScirptModule, SharePoint14Module, StateServiceModule, PublishingHttp-Module, DesignHttpModule, and Session. With the single exception of the DesingHttpModule, this was the same configuration in SharePoint 2010.

The following steps explain the first HTTP request:

1. The user issues a request over the Internet.

2. The HTTP Protocol Stack (HTTP.sys) intercepts the request and passes it to the Svchost.exe.

3. 3Svchost.exe contains the Windows Activation Services (WAS) and the WorldWide Web Publishing Service (WWW Service).

4. WAS requests configuration information from the configuration store, applicationHost.config. This will map virtual directories to physical directories.

5. WWW Service receives configuration information, such as application pool and site configuration.

6. WWW Service uses the configuration information to configure HTTP.sys.

7. WAS starts a worker process for the application pool to which the request was made.

8. Authentication is handled.

9. A request comes in for an ASP.NET page.

10. The request is given to the SharePoint14Module.

11. The page handler is unable to find a precompiled version of the page class on disk, so it must grab the file and give it to the ASP.NET engine for parsing.

12. The HTTP request enters the various SharePoint modules, as outlined in Figure 1-14.

13. The SharePoint14Module will contact either the file system or the content database for the appropriate page class information.

14. The ASP.NET page engine parses the file and generates a page class.

15. The page class is compiled into a .NET assembly and cached on the disk.

16. An instance of the requested page's class is created.

17. The response generated from the requested page class is sent back to the original caller.

You will notice that step 12 actually includes a number of steps, since the HTTP request enters the SharePoint modules. ASP.NET generally expects that the incoming URL will map directly into the file system on the server. As you know, SharePoint makes extensive use of virtual directories that map into the SharePoint Root folder, which is used to return pages that exist in locations like /_layouts/. The modules that are native to ASP.NET are only configured to handle request for resources such as *.aspx* files. Since SharePoint is designed to store files of any type, the SharePoint modules help surface these documents, but only after verifying that the requesting user or process has permission to access the file. The caching mechanisms in SharePoint are required to work differently than the native ASP.NET caches to provide better performance for SharePoint pages. As a result, SharePoint serves most *.aspx* pages in decompile mode. Since SharePoint offers a robust client object model, the modules are also responsible for handing this feature since ASP.NET doesn't have this type of functionality. SharePoint also has a highly configurable request throttling feature, which will honor, restrict, ignore, or reroute requests based on the health of the server. The SPRequestModule, which is the second SharePoint module in the pipeline, is responsible for registering the SharePoint virtual path provider, which serves, as an URL interpreter helping to route user requests to the appropriate file, checks to see if the file is checked out, and resolves the URL to a physical path. The SPRequestModule is also now responsible for handling the new Request Management (RM) feature in SharePoint. If the RM service is running (which is not enabled by default), the RM settings and check to see if Routing or Throttling has been enabled and then routes the request as necessary to a server running the Microsoft SharePoint Foundation Web Application service. The SPRequestModule also evaluates requests to see if they are from mobile devices and forwards those requests to the appropriate mobile page. Finally, the SPRequestModule then determines whether a request should be routed to the SharePoint14Module (*owssvr.dll*) and does some processing of the HTTP headers in the request that is expected by the SharePoint14Module.

In step 13, notice that the SharePoint14Module will contact either the file system or the content database for the appropriate page class information. This is where understanding the structure of IIS comes in handy. URLs with references to the _layouts directory (as shown previously in Figure 1-7) will use the file system. Basic requests for content will extract the data from the content database. The important takeaway here is that as each request is handled by IIS, various files are accessed both on the file system and in the database. Files that are in the database require a greater tax on the system since the SharePoint server will need to access the content database that resides in SQL Server. One of the most expensive hits in the HTTP request is when SharePoint has to pull data from SQL Server, so it is highly recommended that caching features be enabled when appropriate. You will gain an understanding of caching and performance in Chapter 9. One of the decisions you will need to make as you design your SharePoint solution will be to determine how each of these moving pieces should be used together to offer the best solution.

## CHAPTER 2

Introducing Windows PowerShell and SharePoint 2013 cmdlets

In this chapter, you will learn about:

- Exploring the role of Windows PowerShell with Microsoft SharePoint.

- Understanding the benefits of Windows PowerShell.

- Configuring user permissions for Windows PowerShell and SharePoint 2013.

- Examining the Windows PowerShell Management Shells.

- Working with Windows PowerShell cmdlets.

Since the release of Microsoft SharePoint 2010, administrators have needed some form of knowledge about Windows PowerShell. With SharePoint 2013, knowledge of Windows PowerShell has become more of a requirement since Windows PowerShell is replacing the deprecated, but still supported, *Stsadm.exe* command-line utility. As such, it is critical for SharePoint administrators to have strong Windows PowerShell skills. It is well documented that the SharePoint Central Administration web user interface does not allow for full configuration, administration, and management of the SharePoint environment.

It is important to set the proper expectations for this chapter. Although this chapter will introduce essential Windows PowerShell knowledge for SharePoint administrators, it is not intended to provide complete knowledge of Windows PowerShell, the SharePoint 2013 PowerShell cmdlets, and all the possible combination of scripts or uses; to do so would require an entire book, if not more. Instead, this chapter concentrates on giving you the ability to discover and learn the best ways to create powerful management scripting tools, as well as evaluate the numerous online Windows PowerShell snippets available publicly. To refer to the cliché, the purpose of this chapter is to teach you to fish, or, rather be self-sufficient, rather than simply handing you the fish or reviewing every single cmdlet available in Windows PowerShell and the SharePoint 2013 PowerShell library.

It is also important to note that as of January 2010, all Microsoft server products comply with the Microsoft Common Engineering Criteria (CEC), which requires Windows PowerShell support. Therefore, all of the core technologies and the majority of systems that will integrate with SharePoint will also support, if not rely on, Windows PowerShell scripting to configure, manage, and administer their systems as well.

Windows PowerShell is critically important to SharePoint administration, but knowledge of Windows PowerShell fundamentals is a critical skillset for any Microsoft IT professional or any individual using Microsoft products and technologies.

Exploring the role of Windows PowerShell

Windows PowerShell is a task automation tool created by Microsoft to allow users, typically server administrators, to automate and perform tasks on their on-premises SharePoint environment server(s) or while working with SharePoint Online environments. In this section, you will be introduced to a quick history of the tool and then explore the basic syntax.

Brief history of Windows PowerShell

Windows PowerShell 1.0 was first released in conjunction with Windows Server 2008. At the time, it was described as a new task-based command-line shell and scripting language designed especially for system administration. Windows PowerShell is built on the Microsoft .NET Framework and is meant to assist IT professionals to control and automate the administration of the Windows operating system and applications that run on Windows. Windows PowerShell has built-in commands, called *cmdlets* (pronounced "command-lets"), which let Windows PowerShell users manage the computers from the command line.

Windows PowerShell 2.0 was released in conjunction with Windows Server 2008 R2 and Windows 7. However, a downloadable install, known as the *Windows Management Framework,* was also made available for previous versions of the Windows server and client operating systems. The Windows Management Framework not only included Windows PowerShell 2.0, but also the Windows Remote Management (WinRM) 2.0 and Background Intelligent Transfer Server (BITS) 4.0. Arguably, the single most important improvement in Windows PowerShell 2.0 was the introduction of the feature to allow remoting—the ability to run commands on one or more remote computers from a single computer running Windows PowerShell. Windows PowerShell remoting allows for multiple ways of connecting, including interactive (1:1), fan-out (1:many), and fan-in [many:1 by using an Internet Information System (IIS) hosting model]. Additionally, Windows PowerShell 2.0 introduced the Windows PowerShell Integrated Scripting Environment (ISE). The Windows PowerShell ISE is a host application for Windows PowerShell, allowing users to run commands and write, test, and debug scripts in a single Windows-based graphical user interface (GUI) with multiline editing, tab completion, syntax coloring, selective execution, context-sensitive help, and support for right-to-left languages.

Finally, Windows PowerShell 3.0 was released in conjunction and as part of the Windows Server 2012 and Windows 8 operating systems. Again, however, a downloadable version of the Windows Management Framework 3.0 includes Windows PowerShell 3.0. Windows Management Framework 3.0 and is available only for Windows Server 2008 R2 with Service Pack 1 (SP1) and/or Windows 7 with Service Pack 1 (SP1). Additionally, the .NET Framework 4.0+ is a prerequisite requirement install on both Windows Server 2008 R2 SP1 and Windows 7 SP1.

When SharePoint Server 2013 is installed, applicable Windows PowerShell cmdlets are available via the SharePoint 2013 Management Shell. Basically, the SharePoint 2013 Management Shell is simply a Windows PowerShell shell that registers the SharePoint 2013 PowerShell extensions (Microsoft.SharePoint.PowerShell.dll) for use within the shell. Most, if not all, aspects of SharePoint 2013 can be managed via Windows PowerShell and the SharePoint extensions.

Basic Windows PowerShell syntax

To reduce the complexity of Windows PowerShell scripting and syntax, all Windows PowerShell scripts revolve around cmdlets. A cmdlet is a single-feature command consisting of a verb and noun separated by a dash (-) that manipulates objects in Windows PowerShell. Examples include *Get-Help*, *Get-Process*, and *Start-Service* (Verb-Noun). This is very different than other command-line interfaces (CLIs) or shells where commands are comprised of executable programs ranging from basic to complex.

In Windows PowerShell, most cmdlets are simple and designed to be used in combination with other cmdlets. For example, the *get* cmdlets only retrieve data, the cmdlets only establish or change data, the *format* cmdlets only format data, and the *out* cmdlets only direct the output to a specified destination.

Additionally, PowerShell cmdlets have a help file that you can access by typing:

```
PS C:\> Get-Help <cmdlet-name> -Detailed
```

The detailed view of the cmdlet help file includes a description of the cmdlet, the command syntax, descriptions of the parameters, and example(s) that demonstrate use of the cmdlet. However, specific sections of the cmdlet help file can be accessed via specific parameters such as *-Examples*.

In essence, the most important fact to remember in Windows PowerShell syntax is the verb-noun format with required and/or optional parameters.

Understanding the benefits of Windows PowerShell

GUIs, including the SharePoint Central Administration web application and site, typically use common, basic concepts understood by most computer users. A CLI such as Windows PowerShell uses a different approach to expose information. As it is completely text based from the user's perspective, it is important to know command names before using them. However, it is possible to compose complex commands that are equivalent to the features in a GUI environment. It is important to become familiar with commonly used commands and command parameters. Unfortunately, most CLIs do not have patterns that can help the user to learn the interface. Because CLIs were the first operating system shells, many command names and parameter names were not selected using common language or syntax.

Windows PowerShell is designed to improve the command-line and scripting environments by eliminating longstanding challenges and adding new, modern features, including:

- **Discoverability**   Windows PowerShell makes it easy to discover commands and syntax, as well as features.

    For example, to find a list of cmdlets that view and change Windows services, simply type:

    ```
    Get-command *-service
    ```

    After discovering the cmdlet that accomplishes a task, it is possible to learn more about the specific cmdlet by using the *Get-Help* cmdlet. For example, to display help about the *Get-Service* cmdlet, type:

    ```
    Get-Help Get-Service
    ```

    To fully understand the output of the specific cmdlet, pass (also known as "pipe," based on the character being used) the output object to the *Get-Member* cmdlet to see all the members of the returned *Get-Service* output "object." For example, the following command displays information about the members of the object output by the *Get-Service* cmdlet:

    ```
    Get-Service | Get-Member
    ```

- **Consistency**   The consistency of Windows PowerShell is one of its primary assets. For example, knowing how to use the *Sort-Object* cmdlet for one scenario enables the user to know how to use it for other scenarios. It is not necessary to learn different sorting routines for different cmdlets or systems. Additionally, new cmdlet developers can rely on existing cmdlets rather than creating new cmdlets for the same functionality. Windows PowerShell encourages developers to use the framework that provides basic features, as well as be consistent about the usage of the interface.

- **Interactive and scripting environments**   Windows PowerShell is a combined interactive and scripting environment that grants access to command-line tools and COM objects, and also enables access to the power of the .NET Framework Class Library (FCL). This environment improves upon the Windows command prompt (*Cmd.exe*), which provides an interactive environment with multiple command-line tools. It also improves upon Windows Script Host (WSH) scripts, which let you use multiple command-line tools and COM automation objects but do not provide an interactive environment.

- **Object orientation**   Although Windows PowerShell is text-based from an interaction perspective, Windows PowerShell is based on objects, not text. The output of a command is an object. It is then possible to send (or "pipe") the output object of one command to another command as its input. Therefore, Windows PowerShell provides a familiar interface for people with other shell experience, while introducing new object-oriented command-line functionality. In other words, it extends the concept of sending data between commands by enabling a user to send objects, rather than simply text as used in STSADM. This also increases the speed in which cmdlets will execute when compared to its STSADM counterparts.

- **Easy transition to scripting**   Windows PowerShell makes it easy to transition from typing commands interactively to creating and running scripts. It is possible to enter commands at the Windows PowerShell command prompt to discover the commands that perform a task. Once those commands are known and/or tested, save those commands in a transcript or a history before copying them to a file for use as a script. This offers several advantages; the first is that it documents a repeatable process. The second is the speed at which the process can be duplicated.

Although it may be tempting to use the SharePoint 2013 Products Configuration Wizard and/ or the SharePoint Farm Configuration Wizard, most experienced SharePoint professionals, as well as Microsoft, will recommend against the use of wizards in production SharePoint 2013 environments. Additionally, many SharePoint 2013 administrators prefer to utilize the SharePoint 2013 Central Administration web application for making configuration changes to the farm and/or its servers and services.

Utilizing Windows PowerShell to manage and administer the configuration of a SharePoint 2013 environment has many advantages, including:

- **Change control**   It is surprising how many production environments do not maintain a change control log. When configuration changes are done via SharePoint 2013 Central Administration or another graphical interface, creating change control log entries can be extremely difficult and usually incomplete. Short of numerous screenshot captures and/or video files, it can be unclear as to what changes have been made to the environment.

- **Disaster recovery**   One of the most beneficial items of utilizing Windows PowerShell for installation and configuration is maintaining the scripts in the event of a catastrophic system disaster. The saved scripts can be used to quickly re-create the environment in a disaster recovery situation.

- **Documentation**   Most organizations, although directed, fail to maintain proper documentation on their SharePoint 2013 environments. By using Windows PowerShell, it is easy to add the executed scripts from installation, configuration, and change to maintain the documentation of the environment.

- **Fine-tuning configuration**   It should be obvious, but not everything can be done via SharePoint 2013 Central Administration or other GUIs. In fact, only via Windows PowerShell can you potentially access all the possible configurations to ensure maximum efficiency and performance of the SharePoint 2013 environment.

It needs to be pointed out that there are certain cases where Windows PowerShell should and should not be used (the latter very rarely), especially when installing and configuring a SharePoint 2013 environment. The most prominent of these scenarios is when configuring the SharePoint 2013 Search service application. You will see an example of this in the final section of this chapter.

Windows PowerShell 3.0 enhancements

Since you will be working with Windows PowerShell 3.0 in SharePoint 2013, it is important to know about several of the significant features that improve its usability and allow you to better manage environments. With Windows PowerShell 3.0, new core cmdlets have been added to support much of the new functionality of Windows PowerShell 3.0. Since Windows PowerShell 3.0 is built upon .NET Framework 4.0, you can use new classes in Windows PowerShell, including Parallel Computing, Windows Communication Foundation (WCF), and Windows Workflow Foundation (WF).

Module autoloading is a significant enhancement to Windows PowerShell 3.0. When using the *Get-Command* cmdlet, it searches and retrieves all cmdlets and functions from all modules that are installed on the computer system, even if the module is not imported into the current session. Automatic importing of modules is triggered by using the cmdlet in a command, running *Get-Command* for a cmdlet without wildcards, or running *Get-Help* for a cmdlet without wildcards. The automatic loading of modules can be controlled by using the *$PSModuleAutoLoadingPreference* preference variable. The Windows PowerShell 3.0 console improves the tab completion functionality by completing the names of cmdlets, parameters, parameter values, enumerations, .NET Framework types, COM objects, hidden directories, and more.

Arguably, one of most important new features of Windows PowerShell 3.0 is the ability to schedule Windows PowerShell background jobs and manage them both in Windows PowerShell and Task Scheduler. Essentially, scheduled jobs are a combination of Windows PowerShell background jobs and Task Scheduler tasks. Scheduled jobs run asynchronously in the background, like Windows PowerShell background jobs. But, like Task Scheduler tasks, you can run scheduled jobs on a one-time or recurrent schedule or in response to an action or event. You can also view and manage scheduled jobs in Task Scheduler, enable and disable them as desired, use them as templates, run them, and set conditions for which they start automatically. A perfect example would be performing backups of SharePoint on a scheduled basis.

With Windows PowerShell 3.0, support for an updatable, enhanced online help system has been introduced. You can check for and download updated help files for the cmdlets in your modules. The *Update-Help* cmdlet automatically checks and identifies the newest help files, downloads them, validates them, and installs them in the correct language-specific directory for the module. The *Get-Help* cmdlet has been enhanced with a new parameter, *-Online*, which will open the online version of the help topic in your default web browser.

New to Windows PowerShell 3.0 is the ability to utilize persistent, user-managed disconnected sessions, using a PSSession object. The PSSession object is created by using the New-PSSession cmdlet and are saved on the remote computer. Unlike Windows PowerShell 2.0, the PSSession is no longer dependent on the session in which it is created. It is now possible to disconnect from a session without disrupting the commands running in the session. Therefore, you can close the session and even shut down the computer and later reconnect to the remote session from the same or different computer system. Additional cmdlets and parameters have been introduced to support the use of remote, disconnected sessions. However, both the originating (client) and terminating (server) ends of the connection must be running Windows PowerShell 3.0.

These are just a few of the Windows PowerShell 3.0 enhancements that can significantly increase your ability to manage your SharePoint and Windows systems.

Configuring permissions for Windows PowerShell and SharePoint 2013

Depending on whether your SharePoint 2013 environment is hosted on-premises or through SharePoint Online, the administrator who is executing the various SharePoint cmdlets will need a number of permissions. By default, the account that is used to install SharePoint will have the required rights and will be able to provide other accounts with these permissions if needed. The *Add-SPShellAdmin* cmdlet can be used to grant permissions for users to run the 2013 cmdlets, but to be able to execute this cmdlet yourself, you must have membership in both the *securityadmin* fixed server role on the SQL Server instance and the *db_owner* fixed database role on the databases that are to be updated. Additionally, you will also need to be a member of the Administrators group on the server on which you are running the Windows PowerShell cmdlets. The *Add-SPShellAdmin* cmdlet will add a user to the *SharePoint_Shell_Access* role for a specified database. If the role does not exist, it will be created at the time of execution. If no database is provided in the *–database* parameter, then the default behavior is to apply the settings to the Central Administration configuration database. If you use the *-database* parameter, the user is added to the role on the farm configuration database, the Central Administration content database, and the specified database. Using the *-database* parameter is the preferred method because most of the administrative operations require access to the Central Administration content database. In addition to adding the specified user to the *SharePoint_Shell_Access* role for the specified database, the user is also added to the *WSS_Admin_WPG* group on all web servers. In SharePoint 2010, the use of *Add-SPShellAdmin* would also add the user specified by the *–UserName* parameter to the *dbo_owner* role of the database; this is no longer the case in SharePoint 2013. Executing the cmdlet on a particular database will add the user to the *SharePoint_Shell_Access* and *SPDataAccess* roles. The following example will grant a backup administrator account (spAdmin2) the appropriate database permissions to execute SharePoint cmdlets against the database. It is worth noting that you will need to execute the *Add-SPShellAdmin* cmdlet for all database to which you want to grant access:

```
$db = Get-SPContentDatabase Contoso_Content_Main
Add-SPShellAdmin -UserName spAdmin2 -database $db
```

Additionally, the execution policy will be restricted for Windows PowerShell execution. To enable Windows PowerShell execution, you will need to change the execution policy (see Figure 2-1). Remembering your basic format of Windows PowerShell cmdlets, you will use the verb-noun combination of *Set-ExecutionPolicy* with the desired parameters. Setting the execution policy can be scoped out to the individual user (as shown in Figure 2-1), or to the server level (as shown in Figure 2-2).

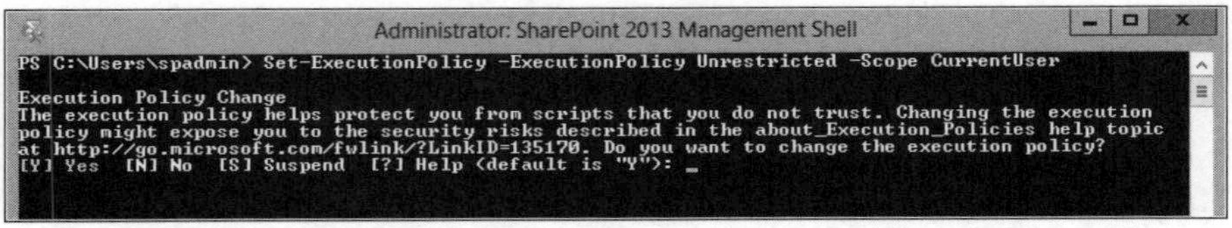

FIGURE 2-1 Users have the ability to set permissions for the execution policy for the current user only.

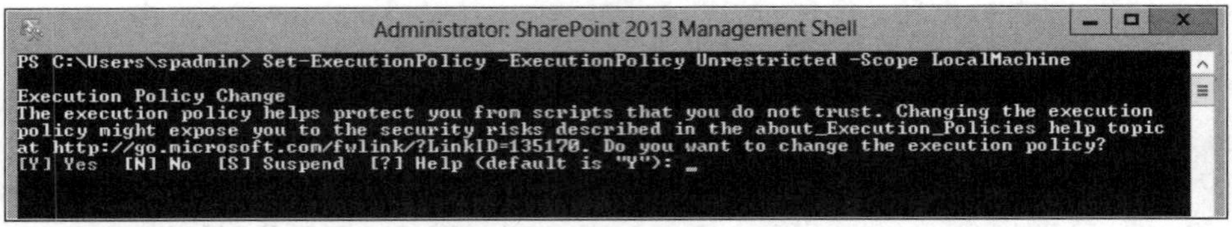

FIGURE 2-2 Users have the ability to set execution policy at the server level.

To run scripts, the minimum required execution policy for SharePoint 2013 is RemoteSigned, although the default policy for Windows PowerShell is Restricted. If the policy is left as Restricted, the SharePoint 2013 Management Shell will change the policy for Windows PowerShell to RemoteSigned. This means that you must select Run As Administrator to start the SharePoint 2013 Management Shell with elevated administrative permissions. This change will apply to all Windows PowerShell sessions.

In regards to SharePoint Online, you must be assigned the global administrator role on the SharePoint Online site on which you are running the Windows PowerShell cmdlets. You will learn more about the SharePoint Online management shell in the next section.

Examining the Windows PowerShell management shells

As a SharePoint professional, you will have a number of tools available to allow you to interact with a particular SharePoint environment. While much of the information in this chapter is directed at executing Windows PowerShell cmdlets in on-premises deployments, SharePoint Online has its own management shell that you should be aware of. The SharePoint Online Management Shell allows the SharePoint professional to manage users, sites, and organizations instead of using the SharePoint Online Administration Center. To set up the SharePoint Online Management Shell environment, you will need to install the Windows Management Framework 3.0 (*http://go.microsoft.com/fwlink/ p/?LinkID=244693*) and the SharePoint Online Management Shell (*http://go.microsoft.com/fwlink/ p/?LinkId=255251*). Once the shell is installed, you will need to execute the *Connect-SPOService* cmdlet similar to the following example. This will need to be done prior to being able to manage users and site collections:

```
Connect-SPOService -Url https://contoso-admin.sharepoint.com
    -credential admin@contoso.com
```

> **Note** If you forget to execute the *Connect-SPOService* cmdlet prior to executing other SharePoint Online cmdlets, you will receive an error message stating that no connection is available.

With the install of SharePoint Server 2013 on premises, you will have direct access to the SharePoint 2013 Management Shell. The SharePoint Management Shell is simply a Windows PowerShell shell with the additional execution of a script to add the necessary Windows PowerShell cmdlet library and shell environmental variables to easily access SharePoint cmdlets and commands. The actual startup script's default location is:

```
C:\Program Files\Common Files\Microsoft Shared\Web Server Extensions\
    15\CONFIG\PowerShell\Registration\SharePoint.ps1
```

However, most administrators will prefer to use the more fully functional Windows PowerShell Integrated Scripting Environment (ISE) included with the Windows Server operating system.

Windows PowerShell can be utilized to run many aspects of Windows Server 2012, and out of the box, there are few ways to run your Windows PowerShell cmdlets on the server. As shown in Figure 2-3, users have the ability to use the default command-line-driven Windows PowerShell environment and add the appropriate snap-ins for what they are trying to accomplish. For example, if a user wanted to use Windows PowerShell to execute SharePoint cmdlets, they would need to add the SharePoint snap-in as follows:

```
PS C:\> Add-PSSnapin Microsoft.SharePoint.PowerShell
```

FIGURE 2-3 You can execute cmdlets with out-of-the-box Windows PowerShell.

Unfortunately, by default, the Windows PowerShell ISE will not include the SharePoint cmdlets. If you attempt to load the snap-in after it has been loaded, it will throw an error. While the error will not halt the execution, you probably don't want to see red text flying by every time you execute your scripts. To eliminate the error, it is common that you will see *–EA 0* at the end of the module name. This is telling Windows PowerShell to handle the error silently. You can use either of the following shorthand examples to load the SharePoint snap-in:

```
PS C:\> asnp Microsoft.SharePoint.PowerShell –EA 0
```

```
PS C:\> asnp *sharepoint* -EA 0
```

However, as seen in Figure 2-1 and Figure 2-2, users can simply open the SharePoint 2013 Management Shell to execute SharePoint-specific cmdlets. The downside to using the shell is that it too is a command-line-driven tool. While there are hundreds of cmdlets, once the snap-in has been loaded, you will be able to select cmdlets by typing the verb and then tabbing (that is, using the Tab key and/or Shift-Tab key combination) through a list of available cmdlets. One improvement over the previous version of Windows PowerShell and SharePoint is that the parameters are now viewable in IntelliSense, making it much easier to be productive with the tool.

With Windows Server 2008 R2, Microsoft introduced the Windows PowerShell ISE. ISE is an environment built for users to have more robust control of their scripts and how the scripts are run. In Windows Server 2008 R2, ISE is a Windows feature that needs to be enabled either manually or by running the following cmdlet:

```
PS C:\> Add-WindowsFeature PowerShell-ISE
```

With Windows Server 2012, ISE is already up and running by default. Figure 2-4 shows the ISE for Windows PowerShell 3.0 in Windows Server 2012.

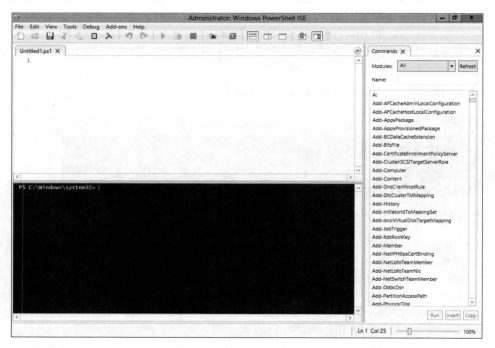

FIGURE 2-4 Windows PowerShell ISE is available by default in Windows Server 2012.

Since the SharePoint 2013 cmdlets and environment variables are not available by default when using the Windows PowerShell ISE, you can either add the SharePoint snap-in or change the profile for either a specific user or for all users. By default, no profiles are present on a fresh install of a server, but they can be modified to preload the SharePoint snap-in.

Selecting a profile to use in Windows PowerShell ISE

Windows PowerShell ISE supports profiles for the current user and all users of Windows PowerShell ISE. It also supports the Windows PowerShell profiles that apply to all hosts. The profile that you use is determined by how you use Windows PowerShell and Windows PowerShell ISE.

If you use only Windows PowerShell ISE to run Windows PowerShell, then save all your items in one of the ISE-specific profiles, such as the CurrentUserCurrentHost profile for Windows PowerShell ISE or the AllUsersCurrentHost profile for Windows PowerShell ISE.

If you use multiple host programs to run Windows PowerShell, save your functions, aliases, variables, and commands in a profile that affects all host programs, such as the CurrentUserAllHosts or the AllUsersAllHosts profile, and save ISE-specific features, like color and font customization, in the CurrentUserCurrentHost profile for Windows PowerShell ISE profile or the AllUsersCurrentHost profile for Windows PowerShell ISE.

Table 2-1 lists profiles that can be created and used in Windows PowerShell ISE. Each profile is saved to its own specific path.

TABLE 2-1 Profile paths for different profile types for Windows PowerShell

Profile Type	Profile Path	
"Current user, Windows PowerShell ISE"	$profile.CurrentUserCurrentHost, or $profile	
"All users, Windows PowerShell ISE"	$profile.AllUsersCurrentHost	
"Current user, All hosts"	$profile.CurrentUserAllHosts	
"All users, All hosts"	$profile.AllUsersAllHosts	

For example, assuming that all users use all hosts for Windows PowerShell for the SharePoint server, you would execute the following Windows PowerShell command in the Windows PowerShell ISE. Be aware that the following example applies to the "All users, All hosts" case, as noted in the $profile.AllUsersAllHosts property of the New-Item cmdlet and powerShell_ise.exe command. You would change the property based upon the desired profile type:

```
if (!(Test-Path $profile.AllUsersAllHosts)) {
    New-Item -Type file -Path $profile.AllUsersAllHosts -Force
}
powershell_ise $profile.AllUsersAllHosts
```

As shown in Figure 2-5, this will open another tab in ISE called profile.ps1, into which you would enter the following code and save the profile file:

```
$ver = $host | select version
if ($ver.Version.Major -gt 1) {
    $host.Runspace.ThreadOptions = "ReuseThread"
}
if ((Get-PSSnapin "Microsoft.SharePoint.PowerShell" -ErrorAction SilentlyContinue) -eq $null) {
    Add-PSSnapin "Microsoft.SharePoint.PowerShell"
}
```

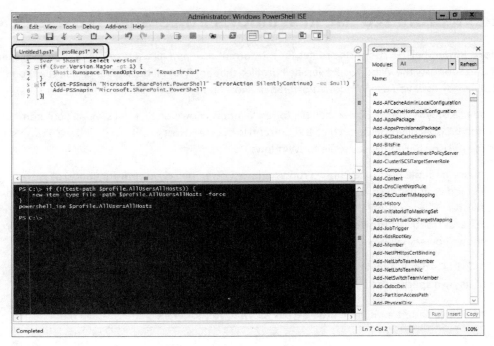

FIGURE 2-5 The process for setting up a default profile in ISE.

> **Note** The SharePoint 2013 Management Shell and the Windows PowerShell console differ in the use of the *ReuseThread* option, which defines how the threading model is used. The use of the SharePoint 2013 Management Shell is defined by the line *{Host.Runspace. ThreadOptions = "ReuseThread"}*, which is in the *SharePoint.ps1* file.

Working with Windows PowerShell cmdlets

As noted previously, all Windows PowerShell cmdlets are verb-noun combinations. And, as one of the specifications for Windows PowerShell is for cmdlets to be discoverable, the most essential cmdlets are those that allow you to discover which cmdlets to use and how to use them.

First and foremost would be to find the appropriate cmdlet. The *Get-Command* cmdlet helps users accomplish this. With the additional optional parameters of *-Noun, -Module, -Syntax*, or others and the ability to use wildcards, the *Get-Command* can be extremely powerful in helping to find the right cmdlet. Additionally, if you are using the Windows PowerShell ISE, you can also use the Commands Add-On (see Figure 2-6), which by default is found on the right side of the Windows PowerShell ISE GUI.

FIGURE 2-6 The default Commands Add-On for Windows PowerShell ISE.

Once the desired cmdlet is determined, use the *Get-Help* cmdlet and/or the *Show-Command* cmdlet. The *Get-Help* cmdlet will display the textual help for the cmdlet specified. The *Show-Command* cmdlet will show a graphical (GUI) window with both specific and common parameters for the command. Figure 2-7 is an example of the *Show-Command* window for the cmdlet.

FIGURE 2-7 The GUI to set the parameter for the *Get-Help* cmdlet.

When using Windows PowerShell, you can keep the cmdlet help references up to date online if you wish. You will be prompted to do this when first using Windows PowerShell, but can always manually force an update using the *Update-Help* cmdlet in any Windows PowerShell shell.

As shown in Figure 2-8, once you have found the cmdlet that you desire, use the *Get-Command -Syntax* cmdlet/parameter combination to get just the syntax of the cmdlets.

```
PS C:\Windows\system32> Get-Command -Syntax Get-Help

Get-Help [[-Name] <string>] [-Path <string>] [-Category <string[]>] [-Component <string[]>]
[-Functionality <string[]>] [-Role <string[]>] [-Full] [<CommonParameters>]

Get-Help [[-Name] <string>] -Detailed [-Path <string>] [-Category <string[]>] [-Component
<string[]>] [-Functionality <string[]>] [-Role <string[]>] [<CommonParameters>]

Get-Help [[-Name] <string>] -Examples [-Path <string>] [-Category <string[]>] [-Component
<string[]>] [-Functionality <string[]>] [-Role <string[]>] [<CommonParameters>]

Get-Help [[-Name] <string>] -Parameter <string> [-Path <string>] [-Category <string[]>]
[-Component <string[]>] [-Functionality <string[]>] [-Role <string[]>] [<CommonParameters>]

Get-Help [[-Name] <string>] -Online [-Path <string>] [-Category <string[]>] [-Component
<string[]>] [-Functionality <string[]>] [-Role <string[]>] [<CommonParameters>]

Get-Help [[-Name] <string>] -ShowWindow [-Path <string>] [-Category <string[]>] [-Component
<string[]>] [-Functionality <string[]>] [-Role <string[]>] [<CommonParameters>]

PS C:\Windows\system32>
```

FIGURE 2-8 An example of using the *Get-Command* together with the *–Syntax* parameter for *Get-Help*.

For more technical information about the cmdlet, use the *Get-Help -Detailed* parameter. For examples of how to use the cmdlet, use the *Get-Help -Examples* parameter, as shown in Figure 2-9. And finally, for the full help file, including all the information on syntax, technical information, and examples, use the *Get-Help -Full* cmdlet/parameter combination.

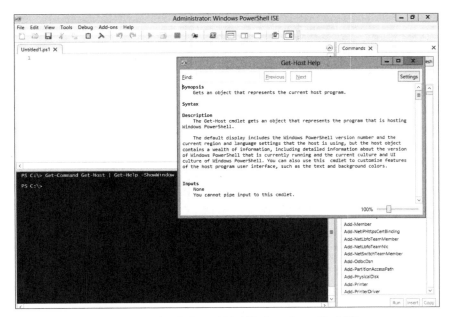

```
PS C:\> Get-Help Get-Help -Examples

NAME
    Get-Help

SYNOPSIS
    Displays information about Windows PowerShell commands and concepts.

    -------------------------- EXAMPLE 1 --------------------------

    PS C:\> Get-Help

    This command displays help about the Windows PowerShell help system.
    -------------------------- EXAMPLE 2 --------------------------

    PS C:\> Get-Help *

    This command displays a list of the available help topics.
    -------------------------- EXAMPLE 3 --------------------------

    PS C:\> Get-Help Get-Alias
    PS C:\>Help Get-Alias
    PS C:\>Get-Alias -?

    These commands display basic information about the Get-Alias cmdlet. The "Get-Help" and "-?" commands display the information on
    a single page. The "Help" command displays the information one page at a time.
    -------------------------- EXAMPLE 4 --------------------------

    PS C:\> Get-Help about_*

    This command displays a list of the conceptual topics included in Windows PowerShell help. All of these topics begin with the
    characters "about_". To display a particular help file, type "get-help <topic-name>, for example, "Get-Help about_Signing".

    This command displays the conceptual topics only when the help files for those topics are installed on the computer. For
    information about downloading and installing help files in Windows PowerShell 3.0, see Update-Help.
    -------------------------- EXAMPLE 5 --------------------------

    The first command uses the Get-Help cmdlet to get help for the Get-Command cmdlet. Without help files, Get-Help display the
    cmdlet name, syntax and alias of Get-Command, and prompts you to use the Update-Help cmdlet to get the newest help files.
    PS C:\> Get-Help Get-Command
```

FIGURE 2-9 The output of the *Get-Help* examples after help has been updated.

Many times, you will see references in the help provided about the *PipeBind* object parameter (see Figure 2-10). As discussed earlier in the chapter, keep in mind that all Windows PowerShell cmdlets return objects. You can assign that object optionally to a Windows PowerShell variable composed of unique alphanumeric combinations preceded by a *$* symbol (for example, *$webApp*). Additionally, you can "pipe" the output object of one cmdlet to the next cmdlet in an execution line using the pipe (|) symbol.

FIGURE 2-10 The Get-Host Help window within Windows PowerShell ISE.

Pipe binding allows you to pass output objects without creating variables when references to objects are necessary to return the desired object. If you believe that you may need a reference to an object later, you can assign it to a variable and then pipe in the variable. It is possible to pass the output object from the first cmdlet to the second, and then the output object from the second to the third, and so on, keeping in mind the object type for each cmdlet may and will probably be different. The key is to ensure the output object type of the cmdlet is the required input object type for the PipeBind object of the next cmdlet.

Discovering SharePoint-specific Windows PowerShell cmdlets

As discussed previously in the chapter, the *Microsoft.SharePoint.PowerShell.dll* file provides the library of almost all SharePoint-specific Windows PowerShell cmdlets. When the *Add-PSSnapin Microsoft.SharePoint.PowerShell* cmdlet is executed—either manually, by opening the SharePoint 2013 Management Shell, or by a *profile.ps1* file for the Windows PowerShell ISE, the references for the SharePoint cmdlets defined in the library are added to the shell environment. Using the *Get-Command* cmdlet with the *-Module* parameter, you can easily get the entire list of SharePoint-specific Windows PowerShell cmdlets, as shown in Figure 2-11. Additionally, you can use the Windows PowerShell ISE Command Add-On and limit the cmdlets in the window to the Microsoft.SharePoint. PowerShell module, as shown in Figure 2-12.

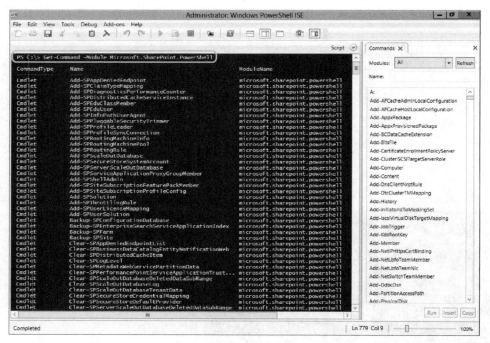

FIGURE 2-11 An example of the output of *Get-Command –Module* for Microsoft.SharePoint.PowerShell.

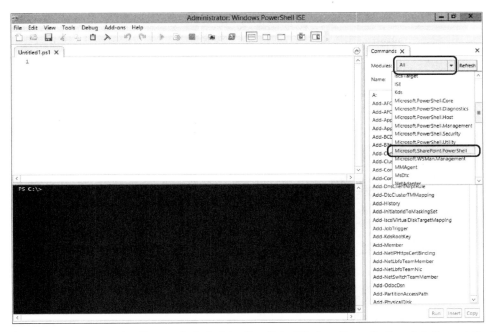

FIGURE 2-12 An example of how to find all of the SharePoint Windows PowerShell cmdlets through the ISE interface.

One of the most interesting tools now available to help with the building of Windows PowerShell scripts is Microsoft TechNet's Windows PowerShell for SharePoint Command Builder (*http://www .microsoft.com/resources/TechNet/en-us/Office/media/WindowsPowerShell/WindowsPower-ShellCommandBuilder.html*). This interactive web-based design (see Figure 2-13) allows you to explore Windows PowerShell cmdlets for different SharePoint platforms, including Microsoft SharePoint Foundation 2010, SharePoint Server 2010, SharePoint Online, SharePoint Foundation 2013, SharePoint Server 2013, and Microsoft Office 365. Additionally, there are a few quick steps available for common functions. The design surface allows for the input of values that will provide the parameters for the cmdlets and, finally, copying to the Clipboard to allow quick pasting in the Windows PowerShell shell.

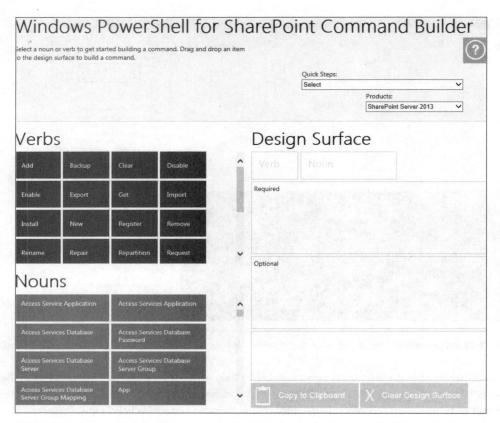

FIGURE 2-13 An image of the Windows PowerShell for SharePoint Command Builder on TechNet.

Another interesting website contains the TechNet documentation providing the index of Windows PowerShell cmdlets for SharePoint 2013 (*http://technet.microsoft.com/en-us/library/ff678226.aspx*). The online index provides all of the SharePoint 2013 cmdlets in both verb and noun order, as well as denoting the new cmdlets for SharePoint 2013 and links to the online documentation for each cmdlet, as shown in Figure 2-14. It is important to note that the cmdlets for on-premises and online are different and the SharePoint Online cmdlets are limited in their functionality, as opposed to the ones provided for on-premises.

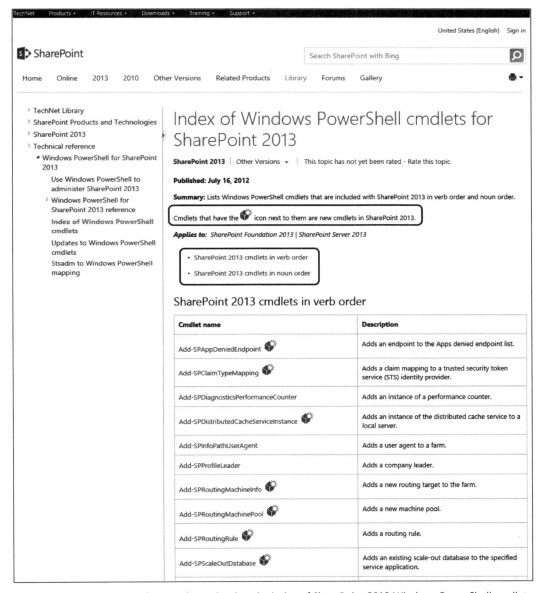

FIGURE 2-14 The webpage from TechNet that has the index of SharePoint 2013 Windows PowerShell cmdlets.

The last tool that you should be aware of is the Microsoft TechNet Script Center (*http://gallery .technet.microsoft.com/scriptcenter*) which is not limited to SharePoint Windows PowerShell scripts; rather, it is a community-driven gallery that provides many Windows PowerShell scripts and *can* be a good place to learn additional scripting techniques. Keep in mind, though, that because anyone can upload scripts to the Script Center, the scripts available should still be examined and tested thoroughly before using.

Working with SharePoint disposable objects

It is important to remember, similar to programming with certain SharePoint objects, the need to dispose—that is, to explicitly call the *IDisposable* interface *Dispose()* method on those objects to release the memory allocation back to the system. Failing to do this in programming, or within Windows PowerShell scripts, can lead to memory leaks, which in turn can lead ultimately to system performance issues or even failure. When using Windows PowerShell to work with certain SharePoint objects, most commonly *SPSite* and *SPWeb* objects, you should ensure proper disposal of the objects.

This need for disposal arises from the use of any object that contains or references an *SPRequest* object. The *SPRequest* object contains a reference to an unmanaged COM object that handles communications with the database server. Any SharePoint or third-party application or Windows PowerShell script that calls upon any object with reference(s) to the *SPRequest* object should be examined to ensure proper disposal.

Windows PowerShell will automatically dispose of objects used in commands that appear on a single line or as part of a piped command. However, if you create a variable that stores a reference to an *SPSite* or *SPWeb* object, you will need to explicitly or manually dispose of the object when you are done working with the variable. Luckily, there are certain tricks, including a couple of important SharePoint cmdlets, to assist you in ensuring proper SharePoint disposable object disposal.

An example of a single line and piping that would not need the object's *Dispose()* method called is:

```
Get-SPWebApplication | Get-SPSite –limit all | ForEach-Object { Write-Host $_.Url }
```

However, as mentioned previously, when using an assigned variable to represent the SharePoint disposable object, you will need to explicitly call the *Dispose()* method like so:

```
$web = Get-SPWeb http://portal.tekfocus.com/it
# Additional PowerShell script working with $web variable
$web.Dispose()
```

Finally, arguably the easiest method is to simply wrap all SharePoint disposable objects using Windows PowerShell within the combination of a *Start-SPAssignment -Global* and a *Stop-SPAssignment–Global* cmdlet pair, as shown here:

```
Start-SPAssignment –Global
# PowerShell script using SharePoint disposable objects
Stop-SPAssignment –Global
```

Any objects defined between the *Start-* and *Stop-SPAssignment –Global* cmdlets will automatically have their *Dispose()* methods called.

Putting it all together

So far in this chapter, you have gained an understanding of the importance of Windows PowerShell in a SharePoint environment and how to ensure that you will be able to both use it from a permission standpoint and explore the hundreds of cmdlets that are available. While it only takes a little tinkering to get an intermediate level of understanding of the Windows PowerShell cmdlets for SharePoint, there are additional advanced tasks in SharePoint that benefit from the use of Windows PowerShell. Prior to diving into some advanced scenarios, you will first explore how to build a simple site. From there, you will get an understanding of how to configure one of the more complex service applications: SharePoint Search.

Creating a sample site (site collection)

In this first example, the key takeaway is the use of variables that are prefixed with the dollar sign ($). While you don't always need to use variables, they do offer some readability to your scripts. Examine the following syntax. The use of SharePoint cmdlets doesn't happen until the final line, where you see the use of the *New-SPSite* cmdlet and a number of parameters that follow. The parameters are prefixed with the hyphen (-).

```
Add-PSSnapin Microsoft.SharePoint.PowerShell -EA 0
$siteURL = "http://portal"
$owner = "Contoso\Administrator"
$template = "BLANKINTERNET#0"
$name = "Portal"
$description = "This is a sample site that was built using PowerShell."
New-SPSite $siteURL -OwnerAlias $owner -name $name -Template $template -Description $description
```

SharePoint 2013 Search service application topology management

SharePoint 2013 uses the web-based interface within the SharePoint 2013 Central Administration web application to show the current status of the search topology. The primary way to change the topology is by using Windows PowerShell. This is a significant change from the previous version, as SharePoint Server 2010 also included a web-based option for changing the topology. The reason for this is that the core search architecture of SharePoint 2013 has a more complex and flexible topology that can be changed more efficiently by using Windows PowerShell. Also, keep in mind, the search capabilities of SharePoint Foundation 2013 have changed and are now based on the same search implementation as SharePoint Server 2013. This provides many improvements, but it also means that the search configuration is very different from the SharePoint 2010 Foundation but similar to SharePoint Server 2013 Search.

For specific information on changing the SharePoint Server 2013 Search service application topology, refer to *http://technet.microsoft.com/en-us/library/jj862356.aspx*, which contains references to Windows PowerShell to modify the SharePoint 2013 Search service application topology.

In this next example, you will see the use of comments. These are notes created by the author and are ignored by the system. These lines begin with the pound sign (#). The script may look a little more daunting than the last, but because of commenting, everything here should make sense to you.

```
Add-PSSnapin Microsoft.SharePoint.PowerShell -EA 0
# Define App Pool Name
$saAppPoolName = "SharePoint Web Services Default"
# Search Specifics, we are single server farm
# Define Search Server Name
$searchServerName = "Contoso-SP3"
# Define Search Application Name
$serviceAppName = "Contoso Search Service Application"
# Define Root for Search Database Names
$searchDBName = "Contoso_Search"
# Assign the Appplication Pool for Service Application Endpoint
$saAppPool = Get-SPServiceApplicationPool $saAppPoolName
# Start Search Service Instances
Write-Host "Starting Search Service Instances..."
Start-SPEnterpriseSearchServiceInstance $searchServerName
Start-SPEnterpriseSearchQueryAndSiteSettingsServiceInstance $searchServerName
# Create the Search Service Application
Write-Host "Creating Search Service Application and Proxy..."
$searchServiceApp = New-SPEnterpriseSearchServiceApplication  -Name $serviceAppName
    -ApplicationPool $saAppPoolName -DatabaseName $searchDBName
# Create the Search Service Proxy

$searchProxy = New-SPEnterpriseSearchServiceApplicationProxy  -Name "$serviceAppName Proxy"
    -SearchApplication $searchServiceApp
# Clone the default Topology (which is empty) and create a new one and then activate it
Write-Host "Configuring Search Component Topology..."
$clone = $searchServiceApp.ActiveTopology.Clone()
# Get the Search Instance Information
$searchServiceInstance = Get-SPEnterpriseSearchServiceInstance | where
    {$_.Server.Address -eq $searchServerName}
# Create the Search Service Administration Component
New-SPEnterpriseSearchAdminComponent –SearchTopology $clone
    -SearchServiceInstance $searchServiceInstance
# Create the Search Service Content Processing Component
New-SPEnterpriseSearchContentProcessingComponent –SearchTopology $clone
    -SearchServiceInstance $searchServiceInstance
# Create the Search Service Analytics Processing Component
New-SPEnterpriseSearchAnalyticsProcessingComponent –SearchTopology $clone
    -SearchServiceInstance $searchServiceInstance
# Create the Search Service Crawler Component
New-SPEnterpriseSearchCrawlComponent –SearchTopology $clone
    -SearchServiceInstance $searchServiceInstance
# Create the Search Service Indexing Component
New-SPEnterpriseSearchIndexComponent –SearchTopology $clone
    -SearchServiceInstance $searchServiceInstance
# Create the Search Service Query Component
New-SPEnterpriseSearchQueryProcessingComponent –SearchTopology $clone
    -SearchServiceInstance $searchServiceInstance
# Activate Search
$clone.Activate()
Write-Host "Search Done!"
```

You can read more about the Search service and its components in the "Search service application" section of Chapter 4, "Understanding the service application model."

As you work with Windows PowerShell, you will undoubtedly need a deeper understanding of its capabilities. While this chapter has given you a good foundation, as well as enough insight into Windows PowerShell to be successful, there are still many elements that have been left out. There are many online references and books that can help you gain a deeper understanding of this material.

## CHAPTER 3

Gathering requirements

In this chapter, you will learn about:

- The importance of gathering requirements.

- Defining information architecture requirements.

- Mapping information architecture requirements to logical components.

- Designing the physical architecture.

- Mapping requirements to SharePoint Online and hybrid implementations.

Microsoft SharePoint has been and continues to be many things to many people. Even today, if someone asks, "What is SharePoint?" each person has a unique idea of what the product can and cannot do. SharePoint is and always will be a platform to be implemented to meet the needs of the organization that it is meant to serve. As such, arguably the most important task of a successful implementation, is to gather all of the requirements that reflect the business goals of the organization to ensure the maximum value is attained with the implementaion of the SharePoint 2013 platform. Ultimately, the reason that everyone seems to have a different interpretation of what SharePoint is, is that a successful implementation should be molded to the needs of each different organization. Therefore, it is important for you, as its designer, to ask the appropriate questions to ensure that you are building a solution that satisfies organizational goals and visions while providing quantifiable value to the people using SharePoint.

In this chapter, you will gain an understanding of the importance of gathering requirements and then take a high-level view of the core components of the product. You will then take those requirements and map them to the logical and physical architectures to ensure a successful solution. Finally, you will examine what options you have with the new Microsoft SharePoint Online offering and discuss possible hybrid solutions. The final section, "Putting it all together," includes some example questions that you can add to your arsenal to help ensure the success of your implementation.

Importance of gathering requirements

At the very basic level of explanations, requirement gathering should be no different than what you typically do in organizing your personal and professional lives. In your life, you may set goals and determine the plan for accomplishing those goals. Typically, the more detailed the goals and plans for accomplishing those goals are, the better chance you have at being successful at meeting those goals. The approach to implementing SharePoint 2013 is no different.

SharePoint 2013 provides many capabilities to organizations and users. Unfortunately, many organizations either attempt to provide too many, if not all, of the capabilities of the platform, or too few, approaching the implementation with little or no clearly defined expectations. The majority of this book covers the technical elements of an implementation and configuration of SharePoint. The skills necessary for a successful gathering of requirements encompasses not only a deep understanding of the technical capabilities of SharePoint 2013, but also a thorough insight into the organization, its functions, and its goals, both tactical and strategic.

Why gather requirements?

All stakeholders of the SharePoint 2013 solution should understand and be able to communicate the importance of the requirement gathering process to both other stakeholders and, ultimately, the users of the proposed solution. Although seemingly based on common sense, you may run across the situation where the organization has decided to proceed with an implementation without a clear understanding of what the implementation is meant to provide to the organization. This leads to frustration with the solution, and possibly to an abandonment of the solution by the very users that the platform is meant to assist. Organizations that have implemented previous SharePoint environments and other enterprise systems without a thorough understanding of the capabilities and value that the platform provides to the users have found many different challenges throughout the lifecycle of the solution, including:

- Failure of implementing relevant enterprise metadata and content types
- SharePoint site "sprawl" or unruly, difficult-to-manage site structure
- Inability to implement future solutions due to initial configuration decisions and actions

An implementation project that fails to properly gather and understand the requirements may cause a "rip-and-replace" reimplementation of the SharePoint platform. The effort, time, and cost of the initial nonrequirement-focused deployment would be, at the very least, wasted.

When to gather requirements

The primary deployment stage within which to gather the requirements is planning. When you finish the planning stage, you should have documented the following:

- An infrastructure design to support your solution
- A detailed description of how you will implement the solution

- A plan for testing and validating the solution

- A site and solution architecture

- An understanding of the monitoring and sustained engineering requirements to support the solution

- A record of how the solution will be governed

- An understanding of how the solution will be messaged to the organization's users to drive adoption of the solution

Be aware, however, as you move through the future deployment stages of development, proof of concept, pilot, user acceptance testing, and, finally, production, you will likely update your requirements and plans. Like most planning, the important thing to remember is to do the *right amount* of planning. Too little can create significant additional work, consume unbudgeted resources, and/or ultimately detract from the overall success of the implementation. At the same time, too much planning can obviously take away time and resources up front, but also prevent corrections during a full deployment cycle.

Planning for success

Initially, the key question to be answered is, "Why are we implementing SharePoint 2013?" A clear, concise answer is the basis for a successful implementation. To that end, it is a question that can rarely be answered solely by the organization's IT professionals. The most valid answer will come from the organizational leaders and the interpretation of their understanding of the organization's goals and objectives. As such, it is critical to identify the individuals who are responsible for the business objectives, especially those to be addressed by a SharePoint deployment. These individuals will typically be identified by project management as key stakeholders. Additionally, more detailed business objectives to be addressed may come from key individuals within specific business or organizational units. The information gathered from these stakeholders is not only the basis for the implementation, but can also provide the initial information to be documented in the governance and information architecture deliverables. Finally, some, if not all, of these stakeholders should also be identified as potential members of the ongoing governance team or board to ensure that the solution continues to meet the needs of the organization throughout its lifecycle.

Metrics for success

If the process for gathering requirements is simply setting goals for the platform, how will you measure the business or organizational success of the SharePoint 2013 implementation? This question must be addressed and clearly answered to ensure that all stakeholders know when the goals of the project have been met. Even if the technology is close to perfect, the platform is not successful unless it has a positive impact on the organization's goals.

Although ideally it is best to use quantifiable metrics, an information management, collaboration, or content management system is difficult to quantify for users. Therefore, look for examples from users and/or other stakeholders to provide the measurable value statements. A specific example with a simple quantitative statement of organizational value at the end can have significant impact and help to measure the success of the project. For instance, a user could say that for a specific task, instead of the previous two days of effort, the task was completed in four hours. Quantitatively, this translates to a reduction of 75 percent effort to accomplish the task. If the task is repetitive and/or completed by multiple users, this can be easily translated to a cost benefit. If 10 users did the same task monthly, with a savings of 12 hours per task execution, the organization could claim the savings of 120 hours each month *for that task alone!* The features offered by SharePoint 2013 are vast, and no one organization will probably use all of them. Implementing SharePoint in an organization may cause people to examine their processes and find better ways of implementing everyday tasks. With the abilities of SharePoint Search, using metadata for documents instead of folders, or even presenting people with electronic workflows, can save time and money.

> **Important** One of the most critical questions to ask is, "What will determine the success of the project?"

Identifying stakeholders

Once the decision has been made to implement SharePoint, the stakeholders have a number of expectations. Whether formally or informally, there is a vision as to what the outcome of deploying SharePoint 2013 will provide to the organization. However, since SharePoint 2013 is meant to empower all users with access to information, and due to the fact that SharePoint 2013 integrates or connects to so many other systems, there are many people and/or groups of people who will have an impact on the success of the implementation. Identifying the individuals or stakeholders having an impact on the successful implementation is the first step in the process of gathering requirements.

In most organizations, the IT department will lead the technical implementation. However, IT is not necessarily fully aware of the organization's goals. In a worst-case scenario of a deployment of an IT product or technology, IT will simply deploy it without guidance from the organization. You may have seen examples where IT has approached a product or technology with a "build it and they will come" mentality. With SharePoint 2013, this approach is extremely dangerous to the overall success of the deployment. As with most business- and/or user-centric solutions, user adoption is paramount to the success of the project. You should always keep in mind that the role of IT is to support the organization and its goals. You could deploy the perfect technical solution, but if the users do not adopt and use it, the project is a failure. However, a successful SharePoint 2013 implementation is still very much dependent on IT.

Who are the other stakeholders? As with most things in a SharePoint 2013 implementation, it depends. It depends on the purpose of the platform. For example, in deploying a self-service portal for company and personnel information, typically the key executive stakeholder will be the corporate communications director and/or the human resources (HR) director. On the other hand, a customer-focused extranet portal may have the chief marketing officer or similar person as its key stakeholder. Each stakeholder may have his or her own agenda and have a number of requirements that need to be met. Typically, SharePoint may not be successful when those needs are captured. A critical error in deploying SharePoint 2013 is attempting to enable all the functionality and features that come with the product in the first iteration of deployment and expecting that it will satisfy the needs of the stakeholders.

Finally, as mentioned earlier, expect the platform to increase functionality over time, preferably in an iterative or phased approach. Therefore, remember that for each phase or iteration, the group of stakeholders may change. Review Table 3-1 for the most common stakeholders that participate in a project.

TABLE 3-1 Potential SharePoint implementation project stakeholders

Stakeholder	Requirements Input
Executive sponsor(s)	Provide the goal/vision of the platform
Content providers	Provide type(s) of information to be made available on the platform
Users	Provide input to ensure that the solution addresses the needs of users
IT department	Provide guidance in complying with IT policies and guidelines, as well as support for connected and/or integrated systems
SharePoint project team	Provide expertise on the platform capabilities, limits, and ease of solution implementation

The more stakeholders there are, the more information you can gather to provide detailed requirements, as well as ensure comprehensive coverage of important objectives. Additionally, you will gather more support for the implementation. Keep in mind that stakeholder and user support is arguably the most important aspect of any SharePoint 2013 deployment.

The inclusion of employees who may not have official titles but are influencers within the organization can help evangelize the solution. These *champions* can be influential in the organization due to how much they're respected. They can be essential in making an implementation successful.

Organizational objectives

The organizational objectives are the goals of the project put in the perspective of the organizational goals. The organizational or business objectives of the SharePoint 2013 solution should be clearly defined, documented, and measurable. Every requirement should have traceability to the objectives of the system. In fact, if a requirement does not have traceability to the objectives, it should be postponed for a later iteration or phase of the solution or removed altogether. Similarly, the implementation's goal should connect to the organizational mission or goal. This simply defines the SharePoint 2013 project's value to the organization.

In addition to organizational objectives, by deploying SharePoint 2013 within an organization, there can be additional value to the organization. These, too, should have traceability to organizational goals. Some of the additional organizational benefits can include:

- Ensuring less time to find and access information that organizational members need to accomplish their work

- Ensuring less time to find and utilize others' skills and expertise

- Consolidation of organizational classification of information

- Minimizing onboarding time for new members until they are productive

- Improving customer service and/or partner collaboration by providing access to internal organizational information

Prioritizing goals

In implementing a platform based on SharePoint 2013, scope can rapidly become an issue. As such, the first step for successful implementations is to prioritize the objectives to be addressed by the system. Ideally, it is best to identify three to five primary capabilities of the platform that will provide the most organizational impact and ensure that they are implemented extremely well. Ensure that the expectations of the platform are clear and communicated to all stakeholders and users early in the project lifecycle. Also, try to keep the complexity of the solution to a minimum by relying on SharePoint 2013 native functionality. By staying within the native functionality boundaries of the platform, especially during the initial iteration cycle, the project schedule and cost will be minimized, furthering the probability of success. During interviews with stakeholders, use the time to explain the out-of-the-box features and receive feedback about whether the native functionality will be acceptable to the user. Finally, ensure that the vision of the solution, not just the initial iteration, is communicated. This is even more critical in the initial iteration of implementation of the SharePoint 2013 platform.

Mapping objectives to functionality

Once the proposed system's objectives (goals) have been defined, the next step is to map the identified, prioritized objectives to SharePoint 2013 functionalities. This is one of the most important responsibilities of the SharePoint 2013 project team and administrators, as a broad and deep knowledge of SharePoint 2013 is critical to accomplishing this successfully. For example, an objective that ensures less time to find and utilize others' skills and expertise could depend, and therefore be mapped to, the native SharePoint 2013 features of user profile search, My Sites, newsfeeds, community sites, and blogs. Another example would be the objective of improving customer service and/or partner collaboration by providing access to internal organizational information. This requirement would map to SharePoint 2013 functionalities of extranet support, web content management, Business Connectivity Services (BCS), and/or mobile access.

> **Note** Implementing a tool should not dictate a process, and the tools selected to enable a process should not dictate the requirements. It is important to remember the requirements first and the technology second.

Deliverables

The requirements-gathering activities will contribute significant key artifacts for the implementation project. Different groups of stakeholders and individuals will have an impact on different deliverables. Optimally, the project team will gain this information from the stakeholder groups. The best method is by interview, capturing the respective information from each group. However, it may be difficult and too cost and time prohibitive to engage every stakeholder group in personal or group interviews. At the same time, communication solely via email can be less informative and limiting to both the stakeholders and the project team. Be flexible in the communication and information-gathering process.

At a minimum, you should deliver usage scenarios, functional requirements, nonfunctional requirements, taxonomy and metadata, content types that will be implemented, and site structure, and then work with them in defining the governance plan and documentation.

Usage scenarios

You should compile a list of usage scenarios that will capture the most common-use cases of the system. Additionally, the list should be prioritized, based on the commonality and criticality of the scenario. The usage scenarios will also provide additional information and basis for governance documentation, user documentation, and training. There is no dependency on other deliverables.

Key stakeholders   All users of the system

Example   A user will access a file from the archive (file share), make edits, and upload to SharePoint, providing metadata for the document.

Functional requirements

Functional requirements are derived from the usage scenarios and therefore are dependent on the completion of the prioritized list of usage scenarios. The list of functional requirements should also be prioritized based on criticality to business impact, commonality, and ease of implementation.

Key stakeholders   Executive sponsorship, business analysts, and SharePoint project team

Secondary stakeholders   System and application administrators of integrated or connected systems

Example   HR information requires a unique retention policy.

Nonfunctional requirements

Nonfunctional requirements are those that do not affect the functionality of the system, but are typically affected by policies and procedures of the organization. These can include organization- or IT-specific guidelines for IT systems such as security, high availability, capacity considerations, etc. Since nonfunctional requirements are not strongly tied to usage scenarios, the gathering of these requirements can be done in parallel with other requirement deliverables.

Key stakeholders   IT management and SharePoint project team

Secondary stakeholders   System and application administrators of integrated or connected systems

Example   All data must be secured via encryption—at rest and during transmission.

Taxonomy and metadata

In SharePoint 2013, the classification of the information stored within the system is more critical than prior versions. Additionally, the classification or taxonomy of the information will typically occur at multiple levels. In a simple organization, this could be implemented via a two-tier system of enterprise- or organization-wide classification and department classification. In more complex and larger organizations, it could have several tiers of classification. While gathering requirements and usage scenarios from users, the primary question to be asked in determining taxonomies will be, "How do you organize your data?" You will find individuals with the same role and/or responsibilities organizing the same type of data differently. With a well-designed taxonomy and metadata, SharePoint 2013 provides the ability for users to find the information as they desire, rather than by a fixed structure. At the same time, this ability can initially be challenging to users who have only dealt with file shares and folder structures. Most users coming from a simple folder structure have used the folder names and/or file names to provide the classification with which they feel most comfortable. At a minimum, the taxonomy and metadata will provide input to content types and site structure and, optionally, the configuration of the Managed Metadata Service (MMS) application of the platform.

> **Key stakeholders** Users and business analysts
>
> **Secondary stakeholders** SharePoint project team
>
> *Example* All documents in the organization must be identified with office location, department, and sensitivity classification.

Content types

Once information types and classification are determined from both usage scenarios and taxonomy and metadata, the content types and hierarchical level of the types can be defined and planned. Similar to taxonomy and metadata and, in fact, so closely related, the content type structure and level at which they are implemented can be at the organization, department, and or specific need level(s). Additionally, this may affect configuration of one or more MMS applications and their corresponding enterprise content type hubs.

> **Key stakeholders** Business analysts, SharePoint project team, and administrators
>
> *Example* Since all documents need to include the office location, department, and sensitivity classification, an enterprise content type will be created as the base document content type for the organization.

Site structure

As mentioned previously, SharePoint 2013 is more reliant on classification of the information than the storage or site structure of the platform. However, performance and system constraints will still affect the overall site structure for a successful deployment. The taxonomy and content type hierarchies will typically have the most impact on the site structure. The best way to describe the importance and relationship of classification and structure is to remember users will only find and use information in one of two ways if they do not already have the location of the information—either via Search or navigable site structure. Therefore, even if the SharePoint 2013 implementation is more reliant than ever on Search via metadata navigation and/or content, site structure is still just as critical.

One important thing to consider is how governance will dictate what users can and cannot do when creating new sites. You probably want to avoid situations where users are allowed to create sites that change the overall structure of the site.

Key stakeholders   SharePoint project team, administrators, and business analysts

Example   While there are a number of ways to organize sites within a specific organization, review Figure 3-1 as an example of how sites may be broken up functionally.

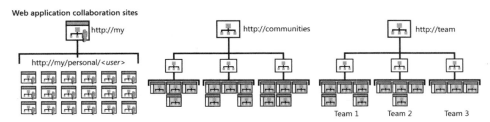

FIGURE 3-1   Site structures should be broken up in functional ways.

Governance plan and documentation

During the discovery of the organizational objectives that the solution is addressing, the initial governance plan should also be considered. Governance will be "living," in that it will and should be constantly changing as the solution matures. It is also essential in keeping the boundaries of use by keeping the platform manageable. It can also minimize the amount of configuration by SharePoint administrators to maintain the governance of the system. This is similar to having a policy within the organization not to browse inappropriate Internet sites. IT could create, administer, and maintain a block and/or accept a list of appropriate Internet sites, but the additional overhead could be significant. Rather, by communicating to all users via an Internet usage policy (governance), the organization can minimize the risk and cost of enforcement. This should be the same approach for SharePoint 2013 and good communication mechanisms of the proper use and purpose of the platform. In the final section of this chapter, you will be presented with a number of sample questions that will help determine the governance needs of an organization.

Key stakeholders   Business analysts, SharePoint project team and administrators, and the IT department

Example   All organizational files to be shared with others will be placed in the SharePoint portal.

Information architecture

Information architecture (IA) has several definitions. It is the structural design of shared information environments. For the intranet and websites, it can be considered the combination of organization, labeling, search, and navigation systems. It is both an art and a science of organizing information within software to support findability and usability. Successful IA addresses all three of the following information access scenarios:

- The user knows where the information is located.

- The user doesn't know where the information is located.

- The user doesn't know if the information exists.

Ignoring the first scenario, which is obvious, the platform provides access to relevant information in a combination of two ways; search and navigable structure.

The enterprise search capabilities native to SharePoint products and technologies has been in the platform for the last several versions. With the new consolidated features of the SharePoint 2013 Search engine, which could be easily be described as a combination of SharePoint Server 2010 Search and FAST Search for SharePoint 2010, the native search capabilities have become more powerful.

The site structure will define the primary navigable structure. However, again, there are improvements within SharePoint 2013 for navigation, allowing for dynamic navigation based on taxonomy. Implementing metadata or taxonomic navigation can be a very powerful tool for the findability and usability of the SharePoint 2013 environment. However, the dependency for successful implementation is a well-defined and planned taxonomy. Additionally, expect difficulty in user adoption of this type of navigation. Most users will have difficulty in moving from a single dimension folder-based structure of files and/or sites to a dynamic presentation of navigation. Additionally, if the information is not "tagged" with the proper taxonomic properties, the navigation structure can fail the organization.

All of the deliverables of the requirement-gathering phase are necessary to complete the IA. However, since you are primarily concentrated on search and navigability, the most important deliverables will be site structure, taxonomy, content types, and usage scenarios. However, functional and nonfunctional requirements, as well as governance, can have an impact on the final IA. Thus, your primary task will be to concentrate on site architecture and taxonomy or metadata architecture.

Benefits of IA

The stakeholders who have made the investment in the SharePoint 2013 environment will expect an intuitive platform for users to find the information being exposed by the solution. Additionally, good IA can have additional benefits, including:

- Reducing IT workload and costs by identifying and potentially removing duplicate or redundant information within the organization.

- Improving user experience and, therefore, adoption by providing intuitive, navigable structure(s) that reduce the amount of time to locate information that users need. As well, users will feel more positive about the system as a whole, driving even more user adoption.

- Minimizing risk of compliance of both internal and external regulations, policies, and procedures.

Site architecture

The site architecture will provide the relationship of the information in SharePoint and, optionally, outside the platform. It will show the relationship between web applications, site collections, sites and, optionally, libraries within the sites. The initial site architecture will typically start with the IA deliverable. Most organizations will be tempted to begin with organizational structure–based site architecture. Although this may benefit smaller, departmental organizations, consider the site architecture options based on usage or flow of information. The primary factors that influence site architecture are:

- **Content responsibility**   Who is creating the content? Who is managing the content? For example, the HR department is responsible for all human resources–related information on the platform.

- **Content security**   If there are specific security requirements for the information, this may cause a separate site hierarchy for the content.

- **Content size**   The amount of information and/or content within a site hierarchy can have an impact on the system as a whole and influence the site architecture.

You should also minimize the depth of the site architecture hierarchy. If a user needs to navigate seven levels to access information, the number of links or clicks can be frustrating to the user. Depending on the use of SharePoint 2013 social features and Office 2013 SkyDrive Pro, this can be minimized for common information. However, users will need training and/or communication surrounding this new functionality.

Some of the other topics that should be examined may include the use of publishing sites versus team sites. While governance may dictate who will modify or review content, the features will need to be determined during the planning phases.

Metadata architecture

Metadata architecture is as critical, if not more critical, than site architecture. It allows for the classification and organization of information in many different ways. Additionally, many of the enhanced SharePoint 2013 IA features rely on good metadata or information descriptors. It can affect relevant search, findability, and organizational compliance, to name a few.

Basically, metadata architecture is the combination of content types, local metadata (columns), and organizational metadata (managed metadata).

Content types are, in fact, primarily defined by the metadata used to define the type of information. The metadata for content types will either be defined at the site (collection) level or at the enterprise (metadata managed) level. With the MMS application, first introduced in SharePoint 2010, you have the ability to manage not only enterprise metadata, but also enterprise content types (that is, content types used across site collections, web applications, and even SharePoint farms). Content types can therefore be defined at the site (collection) level or across the enterprise.

Local metadata consists of two different types of columns: site columns and list columns. Site columns are defined at the site collection level and can be used to help define local (site) content types or be used throughout lists and libraries within the site hierarchy. List columns are defined and only available within the list or library where they are defined and configured.

Managed metadata is metadata that is managed centrally in a SharePoint 2013 MMS application, and optionally available both inside and outside the SharePoint 2013 farm.

Finally, there are very strong advantages of well-designed content type and metadata hierarchies. Since the metadata architecture is hierarchical, changes at a higher level can be optionally passed to lower levels of the hierarchy. This inheritance provides a significant benefit of ease to management and administration for changes in the taxonomy.

User challenges

Arguably, the most difficult part of applying the metadata architecture will be communicating and/or training the users on the benefits and proper use of metadata. Folders, the classic IA cornerstone in legacy information management systems, will still be strongly engrained as the method for organizing information. The classic folder structure was, in essence, the classification of information by location only. However, this structure presents the following problems:

- Folders do not allow for dynamic views of your content.

- Folder structures are fairly immutable or difficult to change.

- Folders assume that everyone accessing the information organizes information in the same manner.

- Folder structures lead to duplicate content, as users may put content in two folders since the content applies to both folders.

Since users will need to change the way they work with information by adopting the process of applying metadata information, it is also extremely critical to communicate the benefits of using metadata to organize information.

Logical architecture

After the completion of the IA, the process moves to creating the logical architecture to support that IA. The logical architecture simply ensures that all the services, service applications, and external systems needed for the IA are available and documented for the implementation of the environment. In a conceptual view, one could imagine the logical architecture as the listing and detailing of all of the building blocks required for the implementation, both internal and external, to the entire SharePoint deployment.

Typically, it is easiest to start by listing the service applications needed, and then understanding and mapping the communication pipelines between the components and/or services listed. Once this is complete, the architect will easily move into the physical architecture and capacity planning of the physical servers to host the services (components) of the complete system. Figure 3-2 illustrates an example of a logical architecture with a dedicated enterprise search farm.

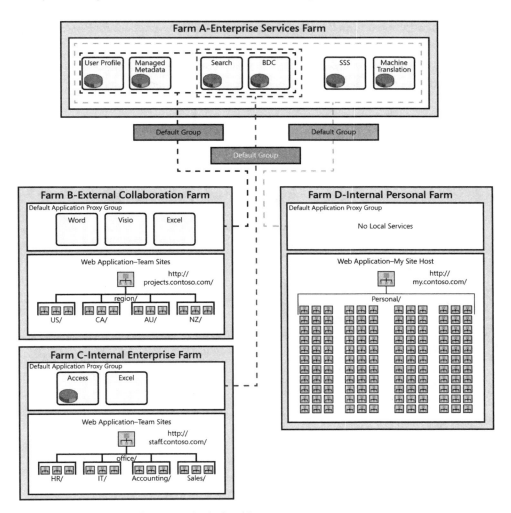

FIGURE 3-2 The diagram illustrates a logical architecture.

Physical architecture

With the logical architecture complete, the next step is to map the logical components (services) to physical servers. Even if the servers are virtualized using Hyper-V or VMWare, the virtual machines are considered, for this phase of design, physical servers. However, the virtual physical hosts need to be considered, if not by the SharePoint technical team, by the administrators managing the virtual environments. It is strongly recommended that virtual guests—physical servers of the SharePoint deployment—utilize dedicated resources such as virtual cores and RAM. Additionally, other factors, such as if and when to utilize hyper-threading (allowing for more CPU cores at a cost of overall CPU capability) or ensuring non-uniform memory access (NUMA) boundaries for RAM, should be considered by the technical architects and/or administrators of the virtual environment.

The physical architecture, as shown in Figure 3-3, will typically show the physical servers, with the services allocated to each server and communication pipelines between the servers.

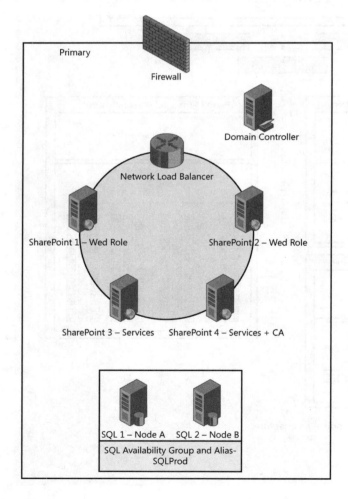

FIGURE 3-3 This diagram illustrates an example of the physical architecture.

Understanding system requirements

SharePoint 2013 supports several installation scenarios. At release, these include the following:

- Single server with a built-in database or single server that uses Microsoft SQL Server

  This scenario should only be used for development and/or evaluation installations of Microsoft SharePoint Foundation 2013.

- Single-server farm installation with built-in database or single server that uses SQL Server

  This scenario is optimal for development and/or evaluation installations of SharePoint Server 2013.

- Multiple server farm installation

  This will be the most common scenario for pilot, user acceptance testing, and/or production deployments of SharePoint Server 2013.

Minimum hardware and software requirements

As the SharePoint platform and its capabilities have increased from previous versions, the minimum hardware requirements have also increased from previous versions. In planning, the technical architect will need to keep these in mind when developing the implementation plan. However, as always, these system requirements should not drive the implementation. The organizational requirements, and therefore the solution requirements, should always have priority over technical requirements.

For the latest guidance on the technical requirements for SharePoint, review http://technet.microsoft.com/en-us/library/cc262485.aspx.

For all of the scenarios listed on the provided resource, the hard disk space for the system drive only provides for the base installation. You must plan for and provide sufficient space for diagnostics including logging, debugging, and other requirements. In production, you must have additional space for other operations. You must maintain, at a *minimum*, two times as much free space as you have RAM. So additional requirements may include:

- Drive space of five times RAM.

- Distributed cache RAM requirements.

- Workflow server farm.

- Office Web Apps farm.

- Search in SharePoint 2013 requires more resources than in the previous version.

- A single-server farm with a number of service applications will require 24 GB of memory.

All servers that belong to a server farm, including database servers, must physically reside in the same datacenter. Redundancy and failover between closely located datacenters that are configured as a single farm ("stretched farm") are not supported in SharePoint 2013, which is a significant change from the previous version.

Most production environments will consist of an implementation based on the multiple server three-tier farm. In this scenario, separate, dedicated database server(s) will be required.

It is important to keep in mind the SharePoint 2013 software boundaries and limits. Expect them to change during the lifecycle of the SharePoint 2013 products and technologies. For more information, visit http://technet .microsoft.com/en-us/library/cc262971.aspx.

Keep in mind that the software and hardware listed above are the *minimum* requirements. Capacity planning, especially from the database perspective, is covered in Chapter 5, "Designing for SharePoint's storage requirements."

SharePoint Online and hybrid architecture considerations

With Wave 15, the emphasis on SharePoint Online is clear. With Microsoft offering a "to the cloud" message and the public release and availability of the new version of Office 365 in February 2013, many organizations are now examining the SharePoint Online platform as an option to provide SharePoint 2013 capabilities to their organizations. Of course, the first and main thing to consider when examining SharePoint Online as an option for deployment is to examine requirements. As stated previously in this chapter, requirements are sometimes very difficult to keep as the goal of all deployments.

When to consider SharePoint Online or hybrid architecture

With either a sole SharePoint Online deployment or a hybrid architecture approach to SharePoint, there are many benefits to considering the cloud-hosted model. Additionally, although SharePoint Online is available as a stand-alone, purchasable Software as a Service (SaaS) model, most organizations will move directly to Office 365, which will include one of the two SharePoint Online plans: Plan 1, sometimes referred to SharePoint Online Standard, or Plan 2, sometimes referred to as SharePoint Online Enterprise. To map to Office 365, SharePoint Online Plan 2 is currently available in Office 365 Plans E1, E3, and E4. However, one of the benefits of SharePoint Online is that the feature set can grow fairly rapidly, especially considering Microsoft communications concerning "rolling releases" of software updates and enhancements to the Microsoft Cloud offerings.

Again, the first things to consider are the features available to organizations from all possible deployment scenarios, especially between on-premises (on-prem) and SharePoint Online. Review Figure 3-4 for an overview of the features and the offerings they map to.

Functional Area	Feature	SharePoint Server Standard	SharePoint Server Enterprise	SharePoint Online (Plan 1)	SharePoint Online (Plan 2)
Apps	App Catalog and Marketplace	New	New	New	New
Collaboration	Team Sites	•	•	•	•
	Work Management	New	New	New	New
	Social	•	•	•	•
	External Sharing			New	New
Search	Basic Search	•	•	•	•
	Standard Search	•	•	•	•
	Enterprise Search		•		•
Content Management	Content Management	•	•	•	•
	Records Management	•	•	•	•
	E-discovery, ACM, Compliance		New		New
Business Intelligence	Microsoft Excel Services, PowerPivot, PowerView		New		New
	Scorecards & Dashboards		•		
	Microsoft Access Services		•	•	•
Business Solutions	Microsoft Visio Services		•		•
	Form-Based Application		•		•
	SharePoint 2013 Workflow		New	New	New
	Business Connectivity Services	•	•		•

FIGURE 3-4 A comparison of SharePoint on-premises and SharePoint Online features.

Arguably, the most attractive feature of moving to a SharePoint Online environment is the lowering of associated overhead of managing the infrastructure, both from a supporting hardware as well as from a manpower perspective. From a financial perspective, the cost associated with providing the functionality for the users shifts from the classic capital expenditure (CAPEX) classification to an operating expense (OPEX) classification. In essence, especially for rapidly changing organizations, the cost for user business productivity software (email, collaboration, instant messaging, VoIP audio and video conferencing, when bundled with Office 365) can be clearly planned on a per-user basis, even for thousands of users. High availability and disaster recovery planning and implementation is already included, which with on-prem (or dedicated hosting) deployments can multiply costs exponentially, if not planned accordingly.

The biggest requirement driving necessity for an on-premises or hybrid deployment is typically business intelligence capabilities. Following right behind the business intelligence requirement seems to be the exposure of line-of-business (LOB) data via BCS. However, exposing LOB data via BCS is quite possible under certain conditions in the hybrid architecture.

If the organizational requirements extend beyond a purely SharePoint Online deployment, there are still more benefits to a hybrid architecture than solely relying on an on-prem deployment. Assuming that the organization subscribes or plans to subscribe to Office 365, SharePoint Online is included in the subscription. At that point, it makes financial as well as common sense to offload as much of the configuration, management, and administration of SharePoint capabilities and functions to reduce the overhead for on-prem deployments.

Hybrid architectures can provide the following:

- **Federated search**   Users in the cloud and the on-premises domain environment will be able to obtain search results that include content from both locations.

- **BCS**   Makes LOB data available to applications for SharePoint and external lists in SharePoint Online.

- **Single sign-on (SSO)**   Users who are connected to either the corporate network or Office 365 have to authenticate only once in a given session to access resources in both the on-premises SharePoint farm and SharePoint Online.

- **Directory synchronization**   User accounts in the on-premises Active Directory Domain Services (AD DS) domain automatically synchronize to Office 365.

- **One-way or two-way server-to-server trust**   A trust relationship between the on-premises SharePoint farm and SharePoint Online that enables secure connections and data flow.

There are three primary architectures when considering hybrid deployments concentrated on providing search and BCS capabilities. From the most basic to the most complex, they are:

- **One-way hybrid search**

  - **SSO**   Users who are connected to the corporate network have to authenticate only once in a given session to access resources in both the on-premises SharePoint farm and SharePoint Online.

  - **Directory synchronization**   User accounts in the on-premises AD DS domain use Active Directory Federation Services (AD FS) to automatically synchronize to Office 365.

  - **One-way server-to-server trust**   A one-way trust relationship is established between SharePoint Online and the on-premises SharePoint farm.

  - **Federated search**   Users in your on-premises domain environment will be able to get search results that encompass content from both locations.

Figure 3-5 gives an example of a one-way hybrid search architecture, showing users who are connected to the corporate network and have access to SharePoint Online.

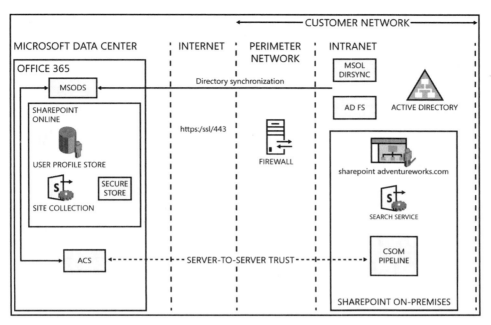

FIGURE 3-5 An example of a one-way hybrid search architecture.

- **Two-way hybrid search**

  - **SSO**   Users who are connected to either the corporate network or Office 365 have to authenticate only once in a given session to access resources in both the on-premises SharePoint farm and SharePoint Online.

  - **Directory synchronization**   User accounts in the on-premises AD DS domain automatically synchronize to Office 365.

  - **Two-way server-to-server trust**   A certificate-based two-way trust relationship is established between the on-premises SharePoint farm and SharePoint Online.

  - **Two-way federated search**   Users in Office 365 and in your on-premises domain environment will be able to get SharePoint Search results that encompass content from both locations.

Figure 3-6 gives an example of a two-way hybrid search architecture showing users who are connected to the corporate network and have access to SharePoint Online.

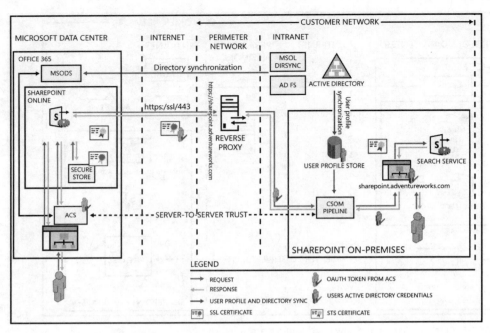

FIGURE 3-6 An example of a two-way hybrid search architecture.

- **Hybrid BCS architecture**

  A SharePoint 2013 BCS hybrid solution provides a bridge for companies that want to take advantage of cloud-based SharePoint Online to access on-premises LOB data while keeping that proprietary data safely maintained on their corporate intranet. The SharePoint BCS hybrid solution does not require opening holes in the firewall to allow traffic through and it does not require you to move your LOB data out into the perimeter network. The SharePoint BCS hybrid solution uses the on-premises BCS services to connect to the LOB data and then, through a reverse proxy, securely publish the endpoint out to the BCS services in SharePoint Online 2013, as shown in Figure 3-7.

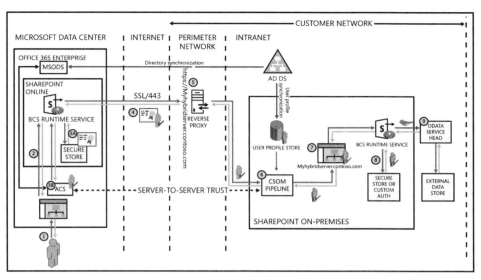

FIGURE 3-7 An example of the hybrid BCS architecture.

Hybrid requirements

Although the SharePoint 2013 technical project team is usually considered to be completely responsible for the deployment of the supporting infrastructure of the system, most organizations will have to include other IT professionals (such as Network Infrastructure, Directory Services, and Certificate Services teams) within their organization to provide the necessary infrastructure requirements to implement a SharePoint 2013 hybrid deployment architecture. Keep in mind, however, that organizations that have already invested in an Office 365 deployment may already have these requirements in place. For example, if an organization has already deployed Exchange Online, either completely online or hybrid, the majority of the prerequisites from an infrastructure perspective should already be in place. It is beyond the scope of this chapter to detail the "how" to deploy the prerequisites, but the following requirements will be necessary:

- AD DS within a functional-level forest of Windows Server 2008, Windows Server 2008 R2, or Windows Server 2012

- On-premises deployment of AD FS 2.0 exposed to the Internet

- On-premises deployment of the Microsoft Online Services Directory Synchronization (DirSync) tool

- An Office 365 Enterprise or SharePoint Online subscription with 15.0.0.4420 as the minimum build number (SharePoint Online Plan 2, Office 365 Enterprise Plan E1, E3, or E4)

- On-premises SharePoint Server 2013 farm that has each of the following configured:

  - Enterprise Search site collection configured with a public external URL (for example, *https://sharepoint.contoso.com*) by using an alternate access mapping

  - An Secure Sockets Layer (SSL) certificate issued by a public root authority

- An App Management Service Proxy installed and published in the SharePoint farm

- A Subscription Settings service application enabled and configured

- A Search service application, configured as appropriate

- A User Profile service application—User profiles contain detailed information about people in an organization. A user profile organizes and displays all of the properties related to each user, together with social tags, documents, and other items related to that user. In the BCS hybrid scenario, it is used to map the users, ACS OAuth credentials to the users' domain credentials.

- A Client-Side Object Model (CSOM) pipeline—The CSOM receives the incoming request from the reverse proxy and maps the OAuth user tokens from ACS to the users' domain credentials.

- A Site/Site collection—A site collection created expressly for the purpose of facilitating all hybrid request communication. The web application that this site collection is in has an alternate access mapping configured.

- BCS Runtime Service SharePoint for on-premises—The BCS Runtime service is the SharePoint service application that manages all BCS functionality, such as administration, security, and communications.

- Secure Store service SharePoint for on-premises—This is the credential-mapping SharePoint service application. In the SharePoint BCS hybrid solution, SharePoint on-premises stores the mapping of the users' domain credentials to the credentials that are used to access the external data source.

- OData service head—The SharePoint BCS hybrid solution only supports the OData protocol. If your external data is not natively accessible via an OData source, you must use Microsoft Visual Studio to build and deploy an OData service head for it.

- A reverse proxy device with an Internet connection that permits unsolicited inbound traffic [for example, Microsoft Unified Application Gateway (UAG) 2010 SP3].

- An Internet domain (such as *tekfocuslab.com*) and access to Domain Name System (DNS) records for the domain

SharePoint Online will need to have the following configured as well:

- BCS Runtime Service Online & Office 365 (O365) Microsoft Online Directory Services (MSODS)—Provides directory services in O365 that you can synchronize with your on-premises AD DS. The synchronization is done through user profile synchronization and allows users to use the same account for both on-premises and cloud authentication.

- SharePoint Online Secure Store service—This is the credential-mapping SharePoint service application. In the SharePoint BCS hybrid solution, SharePoint Online stores an SSL Server certificate that authenticates the SharePoint Online request to the reverse proxy.

- Windows Azure Access Control service (ACS)—This is the Azure security token service that performs authentication and issues security tokens when a user logs on to a SharePoint Online site. It looks up credentials in the MSODS, which has been synchronized with the on-premises AD accounts. This allows the user to use the same set of credentials for both the on-premises and online environments.

Finally, it will be necessary to replace the default token signing certificate for the SharePoint Secure Token service application (one of the default service applications created upon the creation of a new SharePoint Server 2013 farm). It can be replaced with a public certificate, which is recommended, or with a new self-signed certificate that you can create in Internet Information Services (IIS) Manager. A domain-issued certificate *is not supported*.

A hybrid deployment can initially seem to be complex. However, careful planning, approach, and implementation is typically done once, with little maintenance needed.

Putting it all together

As you already hopefully know, gathering, defining, and prioritizing requirements for a system is arguably the most important step in a successful implementation. The balance between planning and actually implementing the system is critical. It is a well-documented fact that there is rarely too much planning. Also, planning will lower the time of implementation if done correctly. Always keep the system requirements as the primary decision-making factors for everything within the implementation. A test implementation will ensure a smooth production implementation. Finally, it is extremely rare to find too much documentation, so ensure that it is created, maintained, and referred to often. This section highlights a number of questions that may enable you, as the Microsoft Share-Point Architect, to gather the requirements that you need to build a successful implementation; while each set of questions is organized into various buckets or individual categories, they may span several.

Planning a successful SharePoint solution strategy

Prior to gathering the requirements for how SharePoint should work, it is important to understand the following:

- Who are the key players involved with the project?

- What are the reporting relationships between the stakeholders?

- Why is each stakeholder involved?

- What are the overall business objectives and vision statements for each?

- How do the business objectives relate to the organization's strategic initiatives and mission?

- Are there any differing goals, conflicts, and so on?

- What will determine the success of the project?

- What processes are in place to maximize and measure user adoption?

- What are the plans for continuing the maintenance and monitoring of the environment?

These questions are more than just "fill in the blanks." These are generally conversation starters to ensure that enough thought has been put into these areas. Oftentimes, these items are overlooked and it is tough to understand if the implementation was successful or not.

It is important to map the overall business objectives to SharePoint functionality early in the process to help decide if SharePoint is a good solution—these cannot be forced.

Planning a governance strategy

Once you have been able to identify who the stakeholders are and how they will be measuring success, you will be able to continue by gaining an understanding of the governance strategy.

One of the first steps in defining a governance strategy is to build a governance team that will include members of IT, Corporate Training, HR, Corporate Communications, Cyber Security, Site Collection administrators, etc. Some example questions that you will find useful when gathering governance requirements include:

- Who will make up the governance board?

- What is the vision statement of the project?

- What are the defined roles and responsibilities?

- What are the policies and standards with regard to:

  - SharePoint content

  - Information design

  - Security

  - Features

  - Navigation

  - Custom code

  - Composite applications

  - Branding

Besides knowing what rules will need to be followed, it is equally important to determine how governance will be enforced.

Planning the IA

The IA of SharePoint describes how content will be organized and accessed. This can be a time-consuming process and should be well planned prior to adding content into SharePoint. Some of the key topics around this area include:

- What type of sites will be included and how will they be accessed?

- What type of content will SharePoint contain?

- Are there any security restrictions on particular content?

- How will users find this information?

- What is the expected user experience?

- How will documents be stored?

- What properties are important for each type of document?

- What are the commonalities of these properties?

- How are the documents being stored prior to moving them to SharePoint?

- Are there any specific policies around document management?

- What managed terms and keywords are expected?

Identifying business processes that will use SharePoint 2013

SharePoint 2013 offers much more than document management. It is important to identify what business processes need to be implemented using the solution as well. It is also important to help the stakeholders understand which processes can be simplified in SharePoint and which ones cannot. The following questions will help identify possible business processes:

- What business processes are tied to content stored in SharePoint?

- Are there any policies around information stored in SharePoint?

- What type of browsers will be supported in the organization?

- Who is responsible for defining the processes?

- Who is responsible for maintaining or creating workflows with SharePoint?

- What composite applications will be available?

- Do you expect to integrate LOB data within SharePoint?

Understanding the security requirements

Security within SharePoint is a critical piece, and understanding the requirements prior to building out the farm is critical to project success. Changes in security requirements can affect how the overall SharePoint farm is constructed and the communication protocols used for each. It is important to gather the following information:

- Who will have access to the system?

- Who will maintain those users?

- How will they access the system?

- Will a user be able to access the system externally? If so, will their rights differ?

- What form of authentication will be used?

- Will the farm contain Personally Identifiable Information (PII) or information that has specific security around it?

- Are there any specific requirements on how the data should be stored? (Transparent Data Encryption [TDE], and so on)

- Are there any specific requirements on how the information should be transported?

- Will certificates be used within the system?

- Will ports be blocked?

- Will antivirus software be configured?

- What server-hardening techniques are expected?

- Are there plans for any gateway or proxy devices?

- What type of load balancers will be used and what protocols do they support?

- Are there any predefined network topologies that we need to be aware of?

- Will Rights Management be required?

- Will compliance and auditing be required?

- What is the planned response to security threats? (governance)

- What are the current password policies?

- What are the current Group Policy Object (GPO) settings?

- Will security groups be maintained in AD and/or SharePoint?

Understanding the business intelligence requirements

Business intelligence requires additional planning over and above what is needed on a typical SharePoint implementation and can be critical in not only dictating how the farm is constructed, but what SQL Server product is used for support. The following items should be considered:

- Do you plan to incorporate any of the following?

  - Reports

  - Charts

  - Dashboards

  - Scorecards

  - Key Performance Indicators (KPIs)

  - Excel Services

- PerformancePoint

- Microsoft Visio

■ Each of these points will need to be planned not only for its existence, but also for the type of data, freshness of data, amounts expected, and so on.

Understanding the role of the Office client

Office has tight integration with SharePoint 2013. The following questions will help you determine the possible Office client solutions:

■ What version of Office is available to the users?

■ Will all users have a copy of Office locally?

■ Do you expect that users will work offline?

■ Do you expect a large number of users to be accessing the same documents?

■ Do you expect coauthoring?

■ Do you expect to support mobile applications?

Understanding the performance and reliability requirements

Once the content of the SharePoint site has been identified, it will be important to gain an understanding of the performance and reliability requirements. The following list of questions will help you determine the appropriate requirements that support performance and reliability:

■ How many concurrent users do you expect?

■ What is your expected growth or adoption rate over the next three years?

■ What is the expected performance metrics?

■ What services do you expect to be available at all times?

■ Do you expect to span geographical areas? Distance?

■ What is the distance from AD to SharePoint to SQL Server?

■ When are your peak hours?

■ Who is responsible for monitoring and maintaining SharePoint? (governance)

■ What is the expected load on the servers?

■ How much RAM can we expect to have on each server?

■ What is the network speed?

■ Are there any specific encryption requirements?

- Will all of the servers be virtual? Vendor? Blade distribution? NUMA boundaries? RAM allocation?

- Describe the load balancers that will be used. Who is responsible for their configuration?

- Is there a budget for Staging and Development servers?

- What is the current software development lifecycle process?

- Are there any concerns about being able to acquire the requested hardware?

- How much time is allocated in the deployment plan for performance and reliability testing?

Every SharePoint 2013 implementation is different, and it is vital to understand the requirements that will help you build a system that will promote success. This section is meant to help trigger requirements that may be critical to the architecture component; you may think of additional questions that help you drive forward to a successful project.

## PART 2

Design considerations for Microsoft SharePoint 2013

## CHAPTER 4

Understanding the service application model

In this chapter, you will learn about:

- Exploring the service application architecture.

- Discovering the service application components.

- Examining the changes in Microsoft Office web applications.

- Reviewing the service applications available in Microsoft SharePoint 2013.

- Exploring service federation.

Microsoft introduced the existing service application architecture with the SharePoint 2010 product. It solved many of the key issues that were present with the SharePoint Service Providers (SSPs) from the Microsoft Office SharePoint Server 2007 (MOSS) product. Those of you who are familiar with how it worked in 2010 will find that the architecture has remained intact. With the release of SharePoint 2013, some of the services have changed, but the overall plumbing works just as it did— both the good and the bad. This chapter will explore the overall service application architecture.

To fully understand how the SharePoint service application model works, you will need to understand the core components of the services. In the next section, you will get a detailed breakdown of how services work and how they work together.

While many of the services remain unchanged, some have been rebuilt from the ground up, and others are completely new. As you review the service applications that are available in SharePoint 2013, you will gain an understanding of what these services do and some design considerations for each. One of the major changes in the product is how Office Web Applications (OWA) is installed and interacts with the SharePoint farm, and this change will be discussed in the "Examining the changes in OWA" section later in this chapter.

Finally, you will learn about cross-farm services or service federation. With the architectures of SharePoint broadening into multiple farms, some organizations will find it useful to have service farms that support a number of SharePoint implementations.

You will then close out the chapter by putting all of the concepts together and building a cross-farm environment that federates the Business Data Connectivity (BDC) service.

Exploring the service application architecture

The service application architecture "plumbing" is basically the same as in SharePoint 2010. Microsoft did introduce some new service applications, and even managed to remove several, but with SharePoint 2013, the service application models are relatively unchanged from SharePoint 2010. Microsoft removed the Web Analytics, Work Viewing, and PowerPoint Viewing services.

Key concepts

The term *service application* has been overused. This makes it difficult for people to understand where the components live and how they function. To really get a handle on what's happening behind the scenes, it's important to know these terms:

- **Service**   The application binaries deployed to the servers in the farm.

- **Service machine instance**   The actual instance of the service running on the server. The service instance also has a Log On As account associated with the instance.

- **Service application**   The logical component that contains the service configuration and management, such as the service application configuration information and the database connection string.

- **Service application proxy**   The interface used by the service consumers for communicating with the service and the load balancer. The proxy is required so that the consumer knows which server to contact and how to consume the actual service. It's important to note that the service application proxy is not a web service or Windows Communication Foundation (WCF) proxy.

- **Service consumer**   Any application or service that consumes the service. If you are using the service application, you are a service consumer.

- **Service proxy groups**   Groups of service applications associated to specific web applications.

You can deploy services in a number of ways, including the Configuration Wizard, Central Administration, or Windows PowerShell. The Configuration Wizard will configure many of the services with their default values. You shouldn't use this for production environments, as there are many services that should be manually configured to ensure success.

In Central Administration, you can configure several services by populating fields associated with them. While you have a little more control than with the Farm Configuration Wizard, most SharePoint professionals will opt to use Windows PowerShell.

Windows PowerShell gives you the most control over the deployment of your service applications into your environment. The provisioning of some of the service applications can be very tricky, but you can still provision them all through Windows PowerShell.

When you configure your SharePoint farms, you get two services created automatically. These are key components for how the services work. These services include:

- The Application Discovery and Load Balancer service application
- The Security Token service (STS) application

Service applications must expose a web endpoint because all of their communications take place over HTTPS. It's also important to know that service applications communicate over TCP ports 32843 (HTTP) and 32844 (HTTPS).

Service applications are consumed by web applications, and each web application can have a specific set of proxy groups assigned to it. In Figure 4-1, you can see that the default proxy group and the secondary proxy group are getting consumed by different web applications and are sharing four service applications.

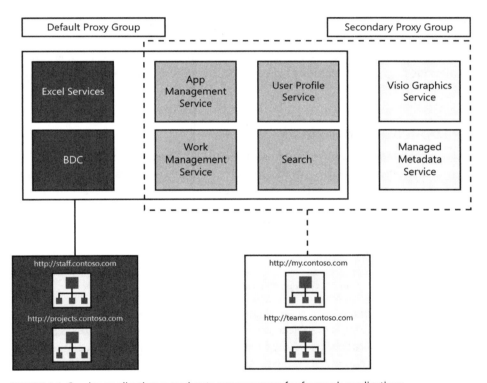

FIGURE 4-1 Service application mapping to proxy groups for four web applications.

Having the ability to pick and choose which proxy groups are assigned to which web application allows you to easily create a service architecture that is as complicated as you require.

Discovering the service application components

Now that you know some of the key terms associated with service applications for SharePoint, let's take a look at what components make up a service application:

- Service application endpoint
- Service application proxy
- Service application implementation
- Database(s)— which are optional

Service application endpoint using the WCF framework

The WCF is a communications framework for sending asynchronous messages between endpoints hosted by Microsoft Internet Information Services (IIS) or hosted within an application such as SharePoint. So when SharePoint services communicate between servers, they use the WCF framework. The complexity of the messages sent over WCF depends on the service using the framework; for example, a message might be as simple as a piece of XML data or as complex as a stream of binary data.

Service application proxies

You can assign a specific service application to an individual web application. The web application uses the service application proxy as a way to connect to the service application because the consuming web application does not talk directly to the service application. You also have the ability to assign a single proxy to multiple proxy groups; however, you are not able to create custom-named proxy groups through Central Administration. To create your new friendly named proxy group, you will have to use the following Windows PowerShell cmdlet, where *"Group Name"* is the name of the proxy group that you wish to create.

```
PS C:\> New-SPServiceApplicationProxyGroup "Group Name"
```

After the new proxy group has been created, users can add service applications to the group through the Central Administration graphical user interface (GUI) or through Windows PowerShell using the *Add-SPServiceApplicationProxyGroupMember* cmdlet. In Figure 4-2, you can see that a custom Application Proxy Group called Staff has been created for the Staff web application.

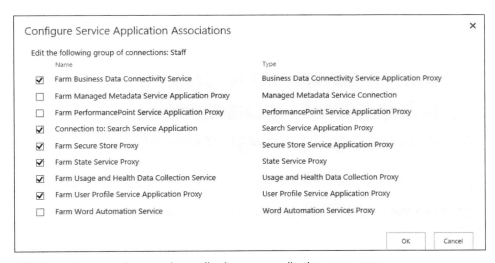

Service Application Associations ⓘ

		View: Web Applications ▾
Web Application / Service Application	Application Proxy Group	Application Proxies
Contoso Staff- 8090 (http://sp-13:8090/)	Staff	Farm Business Data Connectivity Service Connection to: Search Service Application Farm Secure Store Proxy Farm State Service Proxy Farm Usage and Health Data Collection Service Farm User Profile Service Application Proxy
Contoso My Sites- 8070 (http://sp-13:8070/) Contoso Projects- 8080 (http://sp-13:8080/) Contoso Upgrade- 9010 (http://sp-13:9010/)	default	Farm State Service Proxy Farm Usage and Health Data Collection Service Farm Word Automation Service Farm Secure Store Proxy Farm Business Data Connectivity Service Farm Managed Metadata Service Application Proxy Farm PerformancePoint Service Application Proxy Farm User Profile Service Application Proxy Connection to: Search Service Application

FIGURE 4-2 Users have the ability to create custom application proxy groups to keep their service application associations tidy.

By clicking the name (Staff) of the application proxy group, you are able to assign the application proxies (shown in Figure 4-3).

FIGURE 4-3 How to assign a service application to an application proxy group.

Service application implementation

Users have the ability to implement out-of-the-box service applications either through the Central Administration GUI (Development Environment) or through the use of Windows PowerShell; meanwhile, the creation of custom service applications is done through a deployment package. The implementation of service applications can be in dedicated application pools and can be run by different service accounts. When deploying, you can adjust settings or can customize settings after the service application has been implemented. Users have the ability to modify service application proxies through either the administration user interface or through Windows PowerShell.

Database(s) and service applications

A database for a service application is not a requirement; however, for service applications, such as the Search service or the User Profile service, the service application could require more than one database, or for service applications, such as the Microsoft Visio Graphics service or Microsoft Excel, the service might not require any databases. Also, service applications do not need to be implemented as a WCF service. If you deploy your service applications using the Farm Configuration Wizard (into your development environment farm), the database names are automatically created with the service application name, as well as with a GUID. However, when you deploy your service applications into your production environment using Windows PowerShell, you can create user-friendly database names that follow the database naming convention of your organization.

Examining the changes in OWA

The final product that is exposed to the user from the new OWA server is essentially the same as the OWA for SharePoint 2010. They both allow users to view and potentially edit browser-based versions of Microsoft Word, Microsoft PowerPoint, Microsoft Excel, and Microsoft OneNote files. In SharePoint 2010, OWA is a tightly integrated product that must be installed on every SharePoint server in your SharePoint 2010 farm, and it only worked with SharePoint (see Figure 4-4).

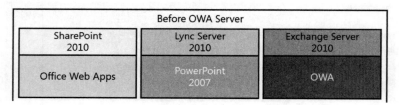

FIGURE 4-4 OWA was tightly integrated with SharePoint 2010, but not with other Microsoft products.

For SharePoint 2013, OWA is now a stand-alone server product, which can be downloaded from *http://tinyurl.com/PCfromDC-OWA*. The new OWA server gives you the ability to scale out and create an entire OWA farm. It also gives you the ability to integrate OWA into other products outside SharePoint. The OWA server works with products and services that support the Web App Open Platform Interface (WOPI) protocol. The new OWA server farm can support accessing files through Microsoft Lync Server 2013, Microsoft Exchange Server 2013, shared folders, and other websites besides SharePoint (Figure 4-5). The OWA server can be installed on one or more physical or virtual server and is free to use as a document viewer (read-only).

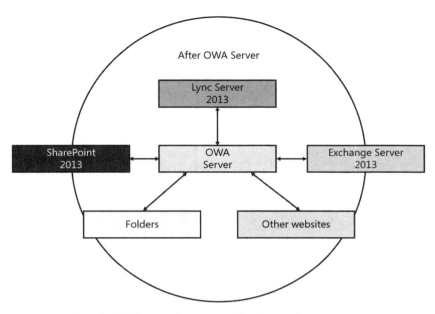

FIGURE 4-5 How the OWA server integrates with other products.

How does it work?

There are not a lot of steps in the process of how OWA functions within SharePoint 2013 (see Figure 4-6).

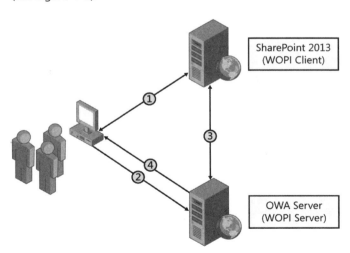

FIGURE 4-6 The steps required to display a document in a web browser using an OWA server through SharePoint.

As you can see in Figure 4-6, there are four steps required to get a document to view within a web browser using the SharePoint 2013 OWA server:

1. The user requests to edit a Word document from a SharePoint library (*GET* method), and SharePoint returns an IFrame (*WopiFrame.aspx*) with information that will be used to redirect to the WOPI server and negotiate the access tokens that OWA will use for the rest of the user session.

2. *POST* to WOPI server to populate a new *wordviewerframe.aspx* IFrame.

3. The WOPI App contacts the WOPI Host to *GET* the document.

4. The WOPI App renders the document in the IFrame and loads a few CSS files, several JavaScript libraries, and the *OneNote.ashx* web handler. After page load, the *OneNote.ashx* web handler will *POST* for approximately 15 seconds.

Examining the changes in workflows

Workflow for SharePoint 2013 continues the theme of breaking out SharePoint 2010 services. The 2010 workflow service is still available in SharePoint 2013 to maintain interoperability post upgrade, but to run a SharePoint 2013 workflow, you must install Workflow Manager (*http://tinyurl.com/PCfromDC-WAWS*). In fact, when creating a workflow in SharePoint 2013, you are only given the ability to create SharePoint 2010 (Figure 4-7) workflows until your SharePoint 2013 farm is bound to the Windows Azure Workflow Server (WAWS).

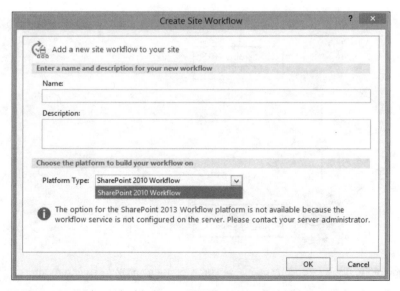

FIGURE 4-7 Without the binding to WAWS, you are limited in your selection of workflow platform types.

By breaking workflow into its own server, WAWS has become a great example of the new SharePoint application model. Workflow communications happen via the core app model technologies, CSOM and REST, and authenticates through OAuth. Like the OWA server, WAWS can run on its own farm, be used to handle workflows for more than one server farm, and work with more than one type of technology (see Figure 4-8). For example, you can run your WAWS farm with a SharePoint 2013 farm and with a Microsoft Project 2013 server farm simultaneously.

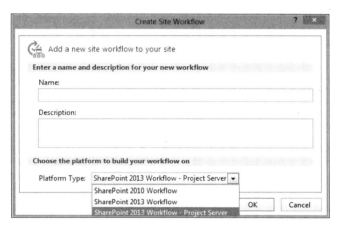

FIGURE 4-8 WAWS can be used to handle the workflow activity of different types of Microsoft farms.

However, unlike OWA, WAWS can be installed on SharePoint servers. Workflow traffic happens over ports 12290 (HTTPS) and 12291 (HTTP) by default. You should set up your WAWS to run over HTTPS—installing WAWS on a domain controller is not supported.

How does it work?

Figure 4-9 shows the steps required for workflow to function within SharePoint 2013.

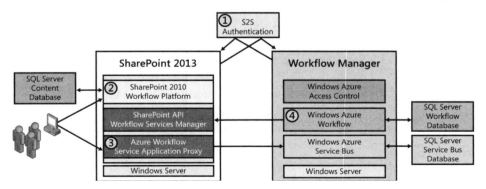

FIGURE 4-9 The way various workflow components talk to each other.

As seen in Figure 4-9, there are several steps that are required for the successful start of a workflow:

1. When setting up the workflow infrastructure, server-to-server (S2S) authentication is created automatically so that OAuth can run correctly when a workflow action starts.

2. To maintain backward compatibility, SharePoint 2013 has the SharePoint 2010 workflow platform already installed. If you are upgrading to SharePoint 2013, then your SharePoint 2010 workflows will simply work out of the box.

3. When the workflow event is triggered, communications to start the workflow happen over Windows Azure Service Bus.

4. The information is then passed to the Azure Workflow Service to send the workflow data back to SharePoint using the REST application programming interface (API).

Discovering the new web service applications available in SharePoint 2013

One of the ways Microsoft improved the functionality of SharePoint 2013 was by improving the functionality of the service applications. As the foundation of how SharePoint operates, there have been new service applications created, improved, and removed or consumed by other service applications.

There are four brand new service applications in SharePoint 2013: the Application Management service, the SharePoint Translation service, Work Management service, and Access Services. Even though there was an Access service in SharePoint 2010, there is now an Access Services 2010 (the old service with a new name), and the new Access Services (a new service with the old name).

Access Services

The Access Services web service application is based on the same service application namesake from SharePoint 2010. Access Services allows users to host Microsoft Access databases in SharePoint 2013 after being built using the Access 2013 desktop client and published into SharePoint. The Access Services for SharePoint 2013 can view and edit the Access 2010 web databases and even republish them into SharePoint 2013. The new service does not just allow you to create a website based on an Access database, but it will create the database schema and logic within a Microsoft SQL Server 2012 instance to store the Access database tables and information. Once the Access database has been provisioned, users will be able to view, edit, and interact with the Access 2013 database through their web browser. Unlike many of the SharePoint Server 2013 application services, Access Services 2013 doesn't expose an API that you can use to develop Access apps in Microsoft Visual Studio. Access 2013 client is the tool that you use to develop Access 2013 apps, as shown in Figure 4-10.

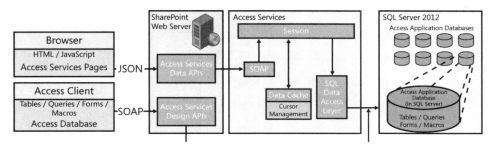

FIGURE 4-10 An example of how Access Services works in SharePoint 2013.

Because the Access Services creates SQL databases and tables to store the Access databases, there are some SQL prerequisites that must be met. You can read more about Access Services and its prerequisites on Microsoft TechNet at *http://social.technet.microsoft.com/wiki/contents/articles/12514 .sharepoint-2013-access-services.aspx*.

How does it work?

The user is using the Access run-time host to access the data from SQL Server 2012 and creating the output in HTML. SharePoint does not create any lists or renderings when using this service. When users accesses their page, they are retrieving the data from SQL using Access Services. When you add an Access database to SharePoint 2013, you will get a brand new SQL database.

The App Management service

With the introduction of the Windows Store came the need for the creation of the Application (App) Management service. The App Management service is responsible for storing and providing the SharePoint app licenses and user permissions, which are stored in its own database. If you purchase an app from the Windows Store, the App Management service will store all of the information about downloaded app licenses. Each time a user tries to use a SharePoint app, the App Management service will query its SQL database to validate that the user has permissions to use the app and that the license is valid (see Figure 4-11).

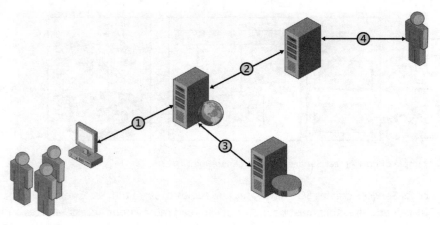

FIGURE 4-11 The App Management service verifies that a user has permission to run the app.

How does it work?

1. The user accesses the web server and opens an app.

2. The App Management proxy queries SQL to get the information about the app.

3. SQL returns information saying that the user and the app are valid and approved.

4. The administrator of the app sets permissions for who can and cannot use the app and manages the app licensing.

The Machine Translation service

The Machine Translation service allows SharePoint to translate content from one language into another through Microsoft Translator. Translator is a cloud-based translation service, so the server that is running the translation service must have the ability to access the Internet. If your organization limits which users can access the Internet, the service account that is running the service will also need permission to access the Internet. The Machine Translation service can run synchronously or asynchronously, or it can stream the translation of documents, pages, or sites. If you are using variations, it is possible to translate pages automatically based on target labels, and Managed Metadata service terms are also included in the variation translation, as shown in Figure 4-12.

The Machine Translation service is supported as a cross-farm (federated) service, is supported over wide area network (WAN) connections, and has its own database.

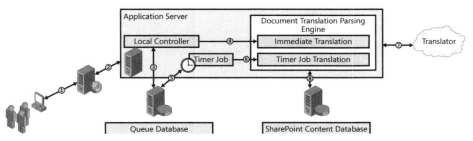

FIGURE 4-12 The Translator service is used with SharePoint to translate between languages.

How does it work?

1. The user accesses the content that needs to be translated from a website, such as a document on demand, or a new site that might have its translation scheduled for overnight.

2. The Machine Translation service proxy passes the information from the web application to the Machine Translation service.

3. The local controller pushes the document into the queue database.

4. The local controller sets the item for immediate translation or for translation using the service timer job.

5. Once the item is added to the document queue database, the item either waits for the timer job or it gets put at the top of the queue for immediate translation.

6. The item is moved from the content database to a local temp folder, where the item's content is parsed from the document by the Document Translation Parsing Engine.

7. The parsed content is sent to Translator for conversion, and the document in the temp folder is updated.

8. Item translation is completed, and content is saved back into the content database.

The WMS application

Task aggregation across multiple platforms within an organization has been a huge thorn in the sides of many people. This new Work Management Service (WMS) gives SharePoint 2013 the ability to take all of the tasks assigned to a person from SharePoint, Exchange, Project, and custom providers and render them in a single location, as shown in Figure 4-13. The WMS is dependent upon the Search service application and the User Profile service application to be provisioned. The service account that is running your WMS application will need full control permissions on the User Profile service application.

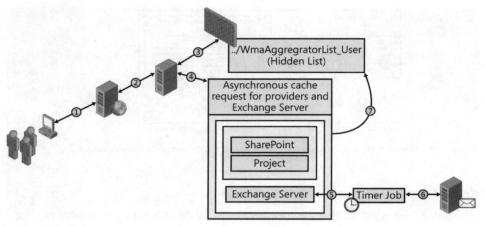

FIGURE 4-13 WMS is used to consolidate all of a person's tasks from various locations.

How does it work?

1. The user goes to his or her My Site URL.

2. The WMS application proxy talks to the WMS on the application server.

3. The user's tasks are displayed based on the information on the WmaAggregatorList_User hidden list.

4. Every 15 minutes, the service application makes a request for the user's task changes from the providers located in the ..*15\CONFIG\WorkManagementService\Providers\ provider.sptasklist .xml* file. Out of the box, only SharePoint will be available in this list, but as you add providers such as Project, the list will be updated.

5. The WMS application starts the timer job to return Exchange tasks.

6. Exchange task data is returned.

7. The user's hidden WmaAggregatorList_User task list gets updated.

Discovering the updated web service applications available in SharePoint 2013

Some of the service applications were tweaked a bit, a few new services were created, and one service application had its historic functionality returned. This section will review the returning service applications that can be created in SharePoint 2013.

Access Services 2010

The Access Services 2010 web service application allows the backward compatibility of existing Access web databases from SharePoint 2010. Access Services 2010 allows users to view, edit, and interact with their Access 2010 databases through their browser. SharePoint does not store the Access Services Access databases in SQL, since this service functions the same as it did in SharePoint 2010.

The BDC service

The BDC service allows users to interact with data that does not live within SharePoint. There are out-of-the-box connectors that allow communication to external databases, such as a SQL database that contains sales data. BDC can publish the external data just like a standard SharePoint list and gives the users the ability to perform standard create, read, update, or delete (CRUD) operations on external line-of-business (LOB) systems (see Figure 4-14).

BDC is supported as a cross-farm (federated) service, is supported over WAN connections, and has its own database.

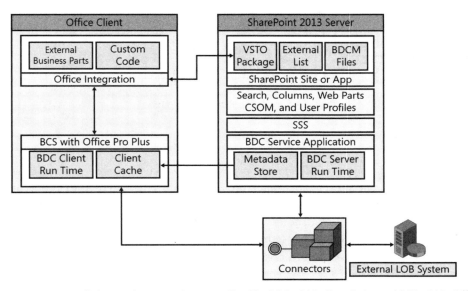

FIGURE 4-14   All the moving parts that are utilized by BDC within SharePoint and BCS within Office.

How does it work?

The one common scenario is to expose external LOB data as a SharePoint list. Another common scenario is using BCS to extend Search to index external LOB systems as well. The first step is usually to create an account used to retrieve the data before entering the credentials into the Secure Store service (SSS). The next step is to create the external SharePoint connector to the LOB data system. This is done by utilizing the built-in connectors or creating a custom connector. The returned data can be used within Search, Web Parts, and even User Profiles, and it can be viewed in a SharePoint list as well.

Excel Services

The purpose of Excel Services has not changed from SharePoint 2010. It still exists to publish Excel work sheets, workbooks, and data within a web browser. However, there have been several enhancements made to Excel Services from a developer perspective, such as updates to the REST API to request data through the Open Data Protocol (ODATA), and to the ECMAScript. There is also a new Excel Interactive View, which uses Excel services to generate Excel tables and chart views on demand, as diagrammed in Figure 4-15.

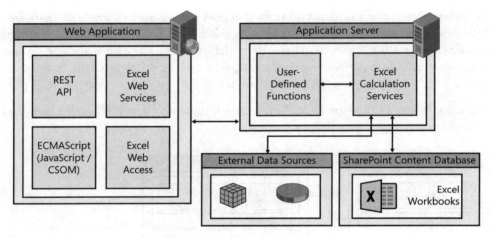

FIGURE 4-15   The parts found within the Excel Services application and proxy.

How does it work?

The purpose of the Excel Services application is to expose Excel workbooks through a web browser. This is done through the Excel Services application proxy, which uses the Excel Services application to grab the data from either a local content database or an external data source. Notice that in SharePoint 2013, you have the option to access the Excel web application proxy through REST and JavaScript. If you are running OWA on your farm, this will create a second version of Excel Services. As you can imagine, having two versions of Excel Services cannot be good. If you want the ability to view and edit Excel documents in a browser, then you will want to stick with OWA; otherwise, if you are interested in the advanced business solutions provided by Excel Services in SharePoint out of the box, then do not use OWA. Choose wisely based on your individual business case.

The MMS application

The Managed Metadata Service (MMS) application makes it possible to use managed metadata and share content types across site collections and web applications. Managed metadata is a hierarchical collection of centrally managed terms that users can define and then use as attributes for items. When you create the MMS application, a centralized term store is created to manage the keywords and terms, which gives the administrator the ability to point other web applications to the centrally managed MMS.

Another feature that is handled by the MMS is the ability to share content types. After creating the MMS and selecting a specific site collection as the content type hub location, users can share content types, such as columns, workflow associations, and policies, from their site collection's content type gallery. It is possible to create multiple MMS and share multiple term stores and content types from multiple site collections, but the question of whether you should deploy more than one MMS would depend on your corporate information architecture. The architecture for MMS is the same as it was for SharePoint 2010.

MMS is supported as a cross-farm (federated) service, is supported over WAN connections, and has its own database.

The PPS application

The PerformancePoint Service (PPS) application allows users to create business intelligence (BI) dashboards, custom reports, filters, tabular data sources, and scorecards (see Figure 4-16). This is the tool that creates all the pretty pictures to show management a quick overview of an organization's health. Using PPS with PowerPivot for SQL Server 2012 rounds off the BI integration stack by extending the capabilities of a user to dive deep into data. PerformancePoint alone will give you the dashboards to alert you of potential issues or trends, and PowerPivot will allow you to analyze (in detail) the source of the issue or trend.

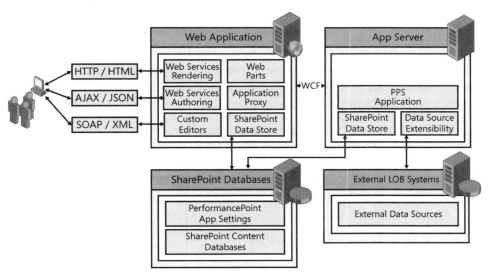

FIGURE 4-16 The PPS application exposes data to the user.

How does it work?

The way that this application exposes data is very similar to Excel Services, except that users have the ability to interact with their data using AJAX and JSON. The proxy service uses the service application to grab the requested data, and then displays the data to the user. The PPS application does not have its own database.

The Search service application

Search is one of the major cornerstones that has made SharePoint a success. For SharePoint 2013, it can be said that the enhancements to the Search service application are not just the best upgrade of the service applications, but probably the best feature of SharePoint 2013. The integration of FAST into SharePoint 2013 Search, as well as shifting the responsibilities from the SharePoint 2010 Web Analytics Service, have made this service application one of the most important features of SharePoint. However, your SharePoint 2013 Search is not just FAST repurposed. Microsoft took the best of SharePoint 2010 Enterprise Search and combined it with the best of FAST to come up with Search for SharePoint 2013. Search is probably one of the most important services within SharePoint 2013, and it is critical to keep this service functioning at peak performance, not only for user satisfaction, but also to help SharePoint administrators keep track of what is happening on the web analytics side of SharePoint. The ability to give the site owners the flexibility to look at the analytics and adjust the search scopes accordingly should help reduce the strain on the administrative staff and make the site owners happier. The Search service application crawls content, maps the information to managed properties, updates analytics, updates the search index, handles user search queries, and displays the query results.

Search is supported as a cross-farm (federated) service and is supported over WAN connections. Search crawls over your corporate WAN to consume the content of your remote farms will eat up your network bandwidth, so plan and crawl accordingly.

How does it work?

The Search service application comprises several components and databases, as shown in Figure 4-17. Just like the other services, before implementing Search, you should take high availability and fault tolerance into account. You should also consider the volume of your content, the estimated page views, and the number of search queries that are going to happen when you architect out your Search service.

SharePoint Search has two system service instances: the SharePoint Search Host Controller and the SharePoint Server Search 15. The SharePoint Search Host Controller is responsible for performing the host deployment and management for the SharePoint Search components on a single host. In a single-server installation, the host controller will start up five Noderunner.exe processes, one for each of the following search components:

- Content processing

- Analytics processing

- Index

- Query processing

- Search administration

This leaves the final component, the crawl component, to be handled by the SharePoint Server Search 15 instance.

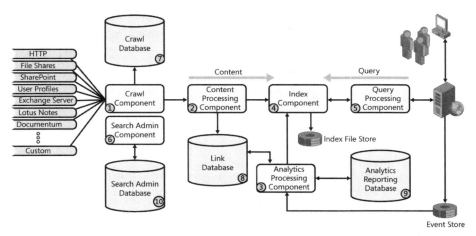

FIGURE 4-17 All these moving parts are required to get the new SharePoint 2013 Search working.

1. The crawl component is responsible for crawling content—not just SharePoint content, but also network folders, webpages, Exchange, and even custom LOB applications (piped items in Figure 4-17). The crawl component is responsible for collecting the content and metadata of the crawled items. To crawl content, the crawl component (crawler) connects to the content source by using the appropriate indexing connector with the appropriate crawl account. After the content has been crawled, the crawl component passes the crawled information to the content processing component for parsing. The crawling and indexing components are now discrete components in SharePoint 2013, where they were not in SharePoint 2010.

2. The content processing component is responsible for processing the crawled items and sending that information to the index component. You still have the ability to use custom iFilters, which are supported through a generic iFilter handler. In SharePoint 2013, you will not have to supply a .pdf iFilter because since it is native to the content processing component. The content processing component also transforms the crawled items into objects that can be included in the search index by parsing the document and document property mappings. This component is also responsible for linguistics processing such as language detection. The content processing component also updates the *Link* database with information about links and URLs. This content processing component is also responsible for generating the phonetic name variations for People Search. The content processing component sends the information to the index component and updates the analytics processing component by directly modifying the *Link* database.

3. The analytics processing component analyzes the crawled items and how users interact with the search results, then updates the search analytics information stored in the *Link* database. The analytics processing component is also responsible for maintaining the usage analytics information. For example, when a user loads a page, the page load event information is stored in the usage files on the web server and then pushed to the event store, where the data will remain until the analytics processing component updates the information in the *Analytics Reporting* database.

4. The index component receives the processed items' information from the content processing component and writes the information to an index file. The index files are stored on a disk in an index replica. The index component is also responsible for handling the incoming search queries, retrieving information from the query processing component, and sending the query result set back to the query processing component. You can divide the search index into separate slices, called *index partitions*, where each index partition holds one or more index replicas. The *search index* is the aggregation of all index partitions. Indexes can be scaled out both horizontally (partitions) or vertically (replicas). Replicas are created for fault tolerance and to help increase the query throughput.

5. The query processing component analyzes and processes the incoming search queries and results. When the query processing component receives a query, it analyzes the query for relevance to help optimize the search precision. The processed query is sent to the index component, which in turn processes that result set before returning the search results to the web server.

6. The search administration component is responsible for running and monitoring the system processes for the search components. The search administration component is also responsible for provisioning and topology changes. Search topology is no longer modifiable through the Central Administration GUI, only through Windows PowerShell.

In SharePoint 2013, there are now four databases for Search out of the box, as compared to three for SharePoint 2010. This should not be too much of a surprise because Search did consume the SharePoint 2010 Web Analytics service. The four databases are as follows:

1. The *Crawl* database still stores the details about crawled items. It also stores historical information, such as the last crawl time, the last crawl ID, and the type of update during the last crawl.

2. The *Link* database stores information (links) gathered by the content processing component. It also stores information about the number of times that people have clicked a search result from the search result page.

3. The *Analytics Reporting* database stores the results of usage analytics and contains the extracted information from the link database. The *Analytics Reporting* database will also store search reports, such as item reports, like the number of views per document over time, or site level reports, like the number of unique visitors over time. Data is aggregated to monthly views every 14 days. A portion of the data is passed to the search index component, such as different view counts.

4. The *Search Administration* database stores search configuration data and the analytics settings. The *Admin* database no longer stores the access control list (ACL). There can be only one *Search Administration* database per Search service application.

You can read more about the Search databases in Chapter 5, "Designing for SharePoint's storage requirements."

SSS

The Secure Store Service from SharePoint 2010 replaced the Single Sign On (SSO) feature in MOSS. SSS is a claims-aware service that stores user names and passwords in an encrypted database. The SSS can store more than just identities and passwords; it can store custom fields as well. The SSS is generally used to store identities and passwords to access external back-end systems within an organization. Within SharePoint, SSS is used to hold the unattended service accounts for other services such as Excel, Visio, PerformancePoint, and PowerPivot services. BCS also uses SSS to store the credentials that it requires to access external LOB data systems.

Before you try to use SSS for the first time, you will need to provide an encryption (passphrase) key, which the SSS will use to encrypt and decrypt credentials stored in its database. It is a good idea to keep a copy of the passphrase in a secure location, such as an encrypted password safe, but you can force a re-encryption of the database based on a new passphrase should you lose your original SSS passphrase. If you are going to force a re-encryption of your SSS database, back it up first. The architecture for SSS is the same as it was for SharePoint 2010.

SSS is supported as a cross-farm (federated) service and is supported over WAN connections, but not recommended across WANs due to the latency created for the applications consuming it. SSS also has its own database.

UPA

The User Profile service application (UPA) stores information about users in a central location, and it can even be set up to synchronize external LOB data to enhance the users' profile data. UPA is required to provision My Sites and enable social features such as Profiles pages, Social Tagging, and Newsfeeds. UPA is also required if you are planning on distributing user profiles across multiple farms. UPA is one service that added functionality by taking features of past deployments and integrating them into the improved SharePoint 2013 UPA. Like in the SharePoint 2007 days, there is once again the ability to run in Active Directory Import (ADI) mode.

Running in ADI mode has its limitations. Since you are not running the User Profile Synchronization (UPS) service, you will not be able to synchronize your user profiles with external data. The UPS for SharePoint 2013 (see Figure 4-18) is the same as it was for SharePoint 2010.

UPA is supported as a cross-farm (federated) service but is not supported over WAN connections. UPA has its own database.

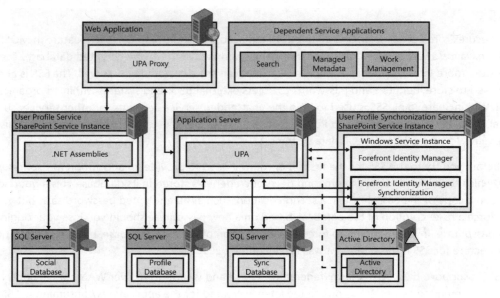

FIGURE 4-18 All these moving parts are required to make UPS and ADI work.

How does it work?

As you can see from Figure 4-18, there are a lot of moving parts in the UPA. Starting with a timer job to synchronize connections to profile sources, the previous figure uses the Forefront Identity Manager (FIM) synchronization service to synchronize Active Directory (AD) to the user profiles within SharePoint. The FIM service updates the *Profile* and *Sync* databases, which are used by the UPA, and exposed to the web application through the proxy. The *Social* database is updated with information about social tags, notes, and ratings as users click through the farm. Having deployed UPS, users are also able to synchronize external LOB data to the user profiles. In SharePoint 2013, the Work Management service application has become dependent upon the successful installation of the UPS. If you have chosen the Active Directory Import route, the timer job for the synchronization connection starts, and the User Profile service starts a bulk import of the user profiles from Active Directory.

VGS

The Visio Graphics service (VGS) allows users to view and refresh Visio diagrams in a web browser. It is the service used to create the Visio diagrams so that you can monitor workflow progress, if enabled, and is a great tool for keeping everyone on the same page regarding how things work. VGS supports the new Visio file format .vsdx, which will allow users to save files directly into SharePoint and not publish them as Visio Web Drawings (.vdw) files. The new service will also natively render Visio macro-enabled drawing (.vsdm) files. One of the other new features within Visio 2013 is the ability to use BCS to refresh external content, tied in with the ability to use SSS for handling authentication. See Figure 4-19 for more information on the architecture of VGS.

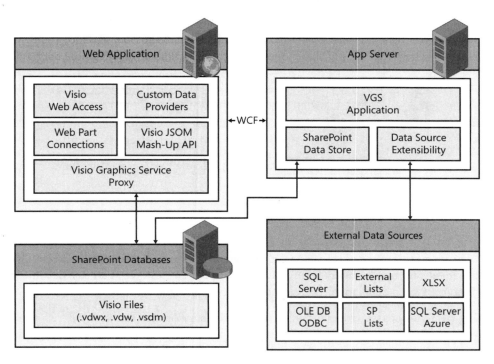

FIGURE 4-19 VGS renders Visio drawings in this way.

How does it work?

The purpose of VGS is to expose Visio drawings through a web browser. This is done through the Visio service application proxy, which uses the Visio service application to grab the data from either a local content database or an external data source.

WAS

The Word Automation service (WAS) performs bulk Word document conversions. The document conversions are automated, unattended server-side conversions. That means that you cannot convert the documents without having custom code written. The conversions can only happen with documents that are a supported "Save As" file type from within the Word client application. In SharePoint 2010, the conversion of Word documents was dependent on the timer service, which could be adjusted to convert documents every minute. In SharePoint 2013, you have the option to create a file conversion request that happens immediately (see Figure 4-20 for more information). Notice that there is a similar architectural layout as the new Machine Translation service. This is not surprising because the Machine Translation service was built using the WAS code. As with the Machine Translation service, the Word Automation service has its own database to store the document queue information.

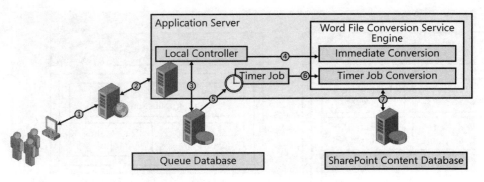

FIGURE 4-20 WAS is used to convert Word documents into other formats.

How does it work?

1. The user accesses the site that has a custom Web Part that starts an automated conversion of documents from a document library. Based on the code for the Web Part, the document can be converted on demand or can be scheduled for overnight.

2. The WAS proxy passes the information from the web application to the WAS.

3. The local controller pushes the document into the queue database.

4. The local controller sets the item for immediate translation or for translation using the service timer job.

5. Once the item is added to the document queue database, the item either waits for the timer job or it gets put at the top of the queue for immediate translation.

6. The item is moved from the content database to a local temp folder, where the file is converted.

7. Item conversion is completed, and the file is saved back into the content database.

Discovering the service applications that SharePoint creates automatically

After you have thrown down the bits for SharePoint, it is time to install Central Administration. Regardless of whether Central Administration was installed via Windows PowerShell or through the SharePoint Products and Configuration Wizard, SharePoint creates a couple of critical service applications for your farm automatically.

The Application Discovery and Load Balancer service

The Application Discovery and Load Balancer service is also known as the *Topology* service, and as its name says, one of the functions of this service is to provide load balancing. However, it is not a network load balancer for your websites (*spWebs*); rather, it is a load balancer for your service applications. This is a round-robin service and is used by the service applications for load balancing and fault tolerance, which allows you to have the same service enabled on different servers for high availability.

The application discovery side of this service occurs when the service application proxy requests an endpoint for a service application from the load balancer. The load balancer maintains a list of the available endpoints for each service application in cache on the consumer and returns the next available endpoint when queried. There is also a timer job that updates the cache that runs every 15 minutes by default. You can manually start a refresh of the endpoints by running the following Windows PowerShell cmdlet:

```
PS C:> Start-SPTimerJob job-spconnectedserviceapplication-addressesrefresh
```

There is more information about service application endpoints in the "Service application endpoint using the WCF framework" section, earlier in this chapter.

STS

The Secure Token service (STS) is another service that is automatically created when you provision your SharePoint farm. The STS is a WCF service (.svc) endpoint that is designed to respond to requests for security tokens and provide identity management.

User authentication in SharePoint 2013

User authentication is the validation of a user's identity against a trusted authentication provider. SharePoint 2013 uses STS to handle the claims-based authentication for user authentication. If the user is authenticated through a claims-based authentication, a claims-based security token is generated by SharePoint STS and converted into an *SPUser* identity (see Figure 4-21).

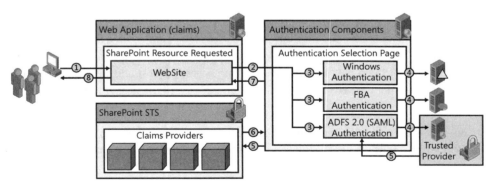

FIGURE 4-21 A user uses STS and claims to become authenticated and access information in SharePoint.

How does it work?

1. The user requests a resource that requires authentication.

2. If the request is not authenticated, the user gets routed to the Authentication Selection page to use the appropriate authentication for that zone.

3. The request is processed by one of the authentication methods. If there is more than one type of authentication provider for the web application, the user will be given a choice of what provider to use for authentication.

4. The user is authenticated by the identity provider.

5. If authentication succeeds, STS generates a claims-based token for the user with the information provided by the identity provider. If additional claims providers are configured, the STS augments the user's token with the claims given by the claims provider.

6. The claims-based token of the user is sent back to the authentication components.

7. The authentication components redirect the request back to the resource address, with the claims-based token issued for the user.

8. The response is sent back to the user. Authentication and authorization are now complete.

S2S authentication in SharePoint 2013

S2S authentication is the validation of a server's request for resources that is based on a trust relationship established between the STS of the server that runs SharePoint 2013 and the STS of another server. For S2S authentication to work, both servers must support the OAuth server-to-server protocol. Examples of on-premises servers that support S2S authentication are SharePoint 2013, Exchange Server 2013, and Lync Server 2013. In Office 365, Azure Workflow service and SharePoint 2013 support S2S.

Because of the established trust relationship, a requesting server can access secured resources on the SharePoint 2013 server on behalf of a specified user account. For example, a server running Exchange Server 2013 can request resources of a server running SharePoint 2013 for a specific user account.

When a server running SharePoint 2013 attempts to access a resource on a server or a server attempts to access a resource on a server running SharePoint 2013, the incoming access request must be authenticated so that the server accepts the incoming access request and subsequent data. S2S authentication verifies that the server running SharePoint 2013 and the user whom it is representing are trusted.

The token that is used for a S2S authentication is a S2S token, not a logon token. The S2S token contains information about the server that requests access and the user account on whose behalf the server is acting.

Exploring service federation

During the architectural design phase of your environment, you should have reviewed the consolidation of existing farms. However, what if you cannot consolidate all of your farms? You do not want to waste server resources by replicating out the same Search service on all of your farms when you could provision a Search service farm to handle search for all of your farms. The primary reason for creating a service farm is to consolidate services into one farm and share the resources across your organization. Another reason to implement a service farm would be for the delegation of service management to different departments or groups, or even an entirely different organization. If you are going to set up a service farm that is going to be accessing other Active Directory domains, a two-way trust is required for UPA—MMS does not require a trust—and the rest of the services will work with a one-way trust. Federating your services will also give you the ability to scale out your services as your farm(s) grow. If you are thinking that you should create a service farm, remember that you need to let the business requirements dictate your decision, not the technology. Just because you can federate your services does not mean that you need to create a service farm.

In SharePoint 2013, there are six services that will federate:

- BDC

- Machine Translation

- MMS

- Search

- Secure Store

- UPA

There were six services that federated in SharePoint 2010 as well; however, the SharePoint 2010 Web Analytics service was consumed by the new Search service. The Machine Translation service is new to service federation with SharePoint 2013.

One advantage of using SharePoint 2013 for your cross-farm services is the ability of the service applications to be consumed by SharePoint 2010. The SharePoint 2013 services that can be consumed by SharePoint 2010 are:

- BDC

- MMS

- Search

- Secure Store

- UPA

The way to create the consumption of a federated service application is the same in SharePoint 2013 as it was in SharePoint 2010. The ability to have a SharePoint 2013 services farm consumed by another farm is started by creating a trust between the two farms. While a lot of work has been done to create S2S trusts within the new SharePoint app model, creating your trust between farms is still certificate based. There are three certificates that must be used to create the trust: the SharePoint Root certificate, which signs the STS certificates; the STS certificate, which signs the claims tokens; and a Secure Sockets Layer (SSL) certificate to keep the service requests encrypted over HTTPS. The way to establish the trust between the two farms is to exchange the Root certificate between servers, and to have the publisher trust the consumer's STS certificate, as illustrated in Figure 4-22.

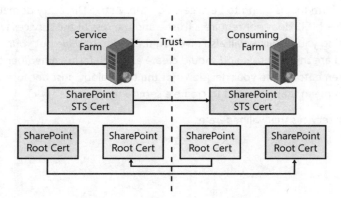

FIGURE 4-22   Trust is created by exchanging certificates between farms.

Once you have set up your service farm, you can assign your default and custom application proxy groups, as shown in Figure 4-23.

The "Putting it all together" section of this chapter offers a demonstration on setting up BCS as a federated service, and you can review the "Putting it all together" section of Chapter 8, "Planning an upgrade strategy," for the deployment of a federated Search farm.

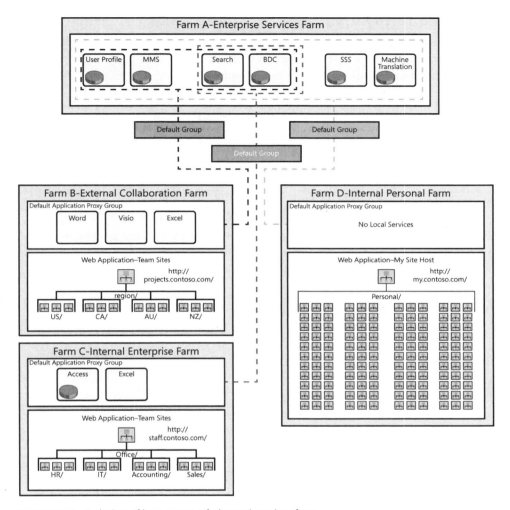

FIGURE 4-23 A design of how to use a federated services farm.

Putting it all together

Now that you understand the principles and architecture behind service applications, it is time to build a service farm. In this scenario, it has been determined that Contoso needs to have a BDC service farm created to help keep business units up to speed and in sync with the corporation's data. The first thing that will need to be accomplished is the creation of the new service farm. It is best to match version numbers between your service farm and your consumer farm.

Creating the farm trust

As previously mentioned, to create a trust between farms, an exchange of certificates needs to take place. From the consumer farm, export the Root and STS certificates. The exporting of the required certificates can only be done using Windows PowerShell:

```
PS C:\> $rootCert = (Get-SPCertificateAuthority).RootCertificate
PS C:\> $rootCert.Export("Cert") | Set-Content C:\consumerFarmRoot.cer -Encoding byte
PS C:\> $stsCert = (Get-SPSecurityTokenServiceConfig).LocalLoginProvider.SigningCertificate
PS C:\> $stsCert.Export("Cert") | Set-Content C:\consumerFarmSTS.cer -Encoding byte
```

The next step will be to export only the Root certificate from the service farm:

```
PS C:\> $rootCert = (Get-SPCertificateAuthority).RootCertificate
PS C:\> $rootCert.Export("Cert") | Set-Content C:\servicesFarmRoot.cer -Encoding byte
```

After the export has completed, copy the consumer Root and STS certificates to the service farm, and copy the Root certificate from the service farm to the consumer farm. From the service farm, establish the trust by importing the Root and STS certificates:

```
PS C:\> $trustCert = Get-PfxCertificate C:\consumerFarmRoot.cer
PS C:\> New-SPTrustedRootAuthority consumerFarm -Certificate $trustCert
PS C:\> $stsCert = Get-PfxCertificate C:\consumerFarmSTS.cer
PS C:\> New-SPTrustedServiceTokenIssuer consumerFarm -Certificate $stsCert
```

From the consumer farm, import the Root certificate only:

```
PS C:\> $trustCert = Get-PfxCertificate C:\servicesFarmRoot.cer
PS C:\> New-SPTrustedRootAuthority servicesFarmRoot -Certificate $trustCert
```

By taking a look within Central Administration | Security | Manage Trust on the consumer (Figure 4-24) and service farms (Figure 4-25), you can verify that you have installed the certificates correctly.

FIGURE 4-24 A list of the consumer farm trust relationships.

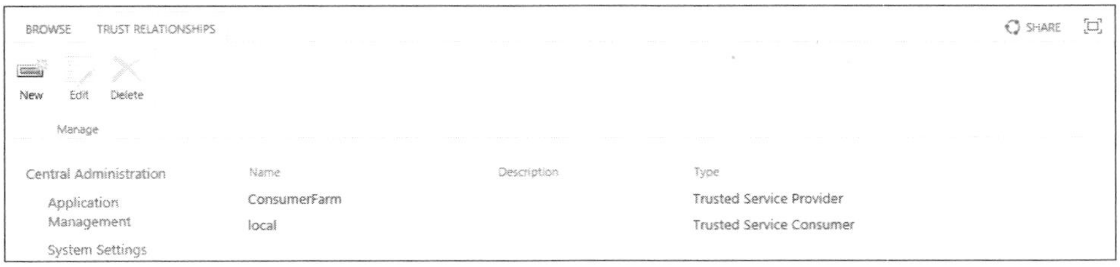

FIGURE 4-25 A list of the provider farm trust relationships.

Configuring the topology service

Because the topology service maintains a list of all of the endpoints for the SharePoint farm, the consuming farm must have access to the publishing farm's topology service. This can be achieved by taking the Farm ID from the consumer farm and giving it permissions on the Topology service application on the service farm. The following Windows PowerShell cmdlet will export the consumer farm's ID:

```
PS C:\> $farmID = (Get-SPFarm).Id
PS C:\> New-Item C:\consumerFarmID.txt -type file -force -value "$farmID"
```

After the file has been created, copy the file to the service farm and run the following Windows PowerShell cmdlet to give the consumer farm access to the service farm's topology service:

```
PS C:\> # Run the following commands on the services farm to set up the trust relationship with
the consumer farm:
PS C:\> $farmID = Get-Content c:\consumerFarmID.txt
PS C:\> $security = Get-SPTopologyServiceApplication | Get-SPServiceApplicationSecurity
PS C:\> $claimProvider = (Get-SPClaimProvider System).ClaimProvider
PS C:\> $principal = New-SPClaimsPrincipal -ClaimType "http://schemas.microsoft.com/
sharepoint/2009/08/claims/farmid" -ClaimProvider $claimProvider -ClaimValue $farmID
PS C:\> Grant-SPObjectSecurity -Identity $security -Principal $principal -Rights "Full Control"
PS C:\> Get-SPTopologyServiceApplication |
PS C:\> Set-SPServiceApplicationSecurity -ObjectSecurity $security
```

The creation of the permission set can be verified by going into Central Administration of the service farm and looking at the permissions for the Application Discover and Load Balancing service application, as shown in Figure 4-26.

FIGURE 4-26   The permissions window for the Topology service.

Publishing your service application

The first step toward being able to publish your service applications is provisioning your service applications. If you have not provisioned the service applications that you wish to publish, you will need to do that first. After you have provisioned the BDC service application and proxy on your services farm, publish the service application by going into Central Administration | Application Management | Manage Service Applications | Business Data Connectivity Service Application | Publish (in the Ribbon).

Clicking Publish will open the Publish Service Application modal dialog box. Change the connection type to HTTPS, and a bit farther down the page, copy the Published URL into Notepad. You will need the URL when it is time to connect to the service (see Figure 4-27). Click OK when you are ready to continue.

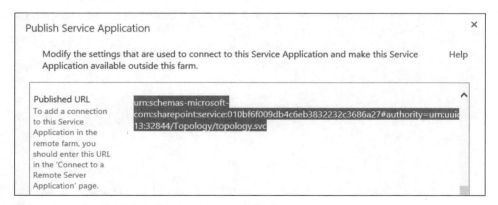

FIGURE 4-27   The Publish Service Application modal dialog box.

Connecting to your service application

From within your consuming farm, select Central Administration | Application Management | Manage Service Applications. If you have already provisioned the BDC service, you should remove it before progressing.

From the Connect drop-down menu, select the BDC service. Don't be fooled by SharePoint exposing all the service applications within the drop-down menu. SharePoint will let you create connections for the App Management and Work Management service applications as well, but that is not supported.

Once the Connect To A Remote Service Application modal dialog box has opened, paste in the URL that you copied when you published the BDC service, as shown in Figure 4-28. If you click OK and run into an error, verify that you have opened port 32844 (HTTPS) if you followed directions, or 32843 (HTTP) if you did not.

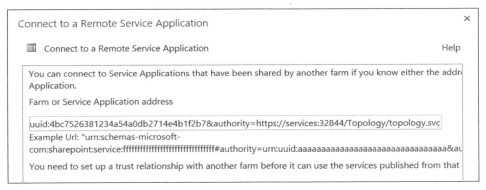

FIGURE 4-28 Enter the URL from the service farm.

After successfully connecting the two farms, your list of service applications should have the connected Topology service and the connected BDC service, as shown in Figure 4-29.

Application Discovery and Load Balancer Service Application Proxy_2019c598-da93-4249-9d79-35caae14a9b9	Application Discovery and Load Balancer Service Application Proxy	Started
Application Discovery and Load Balancer Service Application Proxy_4bc75263-8123-4a54-a0db-2714e4b1f2b7	Application Discovery and Load Balancer Service Application Proxy	Started
Connection to: Farm Business Data Connectivity Service	Business Data Connectivity Service Application Proxy	Started
Connection to: Search Service Application	Search Service Application Proxy	Started

FIGURE 4-29 A list of the remote Topology services and remote service applications.

Setting the service application permissions

Currently, there still is no way to manage the service applications in the service farm from the consumer farm. So, just as when you set the permission for the consumer farm to use the Topology service, it is now time to add the consuming farm's ID to the BDC service. The farm ID is already on the C:\ drive, so all you need to do paste the ID into the permissions window for the BDC service, check the name, add it to the group, and give Full Control, as illustrated in Figure 4-30.

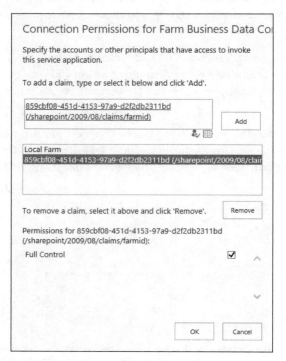

FIGURE 4-30 The modal dialog box is for adding the consuming server's permissions.

The configuration of the BDC service farm is complete, and the consuming farm will treat the service as if it were being run locally.

Service application federation is a valuable tool when it comes to scalability and flexibility in a growing SharePoint 2013 environment. If you need to deploy a service farm, you should now have all the tools to succeed.

## CHAPTER 5

Designing for SharePoint storage requirements

In this chapter, you will learn about:

- The database requirements for Microsoft SharePoint 2013.

- How to initially optimize Microsoft SQL Server for SharePoint 2013.

- Examining the database engine requirements of Microsoft SharePoint Server 2013 platform.

- How to plan for capacity and database system requirements.

- The new Shredded Storage functionality in SharePoint 2013.

- Enabling business intelligence (BI) capabilities within the SharePoint Server 2013 platform.

At its very core, Microsoft SharePoint 2013 is a set of database-driven web applications and services. As such, the database layer is arguably the most important layer of the SharePoint 2013 architecture. Therefore, to produce a highly efficient and performance-based SharePoint 2013 environment, it is critical that the SharePoint architects and administrators understand how to best configure the database layer to provide this functionality. SharePoint 2013 can only utilize Microsoft SQL Server 2008 R2 SP1 and SQL Server 2012 for the database engine supporting the web applications and service applications. Additionally, if business intelligence (BI) capabilities are required in the SharePoint Server 2013 environment, only SQL Server 2012 with SP1 is currently supported.

It is assumed in this chapter that you are working with a full-farm, not a stand-alone, implementation of SharePoint 2013, whether it is a single- or multi-server farm. The stand-alone installation, which unfortunately is the default installation scenario, of SharePoint 2013 installs SQL Server 2008 R2 SP1 Express edition. However, User Profile synchronization does not work with the Express edition. If you intend to use User Profile synchronization with SharePoint Server 2013, you must choose a farm installation, rather than a stand-alone installation. Additionally, SQL Server 2008 R2 SP1 Express edition databases cannot be larger than 10 GB.

This chapter covers the database requirements for a SharePoint 2013 environment. You will be provided the necessary information to initially optimize the configuration of the database engine for SharePoint 2013. You will then be introduced to the individual databases and their role within a SharePoint 2013 deployment. Of course, planning for the capacity and performance of the databases will be discussed, iterating through each of the databases available in a SharePoint Server 2013 environment. You will then be introduced to providing the powerful BI functionality that is unique to SharePoint Server 2013.

Database engine requirements for SharePoint 2013

Currently, SharePoint 2013 only supports the following two versions of SQL Server for use as the database engine:

- 64-bit version of SQL Server 2008 R2 with SP1+ (Standard, Enterprise, or Datacenter edition)

- 64-bit version of SQL Server 2012 (Standard, Business Intelligence, or Enterprise edition)

High Availability (HA) and/or Disaster Recovery (DR) requirements of the SharePoint 2013 implementation will restrict the edition selection for the SharePoint 2013 database engine.

Supported HA/DR options for SharePoint 2013 using the SQL Server 2008 R2 SP1+ database engine include:

- **Failover clustering** Enterprise or Datacenter edition only.

- **Database mirroring** Standard, Enterprise, or Datacenter edition for synchronous mirroring; Enterprise, or Datacenter edition only for asynchronous (also referred to as *high-performance*) mirroring.

- **Log shipping** Standard, Enterprise, or Datacenter edition, but primarily used for DR environments.

 Note Replication is *not* supported for SharePoint 2013.

Supported HA/DR options for SharePoint 2013 using the SQL Server 2012 database engine include:

- **AlwaysOn Failover Cluster Instances** Standard and Business Intelligence editions support a two-node maximum; Enterprise edition supports an operating system maximum.

- **AlwaysOn Availability Groups** Enterprise edition only.

- **Database mirroring (Deprecated)** Standard and Business Intelligence only support Safety Full mirroring mode; Enterprise edition supports all mirroring modes.

- **Log shipping** Standard, Business Intelligence, or Enterprise editions, but primarily used for DR environments.

You should be aware in your planning that database mirroring, although supported in SQL Server 2008 R2 and in the SharePoint 2013 platform, is deprecated in SQL Server 2012. This may provide incentive to utilize SQL Server 2012 and its AlwaysOn capabilities if you're implementing a new environment or upgrading an existing SharePoint environment.

It also should be noted now, though, that for integrated SQL Server BI capabilities in SharePoint Server 2013 (which will be discussed later in this chapter), only SQL Server 2012 with SP1 (Business Intelligence edition or Enterprise edition) is supported. This may move you to decide at implementation time to utilize the database engine of SQL Server 2012 to consolidate and, therefore, simplify the management and administration of the database components to a single version, if possible.

Overview of HA options

As a quick overview, you need to understand the basics of the HA options for the SQL Server database engine. The implementation and design will be covered in more detail in Chapter 10, "Planning your business continuity strategy."

Failover clustering

Failover clustering provides HA support for an entire instance of SQL Server. A *failover cluster* is a combination of one or more nodes, or servers, with two or more shared disks. Applications are each installed into a Microsoft Cluster Service (MSCS) cluster group, known as a *resource group*. At any time, each resource group is owned by only one node in the cluster. The application service has a virtual name that is independent of the node names, and is referred to as the *failover cluster instance name*. An application can connect to the failover cluster instance by referencing the failover cluster instance name. The application does not have to know which node hosts the failover cluster instance.

A SQL Server failover cluster instance appears on the network as a single computer, but has functionality that provides failover from one node to another if the current node becomes unavailable. For example, during a nondisk hardware failure, operating system failure, or planned operating system upgrade, you can configure an instance of SQL Server on one node of a failover cluster to fail over to any other node in the disk group.

A failover cluster does not protect against disk failure. You can use failover clustering to reduce system downtime and provide higher application availability.

Database mirroring

Database mirroring is a solution to increase database availability by supporting almost instantaneous failover. Database mirroring can be used to maintain a single standby database, or mirror database, for a corresponding production database that is referred to as the *principal database*.

Log shipping

Like AlwaysOn Availability Groups and database mirroring, log shipping operates at the database level. You can use log shipping to maintain one or more warm standby databases (referred to as *secondary databases*) for a single production database that is referred to as the *primary database*.

AlwaysOn Failover Cluster Instances

As part of the SQL Server 2012 AlwaysOn offering, AlwaysOn Failover Cluster Instances uses Windows Server Failover Clustering (WSFC) functionality to provide local HA through redundancy at the server-instance level—a failover cluster instance (FCI). An FCI is a single instance of SQL Server that is installed across WSFC nodes and, possibly, across multiple subnets. On the network, an FCI appears to be an instance of SQL Server running on a single computer, but the FCI provides failover from one WSFC node to another if the current node becomes unavailable.

AlwaysOn Availability Groups

AlwaysOn Availability Groups is an enterprise-level HA/DR solution introduced in SQL Server 2012 to enable you to maximize availability for one or more user databases. AlwaysOn Availability Groups requires that the SQL Server instances reside on WSFC nodes. An AlwaysOn FCI can use AlwaysOn Availability Groups to provide remote DR at the database level.

Initial optimization and configuration of SQL Server for SharePoint 2013

It is easy to overlook SQL Server optimizations when configuring the database layer for a SharePoint 2013 environment. However, arguably the database platform is the most critical, for no amount of configuration and/or optimization on the web front ends and application servers can compensate for a poorly performing database layer. As such, careful consideration should be taken when configuring the database layer. Due to the complexity and interoperability of the web applications and service applications, sometimes the configuration and optimization would go against normal database-driven web application development other than SharePoint.

For most SharePoint 2013 implementations, a default installation of SQL Server is not recommended when installing to support a SharePoint 2013 environment. Specifically, there are two settings that should be changed to provide SharePoint 2013 with a proper database engine layer; the default server collation and the max degree of parallelism (MDOP).

SQL Server collation

The Microsoft Knowledge Base (KB) article "Supportability regarding SQL collation for SharePoint Databases and TempDB" (*http://support.microsoft.com/kb/2008668*), states:

> We **do not support** changing the default collation (*Latin1_General_CI_AS_KS_WS*) for SharePoint databases to any other collations (CI, AS, KS, WS).

> We **support** any CI collation for the SQL instance (for master, tempdb databases). However we **recommend** using *Latin1_General_CI_AS_KS_WS* as the instance default collation (master, tempdb databases).

The ability to change this option is found on the Collation tab of the Server Configuration page of SQL Server Setup, as shown in Figure 5-1.

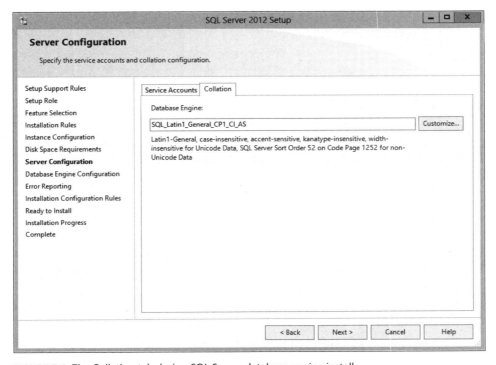

FIGURE 5-1 The Collation tab during SQL Server database engine install.

Additionally, changing the default collation (Latin1_General_CI_AS_KS_WS) for a SharePoint database is not supported. The recommendation is to use Latin1_General_CI_AS_KS_WS as the instance (or server) default collation, although any CI collation for the SQL database engine instance is supported. If the SQL Server instance is dedicated to the SharePoint 2013 implementation, it may be easiest to set the database engine instance collation level to Latin1_General_CI_AS_KS_WS at install, as shown in Figure 5-2.

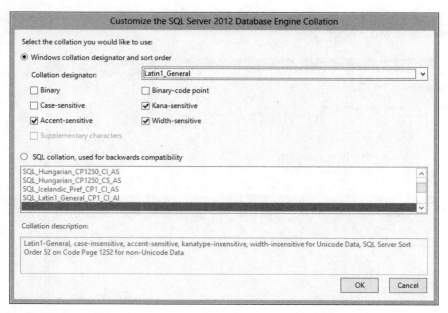

FIGURE 5-2 The recommended SQL Server instance collation setting for supporting SharePoint 2013.

SQL Server MDOP

SharePoint 2013 requires a farm installation to have SQL Server configured for a MDOP value of *1*. The default value is *0*. In fact, if not configured to *1*, the SharePoint 2013 installation and configuration when using Windows PowerShell rather than the SharePoint 2013 Products Configuration Wizard (*Psconfigui.exe*), will fail at the create configuration database step. When an instance of SQL Server runs on a computer that has more than one microprocessor or CPU, it detects the best degree of parallelism (that is, the number of processors employed to run a single statement) for each parallel plan execution. You can use the MDOP option to limit the number of processors to use in parallel plan execution. SQL Server considers parallel execution plans for queries, index data definition language (DDL) operations, and static and keyset-driven cursor populations. It should be noted that SharePoint 2013 will provide a warning and prevent an install if the MDOP is not set to *1* prior to configuration of the farm.

Follow these steps to configure the MDOP option using SQL Server Management Studio:

1. In Object Explorer, right-click a server and select Properties.

2. Click the Advanced node.

3. In the Max Degree Of Parallelism box, select the maximum number of processors, which for SharePoint 2013 will be 1, to use in parallel plan execution, as shown in Figure 5-3.

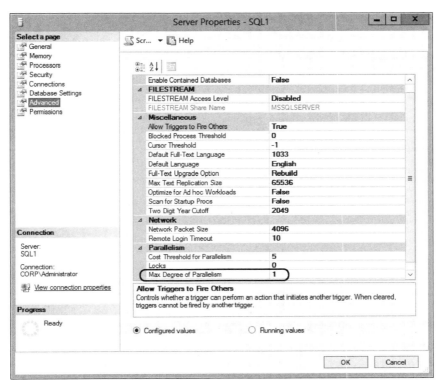

FIGURE 5-3 The process for configuring the MDOP using SQL Server Management Studio.

Follow these steps to configure the Max Degree Of Parallelism option using Transact-SQL:

1. Connect to the database engine.

2. On the Standard bar in SQL Server Management Studio, click New Query.

3. Copy the Transact-SQL code from Figure 5-4 into the query window and click Execute. The Transact-SQL code uses the sp_configure stored procedure to configure the Max Degree Of Parallelism option to 1.

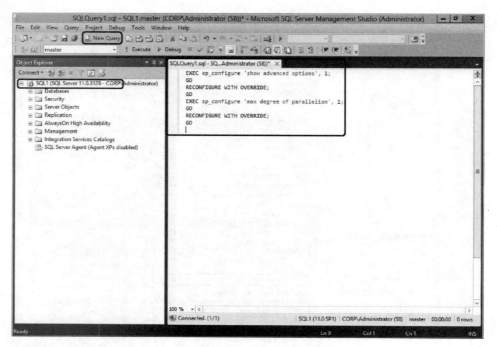

FIGURE 5-4 The query window and query to change the MDOP value to 1.

Additional SQL Server considerations

Some additional considerations should be acknowledged to ensure high performance of the database layer of SharePoint 2013. Although these considerations are not required, they should be considered important general guidelines in maintaining the health of the SharePoint 2013 databases.

Dedicated SQL Server

Probably the most important and the most disregarded rule of thumb is to use a dedicated server running SQL Server for SharePoint 2013. To ensure optimal performance for farm operations, it is recommend that you install SQL Server 2008 R2 with SP1 or SQL Server 2012 on a dedicated server that does not run other farm roles and does not host databases for other applications.

Autocreate statistics

You do not want to enable autocreate statistics on a server that hosts SQL Server for SharePoint 2013. Enabling autocreate statistics is not supported for SharePoint Server. SharePoint Server configures the required settings during provisioning and upgrade. Manually enabling autocreate statistics on a SharePoint database can significantly change the execution plan of a query. The SharePoint databases either use a stored procedure that maintains the statistics (*proc_UpdateStatistics*) or rely on SQL Server to do this.

SQL aliases

Another consideration is to use SQL Server client aliases on SharePoint 2013 servers to reference your SQL Server instance(s). The main reason to use SQL aliases is to help SharePoint find its databases through a consistent name. Regardless of the name of the SQL instance, by using SQL aliases, SharePoint is always expecting its database(s) to be on the same alias name. This allows administrators to move SharePoint databases to new hardware, and then change alias settings and have SharePoint find the new hardware with minimal downtime. A second advantage to using aliases is that you can now use descriptive, friendly names, such as *SP_Content_Alias*, for the server that is hosting your SharePoint content databases.

Configuring a SQL Server client alias

There are essentially three methods of configuring SQL Server client aliases. The method that you choose should be driven by primarily infrastructure and organizational information technology governance. For instance, if the SharePoint 2013 implementation team members are restricted from logging on directly to the servers running SQL Server, it is possible that they would want remote administration capabilities available from the SharePoint servers. In this situation, installing the full set of management tools would be an option. The SharePoint 2013 implementation team could then use the SQL Server Configuration Manager to create and configure the SQL Server client aliases. It is also recommended to create both 64-bit and 32-bit matching aliases in the event that you would want to utilize the SQL client alias to connect to the database instance with a client application such as SQL Server Management Studio or other 32-bit-based client application. If scripting the implementation of the SharePoint 2013 environment with Windows PowerShell, you may want to use scripts to create the SQL Server client aliases directly in the system registry. Of course, the most common method is to use the operating system provided SQL Client Configuration Utility, Cliconfg.exe. The 64-bit version is found in the default location of C:\Windows\SysWOW64\ directory, while the 32-bit version of the utility is found in the default location of C:\Windows\System32\. Each of these three methods is described in this section.

SQL Client Configuration Utility (Cliconfg.exe)   To configure a SQL Server client alias via SQL Client Configuration Utility, follow these steps for both the 64-bit and 32-bit version of the utility:

1. Run C:\Windows\SysWOW64\Cliconfg.exe for 64-bit or C:\Windows\System32\Cliconfg.exe for 32-bit SQL Server client aliases.

2. Click the Alias tab and then click Add, as shown in Figure 5-5.

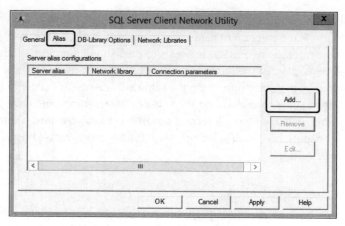

FIGURE 5-5 Use the SQL Server Client Network Utility to configure the client alias.

3. In the Add Network Library Configuration window, type the SQL Alias you want in the Server Alias text box. Select TCP/IP as the Network library, and enter the actual server name in the respective text box of the Connection Parameters section, as shown in Figure 5-6. It is possible to select to either dynamically determine the port or specify a static, preferably nonstandard port.

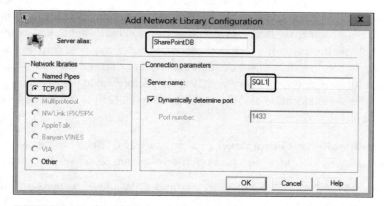

FIGURE 5-6 Use the Add Network Library Configuration to add the client alias.

4. Click OK in the Add Network Library Configuration window and OK in the SQL Server Client Network Utility window.

SQL Server Configuration Manager configuration of SQL Server client aliases To configure a SQL Server client alias via SQL Server Configuration Manager, follow these steps:

1. Verify that the user account that is performing this procedure is a member of either the sysadmin or the serveradmin fixed server role.

2. Run Setup for SQL Server on the target computer, and install the following client components:

   - Connectivity Components

   - Management Tools

3. Open SQL Server Configuration Manager.

4. In the navigation pane, click SQL Native Client Configuration.

5. In the main window, under Items, right-click Aliases and select New Alias.

6. In the Alias - New dialog box, in Alias Name, enter a name for the alias.

7. In Port No, enter the port number for the database instance. Make sure that the protocol is set to TCP/IP.

8. In Server, enter the name of the computer that is running SQL Server.

9. Click Apply, and then click OK.

10. **Verification:** You can test the SQL Server client alias by using SQL Server Management Studio (SSMS), which is available when you install SQL Server client components.

    If you use SSMS to verify, you will need to also create an identical alias in the SQL Native Client Configuration (32bit) | Aliases node, as SSMS is a 32-bit application.

11. Open SSMS.

12. When you are prompted to enter a server name, enter the name of the alias that you created, and then click Connect. If the connection is successful, SSMS is populated with objects that correspond to the remote database.

After you have completed steps 1–12 you should have an alias created within the SQL Configuration Manager similar to Figure 5-7.

FIGURE 5-7 Configure the SQL client aliases via SQL Server Configuration Manager.

Windows PowerShell configuration of SQL Server client aliases   Optionally, you can use Windows PowerShell to create the SQL client alias *after* the installation of both the SharePoint 2013 prerequisites and the SharePoint 2013 binary files (install), but prior to creation of the farm:

```
# SQL Alias name to create
$alias = "SharePointDB"
# Server Name of SQL Server
$server = "SQL1"
# Registry locations for the SQL Aliases
$x86 = "HKLM:\Software\Microsoft\MSSQLServer\Client\ConnectTo"
$x64 = "HKLM:\Software\Wow6432Node\Microsoft\MSSQLServer\Client\ConnectTo"
# Check if the ConnectTo key already exists, and create it if it doesn't.
if ((test-path -path $x86) -ne $True)
{
    New-Item $x86
}
if ((test-path -path $x64) -ne $True)
{
    New-Item $x64
}
# Additional information for creating Registry entry value
$tcpAliasValue = "DBMSSOCN," + $server
# Creation of TCP Aliases registry entries
New-ItemProperty -Path $x86 -Name $alias -PropertyType String -Value $tcpAliasValue
```

```
New-ItemProperty -Path $x64 -Name $alias -PropertyType String -Value $tcpAliasValue
Drive Assignments
```

Depending on the primary purpose of the supported SharePoint 2013 sites, design storage for optimal throughput and manageability by separating and prioritizing your data among the drives of the database server. Ideally, you should place the tempdb database, content databases, usage database, search databases, and transaction logs on separate physical hard disks or Logical Unit Numbers (LUNs) if using a storage area network (SAN) solution.

If the primary purpose of the sites is collaboration-or update-heavy, the storage distribution should adhere to the following prioritized list, with the first items being on the fastest drives:

1. System tempdb data files and transaction logs

2. Content database transaction logs

3. Search databases, except for the Search Administration database

4. Content database data files

If the primary purpose or requirements of the SharePoint 2013 sites are read-centric (such as a records center or portal site), then prioritize the storage distribution on the fastest drives as follows:

1. System tempdb data files and transaction logs

2. Content database transaction data files

3. Search databases, except for the Search Administration database

4. Content database transaction logs

Note that the tempdb SQL Server System database is always the highest priority. As such, as noted previously, it is recommended to utilize dedicated disks for the tempdb files. You should also consider using RAID 10 for the tempdb files. Performance will normally be increased if database data and transaction logs are separated across different disks. If they do share disks due to space, put files that have different usage patterns on the same disk to minimize concurrent access requests. Additionally, if possible, use multiple data files on dedicated disks for heavy-use content databases. Of course, you should proactively monitor and make adjustments as needed to keep content databases below 200 GB or your designated threshold based on information discussed later in the chapter, rather than restrict the database size. Restricting the database size can cause serious, unexpected system issues and related downtime when the capacity defined by a restriction is exceeded.

Proactively managing the growth of data and log files

If at all possible during initial installation and configuration, increase all data files and log files to their expected final size, or schedule times when you will increase the sizes. Consider any changes that would affect database size and make the size change prior to the system change. Autogrowth is enabled by default. However, it is recommended to change the default autogrowth value for new databases from 1 MB to a much larger fixed number. It is not recommended to use a percentage factor for the autogrowth value. As a general rule, the bigger the database, or the bigger it is expected to be, that should drive larger autogrowth increments in the data and log files for the given database. Rather than using autogrowth as a management feature, consider it a risk contingency for unexpected growth. As a good practice, you should maintain at least 25 percent available space across all database data and log drives to accommodate the growth and peak usage patterns for temporary database objects.

Continuously monitoring SQL Server storage and performance

As SQL Server is mission critical to the SharePoint 2013 platform, it is strongly recommended that you continuously monitor the SQL Server storage and performance to ensure that each database is able to deliver the load required of it. Additionally, monitoring over time provides information for future growth and service scenarios. However, ensure that you not only monitor specific SQL Server resources, but also the systems that support the computer running SQL Server, such as the server CPU, memory, cache/hit ratio, and especially the I/O subsystem (disk). Although you can manually monitor the performance counters on the SQL Server system, if an enterprise monitoring solution, such as Microsoft System Center Operations Manager (SCOM) or similar system, is in place, use it to proactively monitor and alert you of issues prior to them resulting in system downtime.

Using backup compression to speed up backups and reduce file sizes

A significant boost to SharePoint 2013 backup operations can be the use of SQL Server backup compression. It is available in SQL Server 2008 R2 SP1 Standard, Enterprise, and Datacenter editions and SQL Server 2012 Standard, Business Intelligence, and Enterprise editions. If you set the compression option in your backup script or configure SQL Server to compress by default, you can significantly reduce the size of your database backups and/or shipped logs.

Overview of SharePoint Server 2013 databases and their roles

The backbone of SharePoint is heavily dependent on SQL Server databases. To maximize efficiency, SharePoint uses many databases to help distribute the workload of the multiple services and corresponding service applications, as well as the user web applications. This section will cover the various databases found within SharePoint Foundation 2013 and SharePoint Server 2013. In the following sections, each available database within the SharePoint platform will be explained and include information on purpose, sizing, scaling, and what to expect with read/write characteristics.

SharePoint Foundation 2013 databases

SharePoint Foundation is the base model of SharePoint 2013, so it does not have all the databases that are associated with SharePoint Server 2013. However, the databases found in SharePoint Foundation 2013 will be found in SharePoint Server 2013.

Configuration database

The configuration database is the "brain" of the SharePoint 2013 farm. It is responsible for maintaining data about the entire farm, including all database, Internet Information Services (IIS) websites, web applications, and solutions. It must be collocated with the SharePoint 2013 Central Administration content database. Typically, it is recommended to initially allocate 2 GB for the configuration database. Over time, it may grow beyond the initial size, but fairly slowly—approximately 40 MB for each 50,000 site collections. Additionally, growth can increase with farm solutions, as they are stored here, and other items, such as administrative Microsoft InfoPath forms. There can be only one configuration database per SharePoint 2013 farm, so it can only be scaled up. The configuration database is read-intensive. The default recovery model is initially set to Full, but it is recommended to be switched to the simple recovery model to restrict the growth of the log file, if possible.

Central Administration content database

The SharePoint 2013 Central Administration content database is similar to any other content database except, of course, that it is the content database of the administration web application. Technically, it should be considered a configuration database. Initially, it is recommended to size the Central Administration content database to at least 1 GB, but platform usage scenarios may grow the database, especially if using integrated SQL Server 2012 SP1 BI functionality in the farm, specifically PowerPivot. Also, because of this characteristic, the read/write characteristics could vary. Similar to the configuration database, the Central Administration database must be scaled up, as only one Central Administration content database is supported per farm. The default recovery model is Full.

If SQL Server 2012 SP1 PowerPivot for SharePoint 2013 is installed, the Central Administration content database also stores the Microsoft Excel worksheets and the PowerPivot data files used in the PowerPivot Management Dashboard. Therefore, if you use PowerPivot for SharePoint 2013 and use the default settings that keep the usage data collection and data refresh history for 365 days, the Central Administration content database will grow over the year.

Content database

The SharePoint 2013 content databases store all content for the user web applications. By default, if no other content databases are added to the web application, all site collections will reside in the original, initial content database created at the time of web application creation. However, administrators can add additional content databases to distribute site collections across different content databases. However, keep in mind, a single site collection cannot span multiple content databases. The content includes documents, files, list data, audit logs, as well as user information. Content database sizing and limits varies significantly, based on two primary factors: usage scenario and the SQL Server storage (disk) subsystem input/output operations per second (IOPS). Microsoft still strongly recommends limiting the size of the content databases to 200 GB, but under certain combinations of usage scenarios and storage system IOPS, sets no explicit limit of what it will support. To surpass the secondary 4 TB supportable limit, the SharePoint 2013 site on the content database must be based on the Document Center or Records Center site template, as well as refrain from using alerts, workflows, link fix-ups, or item-level security on any SharePoint Server 2013 objects in the content database. For scaling, content databases supporting a single site collection must scale up, as a site collection cannot span multiple content databases. However, multiple content databases per web application is supported. The default recovery model for the content database is Full.

One quick note about Remote BLOB Storage (RBS) and database sizing, as there is a significant amount of bad information on the Internet regarding RBS and SharePoint 2013. If you are using RBS, the total volume of the combination of both the RBS storage subsystem and the metadata in the content database must not exceed the 200 GB limit (*http://technet.microsoft.com/en-us/library/cc262787.aspx*).

App Management database

The App Management service application utilizes the App Management database to store the licenses and permissions downloaded from the SharePoint Store or App Catalog. You should scale-up when the database reaches 10 GB. It is only write-heavy during app installation and license renewal. The default recovery model is initially set to Full.

Business Data Connectivity database

The Business Data Connectivity database simply stores connections, external content types, and related objects. As such, the database size is directly proportional to the number of connections to external data. It can only be scaled up within the service application, as only one Business Data Connectivity database is supported per Business Data Connectivity service application. It is read-heavy and has an initial default recovery of Full.

Search service application databases

The SharePoint 2013 Search service application now has four databases to support the new Search service application architecture. Because search is such a critical component of any SharePoint 2013 environment, and with many new areas of functionality dependent on the SharePoint 2013 Search service application, it is important to have a good understanding of each of the databases, their roles, and their performance characteristics in supporting the SharePoint 2013 environment.

Search Administration database

The Search Administration database stores configuration data for the Search service application, including topology, crawl rules, query rules, search schemas at farm, site, and web levels, managed property mappings, content sources, and crawl schedules. Additionally, it stores the Analytics settings for the SharePoint 2013 Search service application. Unlike the previous version's Search Administration database, it no longer stores access control lists (ACLs). Although it is possible to deploy multiple Search Admin components for fault tolerance, there is only one active component, and thus only one Search Administration database, so the database supports only scale-up. It has an equal read/write ratio, and sizing depends on number of search configuration objects contained in the service application. The default recovery model of the Search Administration database is Simple.

Analytics Reporting database

The SharePoint 2013 Search service application Analytics Reporting database stores the results of usage analysis, as well as Search reports. The reports include item reports, such as number of views for an item over time and unique users viewing an item over time, and site-level reports for tenants, site collections, and websites. The data in the site-level reports are aggregated to monthly views every 14 days by default. Typically, the Analytics Reporting database is write-heavy during the default nightly analytics update. It can be scaled both up and out, with the utilization of splitting the database when the database becomes larger than 200 GB. The default recovery model for the Analytics Reporting database is Simple.

Crawl database

The SharePoint 2013 Search service application Crawl database is used by the crawl component and stores information about the crawled items and crawl history tracking, such as the last crawl time, last crawl ID, and the type of update during the last crawl. It should be noted in SharePoint 2013 Search, the crawl and index components are separate, unlike the previous SharePoint Server 2010 Search service application. However, this separation is similar to FAST Search Server for SharePoint 2010 crawl and index components. Each crawl component or server role communicates with all Crawl databases. Additionally, the same host can be distributed across multiple crawl databases. The Crawl database is read-heavy and can be scaled out by creating additional Crawl databases. A new Crawl database should be created for every 20 million items crawled. The default recovery model is Simple.

Link database

The SharePoint 2013 Search service application Link database stores links extracted by the Search service application's Content Processing Component (CPC), as well as information about the number of times that users click a result from the search results. It is write-intensive during content processing. The Link database grows approximately 1 GB per 1 million documents processed and approximately 1 GB per 1 million queries. It should be scaled out with additional Link database(s) for every 60 million documents crawled. You should also add an additional Link database per 100 million expected queries per year. The default recovery model for the Crawl database is Simple.

Secure Store database

The Secure Store database supports the SharePoint 2013 Secure Store service application and stores and maps credentials, such as account names, passwords, and now certificates. It is relatively small, depending on the number of target applications, fields per target application, and number of users stored in each target application defined within the Secure Store service application. If auditing, which is recommended, is turned on, the number of read and write operations against a given target application can affect the database sizing. It has an equal read/write ratio. This database should be scaled up. The default recovery model is Full.

Usage (and Health Data Collection) database

The Usage database is used by the SharePoint 2013 Usage and Health Data Collection service application to store health monitoring and usage data temporarily. It also can be used for reporting and diagnostics. Interestingly, it is the only SharePoint 2013 database to support schema modifications. You can expect the database to be extremely large, depending on several factors, including retention factor, number of items enabled for logging and external monitoring, the number of web applications in the farm, the number of active users, and features enabled in the SharePoint 2013 environment. Unfortunately, this database must only scale up, as only one Usage database in one Usage and Health Data Collection service application is supported per SharePoint 2013 farm. The default recovery model of the Usage database is Simple.

Subscription Settings database

The Subscription Settings database supports the SharePoint 2013 Microsoft SharePoint Foundation Subscription Settings service application, storing features and settings for hosted customers. Unlike the previous version of SharePoint, which used the service application and database only to support multitenancy, the new SharePoint App platform requires the implementation and configuration of the Microsoft SharePoint Foundation Subscription Settings service application. It is relatively small in size and primarily read-intensive. The default recovery model is Full.

SharePoint Server 2013 databases

The following databases are those associated with SharePoint Server 2013, rather than the core SharePoint Foundation 2013 databases. They are available only in their respective edition of SharePoint Server 2013, Standard or Enterprise.

Profile database

The Profile database is one of three databases supporting the User Profile service application. It stores all user profiles, audiences, and activities. It also stores memberships in distribution lists and sites. The primary growth factors include the number of users and the use of news feeds, which grow with user activities. The default setting retains the last two weeks of activities. It is a primarily read-intensive database. Because there is only one Profile database per SharePoint 2013 User Profile service application, the database can only be scaled up. The default recovery model is Simple.

Synchronization database

The User Profile service application Synchronization database stores configuration and staging data for use when the User Profile Synchronization Service is synchronizing user profile data with any number of services. It is important to note that if the new Active Directory Import synchronization connection is used, the Synchronization database still exists but will remain empty. The Synchronization database maintains an equal read/write ratio, while growth is determined by the number of users and systems being synchronized by the User Profile Synchronization service. Because each User Profile service application supports only one Synchronization database, scaling is done via scale-up. The default recovery model is Simple.

Social database

The Social database stores ratings, tags, and comments created by users, along with their respective URLs. Keep in mind, however, that some social information, such as ratings models and settings, is now contained in the content databases, which is a change from the Social database in the previous version. Sizing and growth of the Social database varies greatly and depends primarily on number of tags, ratings, and notes that have been created and used in the environment. Like the other User Profile service application databases, there is only one Social database per service application. Therefore, you would scale up this database. The default recovery model is Simple.

Word Automation database

The Word Automation Services service application uses the Word Automation database to store information about pending and completed document conversions and updates. It is a small database and read-intensive, reading once per conversion item. This database also scales up and has a default recovery model of Full.

Managed Metadata database

Supporting the Managed Metadata service application, the Managed Metadata database stores managed metadata, syndicated content types, and a hierarchical structure for items that are used for tagging content and building site collections. The primary initial sizing and growth factor is based on the amount of metadata and syndicated content types, but considered to be small to medium. It can be scaled up. It is read-intensive and has a default recovery model of Full.

Machine Translation Services database

The Machine Translation service application is a new service application in SharePoint 2013 providing automatic machine translation of files and sites. When a request is sent to the service, either synchronously or asynchronously, it is processed and forwarded to a cloud-hosted machine translation service, where the work is performed and returned. The Machine Translation Services database is small and read-intensive. The default recovery model is Full.

State Service database

The State Service database stores temporary state information for InfoPath Forms Services, Microsoft Exchange Server, the Chart Web Part, and Microsoft Visio Services. It is read-intensive and scales up. Sizing and growth factors are solely dependent on the usage of features within the SharePoint 2013 farm that store data in the State Service database. The State Service database has a default recovery model of Full.

PowerPivot database

The PowerPivot database supports the SQL Server PowerPivot service application. As will be detailed later in the chapter, it requires SQL Server 2012 SP1 SQL Server Analysis Services (SSAS) and SQL Server 2012 SP1 Business Intelligence or Enterprise edition to be installed. The PowerPivot for SharePoint SSAS instance does not need to exist on the servers running SharePoint 2013. When SQL Server 2012

SP1 PowerPivot for SharePoint 2013 is used within the farm, the PowerPivot database stores data refresh schedules, and PowerPivot usage data then is copied from the usage data collection database. Additionally, SQL Server 2012 SP1 PowerPivot for SharePoint 2013 stores more data in the Central Administration Content database and Content databases, as mentioned previously. It is a small, read-intensive database, with typically insignificant growth and a default recovery model of Full.

PerformancePoint Services database

The PerformancePoint Services database stores temporary objects and persisted user comments and settings to support the functionality of the PerformancePoint Services service application. It is a small, read-intensive database that should be scaled up per service application instance. It has a default recovery model of Full.

Access Services 2013

The new Access Services feature is a completely new service application available in SharePoint 2013. There is still the ability to use Access Services 2010, hosted in its own backward-compatible service application within SharePoint 2013, but it is not recommended. Although there isn't a dedicated database for the Access Services 2013 service application per se, it does require SQL Server 2012 to store the user-created Microsoft Access 2013 databases. It is recommended to have a dedicated, separate SQL Server 2012 database engine instance for storing the user-created Access 2013 databases. In addition, it is important to remember to consider the Access 2013 App databases in disaster recovery plans because the content databases only contain links to the Access 2013 App, where the user-created functionality is in its own database.

SharePoint 2013 Integrated Reporting Services databases

When integrating SSRS with SharePoint 2013, there are additional databases needed to provide the functionality of Reporting Services to the SharePoint 2013 farm.

Report Server Catalog

The SSRS Report Server Catalog database stores all report metadata such as report definitions, report history, report snapshots, and report scheduling information. However, report documents are stored in the SharePoint 2013 content databases. The Report Server Catalog database must be located on the same database server as the Report Server TempDB database. It is small, read-heavy, and should only be scaled up. The Report Server Catalog database has a default recovery model set to Full.

Report Server TempDB

The SSRS 2012 for SharePoint 2013 service application uses the Reporting Server TempDB to store all the temporary snapshots currently executing in the environment. It must be located on the same database server instance as the Report Server Catalog database. The sizing and growth can vary greatly, depending on the number and use of cached report snapshots and their caching settings. It is read-intensive and can only be scaled up. It has a default recovery model of Full.

Report Server Alerting

The Report Server Alerting database of the SSRS 2012 for SharePoint 2013 service application is used for storing information about the Data Alerts and run-time data necessary to produce Data Alerts for Reporting Services reports. Data from reports is processed in the database based on the rules in the Reporting Services Alert Definitions. It must also be on the same database server as the Report Server Catalog database and can vary in size depending on the use of Data Alerts within the Reporting Services service application. If used, it will have an equal read/write ratio that is intensive. The recommended scaling method is scaled up to optimize the file I/O and memory consumption. The default recovery model is Full.

SQL Server 2008 R2 (SP1) and SQL Server 2012 system databases

Of the four SQL Server system databases (master, model, msdb, and tempdb), the only significant one to mention supporting a SharePoint 2013 implementation is the tempdb system database. The tempdb database stores temporary objects, such as temporary tables and temporary stored procedures. It is re-created every time that the SQL Server service is started. Due to the heavy use of both reading and writing by the SharePoint 2013 system, it should be located on a fast storage subsystem or disk, separated from other databases. If you use multiple files to reduce the storage contention, it may provide better performance and scalability. The general recommendation or guideline is to create one data file for each CPU core on the server and then adjust for performance from that point. The size is medium or up to 100 GB, depending on the SQL Server database engine activities. Large index rebuilds and/or large sorting operations can cause significant growth. The tempdb should only be scaled up. The default recovery model of the tempdb database is Simple.

SharePoint 2013 database capacity planning

In planning the database tier of SharePoint 2013, usually and hopefully, you will be working with dedicated database administrators. If not, you will be responsible for the performance of the database tier. To optimize performance in the planning of the database tier, the primary concepts are storage capacity and I/O planning. The storage for most SharePoint administrators is straightforward. However, usually the I/O requirements planning knowledge is little to none. As such, we will discuss these two primary factors in moderate depth and provide calculation formulas to assist you in SQL Server database capacity planning for supporting a SharePoint 2013 environment.

SQL Server storage and IOPS

For any SQL Server deployment, not just in supporting SharePoint 2013, it is critical to achieve the highest possible I/O from the storage subsystem, whether the subsystem is a combination of local disk(s) or enterprise SANs. The primary measure of a storage subsystem is usually measured in input/output operations per second (IOPS). Typically, the more disks or arrays of disks and faster disks provide significant increase in IOPS for the storage subsystem. Other factors, such as CPU and memory, can influence, but not compensate for, a poor or slow I/O subsystem. Prior to any production deployment of a SharePoint 2013 farm, it is recommended to benchmark the I/O subsystem. Microsoft provides a free download to analyze the I/O subsystem, called SQLIO (*http://go.microsoft.com/fwlink/p/?LinkID=105586t*). As mentioned previously, because knowledge of I/O subsystem optimization is typically shallow for SharePoint administrators and architects, you will be presented with a walkthrough of SQLIO near the end of this chapter. Additional in-depth information on analyzing I/O characteristics, as well as sizing storage systems for SQL Server database applications, can be found in a white paper available on the SQL Server Customer Advisory Team (CAT) team site (*http://sqlcat.com/sqlcat/b/whitepapers/archive/2010/05/10/analyzing-i-o-characteristics-and-sizing-storage-systems-for-sql-server-database-applications.aspx*).

The basis for every SharePoint 2013 deployment should be configuration, content, and IOPS. The configuration database and Central Administration content databases are small. It is recommended to initially allocate 2 GB and 1 GB, respectively, for the databases. The transaction log for the configuration, however, can be large. Therefore, either change the recovery model for the configuration database from Full to Simple or ensure the backup and truncation of the configuration database transaction logs. Other factors, such as mirroring, could limit your options. For example, database mirroring requires a full recovery model. IOPS requirements for the SharePoint 2013 configuration and Central Administration databases are minimal.

In estimating content database storage, you will use a formula based on the expected number of documents (D), the average size of documents (S), the number of list items (L), and the approximate average number of noncurrent versions of all documents (V). Additionally, you will use a 10 KB value, which is a rough estimate of the amount of metadata required by the SharePoint platform. If metadata is significant in your environment, you may want to increase this value in your calculation. The formula is represented by

$$Content\ database\ size = ((D \times V) \times S) + (10\ KB \times (L + (V \times D)))$$

For example, given the data shown in Figure 5-8, the content database size estimation would be 158 GB.

Variable	Value
# of Documents (D)	187500 (Assumes 7,500 active users and 25 documents per user)
Avg. document size (S)	400KB
# of list items (L)	500,000
# of non-current versions (V) (must be greater than 0)	2 (Assumes max versions allowed is 10)
Database size = (((187,500 x 2)) x 400) + ((10KB x (500,000 + (187,500 x 2))) = 158,750,000KB = 158GB	

FIGURE 5-8 This chart presents how to assign a service application to an application proxy group.

When estimating the IOPS requirement, the planned usage scenario(s) of the SharePoint 2013 platform is the primary factor that influences IOPS needs. Microsoft provides several usage–performance and capacity test results and recommendations for SharePoint 2013 (*http:// technet.microsoft.com/en-us/library/ff608068.aspx*). Ideally, you will find your usage scenario(s) with details. As an option, choose the scenario(s) that most closely resemble your use case requirements.

As an example, to achieve the maximum supported content database server size for all usage scenarios of 4 TB, the disk subsystem IOPS performance must be at least 0.25 IOPS per gigabyte, and optimally at 2 IOPS per gigabyte. In other words, for optimal performance of a 4 TB content database size, the disk subsystem supporting the database would need to be 8,000 IOPS, or a minimum of 1,000 IOPS. As a point of reference, a single 15,000-rpm SAS drive typically performs at 175 to 210 IOPS! As a final note on IOPS, do not simply trust vendor specifications of storage subsystems or drives. Test your system prior to deployment, hopefully using the example at the end of this chapter to baseline your storage subsystem.

The storage architecture selection for the database tier can also be critical in ensuring maximum performance of the environment, whether you are using Direct Attached Storage (DAS), SAN, and Network Attached Storage (NAS). NAS is only supported when using RBS with content database storage, although it should really be avoided for almost all scenarios. All storage subsystems and/ or architectures require a 1-ms ping response and must return the first byte of data within 20 ms. Additionally, each possible storage architecture disk type (for example, SCSI, SATA, SAS, FC, IDE, or SSD) and/or RAID use and type will have an impact on IOPS performance. As a rule of thumb, it is generally recommended to use RAID 10 or other solution that provides similar performance and characteristics.

Enabling SQL Server BI within SharePoint 2013

One of the most compelling features, especially for an intranet scenario, is enabling self-service SQL Server BI capabilities within the SharePoint 2013 platform. First, it should be noted that although the database engine of a SharePoint 2013 farm can be on SQL Server 2008 R2 SP1+ or SQL Server 2012, only SQL Server 2012 SP1 is supported for the SQL Server BI functionality within the SharePoint 2013 platform. Most environments will be multiserver, multitier implementations.

First, our scope of SQL Server 2012 SP1 BI for SharePoint 2013 components includes SQL Server 2012 SP1 PowerPivot (Analysis Services in SharePoint mode) and integrated SQL Server 2012 SP1 Reporting Services for SharePoint 2013. However, the Excel Services application is a prerequisite for PowerPivot and PowerView in SQL Server 2012 SP1 Reporting Services for SharePoint 2013. Assuming that you have a minimum three-server SharePoint Server 2013 Enterprise edition farm, including a Web Front End (WFE), and Application (APP) server, and a Database (SQL) server, the recommended architecture would be to place all the service applications (Excel Services, PowerPivot, and Reporting Services) on the APP server tier. SQL Server 2012 SP1 Analysis Services in SharePoint mode would be installed on the SQL server tier. It could, of course, be placed on a dedicated server. However, the steps are similar in installation and configuration if a dedicated server is used. It is important to note that the Reporting Services add-in is required to be on every server in the SharePoint 2013 farm.

Additionally, a new install or add-in, spPowerPivot.msi, is recommended to be installed on all servers in the SharePoint 2013 farm.

The high-level steps to install PowerPivot for SharePoint 2013 and Reporting Services in SharePoint mode are as follows:

1. Install and configure the Excel Services Application on the APP server.

2. Install Analysis Service in SharePoint mode on the SQL server. You should grant the SharePoint farm and the services account server administrator rights in the Analysis Services instance. As shown in Figure 5-9, the first step is to select Perform A New Installation Of SQL Server 2012.

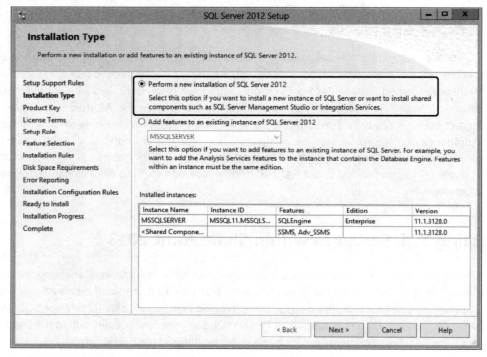

FIGURE 5-9 Specify a new installation for SQL Server PowerPivot for SharePoint in the SQL Server 2012 Setup dialog box.

3. In the Setup Role window, select SQL Server PowerPivot For SharePoint (see Figure 5-10), and then click Next.

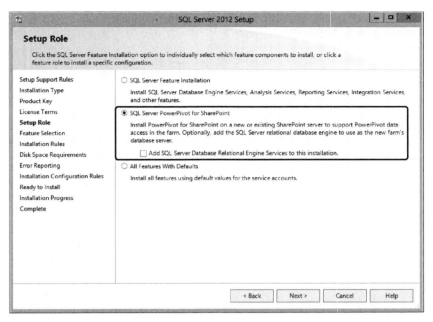

FIGURE 5-10 Specify SQL Server PowerPivot for SharePoint and clear the Database Engine if it is already installed.

4. Verify that the instance name in the Instance Confirmation window is POWERPIVOT, as shown in Figure 5-11.

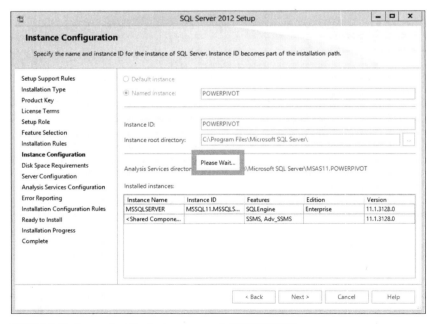

FIGURE 5-11 Ensure that the instance name is POWERPIVOT.

5. In the Server Configuration window, add the SQL Server Analysis Services service account, as shown in Figure 5-12.

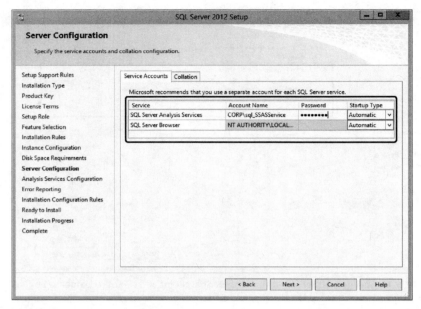

FIGURE 5-12 Specify the service account for SQL Server Analysis Services (PowerPivot for SharePoint).

6. In the Analysis Services Configuration window, add the other administrative accounts that will be using Analysis Services, as shown in Figure 5-13.

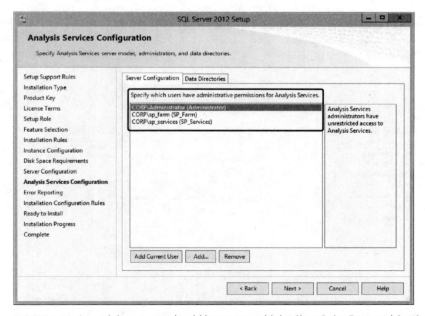

FIGURE 5-13 At a minimum, you should be sure to add the SharePoint Farm and Services accounts.

7. Install the spPowerPivot.msi file, found at *http://www.microsoft.com/en-us/download/details .aspx?id=35577*, on the servers running SharePoint Server 2013, which are APP and WEB servers in this example. Figure 5-14 shows the features selected during the installation of spPowerPivot.msi.

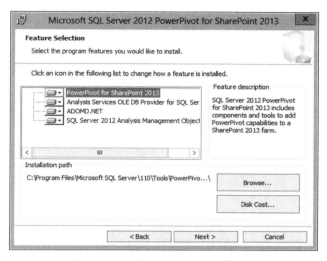

FIGURE 5-14 Make sure to keep defaults for all necessary libraries.

8. You will begin the process of registering the Analysis Services instance with the Excel Services application in SharePoint 2013 Central Administration by configuring the Data Model Settings of the Excel Services application, as shown in Figure 5-15.

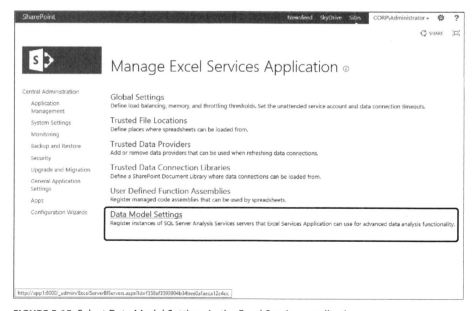

FIGURE 5-15 Select Data Model Settings in the Excel Services application.

9. After clicking Data Model Settings, the Excel Services Application Data Model Settings page will open. Click Add Server to add the server running the SSAS, as shown in Figure 5-16.

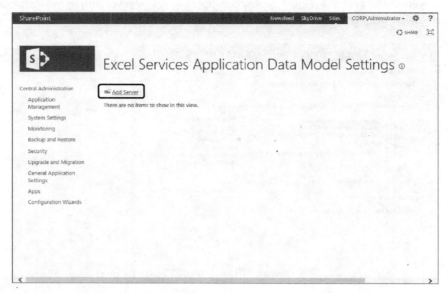

FIGURE 5-16 Click Add Server to add/register the PowerPivot instance.

10. Clicking the Add Server link will open the Excel Service Application Add Server page (shown in Figure 5-17), where you will supply the server and instance of the SQL Server 2012 SP1 PowerPivot instance.

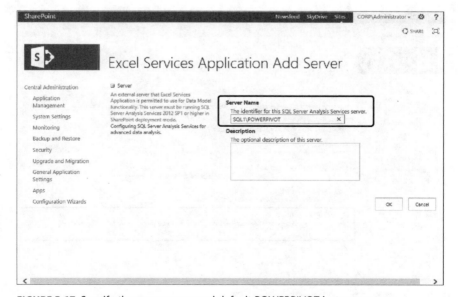

FIGURE 5-17 Specify the server name and default POWERPIVOT instance name.

11. From the Start menu of the SharePoint server, run the PowerPivot for SharePoint 2013 configuration as the account that was used to install the instance of SharePoint 2013, as shown in Figure 5-18.

FIGURE 5-18 Run the PowerPivot for SharePoint 2013 Configuration as the account that installed SharePoint 2013.

12. In the Run As Different User dialog box, enter the user name and password combination for your SharePoint 2013 install account. Next, the PowerPivot Configuration Tool window will open. If this is your first installation of PowerPivot for SharePoint on this server, select Configure Or Repair PowerPivot For SharePoint and click OK, as shown in Figure 5-19.

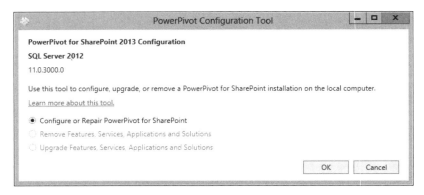

FIGURE 5-19 Continue to configure PowerPivot for SharePoint.

13. The next window that opens is where you will put in your PowerPivot for SharePoint configuration settings. After the settings have been entered, click Validate before proceeding, as shown in Figure 5-20.

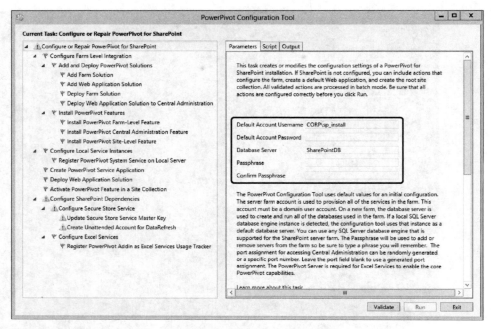

FIGURE 5-20 Specify the information and then validate the settings.

As shown in Figure 5-21, after the PowerPivot for SharePoint settings have been validated, if you click the Script tab, you have the ability to view and/or save the configuration settings as a Windows PowerShell script.

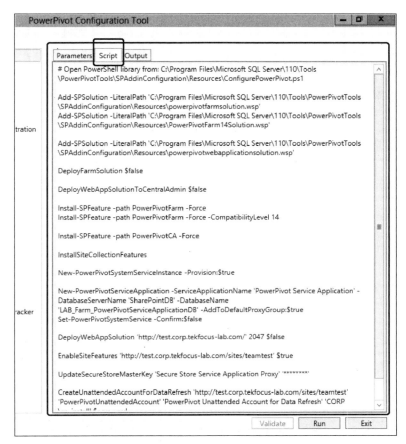

FIGURE 5-21 The Script tab provides the Windows PowerShell executed to perform the configuration.

Now that SQL Server 2012 PowerPivot for SharePoint has been installed and configured within the SharePoint 2013 farm, you will proceed to install and configure SSRS 2012 for SharePoint 2013 in Integrated mode. For the following steps, it is assumed that you are installing SQL Server 2012 SP1 Reporting Services on the APP server and the SQL Server 2012 SP1 Reporting Services add-in on all other SharePoint servers—in this case WFE. Prior to doing the next steps, ensure that you have the media for SQL Server 2012 SP1 available to both the APP and WFE servers.

14. To install Reporting Services in SharePoint mode and the Reporting Services add-in on the SharePoint APP server, you will need to start a new SQL Server 2012 SP1 installation and install a new SQL Server feature, as shown in Figure 5-22. (The procedure for entering the product key and accepting the end user license agreement (EULA) is skipped in these steps.)

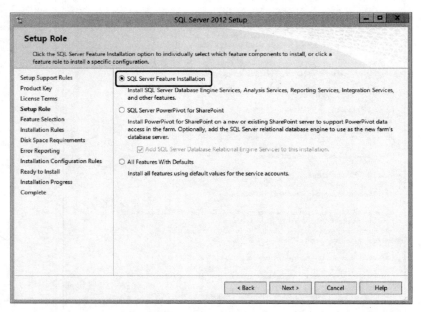

FIGURE 5-22 When installing Reporting Services, you must select SQL Server Feature Installation.

15. After clicking Next, select Reporting Services - SharePoint and Reporting Services Add-in For SharePoint Products from the Share Features section of the Feature Selection window, as shown in Figure 5-23.

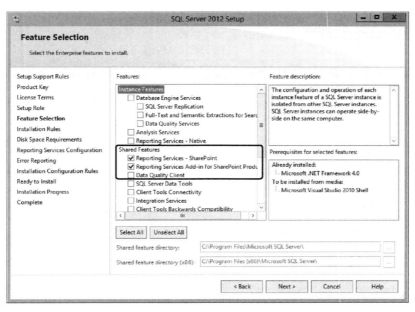

FIGURE 5-23 For the APP server, specify both the Reporting Services – SharePoint and Reporting Services Add-in For SharePoint options.

16. For this example, the Reporting Services add-in will be installed on the remaining SharePoint 2013 web server by adding the feature in the same manner as step 14. However, on the web server, only the Reporting Services add-in will be installed, as shown in Figure 5-24.

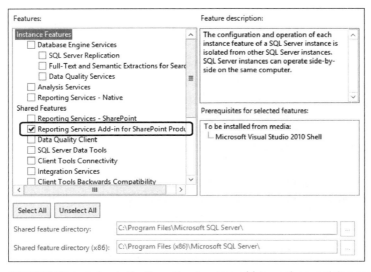

FIGURE 5-24 Install only the Reporting Services add-in on the remaining servers.

17. Configure the SSRS service application by going into Central Administration and adding a new SSRS service application, as shown in Figure 5-25.

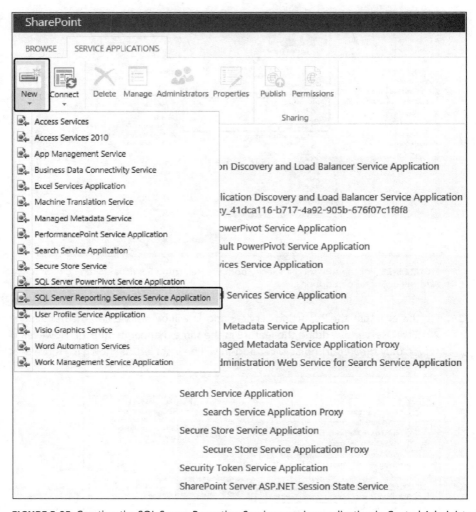

FIGURE 5-25 Creating the SQL Server Reporting Services service application in Central Administration.

18. When the Create SQL Server Reporting Services Service Application modal dialog box opens, add the configuration information required to create the service application, as shown in Figure 5-26.

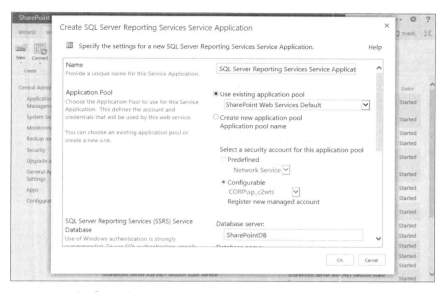

FIGURE 5-26 Configure the SQL Server Reporting Services service application initially.

19. After provisioning the SSRS service application, you'll need to run a script on the server running SQL Server that is hosting the database engine for SSRS that is created for you. To do this, click the Download Script button shown in Figure 5-27.

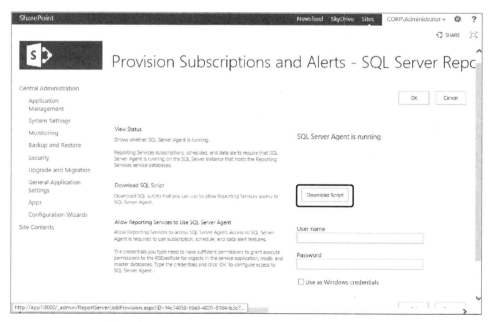

FIGURE 5-27 To provide subscriptions and alerts, download the autogenerated Transact-SQL script and execute it on the database engine server.

20. Activate the Power View Integration site collection feature in site collections where you will use Power View, as shown in Figure 5-28.

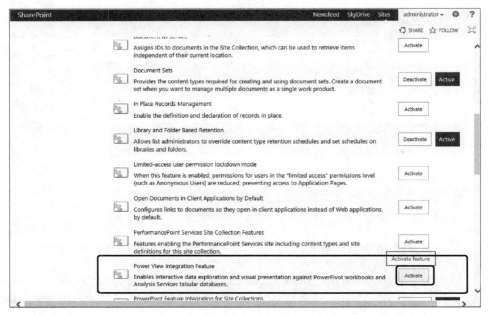

FIGURE 5-28 Activate the Power View Integration site collection feature in the desired site collection(s).

You can now create a site and test the BI functionality.

As a last note, you may want to consider enabling Kerberos and delegation throughout the farm and external data sources so that users' credentials can be passed and used for authentication to the external systems that are acting as the data sources for the BI functionality. Setting up Kerberos in a SharePoint Server 2013 environment is beyond the scope of this chapter.

Shredded Storage in SharePoint 2013

New to SharePoint 2013 is the concept and functionality of Shredded Storage. Shredded Storage is an improvement in the storage management of Binary Large Objects (BLOBS). Specifically, Shredded Storage improves data I/O and reduces the utilization of computing when making *incremental* changes to a file in SharePoint 2013. The Shredded Storage functionality occurs between the servers running SharePoint 2013 and the SQL Server database engine supporting the SharePoint 2013 farm. It is important to note that it is distinct, but it complements the Cobalt protocol functionality between the Microsoft Office clients and SharePoint servers introduced in the previous SharePoint 2010 and Office 2010 platform. In a new SharePoint 2013 implementation, Shredded Storage is enabled by default and cannot be disabled.

In the previous version of SharePoint, the file was completely loaded to the web server, where the merge operation occurred and then was completely written back to the SQL Server database. Shredded Storage improves this process by breaking the file (BLOB) into smaller, separate BLOBs, which are stored in a new database table named *DocStreams*. Each BLOB in the *DocStreams* table contains an identifier that aligns with the source BLOB when merged. When the client updates a file, only the smaller BLOB(s) associated with the updated data are updated. This update occurs on the SQL server rather than in the web server layer. This optimization can result in increased performance of file operations of SharePoint 2013 by approximately two times compared with SharePoint 2010.

FileWriteChunkSize is a new property in SharePoint 2013 similar to the *FileReadChunkSize* property introduced in SharePoint 2010 and associated with the BLOB cache enabled on SharePoint 2010 servers. The *FileWriteChunkSize* property can allow the control the size of the smaller, "shredded" BLOBs. It can be modified by a SharePoint 2013 farm administrator but should be done only after thorough testing in a nonproduction environment.

The most noticeable increase in decreased storage capacity with Shredded Storage in SharePoint 2013 is in the utilization of versioning within a document library. However, it is still recommended to utilize the "classic" storage capacity estimation process for determining initial SQL Server storage in supporting SharePoint 2013.

Putting it all together

Now that you have an understanding of SQL Server optimization techniques and how SharePoint uses the SQL Server databases, you should be able to go off and use the information from the previous sections to optimize your SQL Server environment. Optimizing SQL Server is great, and you can tweak your server settings until you have optimized every aspect of your SQL Server configuration; but what if you have a slow back channel to your hard drives? Do you know the latency and throughput that you are getting from your SharePoint box through to your SQL Server storage? Your throughput, latency, and drive read/write speeds are important to know before you set up your environment to make sure that your entire SQL Server environment is going to be working correctly.

You should have a baseline for your farm's information before and after you make changes, such as page load times, before adding a new Web Part or branding. You should also know your baseline numbers for disk drive performance before you set up your SharePoint farm. Knowing that your infrastructure is solid and can perform under heavy utilization is very important because you do not want a slowdown in the performance of SharePoint because of latency issues to your SAN. And probably the most important reason for you to have baseline numbers is so that the next time your network administrator claims to have tweaked the iSCSI network, you can know for sure. Another reason to understand your disk subsystem is to be able to explain and prove to your bosses what happens behind the scenes when they want to change the max file upload size to 1,500 MB. The default maximum file size is 250 MB, and the file size limit is configurable to expand up to 2,047 MB (2 GB); knowing the effects that changing the default maximum file size will have on your environment is very important before you make those kinds of changes.

Introducing SQLIO

To help determine your key metrics for your disk drive I/O performance, Microsoft has a free utility called SQLIO. It is a command-line tool that is not very user friendly—and don't let the name fool you, as it really has nothing to do with SQL. While it does not deal with SQL Server directly, it will allow you to determine the I/O capacity of your SQL Server hard drives. This disk subsystem benchmark tool will test your IOPS by moving files from Point A (SQL Server or SharePoint Server) to Point B (Disk Subsystem) of a specific size for a specific amount of time. Both file size and length are determined through settings, as well as the number of threads and number of requests. Keep in mind that your disk subsystem does not have to be a separate storage device; it could be your local drive array (hopefully RAID 10). Having insight into your local drive array is just as critical as knowledge of your SAN because things can go wrong internally just as easily as with your external devices.

You can download SQLIO from *http://tinyurl.com/PCfromDC-SQLIO*.

Testing your SQL Server internal drives

For this example, the initial test environment is going to be using three local drives for testing, as shown in Figure 5-29.

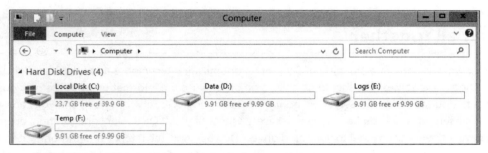

FIGURE 5-29 This window shows the hard drives that will be tested with SQLIO.

After downloading and installing SQLIO onto your server running SQL Server, go to the install location and open the Param.txt file. The default location of this file is C:\Program Files (x86)\SQLIO\ Param.txt. After you open the file, there are some settings that will need to be changed (see Figure 5-30). The Testfile.dat file needs to be created in the drive location that you wish to test. In the SQLIO folder, there is also a Readme.txt document that has a lot of useful information about SQLIO, as well as a file called Using SQLIO.rtf, and both should be read.

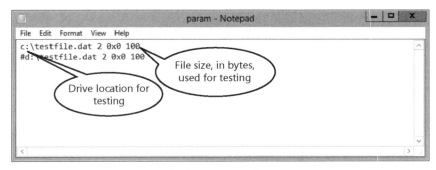

FIGURE 5-30 The default setting for the Param.txt file.

You will want to change the settings to match your desired testing drive locations. This initial test is going to be testing the D:\, E:\, and F:\ drives with a 1 GB file, so the Param.txt file has been modified, as shown in Figure 5-31.

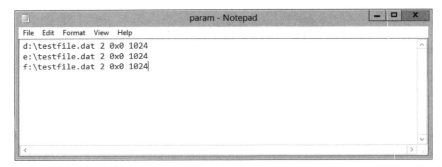

FIGURE 5-31 Modify the settings to match the drive layout and desired file size.

At this point, you will create the Testfile.dat files in the root of the drives and review the output file. You will need to open a command prompt as an administrator and go to the SQLIO folder. Once you have reached the SQLIO folder, run the following command from the command prompt:

```
C:\Program Files (x86)\SQLIO> sqlio -kW -t1 -s120 -dD -o1 -frandom -b64 -BH -LS -Fparam.txt >
c:\outfile.txt
```

Figure 5-32 shows what the variables within the command mean.

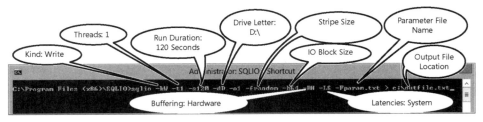

FIGURE 5-32 The labels explain the commands used to assign a service application to an application proxy group.

Running this command will create a text file of the output from SQLIO called Outfile.txt and put it in the root of the C:\ drive. This output file (shown in Figure 5-33) provides the cumulative data for the three drives that are being tested.

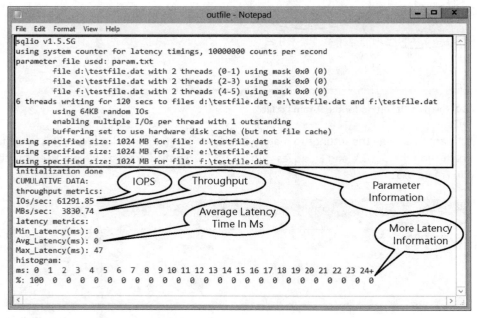

FIGURE 5-33 The output of the SQLIO test.

The desired outcome of testing your SQL Server drives, however, is to test each individual drive. This way, you have the ability to determine which is the fastest drive and put the TempDB on that drive. As you can see from the parameter information in Figure 5-34, the 1,024-MB Testfile.dat files have been created for each drive, which will be used to conduct the following test. To get the results of testing one drive, you will need to run the following command to test the D:\ drive, as shown in Figure 5-34:

```
C:\Program Files (x86)\SQLIO> sqlio -kW -t2 -s120 -dD -o1 -frandom -b64 -BH -LS Testfile.dat >
c:\outfile-D.txt
```

FIGURE 5-34 These commands are used to test the drives, along with the output file information.

A similar test will be run on the E:\ drive (as shown in Figure 5-33) with the following command:

```
C:\Program Files (x86)\SQLIO> sqlio -kW -t2 -s120 -dE -o1 -frandom -b64 -BH -LS Testfile.dat >
    c:\outfile-E.txt
```

And finally, a similar test will be run on the F:\ drive (also shown in Figure 5-33) with the following command:

```
C:\Program Files (x86)\SQLIO> sqlio -kW -t2 -s120 -dF -o1 -frandom -b64 -BH -LS Testfile.dat >
    c:\outfile-F.txt
```

The output of the D:\, E:\, and F:\ drives is shown in Figure 5-35.

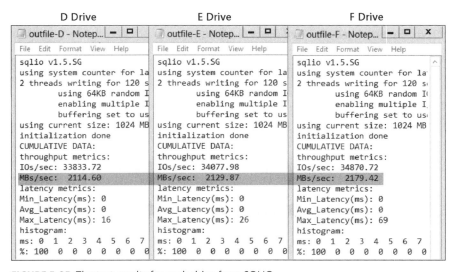

FIGURE 5-35 The test results for each drive from SQLIO.

In this configuration of SQLIO, the fastest drive is the F:\ drive because it has the highest number of IOs/sec and the highest throughput in MB/sec. There is a direct correlation between IOPS and throughput. You will never have a high throughput if your IOPS value is low.

Testing your iSCSI network drives

SQLIO really shines when it comes to testing your iSCSI network because SQLIO does such a good job of tracking latency. Ideally, your average latency for your testing should not be above 20 ms, and even if you are having latency results that are at 0 ms and 40 ms to average you out to 20 ms, you do have a problem somewhere in your chain. For this test, the drive configuration has three SAN drives (shown in Figure 5-36) on the server running SQL Server.

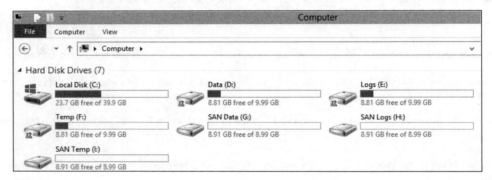

FIGURE 5-36 The local hard drives and attached iSCSI drives are shown here.

At this point, there are two ways to create the Testfile.dat file in the new drives. You can either modify the Param.txt file to include the new drives and rerun the script above, or you copy/paste the Testfile.dat file from an existing location into the new SAN drives.

Now that the Testfile.dat files have been put into the SAN drives, run the following commands to test the drives and create the output files:

```
C:\Program Files (x86)\SQLIO> sqlio -kW -t2 -s120 -dG -o1 -frandom -b64 -BH -LS Testfile.dat >
    c:\outfile-G.txt
C:\Program Files (x86)\SQLIO> sqlio -kW -t2 -s120 -dH -o1 -frandom -b64 -BH -LS Testfile.dat >
    c:\outfile-H.txt
C:\Program Files (x86)\SQLIO> sqlio -kW -t2 -s120 -dI -o1 -frandom -b64 -BH -LS Testfile.dat >
    c:\outfile-I.txt
```

The output files from this test, shown in Figure 5-37, will be drastically different compared to the results from testing the local SQL Server drives, shown in Figure 5-35.

```
outfile-G - Notep...            outfile-H - Notep...            outfile-I - Notepad

File  Edit  Format  View  Help  File  Edit  Format  View  Help  File  Edit  Format  View  Help

sqlio v1.5.SG                   sqlio v1.5.SG                   sqlio v1.5.SG
using system counter for la     using system counter for la     using system counter for la
2 threads writing for 120 s     2 threads writing for 120 s     2 threads writing for 120 s
        using 64KB random I             using 64KB random I             using 64KB random I
        enabling multiple I             enabling multiple I             enabling multiple I
        buffering set to us             buffering set to us             buffering set to us
using current size: 1024 MB     using current size: 1024 MB     using current size: 1024 MB
initialization done             initialization done             initialization done
CUMULATIVE DATA:                CUMULATIVE DATA:                CUMULATIVE DATA:
throughput metrics:             throughput metrics:             throughput metrics:
IOs/sec:  6207.20               IOs/sec:  6311.97               IOs/sec:  6611.81
MBs/sec:   387.95               MBs/sec:   394.49               MBs/sec:   413.23
latency metrics:                latency metrics:                latency metrics:
Min_Latency(ms): 0              Min_Latency(ms): 0              Min_Latency(ms): 0
Avg_Latency(ms): 0              Avg_Latency(ms): 0              Avg_Latency(ms): 0
Max_Latency(ms): 18             Max_Latency(ms): 640            Max_Latency(ms): 14
histogram:                      histogram:                      histogram:
ms: 0  1  2  3  4  5  6  7      ms: 0  1  2  3  4  5  6  7      ms: 0  1  2  3  4  5  6  7
%: 99  1  0  0  0  0  0  0      %: 99  1  0  0  0  0  0  0      %: 99  0  0  0  0  0  0  0
```

FIGURE 5-37 The output files from testing the three iSCSI drives are shown here.

Testing your SQL Server drives from SharePoint

To test the latency between your SharePoint environment and your SQL Server disk subsystem, shared storage will need to be enabled on the storage drives on your server running SQL Server; basically all the drives except for the operating system. Once there is a share name established for each drive, go to the server running SharePoint and create mapped drives to the new shares. After creating your mapped drives, install SQLIO on the SharePoint box, and then run the same commands you ran previously (if the mapped drives match):

```
C:\Program Files (x86)\SQLIO> sqlio -kW -t2 -s120 -dD -o1 -frandom -b64 -BH -LS Testfile.dat >
    c:\outfile-D.txt
C:\Program Files (x86)\SQLIO> sqlio -kW -t2 -s120 -dE -o1 -frandom -b64 -BH -LS Testfile.dat >
    c:\outfile-E.txt
C:\Program Files (x86)\SQLIO> sqlio -kW -t2 -s120 -dF -o1 -frandom -b64 -BH -LS Testfile.dat >
    c:\outfile-F.txt
C:\Program Files (x86)\SQLIO> sqlio -kW -t2 -s120 -dG -o1 -frandom -b64 -BH -LS Testfile.dat >
    c:\outfile-G.txt
C:\Program Files (x86)\SQLIO> sqlio -kW -t2 -s120 -dH -o1 -frandom -b64 -BH -LS Testfile.dat >
    c:\outfile-H.txt
C:\Program Files (x86)\SQLIO> sqlio -kW -t2 -s120 -dI -o1 -frandom -b64 -BH -LS Testfile.dat >
    c:\outfile-I.txt
```

The output files from this test, shown in Figure 5-38, will be drastically different from running this test directly from SQL Server, which were shown in Figure 5-35. Notice that for every added piece of equipment, IOPS reduces, and there is also a reduction in throughput.

D Drive
```
outfile-D - Notep...
File  Edit  Format  View  Help
sqlio v1.5.SG
using system counter for la
2 threads writing for 120 s
        using 64KB random I
        enabling multiple I
        buffering set to us
using current size: 1024 MB
initialization done
CUMULATIVE DATA:
throughput metrics:
IOs/sec:  6731.09
MBs/sec:    420.69
latency metrics:
Min_Latency(ms): 0
Avg_Latency(ms): 0
Max_Latency(ms): 14
histogram:
ms: 0  1  2  3  4  5  6  7
%: 100 0  0  0  0  0  0  0
```

E Drive
```
outfile-E - Notep...
File  Edit  Format  View  Help
sqlio v1.5.SG
using system counter for la
2 threads writing for 120 s
        using 64KB random I
        enabling multiple I
        buffering set to us
using current size: 1024 MB
initialization done
CUMULATIVE DATA:
throughput metrics:
IOs/sec:  6742.90
MBs/sec:    421.43
latency metrics:
Min_Latency(ms): 0
Avg_Latency(ms): 0
Max_Latency(ms): 16
histogram:
ms: 0  1  2  3  4  5  6  7
%: 100 0  0  0  0  0  0  0
```

F Drive
```
outfile-F - Notep...         X
File  Edit  Format  View  Help
sqlio v1.5.SG
using system counter for la
2 threads writing for 120 s
        using 64KB random I
        enabling multiple I
        buffering set to us
using current size: 1024 MB
initialization done
CUMULATIVE DATA:
throughput metrics:
IOs/sec:  6314.39
MBs/sec:    394.64
latency metrics:
Min_Latency(ms): 0
Avg_Latency(ms): 0
Max_Latency(ms): 54
histogram:
ms: 0  1  2  3  4  5  6  7
%: 99  1  0  0  0  0  0  0
```

G Drive
```
outfile-G - Notep...
File  Edit  Format  View  Help
sqlio v1.5.SG
using system counter for la
2 threads writing for 120 s
        using 64KB random I
        enabling multiple I
        buffering set to us
using current size: 1024 ME
initialization done
CUMULATIVE DATA:
throughput metrics:
IOs/sec:  3171.96
MBs/sec:    198.24
latency metrics:
Min_Latency(ms): 0
Avg_Latency(ms): 0
Max_Latency(ms): 25
histogram:
ms: 0  1  2  3  4  5  6  7
%: 96  2  1  0  0  0  0  0
```

H Drive
```
outfile-H - Notep...
File  Edit  Format  View  Help
sqlio v1.5.SG
using system counter for la
2 threads writing for 120 s
        using 64KB random I
        enabling multiple I
        buffering set to us
using current size: 1024 MB
initialization done
CUMULATIVE DATA:
throughput metrics:
IOs/sec:  3128.30
MBs/sec:    195.51
latency metrics:
Min_Latency(ms): 0
Avg_Latency(ms): 0
Max_Latency(ms): 16
histogram:
ms: 0  1  2  3  4  5  6  7
%: 96  3  1  0  0  0  0  0
```

I Drive
```
outfile-I - Notepad         X
File  Edit  Format  View  Help
sqlio v1.5.SG
using system counter for la
2 threads writing for 120 s
        using 64KB random I
        enabling multiple I
        buffering set to us
using current size: 1024 MB
initialization done
CUMULATIVE DATA:
throughput metrics:
IOs/sec:  3269.79
MBs/sec:    204.36
latency metrics:
Min_Latency(ms): 0
Avg_Latency(ms): 0
Max_Latency(ms): 650
histogram:
ms: 0  1  2  3  4  5  6  7
%: 97  2  0  0  0  0  0  0
```

FIGURE 5-38 A comparison of the local drive to the iSCSI drives on the server running SQL Server.

Stress testing your SQL Server drives

You have now completed a single test run using only a single set of parameters on your SQL Server drives. To really stress-test your drives, you will want to create a batch file that has different settings for use with the same Testfile.dat file. There is an excellent article at *http://sqlserverpedia.com/wiki/ SAN_Performance_Tuning_with_SQLIO* with instructions on not only how to create and run such a script, but also how to import the results into your server running SQL Server.

Disk subsystem performance information

Analyzing your disk performance is not easy, and it takes a lot of patience and experience to really understand how everything works and how to optimize your drives. If you would like more information about disk subsystem performance analysis, you can download a white paper from Microsoft called "Disk Subsystem Performance Analysis for Windows," at *http://msdn.microsoft .com/en-us/windows/hardware/gg463405.aspx*. While the paper is a bit old, it still has a lot of useful information.

After reading through this chapter, you should now have a better understanding of how important SQL Server tuning and optimization is for your SharePoint environment. SQL Server will run just fine out of the box without any tweaking, but it comes at the cost of SharePoint not running optimally either. Tuning your server running SQL Server before SharePoint is installed, as well as maintaining a vigilant watch over your SQL Server environment after SharePoint has been up and running, will help keep your SharePoint farm running as fast as possible.

## CHAPTER 6

Mapping authentication and authorization to requirements

In this chapter, you will learn about:

- Analyzing authentication options.

- Examining the SharePoint authentication components and methodologies.

- Investigating authentication services.

- Exploring authorization features.

As you review the requirements for your Microsoft SharePoint 2013 implementation, you have undoubtedly documented a number of them that would fall into the authentication and authorization aspects of SharePoint. In short, authentication (AuthN) is the mechanism to identify users securely, whereas authorization (AuthZ) is a decision about what access is given to an authorized user. The topics of AuthN and AuthZ can be quite long, and it is easy to get lost in all of the details. In this chapter, you will analyze the various authentication options by examining the trusted subsystem and impersonation/delegation. You will then examine the role of claims-based authentication in SharePoint 2013 and examine the role of services that aid in passing authentication details. Finally, you will explore the authorization features that are available in SharePoint.

Analyzing AuthN options

Fundamentally, any application platform will use one of two models for authentication: trusted subsystem or impersonation/delegation. A trusted subsystem is a service that will validate the credentials of the user but, from that point forward, access all of the resources using a service account identity. This type of model allows you to perform actions like connection pooling and caching. If you look at the application pools in Internet Information Services (IIS), the trusted subsystem model allows you to use a service account without storing the credentials in a plain-text file, thus compromising your accounts. Ultimately, SharePoint serves as a trusted subsystem using Windows credentials. This is evident when you have to install SharePoint with a domain account or grant the application pool permission to access the databases in Microsoft SQL Server.

Alternatively is impersonation, or delegation, which facilitates access to back-end resources with the credentials supplied by the information worker. This type of model allows the system to do end-to-end auditing by recording which rows in the database have been accessed by which users, but it doesn't offer actions like connection pooling and caching because each request is from a different user. This model is very useful for configuring business intelligence (BI) solutions, such as those that leverage the Business Connectivity Services (BCS) service application.

Claims-based authentication basically takes both of these models and merges them. Consequently, you will see similarities between claims-based authentications and the trusted subsystem, as well as identity management features similar to those available with the impersonation/delegation models. Claims-based authentication is used by SharePoint whether or not the user selected it for the web application. The core service application infrastructure uses claims-based authentication for internal communications. In SharePoint 2013, while Classic mode authentication is still available through Windows PowerShell, it is no longer an option through the UI. In fact, Classic mode authentication has been deprecated in the product and should not be expected to be carried forward—although there are still some advanced authentication features that will work only in Classic mode.

In this section, you will examine the various forms of authentication that are available within SharePoint 2013 and will learn enough information about each that will enable you, as the SharePoint architect, to map authentication strategies to the business requirements. This chapter will explore the following:

- Windows authentication

- Anonymous authentication

- Claims providers

- Security Assertion Markup Language (SAML) token-based authentication

- Server-to-server (S2S) and OAuth authentication

Windows authentication

The trusted subsystem authentication that is used in SharePoint 2013 validates the credentials of the information worker, and then accesses all of the resources using a service account identity. Windows authentication can be further broken down into four protocols: Basic, Digest, Windows NT LAN Manager (NTLM), and Kerberos. The last two protocols are the most common.

Basic

The first of the four supported authentications in SharePoint is Basic authentication. It requires that the information worker provide valid credentials to access the SharePoint content and is supported with all major browsers. One of the benefits of Basic authentication is that it works across firewalls and proxy servers and can be used in conjunction with Kerberos, enabling the delegation of security credentials.

A drawback of Basic authentication is that the passwords are transmitted in an unencrypted base64-encoded format across the network. If this type of configuration is chosen, it is highly recommended that the connection between the client and the server be encrypted by using Secure Sockets Layer (SSL) and Transport Layer Security (TLS).

Digest

Digest authentication also works well with proxy servers and firewalls but is only supported by Microsoft Internet Explorer 5.0 and later, which isn't a problem with SharePoint since it requires Windows Internet Explorer 8, Internet Explorer 9, Internet Explorer 10, or the latest released versions of Google Chrome, Mozilla Firefox, or Apple Safari. Digest authentication uses a challenge/response mechanism, and instead of sending a password over the network, it sends a hash (also known as a *digest*). Digest requires storing passwords in clear text using a reversible encryption and should also utilize SSL/TLS encryption. Digest authentication cannot be used in conjunction with Kerberos and therefore does not support delegation of security credentials.

NTLM

NTLM credentials are obtained when a user accesses a system, and consist of a domain name, user name, and a one-way hash of the password. NTLM uses an encrypted challenge and response to authenticate without having to send credentials over the network. This is done by the client computing a cryptographic hash of the password and passing it on to the server. The NTLM process is as follows:

1. The user sends an HTTP *GET* request to the server.

2. *HTTP:401 WWW-Authenticate: NTLM* is returned from the server to the client in the response header.

3. In interactive authentication, the user provides his or her credentials.

4. The client computer generates the cryptographic hash.

5. The client sends the requestor's domain name and user name in plain text over the wire.

6. The server sends over a challenge that consists of a randomly generated 16-byte character string called the "nonce."

7. The client receives the challenge and forms a response that consists of the encrypted challenge along with a hash of the user's password.

8. The server then sends the previously formed response to the domain controller.

9. The domain controller retrieves the user's hashed password from the Security Account Manager (SAM) database and encrypts the challenge based on hash.

10. The domain controller then compares the server-generated encrypted challenge to the response. If they are the same, authentication is successful. This is a symmetric comparison.

11. If nothing else fails, an *HTTP 200 OK* response is returned to the client.

NTLM is the default authentication of SharePoint 2013, but this doesn't mean that it is the best. Deciding whether or not to use NTLM will be defined by the business requirements and possibly the physical architecture of the servers that are supporting the farm. Under most conditions, you may find that NTLM is not the option that offers the highest performance. Once you have created a SharePoint web application, you can view the authentication that is being used by reviewing the security logs, as shown in Figure 6-1. You can locate these logs by visiting Server Manager | Diagnostics | Windows Logs | Security.

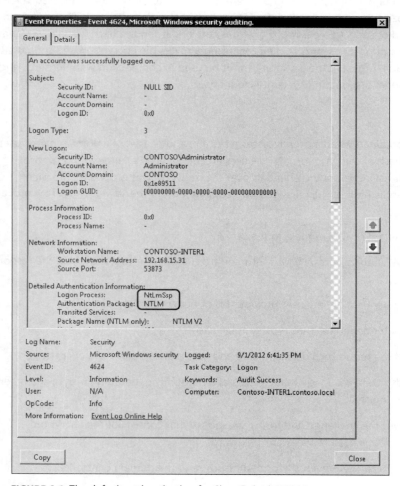

FIGURE 6-1 The default authentication for SharePoint is NTLM.

Not only does NTLM not perform well, it also doesn't scale well. The alternative is to use Negotiate, which is a security support provider that analyzes the HTTP request and uses the best form of authentication possible. This means that if only NTLM is available or Kerberos isn't configured correctly, NTLM is used. If Kerberos is available, then Negotiate will use it. Kerberos can be much faster than NTLM, and in most cases, it's second only to Anonymous Access, which doesn't do any validations at all.

Negotiate (Kerberos)

Kerberos is a ticket-based protocol. Tickets are obtained from the Kerberos Key Distribution Center (KDC), which is typically a domain controller, and are presented to servers when connections are established. The Kerberos ticket is sent in place of the user's credentials, and thus is more secure. The Kerberos process is as follows:

1. The user sends an HTTP *GET* request to the server.

2. *HTTP:401 WWW-Authenticate: Negotiate* or *HTTP:401 WWW-Authenticate: Kerberos* is returned from the IIS server to the client in the response header.

3. The client requests a service ticket from the KDC.

4. The KDC sends the service ticket to the client.

5. The client sends a Kerberos Application Request message to the server that contains an encrypted key sent by the KDC, the service ticket, and a flag indicating whether mutual authentication should be used. (Mutual authentication means that both the server and the client must verify their respective identities before performing any application-specific functions.)

6. The server receives the Kerberos Application Request message, decrypts the ticket, and extracts the user's authorization data and session key; the server uses the session key from the ticket to decrypt the authenticator message and evaluate the time stamp inside.

7. The server uses the session key to encrypt the time from the user's authenticator message and returns the result to the client in a Kerberos Application Reply message.

8. The client receives the Kerberos Application Reply message and decrypts the server's authenticator message with the session key it shares with the server and compares the time stamp with the one from the Kerberos Application Request message sent to the server.

9. If the time stamps match, then the service is considered validated and the HTTP *GET* request is attempted again with the server's authenticator message.

10. If nothing else fails, an *HTTP 200 OK* response is returned to the client.

If you review the IIS log files, you will notice that both NTLM and Kerberos requests initially receive a 401 (unauthorized) message at the beginning of the request. A Kerberos service ticket is valid for approximately 10 hours by default, meaning that it does not have to re-authenticate for each request during that period of time. One of the key aspects of using Kerberos is that the web application barely communicates with the domain controller, thereby significantly reducing the load on the domain controller as compared to NTLM authentication, which must query the domain controller for each request.

While Negotiate is used to configure Kerberos, you do not configure Kerberos simply by selecting Negotiate. This is often misunderstood because Negotiate and Kerberos appear to be the same thing when you're creating a new SharePoint web application. As previously mentioned, if the web application is configured for Negotiate all requests will attempt to be authenticated using Kerberos, however NTLM will be used if Kerberos fails. You will learn how to configure Kerberos in the next section. Examine Table 6-1 to review the differences between NTLM and Kerberos.

TABLE 6-1 Differences between NTLM and Kerberos

Feature	NTLM	Kerberos
Cryptography	Symmetric or encrypted challenge	Symmetric and/or asymmetric
Trusted party	Domain controller	Domain controller with KDC, domain controller, and Enterprise Certificate Authority
Supported clients	Microsoft Windows 9x, Windows Me, Windows NT 4, Windows 2000, and later	Windows 2000 and later
Authentication mechanism	Slow Authentication (passthrough)	Ticketing
Mutual AuthN	No	Yes
Delegation	No	Yes
Open standard	No, proprietary	Yes
Data protection	Hash	Cryptographic

More Info Windows Server 2012 introduced a number of Kerberos improvements. For more information on this topic, please refer to "What's New in Kerberos Authentication" at *http://technet.microsoft.com/en-us/library/hh831747.aspx.*

Configuring Kerberos in SharePoint

Configuring SharePoint to use Kerberos is fairly straightforward but has been known to offer even the most skilled SharePoint professional challenges from time to time. When implementing Kerberos within a SharePoint environment, there are three areas that may need to be configured based on the requirements: SQL Server communication, SharePoint web applications, and service applications.

Prior to diving into exactly how you configure Kerberos, let's first take a look at the minimum requirements to implement it—most of which are already met due to the minimum requirements of SharePoint.

- Windows 2000 or later
- An Active Directory domain
- Domain Name System (DNS)
- A TCP/IP network
- Service Principal Names (SPNs)
- A consistent time service

As mentioned previously, the Kerberos service ticket is valid for about 10 hours by default, so having a consistent time service is going to be imperative. SharePoint requires the first four items listed previously, so the last piece to focus on is the SPNs. The SPNs are the hurdle that seems to trip up most people. They are not difficult, but they are unforgiving when configured incorrectly. You will examine the SPN and the syntax here in a moment.

You must first ensure that the SharePoint servers are configured for delegation. To do this, choose Active Directory Users And Computers and select Properties of the servers hosting SharePoint. By default, they will be set to the first option. Select Trust This Computer For Delegation To Any Service (Kerberos Only), as shown in Figure 6-2. SharePoint delegation is done on a case-by-case basis, based on the requirements that will require service account credentials to be passed across machine boundaries.

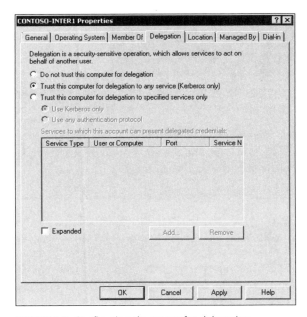

FIGURE 6-2 Configuring the server for delegation.

You can now turn your attention to the SPNs. Here are the guidelines to remember for configuring SPNs:

- You can run *setspn* from a command window or a Windows PowerShell window.

- *-S* will create a new SPN after it verifies that the SPN doesn't already exist (see Figure 6-3).

- *-A* will add the SPN without checking if the SPN exists. (*-S* is recommended.)

- *-D* will remove an existing SPN.

- *-L* will list the currently registered SPNs on the computer.

- Use *http/* whether you are using HTTP or Hypertext Transfer Protocol Secure (HTTPS) when creating the SPN.

- Configure the SPN to use the application pool account for the SharePoint web application.

- If you're using a nondefault port, the port number should be included. Nondefault ports are not recommended.

- Configure SPNs for both NetBIOS names and fully qualified domain names (FQDNs).

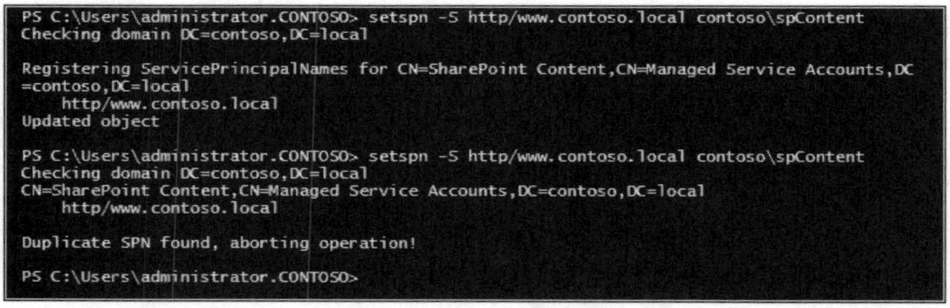

```
PS C:\Users\administrator.CONTOSO> setspn -S http/www.contoso.local contoso\spContent
Checking domain DC=contoso,DC=local

Registering ServicePrincipalNames for CN=SharePoint Content,CN=Managed Service Accounts,DC
=contoso,DC=local
    http/www.contoso.local
Updated object

PS C:\Users\administrator.CONTOSO> setspn -S http/www.contoso.local contoso\spContent
Checking domain DC=contoso,DC=local
CN=SharePoint Content,CN=Managed Service Accounts,DC=contoso,DC=local
    http/www.contoso.local

Duplicate SPN found, aborting operation!

PS C:\Users\administrator.CONTOSO>
```

FIGURE 6-3 The -*S* parameter checks the domain prior to creating the SPN and if the SPN exists, the process will abort.

Your next step is to create the SPN for your SharePoint web application. In this example, the SharePoint web application URL is *http://www.contoso.local,* and the application pool account is *contoso\spContent*. The syntax for this particular setup will look like Listing 6-1.

LISTING 6-1 Web application *setspn* syntax

```
setspn -S http/www.contoso.local contoso\spContent
```

The syntax is critical and must be in the format of *protocol/host:port*. Listing 6-2 shows an example of this format for SQL Server communications.

LISTING 6-2 SQL Server *setspn* syntax

```
setspn -S MSSQLSvc/sql.contoso.local:1433 contoso\sqlService
```

Revisit the Active Directory Users And Computers and find the application pool account that was used to create the SPN. If the SPN has been created, a Delegation tab will be visible. Click the tab and select Trust This User For Delegation For Any Service (Kerberos Only), as shown in Figure 6-4. Then click OK.

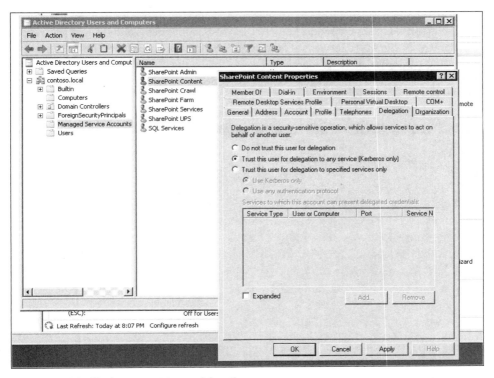

FIGURE 6-4 Modify the account to use delegation.

You can change the authentication of a SharePoint web application at any time, so if you elected not to select Negotiate when you created the web application, you can do so by visiting the Authentication Providers available on the ribbon of the Web Application list in Central Administration. Once there, you will be able to select the appropriate option, as shown in Figure 6-5.

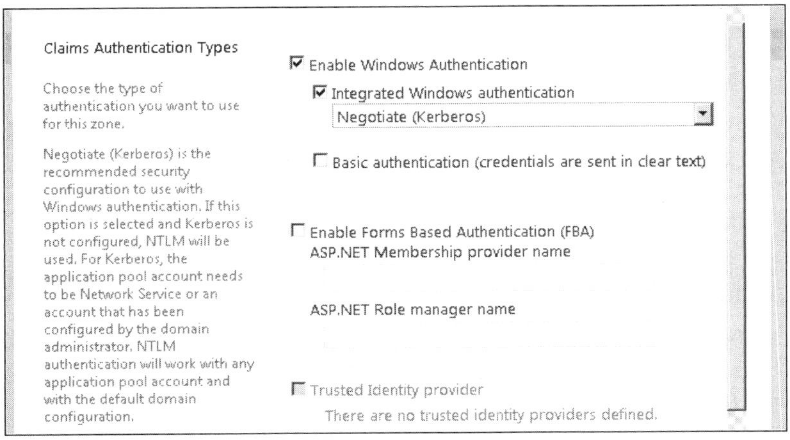

FIGURE 6-5 Kerberos configuration requires the Windows authentication of Negotiate.

Once all configurations are made, go to the Windows Event Log and review the Windows security audit success entry. The log should report Kerberos for the Logon Process and the Authentication Package, as shown in Figure 6-6. Server and account delegation are not required for the web application to use Kerberos tickets. As mentioned earlier, it is only required when crossing machine boundaries; a typical scenario is passing credentials back to SQL Server or configuring Microsoft Excel services.

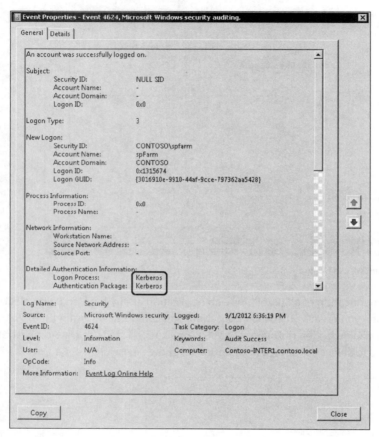

FIGURE 6-6 Once the SPN is configured, the Logon Process and Authentication Package should report Kerberos.

Classic mode vs. Claims mode

Some SharePoint 2010 implementations may be upgraded to SharePoint 2013 and left as Classic mode authentication web applications. In SharePoint 2013, some features will work only if the SharePoint web application is in Claims mode. Some of these features include OAuth authentication and the new Server-to-Server (S2S) authentication (which you'll learn about later in this chapter). It is recommended that all SharePoint web applications be configured in Claims mode so that the full suite of features of SharePoint 2013 will be available. However, there are some advanced authentication scenarios that are still only available in Classic mode. One example is with the use of BCS. BCS operates within the W3WP process and is unable to use the Claims to Windows Token Service (C2WTs). This restricts you to use classic mode under certain circumstances. If you are using features such as this in your web application, you will lose this functionality if you change to Claims mode.

In addition to the various authentication features, keep in mind that Windows authentication is a function of both Classic and Claims mode web applications. It is important to understand that just because a web application is in Claims mode does not mean it cannot use Windows authentication. In short, Classic mode authentication can only support Windows authentication, while Claims mode can support a wide variety of authentication models, including Windows authentication.

With that said, how are you supposed to get your Classic mode SharePoint web applications into Claims mode?

Converting Classic mode to Claims mode

If you converted Classic mode SharePoint applications to Claims mode in the 2010 product, you are already familiar with the *MigrateUsers()* method that was available from the *SPWebApplication* object. This method has been depreciated in SharePoint 2013 and replaced with a new Windows PowerShell cmdlet: *Convert-SPWebApplication*.

Convert-SPWebApplication is designed to convert the authentication mode of a SharePoint web application from Windows Classic to Windows Claims authentication mode and migrate the user accounts associated with the web application to claims-encoded values. The claims-encoded values in SharePoint 2010 contained syntax similar to *i:0#.w* or *c:0!.s* prior to the domain or Windows account value. If users had more than one instance of an account in the UserInfo table, they would often see this type of encoding, and although it seems very random, you can tell a great deal from the characters that the encoding contained. You will learn about the claims-encoding syntax and the new customization process available in SharePoint 2013 later in this chapter.

To upgrade a SharePoint 2010 Classic mode application to a SharePoint 2013 Claims mode application, do the following:

1. Create a SharePoint web application in SharePoint 2013 that uses Classic mode authentication. Remember that this must be done using Windows PowerShell since the Classic mode option has been removed from the UI in SharePoint 2013.

2. Make a copy of the SharePoint 2010 content database and attach it using the *Mount-SPContentDatabase* to the newly created SharePoint 2013 web application. This will upgrade the database to the 2013 format. (For more information on upgrades, see Chapter 8, "Upgrading your SharePoint 2010 environment.")

 Note It is recommended that you review your content after executing the *Mount-SPContentDatabase* cmdlet to ensure that the site is working as expected. If you perform too many steps before reviewing your content and there is a problem it may be difficult to troubleshoot any issues that arise.

3. Run the *Convert-SPWebApplication* cmdlet on the SharePoint 2013 web application. This will convert the authentication mode from Classic to Claims and migrate the user accounts to use claims encoding. When this cmdlet is executed, you will be prompted with two continuation messages: one stating that the operation may take a long time and the service will be unavailable, and the other letting the admin know that the user performing the operation will be given full rights to the web application.

4. Once the cmdlet has completed, the authentication mode for the SharePoint web application will be Claims and the user accounts have been converted to use claims encoding. If there are any issues, they will be available in the ULS logs for review.

As an alternative to the preceding method, you could simply attach the 2010 content database to an existing SharePoint 2013 web application and run the *Convert-SPWebApplication*. However, you would be skipping some critical testing stages that could possibly introduce problems.

 Note SharePoint 2013 does not support converting a web application from Claims authentication mode to Classic authentication mode. The *-To* parameter of the Convert-SPWebApplication cmdlet only accepts Claims.

Anonymous authentication

Anonymous authentication is an authentication type that does not validate the user who is accessing the site. Anonymous authentication is generally used for web-facing implementations when the information is for public review. Since no validation checks are performed, anonymous authentication is the fastest of the authentication options and offers some caching benefits that you will learn about in Chapter 9, "Maintaining and monitoring Microsoft SharePoint."

Anonymous authentication is configured in two steps. The first step requires the SharePoint farm administrator to enable anonymous access at the SharePoint web application level, as shown in Figure 6-7. This can be done either at the time of creating the web application or any time afterward.

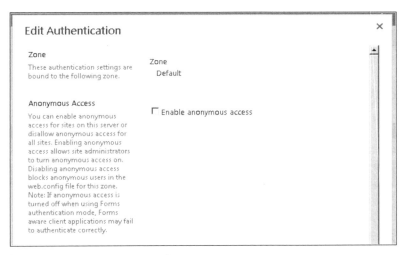

FIGURE 6-7 Edit authentications for anonymous access.

Once anonymous access has been enabled at the web application, the content owner can complete the configuration by accessing the site permissions on the site settings page. The content owner will see the Anonymous Access option available in the SharePoint ribbon. This option will allow users to either access the entire website, only list and libraries, or disable anonymous access altogether, as shown in Figure 6-8.

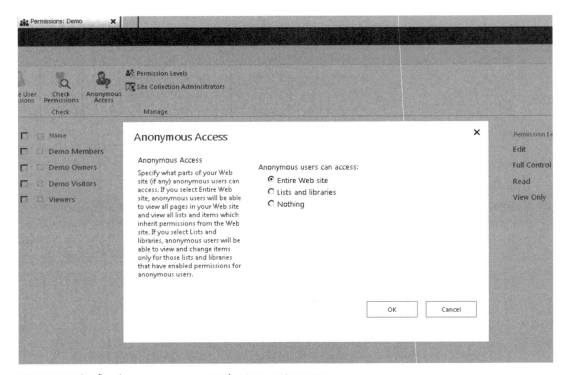

FIGURE 6-8 Configuring anonymous access is a two-part process.

Anonymous access is a two-part process, and by default, it is disabled at all levels. Take extreme caution when turning on this feature in SharePoint. All content will be accessible to anyone who can access the sites URL.

Claims-based authentication

Thus far in this chapter, you've learned that Claims is the default authentication type in SharePoint 2013 and how to convert a Classic mode web application to Claims mode, but it may not be clear what a claim actually is. With Windows authentication, a user identity is configured in Active Directory Domain Services (AD DS) and supports having a number of attributes that are associated to each user. The user is either challenged for their credentials when they log on to their client computer or when they attempt to access SharePoint. The downside of this type of authentication is that if additional information about the user is required (roles, group membership, etc.), additional AD DS requests may be required. This approach doesn't necessarily scale well with advanced authentication providers over Internet or cloud-based solutions. A solution to this problem is to use a claims-based token that you obtain from a trusted identity provider and that contains a set of claims about the users. Each of the claims can contain the critical pieces of data about the user such as name, birthdate, role, group membership, or even an email address that can then be used to give the user access to content based on the claim without going back to AD DS.

To further simplify how a claim works, here's a real-world example: air travel. When someone goes to book travel on an airplane, he or she is asked for a form of identification. This piece of identification is used to tie the person flying to a particular boarding pass. The soon-to-be airline passenger then takes the identification and the boarding pass to security (since both are required for passage). Once the passenger has been validated through security, only the boarding pass is needed to access the resources (in this case, the airplane).

Claims-based identities are built on a set of Microsoft .NET Framework classes known as the Windows Identity Foundation (WIF). The WIF is comprised of a number of standards that enable it to work across technology boundaries. These standards include WS-Federation 1.1, WS-Trust 1.4, and SAML 1.1, as described in Table 6-2.

TABLE 6-2 Standards used in Claims authentication

Standard	Description
WS-Federation 1.1	Provides flexible architecture with separation between trust mechanisms, security token formats, and the protocol for obtaining tokens
WS-Trust 1.4	Specifies how security tokens are requested and received
SAML Token 1.1	Identifies the XML that represents claims

Here's an example of the steps that a typical claims request would go through:

1.   The client (a web browser or Microsoft Office 2013) submits a resource request to SharePoint.

2.   SharePoint responds and tells the client that it is unauthenticated and passes a URL to the client via a 301 redirect so that the client knows where to go to get authenticated.

3. The client requests authentication from the Identity Provider Security Token Server (IP-STS).

4. IP-STS returns a security token (SAML 2.0, SAML 1.1, SWT, and JWT) to the client.

5. The client passes the newly acquired security token back to the SharePoint STS, otherwise known as the relying party (RP).

6. The SharePoint STS decides if it trusts the issuer of the token, and if so, performs claims augmentation, which generates a new SharePoint claims token that is sent back to the client.

7. The client passes the new token to the target SharePoint application.

8. SharePoint then converts the augmented claim into a *SPUser* object, and the rest is business as usual.

In SharePoint 2013, if Claims mode authentication is being used, all authentication forms (Windows Identity, Forms Based Authentication, or SAML 1.1) are augmented into a SAML token, which is then converted into a *SPUser* object inside SharePoint. If Classic mode is being used, the Windows Identity is converted straight into a *SPUser* object inside SharePoint.

One of the major improvements in SharePoint 2013 is that SharePoint tracks *FedAuth* cookies in the new Distributed Cache Service. In SharePoint 2010, each web server had its own copy, which meant that if users were redirected to a different web server, they would have to re-authenticate. With this improvement, sticky sessions are no longer required when using SAML claims.

Another feature in SharePoint 2013 is the ability to choose the characters for the claim type and prepopulate the custom claim types and characters across all SharePoint farms. The order in which the claim providers are installed is no longer a factor.

Forms-based authentication (FBA)

Starting with the SharePoint 2010 product, Forms-based authentication (FBA) became a claims-based identity management system based on ASP.NET membership and role provider authentication. FBA offers a number of flexible solutions by storing user credentials in a database or Lightweight Directory Access Protocols (LDAP) data such as Sun ONE, Novell Directory Services (NDS), or Novell eDirectory.

FBA in SharePoint prompts the user for credentials using a web-based logon. Once the user has successfully been authenticated, the system issues a cookie that is used for subsequent authentication requests.

Configuring FBA for SharePoint 2013 is exactly the same process as for SharePoint 2010. This process includes the following high-level steps:

1. Create a new Claims mode SharePoint web application that enables FBA, or enable FBA in a current Claims-mode web application.

2. Type a value specifying the provider in ASP.NET Membership Provider Name.

3. Type a value specifying the role in ASP.NET Role Manager Name.

4. Modify the *web.config* file of the Central Administration to contain a connection string, role, and membership provider using the same ASP.NET Membership Provider names in step 2 and 3.

5. Configure the Security Token Service *web.config* file to contain a connection string, role, and membership provider.

6. Configure the *web.config* file of the SharePoint web application to contain a connection string, role, and membership provider.

Optionally, you may choose to create a new SharePoint web application using Windows PowerShell. The syntax is provided in Listing 6-3. The modifications of the *web.config* files will still need to be done. It is important to remember that these files need to be changed on each of the servers that are hosting the SharePoint web applications.

LISTING 6-3 Create a new web application that uses FBA using Windows PowerShell

```
$ap = New-SPAuthenticationProvider -Name <Name> -ASPNETMembershipProvider
<Membership Provider Name> -ASPNETRoleProviderName <Role Manager Name>
$wa = New-SPWebApplication -Name <Name> -ApplicationPool <ApplicationPool>
-ApplicationPoolAccount <ApplicationPoolAccount> -Url <URL> -Port <Port>
-AuthenticationProvider $ap
```

Note Steve Peschka has released a new update to his FBA Configuration Manager for this release of SharePoint. If you are looking for a great way to implement FBA without much hassle, this tool is definitely worth investigating. You can find it at *http://blogs.technet .com/b/speschka/archive/2012/07/28/fba-configuration-manager-for-sharepoint-2013.aspx*.

Be aware that FBA sends user account credentials over the network as plain text, so only configure it on SharePoint web applications that have SSL encryption between the client and SharePoint server.

SAML token-based authentication

SAML token-based authentication in SharePoint 2013 uses the WS-Federation Passive Requestor Profile (WS-F RPR), included in the WS-Federation specification, and the SAML 1.1 protocol. The WS-Federation model is applied to passive requestors, which include web browsers supporting the HTTP protocol by defining an integrated model for providing authentication and authorization across trust realms and protocols. Passive requestors require a secure service (SSL/TLS or HTTP/S) that will ensure that the claims requestor is actually making the request. One way to configure a SAML token-based authentication environment is to use Active Directory Federation Services (ADFS) 2.0 or Microsoft Live ID. Prior to examining the communication path of SAML token-based authentication, read the descriptions in Table 6-3 to get an understanding of the components that are included in a SAML token-based architecture.

TABLE 6-3 SAML token-based authentication components

Component	Description
SharePoint Security Token Service	Creates the SAML tokens that the farm uses. This is an automatic service that is provisioned when the SharePoint farm is created. It's used for all SharePoint web application Claims-based authentications (Windows authentication, FBA, and SAML) and inter-farm communications between services.
Identity provider Security Token Service (IP-STS)	A service that authenticates a client and issues SAML tokens on behalf of users who exist in a particular user directory. This service is typically found in the client's domain and, in the case of SharePoint 2013, contains a list of SAML-configured web applications that will rely on this service.
Relying Party Security Token Service (RP-STS)	Each SharePoint 2013 web application that is configured for SAML token-based authentication is added to the IP-STS server as an RP-STS entry.
Token-signing certificate	A certificate that is exported from the IP-STS and imported in to the SharePoint 2013 Trusted Root Authority list.
SPTrustedIdentityTokenIssuer	An object on the SharePoint 2013 farm that includes values that are used to communicate with and receive SAML tokens from the IP-STS. It is replicated across the servers in the SharePoint farm.
Identity claim	The claim from a SAML token that is unique to the user. Only the IP-STS owner will know which value in the token will be unique for each user, like an email address.
Realm	The URL or URI that is associated with a SharePoint web application.
Other claims	Additional claims that describe the user such as roles, user groups, age, etc.

To summarize Table 6-3, SAML token-based authentication in SharePoint 2013 web applications are configured to point to one or more IP-STS. The IP-STS authenticates a particular user that is located in the user directory. The IP-STS issues SAML tokens, which contain the identity claim and optionally other claims, that are then returned to the requesting web application, who serves as the relying party STS (RP-STS). The web application then uses the claims inside to decide whether or not to grant access (AuthZ) to the requested resource. Figure 6-9 is a graphical representation of the SAML token-based authentication.

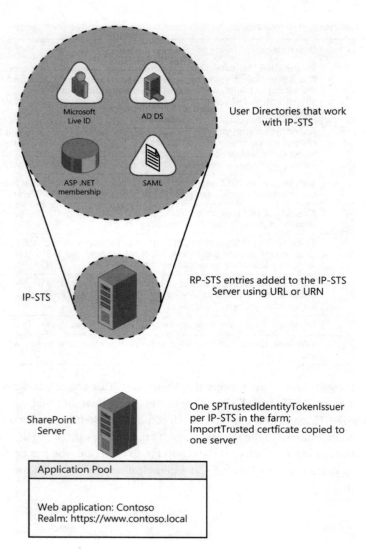

FIGURE 6-9 SAML token-based authentication.

When you're configuring SharePoint web applications to use SAML token-based authentication, it is important to know that *SPTrustedClaimProvider* will not provide search functionality into the IP-STS and will automatically resolve anything entered in the People Picker control whether or not it is a valid user, group, or claim. This is due to the lack of standards on how this information is to be obtained.

In SharePoint 2013, you are now allowed to have multiple token-signing certificates. This is useful in S2S scenarios and also allows you to bypass any downtime associated with certificate expirations since now the certificates can overlap.

Once the token-signing certificate is used to create a *SPTrustedIdentityTokenIssuer*, it cannot be used to create another one. If the token-signing certificate is to be used to create a new *SPTrustedIdentityTokenIssuer*, the existing one must be disassociated from all SharePoint web applications and then deleted. Once the *SPTrustedIdentityTokenIssuer* has been created, additional realms can be associated. The realm must then be added to the IP-STS as a relying party.

> **More Info** For a step-by-step walkthrough on configuring a SAML token-based authentication SharePoint environment, visit *http://technet.microsoft.com/en-us/library/hh305235(v=office.15)*.

The *SPTrustedIdentityTokenIssuer* object, as shown in Figure 6-10, has a number of important parameters. It can only contain a single identity claim, *SignInURL* parameter, and *Wreply* parameter, but it can contain multiple realms and claim mappings. The *SignInURL* parameter specifies the location of the IP-STS that the user will be redirected to in order to complete the authentication. Depending on the type of IP-STS you're using, a *Wreply* parameter may also be required. *Wreply* is a Boolean value that has a default value of *false*.

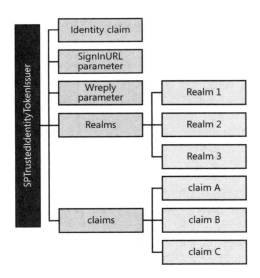

FIGURE 6-10 Important parameters of the *SPTrustedIdentityTokenIssuer* object.

> **Caution** The *SPTrustedIdentityTokenIssuer* contains a property named *MetadataEndPoint*. Steve Peschka wrote a blog post warning against the manual manipulation of this property because it can cause your SharePoint farm to be nonfunctional beyond the point of repair.

One of the new improvements for SharePoint 2013 is that network load balancing no longer requires single affinity when using Claims-based authentication. Prior to 2013, single affinity was required to ensure that the user session would "stick" to one server to avoid the user from being prompted for additional authentication.

OAuth authentication

OAuth is an open protocol for secure authorization (AuthN) and is the core infrastructure in both the new app authentication and S2S authentication models. Before going into the specifics of each of these, you will learn what OAuth is and isn't. In SharePoint 2013, OAuth is used to establish a trust between two applications and the identity of a particular principal, application or user. In regards to App authentication this enables users to approve an application (during the installation process of the app) to act on their behalf without sharing their user name and password. Not sharing user credentials is a key aspect; this allows a user to authorize access to a scope of resources (documents, pictures, etc.) for a specified duration of time and not necessarily everything the user would have access to. OAuth also provides trusts between cross-farm services like the remote SharePoint Search index feature or extra-farm servers like Microsoft Lync or Microsoft Exchange Server.

OAuth provides access tokens, which are used for application authentication, as opposed to sign-in tokens, which support user sign-in. User authentication, as mentioned in the previous section, is handled by the *SPTrustedIdentityTokenIssuer*.

Since OAuth is going to be used for a number of scenarios in SharePoint 2013, it is important to consider how the users will access the system. When SharePoint uses OAuth, it is passing around a cookie that contains an access token and therefore is vulnerable to unauthorized reuse. It is recommended to protect the token using SSL in production environments. SSL is a requirement for web applications that are deployed in scenarios that support S2S authentication and App authentication.

App authentication

In Chapter 1, "Understanding the Microsoft SharePoint 2013 architecture," you were introduced to the SharePoint App model as the new standard in deploying customizations to SharePoint. They are deployed from the Corporate Catalog or Office Marketplace and offer flexible and reusable options for any SharePoint deployment type On Premise, Hybrid, or SharePoint Online. During the creation of the application, the developer configures the app manifest file, which specifies the permissions the application needs to perform its functions; the application will then request these permissions as it is being installed. Users can only grant the permission that they have. Therefore, the user who is installing the app must be able to grant the required permissions or the installation of the app will fail. There are five opportunities to manage app permissions:

- During the installation

- When a user gives consent through the UI

- When permission by a tenant admin or website admin is explicitly granted

- During an app request for new permissions

- During app removal

The app uses permission requests that will request both the rights and the scope that is required. The scopes that are supported in SharePoint for content databases include site collection (SPSite), website (SPWeb), list (SPList), and Tenancy. Additionally, there are other scopes for search queries, accessing taxonomy data, user profiles, etc. Once the scope has been defined, as shown in Figure 6-11, the permission rights will define what an app is permitted to do within that particular scope. For content, SharePoint supports Read-Only, Write, Manage, and Full Control—these rights are not customizable. Once the application has been provisioned the rights for the app can only be revoked, but not changed. Uninstalling the app will remove all of its permissions.

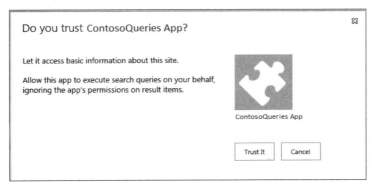

FIGURE 6-11 The app requests permissions when being added.

In regards to the cloud, if an organization wishes to utilize cloud-hosted apps, communication between the app, SharePoint 2013, the authorization server, and the user must take place. For the sake of this discussion, our SharePoint farm is hosted in the Fabrikam company domain, the app is hosted on Contoso.com, and the authorization server is Windows Azure Access Control Service (ACS). The app (hosted on Contoso.com) uses the SharePoint client object model (CSOM) or REST endpoints with CSOM to make calls to the SharePoint farm (hosted in the Fabrikam domain). The SharePoint farm will request a context token from ACS that it can send to the Contoso.com server which, in turn, uses the context token to request an access token from ACS as part of the OAuth transaction process. The app hosted on Contoso.com then uses the access token to communicate back to the SharePoint farm. It is important to note that Internet access to ACS is required, and access to the SharePoint farm is required from the Internet for this to work. You will now examine this process in more detail. The following steps are depicted in Figure 6-12.

1. A user accesses a SharePoint 2013 web application where a particular app is installed. The app is a Contoso.com app, and the UI elements on the SharePoint page come from the app.

2. SharePoint detects that there is a component from the Contoso.com app on the page and must get a context token that it can send to the Contoso.com app; SharePoint requests a context token from ACS.

3. ACS returns the signed context token that contains an app secret that only ACS and the Contoso.com app share.

4. SharePoint renders the page and passes the context token to the app's visual component (IFrame).

5. The IFrame causes the browser to request a page from Contoso.com and sends the context token to Contoso.com.

6. Contoso.com validates the signature on the context token by reviewing the app secret. Contoso.com makes a request to ACS for an access token so that it can talk back to SharePoint.

7. ACS returns an access token to the Contoso.com server and Contoso.com can cache this access token to alleviate further communications. By default, access tokens are good for a few hours at a time.

8. Contoso.com can use the access token to make a web service call or CSOM request to SharePoint, passing the OAuth access token in the HTTP Authorization header.

9. SharePoint responds to Contoso.com with any information it requests.

10. Contoso.com renders the content as per the user request in step 1.

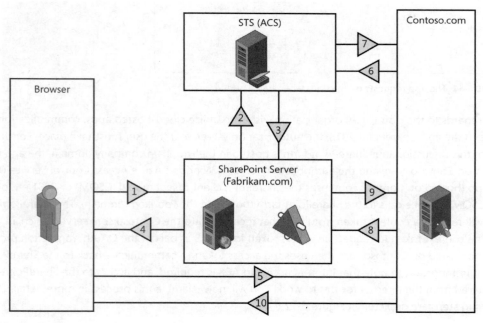

FIGURE 6-12 OAuth and cloud-hosted apps.

In this scenario, the OAuth flow is relying on ACS to provide a secret to get an access token from ACS. In the event that ACS is not being used, the app creates an access token using the app's trusted certificate.

After an app has been installed in the farm, you can retrieve a list of app principals by viewing the *appprincipals.aspx* page in the SharePoint 2013 (15) root folder at *http://www.fabrikam.com/_layouts/15/appprincipals.aspx*.

Additionally, you can also retrieve app registration information by viewing the *appinv.aspx* page located in the layouts folder at *http://www.fabrikam.com/_layouts/appinv.aspx*.

S2S authentication

S2S provides application to application authentication using OAuth and involves using "well-known app principals" (Exchange Server 2013, Lync Server 2013, multitenant workflow, and SharePoint 2013) to delegate a user identity that SharePoint 2013 will accept. The SharePoint S2S authentication is dependent on the User Profile Application (UPA) to construct a user token that describes the user whose content the application is requesting. In order for this process to be successful, SharePoint will communicate with the UPA and extract the user principal name (UPN), Simple Mail Transfer Protocol (SMTP), and Session Initiation Protocol (SIP) attributes and create the token that can be handled through OAuth to authenticate with the back-end server application. Some examples include Exchange Server requesting information from SharePoint, Windows Azure hosted workflows, a SharePoint timer job asking Lync or Exchange Server for information.

For cloud-based services, ACS acts as a trust broker to enable cross-server communications. In on-premise deployments, this can be configured by using the JavaScript Object Notation (JSON) metadata endpoint of the other S2S-compliant service to establish the trust relationship; this can be done using the *New-SPTrustedSecurityTokenIssuer* cmdlet, as shown in Listing 6-4.

LISTING 6-4 Create a trust between SharePoint and a S2S-compliant service

```
New-SPTrustedSecurityTokenIssuer –MetadataEndpoint
"https://<AuthorityComponent>/_layouts/15/metadata/json/1" –IsTrustBroker –Name
"<FriendlyName>"
```

Note The SharePoint STS uses and consumes the federation metadata endpoint in a JSON format, which allows SharePoint and identity providers to exchange content; AD FS 2.0 does not currently support this format.

Claims encoding

Most Windows users are familiar with the classic NETBIOS user names as they are often used to log on to most corporate computers. The user name is in the format *DOMAIN\user* (or *PROVIDER:user* for FBA). While this format worked well for standard authentication models, they were not sufficient for the Claims-based authentication model introduced in SharePoint 2010. As SharePoint 2013 expands on the role of the Claims model with the emergence of OAuth, understanding the enigma behind the claims-encoding cast of characters may help many SharePoint administrators understand when and why they see these characters in the environment. For example, as shown in Figure 6-13, the SharePoint web application policy shows the SharePoint search crawling account as *i:0#.w|contoso\ spsearch*.

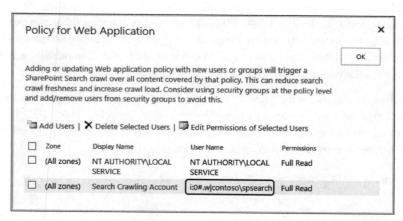

FIGURE 6-13 Viewing the policy for a web application shows an example of claims encoding.

There is little available information from Microsoft on this protocol. Wictor Wilén composed a fantastic blog post on how claims encoding works in SharePoint, and the figure he used in his blog, as shown in Figure 6-14, simplifies what each of these characters means.

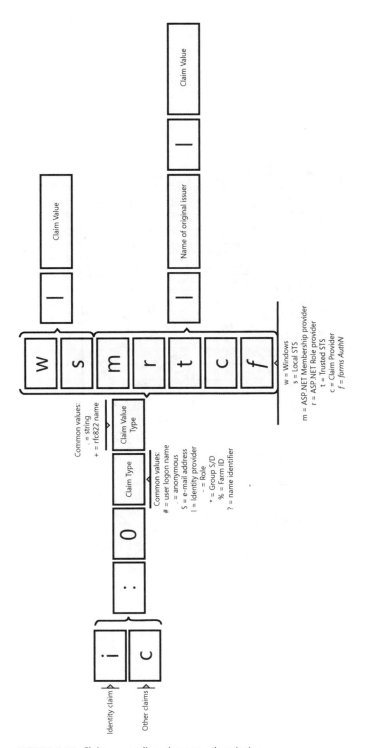

FIGURE 6-14 Claims encoding character description.

Using Figure 6-14, you will reexamine the claims identifier mentioned here: *i:0#.w|contoso\spsearch*. As you can see, the first character can specify an identity claim (*i*) or any other type of claim (*c*).

The second character, represented by the colon (:), is a fixed character, as is the third character, the zero (*0*). The fourth character is the claim type. There are a wide variety of constants that are used to define well-known claim types that are supported by WIF. Some of the most common include user name (#), email (5), role (-), group SID (+), and farm ID (%). For a full list, you can use the *Get-SPClaim-TypeEncoding* cmdlet; the output is shown in Figure 6-15.

```
EncodingCharacter ClaimType
----------------- ---------
              @ http://schemas.xmlsoap.org/ws/2005/05/identity/claims/otherphone
              ? http://schemas.xmlsoap.org/ws/2005/05/identity/claims/nameidentifier
              > http://schemas.xmlsoap.org/ws/2005/05/identity/claims/name
              = http://schemas.xmlsoap.org/ws/2005/05/identity/claims/mobilephone
              < http://schemas.xmlsoap.org/ws/2005/05/identity/claims/locality
              9 http://schemas.xmlsoap.org/ws/2005/05/identity/claims/homephone
              8 http://schemas.xmlsoap.org/ws/2005/05/identity/claims/hash
              7 http://schemas.xmlsoap.org/ws/2005/05/identity/claims/givenname
              6 http://schemas.xmlsoap.org/ws/2005/05/identity/claims/gender
              5 http://schemas.xmlsoap.org/ws/2005/05/identity/claims/emailaddress
              4 http://schemas.xmlsoap.org/ws/2005/05/identity/claims/dns
              3 http://schemas.xmlsoap.org/ws/2005/05/identity/claims/denyonlysid
              2 http://schemas.xmlsoap.org/ws/2005/05/identity/claims/dateofbirth
              1 http://schemas.xmlsoap.org/ws/2005/05/identity/claims/country
              0 http://schemas.xmlsoap.org/ws/2005/05/identity/claims/authorizationdecision
              / http://schemas.xmlsoap.org/ws/2005/05/identity/claims/authentication
              . http://schemas.xmlsoap.org/ws/2005/05/identity/claims/anonymous
              - http://schemas.microsoft.com/ws/2008/06/identity/claims/role
              + http://schemas.microsoft.com/ws/2008/06/identity/claims/groupsid
              * http://schemas.microsoft.com/ws/2008/06/identity/claims/primarygroupsid
              ) http://schemas.microsoft.com/ws/2008/06/identity/claims/primarysid
              ( http://sharepoint.microsoft.com/claims/2009/08/isauthenticated
              ' http://schemas.microsoft.com/sharepoint/2009/08/claims/processidentitylogonname
              & http://schemas.microsoft.com/sharepoint/2009/08/claims/processidentitysid
              % http://schemas.microsoft.com/sharepoint/2009/08/claims/farmid
              $ http://schemas.microsoft.com/sharepoint/2009/08/claims/distributionlistsid
              # http://schemas.microsoft.com/sharepoint/2009/08/claims/userlogonname
              " http://schemas.microsoft.com/sharepoint/2009/08/claims/userid
              ! http://schemas.microsoft.com/sharepoint/2009/08/claims/identityprovider
              n http://sharepoint.microsoft.com/claims/2012/02/claimprovidercontext
              m http://schemas.microsoft.com/office/2012/01/sip
              l http://schemas.microsoft.com/office/2012/01/smtp
              k http://schemas.microsoft.com/office/2012/01/nameidissuer
              j http://schemas.microsoft.com/office/2012/01/upn
              i http://schemas.microsoft.com/office/2012/01/nameid
              h http://sharepoint.microsoft.com/claims/2009/08/provideruserkey
              g http://schemas.xmlsoap.org/ws/2005/05/identity/claims/webpage
              f http://schemas.xmlsoap.org/ws/2005/05/identity/claims/uri
              e http://schemas.xmlsoap.org/ws/2005/05/identity/claims/upn
              d http://schemas.xmlsoap.org/ws/2005/05/identity/claims/thumbprint
              c http://schemas.xmlsoap.org/ws/2005/05/identity/claims/system
              b http://schemas.xmlsoap.org/ws/2005/05/identity/claims/surname
              a http://schemas.xmlsoap.org/ws/2005/05/identity/claims/streetaddress
              ` http://schemas.xmlsoap.org/ws/2005/05/identity/claims/stateorprovince
              _ http://schemas.xmlsoap.org/ws/2005/05/identity/claims/spn
              ^ http://schemas.xmlsoap.org/ws/2005/05/identity/claims/sid
              ] http://schemas.xmlsoap.org/ws/2005/05/identity/claims/rsa
              \ http://schemas.xmlsoap.org/ws/2005/05/identity/claims/privatepersonalidentifier
              [ http://schemas.xmlsoap.org/ws/2005/05/identity/claims/postalcode
```

FIGURE 6-15 The output for the *Get-SPClaimTypeEncoding* cmdlet.

As custom claim providers are added to SharePoint 2013, the need for claim types that are not predefined may be needed. To facilitate this need, SharePoint offers the *New-SPClaimTypeEncoding* cmdlet. This cmdlet not only allows you to add a new claim type but also allows you to specify an *-EncodingCharacter*. Prior to this cmdlet, SharePoint generated its own encoding character that made it difficult to use the same claims provider with the same encoding across farms.

The next value, the claim type value, is also defined by the WIF, and like the claim type, has a long list of values. Some of the most common values include string (.) and rtc822 name (+).

The sixth character specifies the origination of the claim and includes the following: Windows (*w*), Local STS (*s*), ASP.NET Membership provider (*m*), ASP.NET Role provider (*r*), trusted STS (*t*), claim provider (*c*), and forms AuthN (*f*). The seventh character is a pipe that is either followed by the claim value or the name of the original issuer followed by a pipe and claim value.

Examining SharePoint authentication components and methodologies

SharePoint has a number of authentication components and methodologies that are important to understand as you map user requirements to architecture solutions. In Microsoft Office SharePoint Server (MOSS) 2007, the primary way to share the same SharePoint content with users that required multiple forms of authentication was through the use of zones. These zones, which required their own IIS web application, mapped to one or more alternate access mappings (AAMs). As the SharePoint product matured, new ways to share access and content became important. In this section, you will learn more about the importance of authentication zones and how AAMs relate to them. AAMs offer your architecture designs a way to use multiple URLs to access the same content. You will then turn your focus to site collection host headers, as the recommended way to expose your SharePoint sites to the users who depend on them.

Authentication zones

Authentication zones in SharePoint offer a way to present the same sites in a web application to alternate logical paths. Each SharePoint web application can contain up to five zones: Default, Intranet, Internet, Extranet, and Custom. While these names may seem fairly descriptive in the function they perform, it is important to understand that the names are merely labels. But while the names themselves don't necessarily mean anything, how the web applications are built and which zones they share with other web applications are critical.

When a SharePoint web application is created, it is automatically associated with the Default zone. In order to use an additional zone, you would either extend the web application from central administration or the *New-SPWebApplicationExtension* cmdlet, as shown in Listing 6-5. When extending a SharePoint web application, a new IIS web application is mapped to the existing SharePoint content database. Creating the new IIS web application ensures that the new application has its own set of *web.config* files, IIS bindings, and protocols. This allows for the configuration of various authentication methods like classic Windows NTLM on one zone and Claims FBA on the other. Each SharePoint web application will then have its own internal AAM, as you'll see in the next section.

LISTING 6-5 The *New-SPWebApplicationExtension* cmdlet

```
Get-SPWebApplication http://www.contoso.local | New-SPWebApplicationExtension
-Name "ExtranetSite" -SecureSocketsLayer -Zone "Extranet" -URL "https://extranet
.contoso.local"
```

In SharePoint 2013, most new web applications will utilize the Claims mode option for the various reasons outlined earlier in this chapter. Claims mode also allows the ability to have multiple authentications on the same zone. This would allow for having corporate partners access the default zone using SAML token-based authentication, individual partners using FBA, internal employees using various AD DS implementations, and having SharePoint search crawl the web application with AD DS Windows NTLM.

There are some important things to know about zones and SharePoint search. If Windows authentication is not selected on any zone of the web application, search crawling for that particular web application will be disabled. Please note that NTLM is not required so long as you have Windows authentication enabled; the search crawls will work as expected. This is a contradiction to the statement in the UI, but you will find that the functionality works with Kerberos as well. In addition, if multiple zones are being used, and the user submits a search query for content inside another web application, the URL of the corresponding zone of the other web application will be used in the search results. When you are extending SharePoint web applications to other zones, ensure that the user experience is as intended.

It is important to remember that if you are making changes to a *web.config* file in one IIS web application (zone), the change may need to be made in the other zones as well.

AAMs

As mentioned in the previous section, when you extend a SharePoint web application to another zone, an AAM is automatically created for the selected zone, as shown in Figure 6-16. Up until SharePoint 2013, the use of AAMs was considered the mainstream approach of extending SharePoint content to other URLs. In SharePoint 2013, the use of AAM is being discouraged in the place of host header site collections (see the next section).

Alternate Access Mappings

Edit Public URLs | Add Internal URLs | Map to External Resource

Internal URL	Zone	Public URL for Zone
http://contoso-sp2:2013	Default	http://contoso-sp2:2013
http://www.contoso.local	Default	http://www.contoso.local
https://extranet.contoso.local	Extranet	https://extranet.contoso.local
http://search.contoso.local	Default	http://search.contoso.local

FIGURE 6-16 SharePoint zones and AAMs.

Path-based sites and AAMs are not totally obsolete. There are a few scenarios when their use is recommended over the site collection host headers:

- When the SharePoint web application requires the Self-Service Site Creation feature, which is hard-coded to create only path-based sites

- When additional security is required by multiple web apps with separate app pools

Self-Service Site Creation

The Self-Service Site Creation (SSSC) feature in SharePoint allows users who have the "Use Self-Service Site Creation" right to create site collections or new site by using the Start A New Site link in their personal menu. This feature is turned on in the web application management page inside Central Administration, as shown in Figure 6-17. Microsoft has made new investments in the SSSC feature in SharePoint 2013. Some of the improvements include:

- The ability to specify a custom form when creating a new site. This can give the user the option of selecting a template other than a team site.

- The ability to specify a new site collection or new site.

- The ability to specify the inclusion under which new sites should be created.

- The ability to define policies in a content-type hub and associate them with the new site collection.

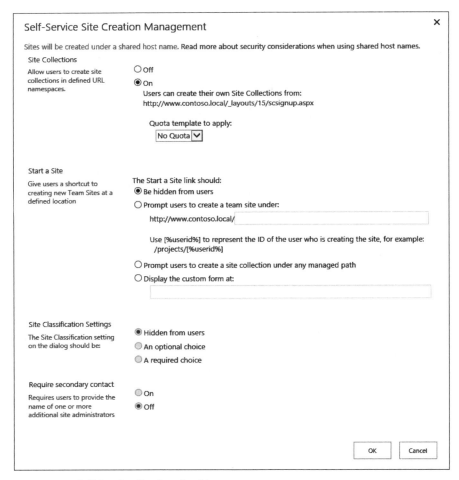

FIGURE 6-17 Self-Service Site Creation Management.

Note The SSSC feature is automatically enabled on site collections that are created by the farm creation wizard.

Site collection host headers

As discussed in Chapter 1, SharePoint 2013 supports both path-based and host-named site collections; to gain an understanding of the differences between them, refer back to that chapter. New implementations should consider the use of site collection host headers. Site collection host headers allow for the configuration of multiple URLs with a single site collection. The management of this feature can be done using the *Get-SPSiteUrl*, *Set-SPSiteUrl,* and *Remove-SPSiteUrl* cmdlets. Site collection host headers can be used only with host header site collection, as opposed to path-based site collections. Remember that path-based site collections are the ones that include managed paths like *sites*.

SharePoint authentication zones can still be used in conjunction with the URLs if alternate authentication is needed between the site collection host headers. The site collection host headers will be associated with only the default zone. Since you have the ability to associate a number of URLs to a single zone, it creates a more scalable solution than what AAMs offered.

Investigating authentication (AuthN) services

There are a number of authentication services that, when planned correctly, offer a wide variety of solutions that allow SharePoint 2013 to interact with external systems. These systems may include any number of databases that are providing critical data. In this section, you will learn about the Claims to Windows Token Service (c2WTS), which extracts a UPN from a claim and passes it on as a Windows identity. You will then learn about the Secure Store Service (SSS), which stores credentials to other systems and offers a simplified way of providing access to those systems. Finally, you will learn how BCS can be used to access external data.

Claims to Windows Token Service (c2WTS)

In SharePoint 2013, there are a number of services that do not support claims and need to have the credentials translated from Windows claims-based credentials to Windows credentials. These services include Excel services, PerformancePoint services, Microsoft InfoPath Forms services, and Microsoft Visio services. These services must rely on the Claims to Windows Token Service (c2WTS), which is a feature of WIF, to extract the UPN claims from non-Windows security tokens, such as SAML and X.509 tokens, and generate impersonation-level Windows security tokens. The Windows security tokens are then passed to back-end resources using Kerberos-constrained delegation, which means that a service can impersonate an authenticated client's identity and pass those credentials to another server. Claims-based authentication can also be used to delegate client credentials, but requires the back-end application to be claims aware, which is not the case when dealing with SQL Server. Once the c2WTS converts the claim-based credentials to Window credentials, the back-end system then performs its own authentication. Relying party applications running as the local system account do not require c2WTS. Furthermore, service applications that are accessed through web applications and use SAML claims or FBA claims do not use the c2WTS service; it can only be used if the incoming authentication method is either Windows Claims or Windows Classic mode.

When using SharePoint 2013 and the services mentioned earlier (Excel services, PerformancePoint services, InfoPath Forms services, and Visio services), the data sources must reside in the same Windows domain. Although Windows Server 2012 does allow constrained delegation across domain and forest boundaries, the limitation of accessing the data sources in another domain falls on the c2WTS. Additionally, the Business Data Connectivity service will not leverage the c2WTS as it runs within a *W3WP.exe* process.

The c2WTS can be enabled within Central Administration in the Service Application section under Managed Services On Server. Select the server(s) that is to run the service and click Start. Alternatively, you can use the Windows PowerShell similar to the example in Listing 6-6.

LISTING 6-6 Start the c2WTS with Windows PowerShell

```
$svc = Get-SPServiceInstance -Server $env:computername | `
where {$_.TypeName -eq "Claims to Windows Token Service"}
if ($svc.Status -ne "Online") {
    $svc | Start-SPServiceInstance
}
```

By default, the c2WTS service is started using the Local System account. In order to take full advantage of the capabilities, a domain account should be used. This account will also need to have local administration rights, so it should be an isolated account. This can be done either by using Windows PowerShell or through Central Administration's Configure service accounts (shown in Figure 6-18) in the security section. We will go into more detail on SharePoint's service accounts in Chapter 7, "Designing for platform security."

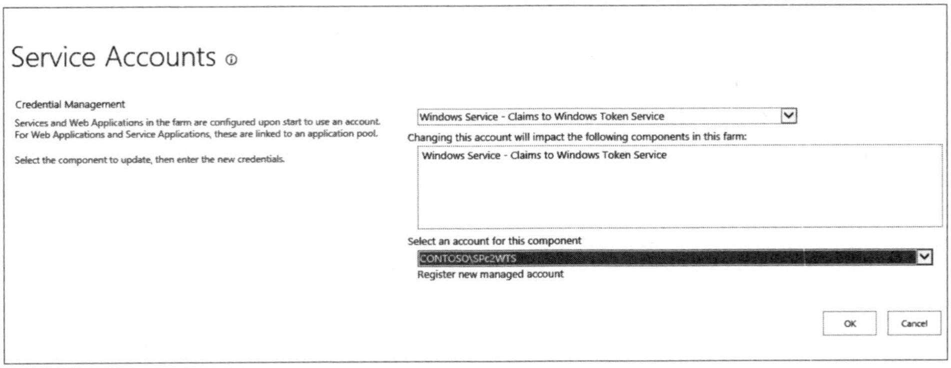

Service Accounts ⓘ

Credential Management

Services and Web Applications in the farm are configured upon start to use an account. For Web Applications and Service Applications, these are linked to an application pool.

Select the component to update, then enter the new credentials.

Windows Service - Claims to Windows Token Service ▾

Changing this account will impact the following components in this farm:

Windows Service - Claims to Windows Token Service

Select an account for this component

CONTOSO\SPc2WTS ▾

Register new managed account

OK   Cancel

FIGURE 6-18 The c2WTS account should be a domain account.

Secure Store Service (SSS)

The Secure Store Service (SSS) is an authorization service that runs on a SharePoint server and provides a credentials cache that can be used to access external data sources. These credentials are stored in a collection of data called a *target application*. A target application contains the following user-defined data:

- Individual or group mapping

- Fields to store in the Secure Store database, including a Windows user name, Windows password, and any other fields that may be required for authentication

- Users who have administration rights to the target application

Each target application has a unique application ID that is used when referencing the collection. This ID is used in external applications such as Microsoft SharePoint Designer and Excel services.

The SSS is a claims-aware service and can accept security tokens and decrypt them to get the application ID, and then use the application ID to do a lookup from the credentials cache. These credentials are then used to authorize access to the specified resources. The SSS is commonly used in conjunction with Excel services, Visio services, PerformancePoint services, BCS, custom web services, and ACS. BCS supports Anonymous, Basic, Windows, and Custom authentication to OData services when it is used with SSS.

Due to the sensitive nature of the credentials in the SSS, it is recommended that the service use a separate application pool that is not used by other services.

In SharePoint 2010, this service was only available in the Enterprise version but with the release of SharePoint 2013, it is available to all versions (including SharePoint Foundation).

Business Connectivity Services (BCS)

SharePoint has a number of services under the Business Data Connectivity infrastructure that enables external data to be surfaced through the product using external content types. External content types are reusable collections of metadata that contains data definitions, connectivity information, and actions that can be performed through the connection to an external line of business systems.

The BCS service application was first introduced in Chapter 4, "Understanding the service application model." In that chapter, you will see some of the authorization components that will be important to understand how they interact with line-of-business (LOB) systems. BCS supports different security models for accessing services and databases: pass-through authentication and RevertToSelf authentication.

Pass-through authentication refers to the ability of the operating system to pass a client's authentication information to an external system. When using pass-through, it is important to understand the web application's authentication method because it will affect how the user's credentials are passed to the external systems. When using NTLM, pass-through authentication will use the application pool identity. When using Kerberos, the identity of the user accessing the SharePoint site is used.

By default, the RevertToSelf authentication is disabled because it poses a potential security risk and therefore is not supported in hosted environments. Using RevertToSelf accesses resources as the application pool account of the SharePoint web application. A malicious developer could point the service endpoint back to SharePoint and use the elevated privileges of the application pool account to circumvent security restrictions. The application pool account has enough privileges to make itself an administrator. The SSS is recommended, because it nullifies the need to use the RevertToSelf option, but the SSS is not available if the users are accessing the system anonymously. In SharePoint Foundation 2010, SSS wasn't available and the RevertToSelf option helped in some authentication scenarios. However now, in SharePoint 2013, SSS is available in all stock-keeping units (SKUs), and the need for RevertToSelf in those instances has been removed.

In order to enable RevertToSelf, use Windows PowerShell to configure the *RevertToSelfAllowed* property on the BCS service application object, as shown in Listing 6-7.

LISTING 6-7 *RevertToSelf*

```
PS C:\> $bcs = Get-SPServiceApplication | where {$_.TypeName -eq "Business Data
Connectivity Service Application"}
PS C:\> $bcs.RevertToSelfAllowed = $true
PS C:\> Write-Host "The value of RevertToSelf is now " $bcs.RevertToselfAllowed
```

Exploring authorization (AuthZ) features

SharePoint 2013 has a number of features that enable site collection administrators and site owners to configure the authorization of users and content in their sites. In this section, you will examine the features that are configured outside the bounds of the typical SharePoint site collection administrator so that they can be planned for and configured during the design phase of the SharePoint farm. This will be followed by an exploration of application policies, the people picker, configuring connections to ACS, and the new Sharing option.

Application policies

SharePoint has a number of user access levels that offer granularity of how access to the platform is allowed or denied. A SharePoint web application can contain thousands of site collections, and modifying the policy for each of them would require a great deal of time. The SharePoint web application policies, located in Central Administration and shown in Figure 6-19, allow the farm administrator to manage user permission policies and permission policies for anonymous users, and permission policy levels.

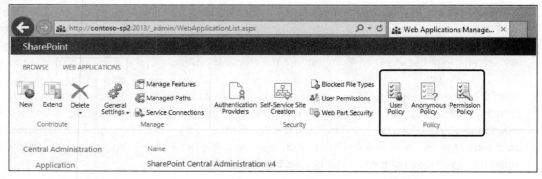

FIGURE 6-19 The SharePoint web application policies allow the farm administrator to configure and manage a number of options.

As discussed earlier in this chapter, a SharePoint web application can be configured across a number of authentication zones. When a SharePoint web application is extended to use a new zone, it creates a new web application in IIS. Since up to five zones can be used, it is foreseeable that a particular SharePoint web application may span a number of zones. With this being the case, the user permission policy allows the farm administrator to configure user policies across all zones at once or isolate a specific zone. This may be useful if you allow certain access within a company's intranet but not over the Internet.

The user permission policy has a unique option that is not seen anywhere else in SharePoint, which enables the farm administrator to deny access explicitly. The permission allows for Full Control, Full Read, Deny Write, and Deny All configurations. You can configure custom permissions by selecting Permission Policies and selecting Allow or Deny for the permissions described in Table 6-4.

TABLE 6-4 Permission policies

Permission	Description
Manage Lists	Create and delete lists, add or remove columns in a list, and add or remove public views of a list.
Override List Behaviors	Discard or check in a document that is checked out to another user, and change or override settings that allow users to read/edit only their own items.
Add Items	Add items to lists and add documents to document libraries.
Edit Items	Edit items in lists, edit documents in document libraries, and customize Web Part pages in document libraries.
Delete Items	Delete items from a list and documents from a document library.
View Items	View items in lists and documents in document libraries.
Approve Items	Approve a minor version of a list item or document.
Open Items	View the source of documents with server-side file handlers.
View Versions	View past versions of a list item or document.
Delete Versions	Delete past versions of a list item or document.
Create Alerts	Create alerts.

Permission	Description
View Application Pages	View forms, views, and application pages. Enumerate lists.
Manage Permissions	Create and change permission levels on the website and assign permissions to users and groups.
View Web Analytics Data	View reports on website usage.
Create Subsites	Create subsites such as team sites, Meeting Workspace sites, and Document Workspace sites.
Managed Website	Grants the ability to perform all administration tasks for the website, as well as manage content.
Add and Customize Pages	Add, change, or delete HTML pages or Web Part pages, and edit the website using a Microsoft SharePoint Foundation–compatible editor.
Apply These and Borders	Apply a theme or borders to the entire website.
Apply Style Sheets	Apply a style sheet (.css file) to the website.
Create Groups	Create a group of users that can be used anywhere within the site collection.
Browse Directories	Enumerate files and folders in a website using SharePoint Designer and Web DAV interfaces.
User Self-Service Site Creation	Create a website using Self-Service Site Creation.
View Pages	View pages in a website.
Enumerate Permissions	Enumerate permissions on the website, list, folder, document, or list item.
Browse User Information	View information about users of the website.
Managed Alerts	Manage alerts for all users of the website.
Use Remote Interfaces	Use Simple Object Access Protocol (SOAP), Web DAV, the Client Object Model, or SharePoint Designer interfaces to access the website.
Use Client Integration Features	Use features that start client applications. Without this permission, users will have to work on documents locally and upload their changes.
Open	Allows users to open a website, list, or folder in order to access items inside that container.
Edit Personal Information	Allows a user to change his or her own user information, such as adding a picture.
Manage Personal Views	Create, change, and delete personal views of lists.
Add/Remove Personal Web Parts	Add or remove personal Web Parts on a Web Part page.
Update Personal Web Parts	Update Web Parts to display personalized information.

When the SharePoint search service application is provisioned, an entry into the web application policy is created for the Search Crawling Account. By default, this is typically the SharePoint farm account. After provisioning the search and changing the Search Crawling Account, the farm administrator will see Full Read entries in the web application policy for both the farm account and the newly added Search Crawling Account. The farm account can be removed safely from this list. In scenarios where search is configured using federated (cross-farm) services, the Search Crawling Account will need to be added manually. An example of what a typical policy may look like is shown in Figure 6-20.

The farm administrator also has the ability to configure anonymous policies, which provide options to Deny Write or Deny All to one or more zones for unauthenticated users.

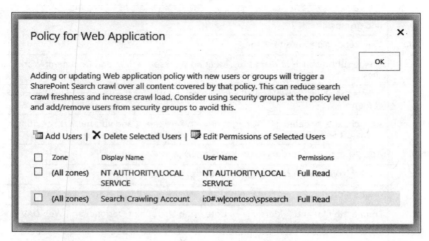

FIGURE 6-20 The web application policy gives permission to the Search Crawling Account.

The People Picker

The People Picker control in SharePoint is used to select claims, groups, or users for specific functions. It is used to grant permissions at the site, library, list, folder, or item level, as well as in the web application policies (mentioned previously) to restrict certain claims, groups, or users in various scenarios. In most cases, the People Picker aids in finding and selecting objects but is dependent on the authentication method used by the SharePoint web application. The Central Administration's *web.config* file must be modified when configuring FBA because it allows the farm administrator to pick objects for the web application policies, farm administrators, or site collection administrators from within Central Administration.

The People Picker control can be configured using Windows PowerShell and the properties that are available through the *PeoplePickerSettings* object on the SharePoint web application, as shown in Listing 6-8.

LISTING 6-8 People Picker and Windows PowerShell

```
PS C:\> $wa = Get-SPWebApplication http://www.contoso.local
PS C:\> $wa.PeoplePickerSettings
SearchActiveDirectoryDomains                        : {}
ActiveDirectoryCustomQuery                          :
ActiveDirectoryCustomFilter                         :
OnlySearchWithinSiteCollection                      : False
PeopleEditorOnlyResolveWithinSiteCollection         : False
DistributionListSearchDomains                       : {}
ActiveDirectorySearchTimeout                        : 00:00:30
NoWindowsAccountsForNonWindowsAuthenticationMode    : True
ServiceAccountDirectoryPaths                        : {}
ReferralChasingOption                               : None
ActiveDirectoryRestrictIsolatedNameLevel            : False
AllowLocalAccount                                   : True
UpgradedPersistedProperties                         :
```

It is important to understand about how the People Picker control works with claims providers. You will find when using the providers for Windows authentication and FBA, the People Picker functionality works as one would expect. It searches the user store and resolve users, groups, or claims. When working with SAML claims, however, the default provider will not search the partner location and resolve the claim objects. The farm administrator will notice that every value entered will be resolved, so it is critical to understand the data that is coming back; this can be overcome by implementing a custom solution. SharePoint 2013 has improved its logging features for Claims-based authentication, but it may be necessary to use a tool like Fiddler to inspect the traffic.

Depending on the farm configuration, additional planning may be needed to ensure optimum performance when pulling back objects from the authentication provider. Here are some things you should consider:

■ Do users need to query across a forest or domain?

■ What is the DNS name for each forest or domain that needs to be queried?

■ What trusts are set up between the forests and domains?

Based on the requirements, the farm administrator may want to filter specific objects so that a smaller amount of data is populating the People Picker control. This can be done at the site collection level by using the *UserAccountDirectoryPath*.

Sharing

SharePoint 2013 offers a new Sharing feature to provide access to members outside of the typical SharePoint user base. This option is only available for administrators if the Outbound SMTP Server and the From Address is configured within Central Administration. This is because the feature uses emails for notifying the involved parties that they have access to the system.

The Sharing feature, when available, will be visible in the upper-right corner on the default master page. This will allow an email to be sent to the involved party, while at the same time, setting their access level to the SharePoint object, as shown in Figure 6-21.

With the release of SharePoint 2013, there are a number of options for sharing documents and sites:

- You can store personal documents in a SkyDrive Pro library. All of the documents in the library are private until you decide to share them.

- Invite people to share specific data and control what they can do with them using the "Share" feature and sending out a guest link using a personalized email invitation to the site or document library.

FIGURE 6-21 The Sharing feature allows access to members outside of the typical SharePoint user base.

Putting it all together

Now that you know about the various SharePoint 2013 authentication types and features, it's time to see how you would use them in a business scenario. Consider a fictitious private security company called Contoso Security that works for state and local government agencies. The company would like to have a collaboration environment that provides security officers in the field access to corporate resources. Contoso Security would also like to provide read-only access to several other security agencies. Contoso Security doesn't want to maintain the credentials for the partnering agencies in its AD DS and would like each partner to be responsible for their own people who will access the system.

Contoso Security has a number of LOB systems that provides useful data. One of the requirements for the system is that the data must be available for both internal and external users. Some of the data may be required for criminal cases and Contoso Security would like to be able to search information in both SharePoint and Exchange Server and be able to put legal holds on pertinent information.

In addition to many of the SharePoint collaboration features that are provided out of the box, Contoso Security would like to be able to manage SharePoint tasks and emails in either the Microsoft Outlook client or SharePoint.

Some of the information may need to be shared with individuals outside of the security agencies. Contoso Security would like to be able to enable access to these individuals without having to augment their AD DS users.

Northwind Traders has a number of .NET developers working for the company and would like to have them design custom software that will help security officers in the field streamline some of their everyday processes. Northwind Traders will be providing the solution to Contoso Security through the app store using ACS.

To begin with, you are presented with a possible solution that will satisfy the need to collaborate with outside agencies. Contoso Security has the option for hosting its environment in either the cloud or on the premises. For this discussion, you will focus on an on-premise solution.

Contoso Security would like to provide read-only access to partnering agencies without having to maintain their credentials. In order to satisfy this requirement, Contoso Security has elected to utilize ADFS 2.0, which was briefly mentioned in the "SAML token-based authentication" section earlier in this chapter. The web application then uses the claims inside to decide whether or not to grant access (AuthZ) to the requested resource. In the case of Contoso Security, it will be accepting all claims from the partner agencies and have assigned them visitor permissions. An example of the topology is shown in Figure 6-22.

The next AuthN and AuthZ requirement is the use of LOB data. SharePoint has a number of ways to provide this, but the easiest way is to create external content types using either Microsoft Visual Studio or SharePoint Designer. The external content type is a reusable collection of metadata that contains data definitions, connectivity information, and actions that the security officer will use to connect to external line of business systems. The data continues to reside within the LOB system and SharePoint queries the data as needed. Depending on the type of system, SSS (which is claims aware) can be used to tie a group of users to a specific account. The BCS will then use the SSS setup to surface the data in SharePoint.

Contoso Security has a number of other requirements that are similar in their solution. The requirements to search for eDiscovery data and be able to interact with tasks and emails from either the Outlook or SharePoint side would benefit from using the S2S enhancements added to the 2013 series of products.

The new Sharing feature in SharePoint 2013 allows for sharing content to external users without having to add the users into Active Directory, but it must be set up by the SharePoint administrator since it utilizes emails for communication; remember that this can be done on SharePoint sites or documents with a select group of people through the "Selective People" link.

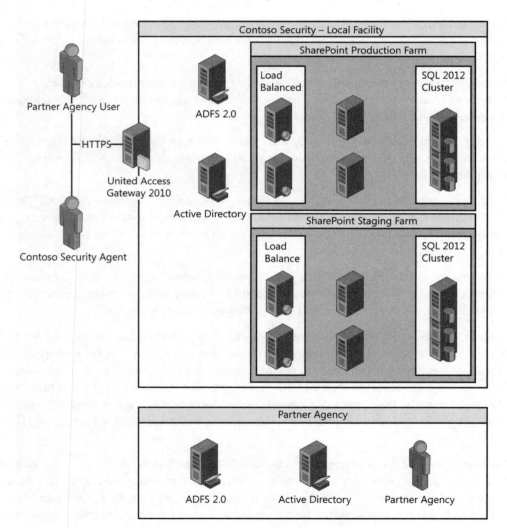

FIGURE 6-22 Server topology for Contoso Security.

Finally, Contoso Security can leverage third-party solutions that are deployed to the Corporate Catalog or Office Marketplace for any SharePoint deployment: On Premise, Hybrid, or SharePoint Online. An example of what the information flow would look like is shown in Figure 6-23.

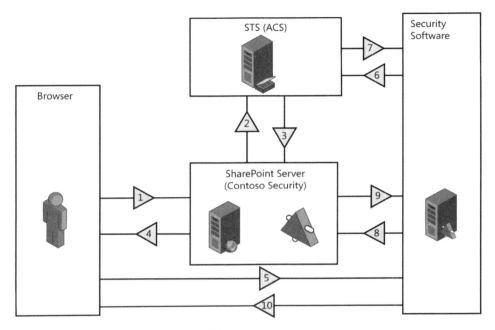

FIGURE 6-23 A custom solution using the OAuth model.

If Contoso Security wishes to utilize cloud-hosted apps, communication between the app, SharePoint 2013, the authorization server, and the security officers must take place. The security officers would access their collaboration data in the Contoso Security farm and the development solution would be hosted by Northwind Traders ; the authorization server is Windows Azure ACS. The Contoso Security farm then uses the CSOM or REST endpoints to make calls into the hosted Northwind Traders applications. The SharePoint farm will request a context token from ACS that it can send to the third-party server, which in turn uses the context token to request an access token from ACS as part of the OAuth transaction process. The app hosted on the third-party server then uses the access token to communicate back to the Contoso Security SharePoint farm and renders the app to the user through the SharePoint browser.

To recap, your solution now allows partner agencies to authenticate into the system without having to store partner credentials inside the Contoso Security Active Directory. Sites and documents can be "shared" with outside resources. eDiscovery can be used to search for information in both SharePoint 2013 and Exchange 2013. Using BCS and SSS in tandem allows for flexible solutions that can display external data in SharePoint. Finally, the new SharePoint App model provides a robust solution for allowing a wide variety of solutions that are hosted outside of SharePoint but still have access to data inside SharePoint using various client-side options.

## CHAPTER 7

Designing for platform security

In this chapter, you will learn about:

- Preventing, tracking, and reporting on Microsoft SharePoint installations.

- Understanding communications and encryption.

- Planning for and configuring Microsoft SQL Server Transparent Data Encryption.

- Installing SharePoint using least privileges.

- Understanding roles and group permissions.

Microsoft SharePoint deployments are managed at the farm level. With the product growing in popularity, it may be necessary for system administrators to be able to track SharePoint installations or prevent them from being added to the corporate intranet. In this chapter, you will learn how to apply those features so that it is easier to know when new farms are created.

When you went through the requirements gathering phase, you no doubt had requirements that were directly related to platform security. In this chapter, you will gain an understanding of what it takes to protect not only the SharePoint web interface, but the communications from the information worker all the way back to the database. But is this enough? What exactly is platform security, anyway?

A reasonable definition for platform security would be a security model that is used to protect all aspects of a particular system; in the case of SharePoint, this not only includes the features that are available through the web interface but also the data at rest. You will learn about how to plan for and configure Microsoft SQL Server Transparent Data Encryption (TDE) to protect the data at rest.

Once you have an understanding of how to track installations and protect the data leaving the clients all the way to where it rests in the database, it will be time to examine techniques for limiting which accounts have access to various parts of the system and learning the tradeoffs you make for incorporating least privileges in a SharePoint environment. This will then take you inside Central Administration, where you will focus on the various accounts used by the system, general security options, and information policy.

Security is always a hot topic when it comes to SharePoint, and rightfully so; organizations place their trusted business documents into the system, and it is important for them to feel that the system is safe and secure. With the growing concerns of security, and with regulations helping to keep data private, platform security is undoubtedly one of the most important concepts that you can implement into your SharePoint 2013 farms. In the final section of the chapter, you will review a scenario that will help put many of the concepts in place so that you can assure the stakeholders that their information is safe.

Preventing, tracking, and reporting on SharePoint installations

Installing SharePoint 2013 on a computer that uses a client operating system is not supported; this was not the case with the 2010 product. With Microsoft SharePoint Foundation being freely available, it was not uncommon for rogue SharePoint farms to take root and grow. SharePoint is installed and managed at the farm level, and one SharePoint deployment has no information about another farm that may exist in the same enterprise. Because there is no enterprise-wide way to know where SharePoint farms are being created, you may need to prevent (or at least track) where new farms are being created. In this section, you will not only learn how to perform both of these operations, but also how to review where SharePoint is installed once these options have been implemented.

Preventing SharePoint installations

You can prevent users from installing SharePoint by using Group Policy in Active Directory services. To do so, update the following key on all of the servers:

HKLM\Software\Policies\Microsoft\Shared Tools\Web Server Extensions\15.0\ SharePoint\DWORD DisableInstall

To block installations, set DWORD *DisableInstall=00000001*.

You can use Windows PowerShell to add the registry value to the Group Policy on the server hosting the Active Directory services (see Listing 7-1).

LISTING 7-1 Group Policy

```
Set-GPRegistryValue -Name "Default Domain Policy" -Key "HKLM\Software\Policies\
Microsoft\Shared Tools\Web Server Extensions\15.0\SharePoint" -ValueName
"DisableInstall" -Type DWORD -Value 1
```

Once the keys are set to disable, you will see a Setup Errors message, as shown in Figure 7-1.

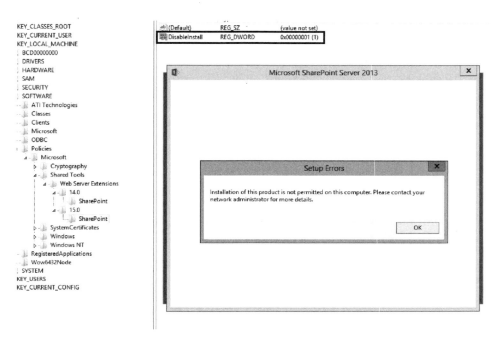

FIGURE 7-1 SharePoint installation is not permitted.

If you had a group policy to block SharePoint 2010 (14.0), you will need to create a new one for version 15.0. The installation process doesn't check the status of the previous version. Because this is a Group Policy Object (GPO) setting, it is possible to circumvent the process by modifying the registry and changing the value to zero or deleting it altogether. So trying to control installations solely by blocking them may not offer a complete solution, but it will stop people who do not understand how the feature works.

Tracking SharePoint installations

SharePoint has the ability to work in conjunction with Active Directory Service Connection Points to identify SharePoint products used in an organization. As with the blocking of installations, the tracking of installations doesn't offer a complete solution either. Once configured, SharePoint installs that are done with the SharePoint Products Configuration Wizard will have a marker injected into the service connection point; however, installations using Windows PowerShell will not do this by default. So relying on this feature to keep track of every SharePoint farm will be unreliable. With that being said, these markers can be added via Windows PowerShell, after the fact, or be added to the installation scripts.

To create a service connection point container to track installations, follow these steps:

1. On the domain controller, open ADSI Edit.

2. On the Action menu, click Connect To and connect to the domain in which you are tracking installations.

3. Expand the domain name and then click CN=System.

4. Right-click in the white area, click New, and then click Object.

5. In the dialog box, click Container and then click Next.

6. In the value box, type **Microsoft SharePoint Products** as the container name and click Next.

7. Click Finished.

8. Right-click the Microsoft SharePoint Products container that you just created and click Properties.

9. On the Security tab, click Add.

10. Add all Authenticated Users or Everyone and give them write permission to the container. If a particular individual doesn't have write access, that person will still install SharePoint, but the marker will not be created.

11. On the group that you just entered, click Advanced.

12. In the Permission entries box, select the name or group you just added and click Edit.

13. In the Permission Entry for Microsoft SharePoint Products dialog box, select the Allow check box for Create *serviceConnectionPoint* Objects (as shown in Figure 7-2), and click OK.

FIGURE 7-2 Showing that it's allowed to create *ServiceConnectionPoint* objects.

Once the service connection point has been created and the permissions have been set, all installations using the SharePoint Product Configuration Wizard will be automatically tracked. In order to track installations using Windows PowerShell, you can use the *Set-SPFarmConfig* cmdlet, as shown in Listing 7-2.

LISTING 7-2 Set-SPFarmConfig

```
Set-SPFarmConfig -ServiceConnectionPointBindingInformation
StringwithBindingInformationa
```

You can modify the string value of the *-ServiceConnectionPointBindingInformation* with a more meaningful value, such as *Get-SPTopologyServiceApplication | select URI*. This will return the Uniform Resource Identifier (URI) of the farm topology service (in this case, *https://contoso-sp1:32844/Topology/topology.svc*). Or you can simply use the host parameter of the URI. You can use the same cmdlet and parameters to update the connection string at any time.

If you are responsible for maintaining the Windows PowerShell scripts within your organization, you can simply add the *Set-SPFarmConfig* cmdlet to the end of your farm installation script, and installations using those scripts will be tracked.

The tracking information can be deleted using the *-ServiceConnectionPointDelete* parameter on the *Set-SPFarmConfig* cmdlet.

Reporting SharePoint installations

Once the service connection points are configured correctly, you can either review the markers created in Active Directory Domain Services (AD DS) by reviewing the Microsoft SharePoint Products container or by using the Windows PowerShell script shown in Listing 7-3—that will list all SharePoint farms with Active Directory markers.

LISTING 7-3 Reporting installations

```
$containerPath = 'LDAP://CN=Microsoft SharePoint Products,CN=System,DC=contoso,D
               C=local'
$entry = New-Object DirectoryServices.DirectoryEntry $containerPath
$searcher = New-Object DirectoryServices.DirectorySearcher
$searcher.SearchRoot = $entry
$searcher.Filter = "(objectClass=serviceConnectionPoint)"
$searcher.FindAll() |  % { New-Object PSObject -Property $_.Properties } | select
servicebindinginformation, whencreated, whenchanged
```

Encrypting communications

As you learned in Chapter 6, "Mapping authentication and authorization to requirements," there are a number of situations that require encryption, whether they be between the client and server or between the various servers that make up your SharePoint farm. There are many places in SharePoint that transmit credentials in clear text, and you should use Transport Layer Security (TLS) to encrypt the credentials—Secure Sockets Layer (SSL) is the most common way to implement this. When creating or modifying information about a Managed Account, if the Central Administration site is not encrypted, you will see the following message:

> Warning: this page is not encrypted for secure communication. User names, passwords, and any other information will be sent in clear text.

An example of this has been provided in Figure 7-3. Central Administration is often overlooked when considering platform security, and it is undoubtedly the most important web application to secure. Many organizations remote into the server that hosts the web application to make modifications, but you must remember that it can be accessed from any computer within the domain, just like any other web application.

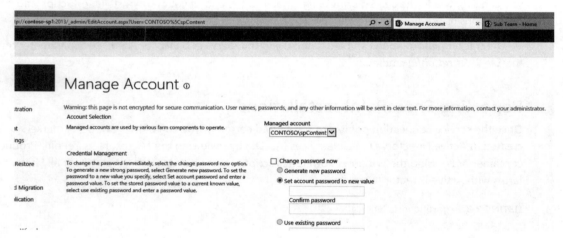

FIGURE 7-3 The text below "Manage Account" is a a clear text warning.

You will learn more about encrypting your SharePoint sites using SSL as you progress through this chapter.

Certification Authorities (CAs)

You will need to obtain a certificate from a certification authority (CA) in order to secure server communications. For production systems that have a public reach (Internet), this is best done through a public CA; these cost money, however, so for internal (intranet) web applications, you may find it best to use a Domain CA, which is a role under Active Directory Certificate Services. This will allow you to create internal certificates as needed.

There are several types of certificates that are worth mentioning at this point: standard SSL and wildcard SSL certificates. Standard SSL is valid for a particular named domain or subdomain and is very specific. Wildcard SSL certificates can be used for all subdomains and subdirectories of a particular domain, giving you more flexibility, and is often cheaper than buying many public standard SSL certificates. To generate the wildcard SSL, you need to use *.*domain.com* in the common name. It is worth noting that many organizations believe that wildcard certificates introduce security risks, so you should verify if they are allowed in your organization. This chapter will use a Domain CA for all SSL examples, and a walkthrough of securing Central Administration communications will be demonstrated in the "Putting it all together" section at the end of the chapter. A third option, which we do not cover, is the use of UCC Certificates; these will allow for multiple domains.

> **Note** Alternatively, you could decide to use a Self-Signed Certificate, but these are not trusted throughout the domain, and you will need to import the certificates. The Domain CA is a better option in most cases.

Communication between the client and server

Communications that are passed without encryption can be compromised with tools such as WireShark. In order to protect your environment, you should consider using SSL for each web application in your farm. In order to do this, you must first obtain your certificate from either a public CA or use a Domain CA. For the sake of this example, *team.contoso.local* will be used and will use a Domain CA.

The first step is to visit Microsoft Internet Information Services (IIS), click the server node in the left pane, and double-click Server Certificates in the center pane. This will show you all the certificates in the center pane and provide new actions in the right pane. From here, you need to select Create Domain Certificate and fill in the certificate form, as shown in Figure 7-4.

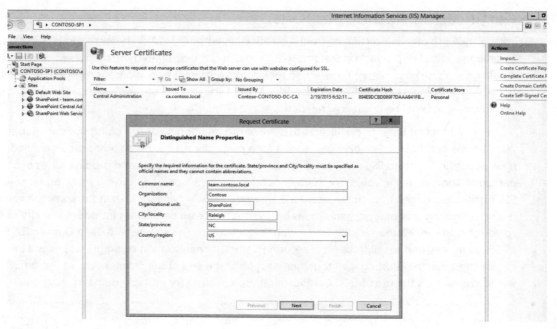

FIGURE 7-4 Requesting a Domain CA.

If the certificate process is successful, you will now have a certificate that you can use with your SharePoint web applications. Whether you are creating a new SharePoint web application or converting one, the overall steps are the same. To convert an existing site to use SSL, you may find it easiest to re-create the SharePoint web application. This does not only require keeping the content database but also the Web.config file in case there are any configuration changes to your existing web application. When deleting the web application, make sure you only delete the IIS web application.

Create a new SharePoint web application. The key values will be the Port, Host Header, and the use of SSL, as shown in Figure 7-5. If your Central Administration site is not encrypted, you will see a warning across the top of the form that the credentials will be sent in clear text.

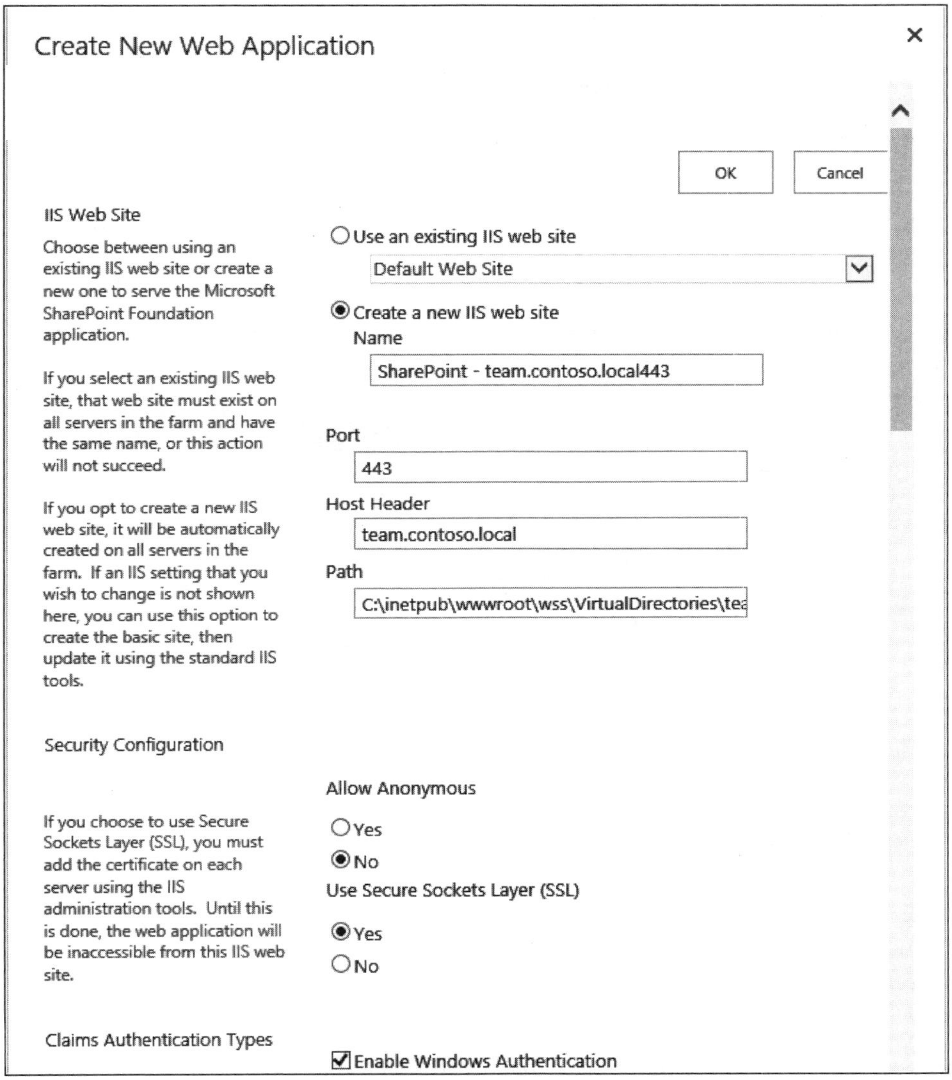

FIGURE 7-5 The Create New Web Application form.

Once the web application has been created, you will find that it is inaccessible. This is because the site needs the certificate associated with its HTTPS binding. This is illustrated in Figure 7-6.

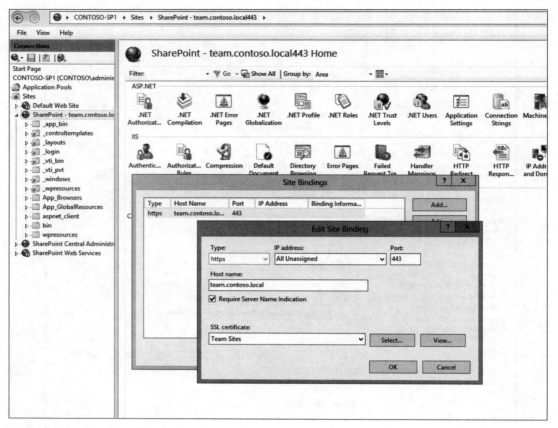

FIGURE 7-6 The Edit Site Binding dialog box.

If you plan to have a number of sites that use port 443 with multiple certificates, you will need to check the box for Require Server Name Indication; this allows multiple secure websites to be served using the same IP address. Because you will undoubtedly be securing all of your SharePoint sites in conjunction with Central Administration, you will want to check this every time.

After you have associated the certificate with the IIS binding, your site should work as expected over HTTPS. If you would like to associate the certificate using Windows PowerShell, review Listing 7-4.

LISTING 7-4 Windows PowerShell for IIS binding

```
$siteName = "SharePoint - team.contoso.local443"
$certName = "Team Sites"
# Get the site using the site name and remove the existing binding
Get-WebBinding -Name $siteName | Remove-WebBinding
# Get the certificate using the Cert Name
$cert = get-childitem cert:\LocalMachine\my | where-Object {$_.FriendlyName -like
$certName}
# Update the binding
$cert | New-Item -Path "IIS:\SslBindings\!443!team.contoso.local"
```

Important Your binding information will vary from the examples in this book. To review all of the certificates and retrieve their FriendlyName values, use the following code:

```
#get-childitem cert:\LocalMachine\my | ft issuer, subject, notafter, FriendlyName
```

Server-to-server communication

Now that you have mastered encrypting the data between the client and the SharePoint server processing the web requests, it is time to focus on the communications between the servers running SharePoint and the servers running SQL Server. SSL and Internet Protocol security (IPsec) can be used to protect communication between servers by encrypting traffic. The choice of which method to use will depend on the specific communication channels you are securing and the benefits and tradeoffs that are appropriate for your organization.

SharePoint server communications

Many organizations like to close any ports that are not in use, and if the security team is unaware of SharePoint server communications, it can hinder the ability of SharePoint to operate correctly. The following list of ports outlines the critical ones that must be planned for:

- Standard web traffic is generally over the default ports of TCP 80, TCP 443 (SSL).

- Ports used by the search index component: TCP 16500-16519 (intra-farm only).

- Ports required for the AppFabric Caching Service: TCP 22233-22236.

- Ports required for Windows Communication Foundation communication: TCP 808.

- Ports required for communication between web servers and service applications (the default is HTTP):

  - HTTP binding: TCP 32843.

  - HTTPS binding: TCP 32844.

  - Net.tcp binding: TCP 32845 (custom service applications).

- Ports required for synchronizing profiles between SharePoint 2013 and AD DS on the server that runs the Forefront Identity Management agent:

  - TCP 5725.

  - TCP&UDP 389 (LDAP service)

  - TCP&UDP 88 (Kerberos)

  - TCP&UDP 53 (DNS)

  - UDP 464 (Kerberos Change Password)

- Default ports for SQL Server communication: TCP 1433, UDP 1434. If these ports are blocked on the computer running SQL Server (recommended) and databases are installed on a named instance, configure a SQL Server client alias for connecting to the named instance.

- SharePoint Foundation User Code Service (for sandbox solutions): TCP 32846. This port must be open for outbound connections on all web servers. This port must be open for inbound connections on web servers or application servers where this service is turned on.

- Simple Mail Transfer Protocol (SMTP) for email integration: TCP 25.

- Workflow Manager:

  - HTTP binding: TCP 12291.

  - HTTPS binding: TCP 12290.

Marek Samaj recently published a blog post that contained an illustrated overview of the SharePoint 2013 farm communications (see Figure 7-7).

SSL and SQL Server

Enabling SSL encryption increases the security of the data transmitted across networks between instances of SQL Server and other applications. This sounds like something you would want to do all the time, right? It might be, but keep in mind that that enabling encryption will slow performance. When all of the traffic is encrypted using SSL, the following additional processes are required:

- At connection time, an extra network round trip is required.

- Packets sent from the application must be encrypted by the client and decrypted by the instance of SQL Server.

- Packets sent from the instance of SQL Server must be encrypted by the server and decrypted by the application.

With this in mind, you will probably not find a noticeable impact by implementing SSL, but load testing should be done to ensure that you are getting the metrics that you expect. For more information, see Chapter 11, "Validating your architecture."

To configure a SQL Server instance to use SSL, start the SQL Server Configuration Manager. You can get there by opening the Microsoft Management Console (MMC) (type MMC in the Run dialog box). On the Console menu, click Add/Remove Snap-in. Click Add | Certificates | Add. Then select the Computer Account | Local Computer. Click Finished.

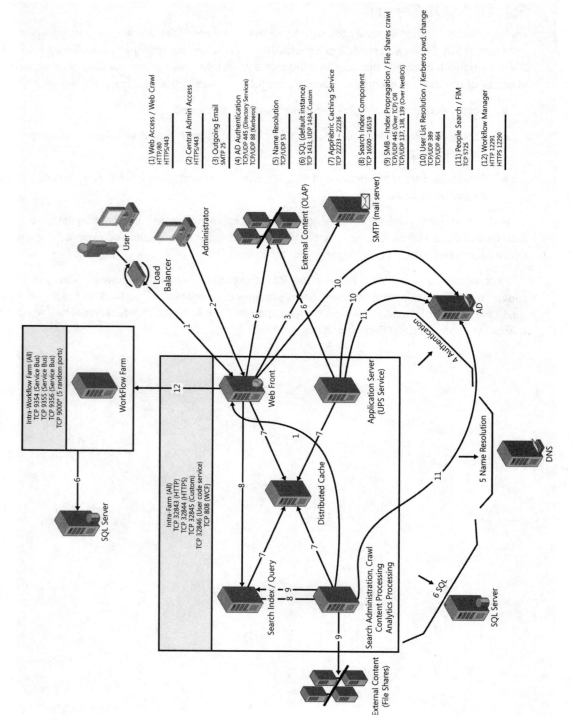

FIGURE 7-7 SharePoint 2013 ports and protocols.

Once you have the Certificates snap-in ready, select the Personal folder in the left pane and expand the arrow in the right pane to show All Tasks, as shown in Figure 7-8. Then select the option to Request New Certificate.

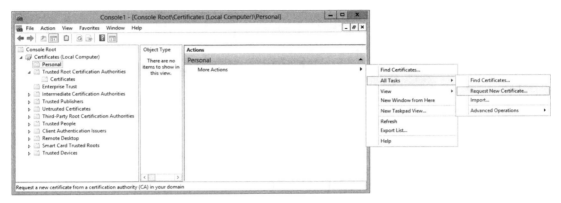

FIGURE 7-8 Requesting a new certificate using MMC.

The next screen of the Certificate Enrollment process has you select a certificate enrollment policy. It should be defaulted to Active Directory Enrollment Policy, so you can click Next. This screen will be followed by a dialog box that allows you to request various certificates. You will want to select Computer | Enroll. You should be greeted with a successful message. You can then review the Personal Certificates and see a newly issued certificate, as shown in Figure 7-9.

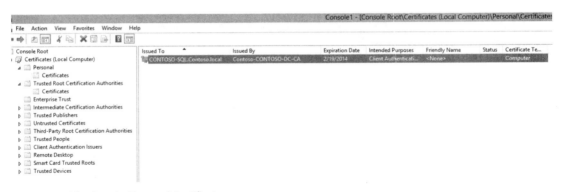

FIGURE 7-9 Viewing the Personal Certificates.

Now open the SQL Server Configuration Manager. You will see a list of services in the left pane. Expand the SQL Server Network Configuration, and then right-click Protocols For MSSQLSERVER (also in the left pane) | Properties. You should see a properties window open, as shown in Figure 7-10.

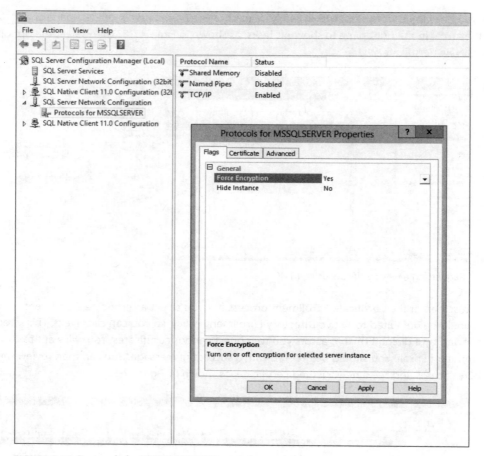

FIGURE 7-10 Protocols for MSSQLSERVER Properties.

The next two steps are to change the Force Encryption property to Yes and then select the newly created certificate on the Certificates tab. With the Force Encryption flag now set to Yes, all server/client communication is encrypted, and clients that cannot support encryption are denied access. Encryption can still happen if the flag is set to No, but it is not required. You will be configuring the application side in a few moments, but first you will need to assign the appropriate permissions to the newly created certificate. This can be done by clicking the More Actions menu associated with the server in the right pane. The certificate in this example would be Contoso-SQL.contoso.local. Click the All Tasks menu, followed by the Managed Private Keys menu item. You will then add the service account that the SQL Server instance is running under and give Read permission to the certificate, as shown in Figure 7-11.

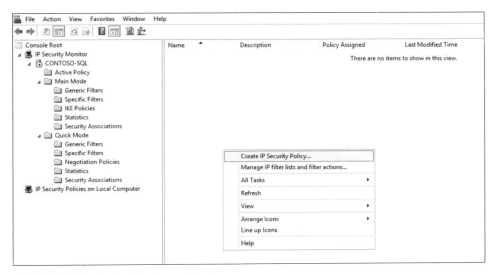

FIGURE 7-11 Permissions for the certificate.

You will then need to restart the SQL Server service. If you fail to give the SQL Server service account Read permissions for the certificate, your SQL Server instance will fail to restart. You can now refresh the pages in SharePoint, and everything should be working as expected.

IPsec IKEv2

IPsec protects the communication channel between two servers and can restrict which computers can communicate with each other. Not only can IPsec be used to encrypt traffic to and from the SQL Server instances, as SSL does, it can also be used to encrypt traffic between the SharePoint servers. IPsec allows you to restrict communication to specific protocols and TCP/UDP ports. In order for a SharePoint farm to be a good candidate for IPsec, all servers will need to be contained on one physical local area network (LAN) to improve IPsec performance, and the servers should be assigned static IP addresses.

With the release of Windows Server 2012, Internet Key Exchange version 2 (IKEv2) support has been extended and now supports end-to-end transport mode connections and interoperability with other operating systems that use IKEv2 for end-to-end security. These options can coexist with existing policies that deploy AuthIP/IKEv1 and certificate authentication. IKEv2 does not have a user interface and is only configurable through Windows PowerShell. IKEv2 was available in Windows Server 2008 R2 as a virtual private network (VPN) tunneling protocol that supported automatic VPN reconnection.

The first step in the process is to establish a connection security rule that uses IKEv2 for communication between two computers (Contoso-SP1 and Contoso-SQL) that are joined to the *contoso.local* domain. You can do this by using the code in Listing 7-5. You will need to already have a public key infrastructure (PKI) in place for computer authentication.

LISTING 7-5 IKEv2 security rule

```
# Create a Security Group for the computers that will get the policy
$pathname = (Get-ADDomain).distinguishedname
New-ADGroup -name "IPsec client and servers" `
-SamAccountName "IPsec SharePoint" -GroupCategory security `
-GroupScope Global -path $pathname

# Add test computers to the Security Group
$computer = Get-ADComputer -LDAPFilter "(name=Contoso-SP1)"
Add-ADGroupMember -Identity "IPsec SharePoint" -Members $computer
$computer = Get-ADComputer -LDAPFilter "(name=Contoso-SQL)"
Add-ADGroupMember -Identity "IPsec SharePoint" -Members $computer

Important In order to use the Group Policy cmdlets on a server not hosting this
role, you will need to install the GPO module and execute the import-module
GroupPolicy.

# Create and link the GPO to the domain
$gpo = New-gpo IPsecRequireInRequestOut
$gpo | new-gplink -target "dc=contoso,dc=local" -LinkEnabled Yes

# Set permissions to security group for the GPO
$gpo | Set-GPPermissions -TargetName "IPsec SharePoint" `
-TargetType Group -PermissionLevel GpoApply -Replace
$gpo | Set-GPPermissions -TargetName "Authenticated Users" `
-TargetType Group -PermissionLevel None -Replace

Important These cmdlets are new for Windows Server 2012.

#Set up the certificate for authentication
$gponame = "contoso.local\IPsecRequireInRequestOut"
$certprop = New-NetIPsecAuthProposal -machine -cert `
-Authority "DC=local, DC=contoso, CN=contoso-dc"
$myauth = New-NetIPsecPhase1AuthSet -DisplayName "IKEv2SPPhase1AuthSet" `
-proposal $certprop -PolicyStore GPO:$gponame

#Create the IKEv2 Connection Security rule
New-NetIPsecRule  -DisplayName "SharePoint IKEv2 Rule" `
-RemoteAddress any -Phase1AuthSet $myauth.InstanceID `
-InboundSecurity Require -OutboundSecurity Request `
-KeyModule IKEv2 -PolicyStore GPO:$gponame
```

The script creates a security group called *IPsecSharePoint* and adds *contoso-sql* and *contoso-sp1* as members. It will then create a GPO called *IPsecRequiredInRequestOut* and links it to the *contoso.local* domain. The script then sets the permissions to the GPO so that they apply only to the computers in *IPsecSharePoint* and not to Authenticated Users. The script finishes by creating the IKEv2 connection security rule called SharePoint IKEv2 Rule.

You can now verify the configuration by examining the left pane of the Windows Firewall With Advanced Security snap-in. Click Connection Security Rules, and verify that there is an enabled connection security rule with the specified name, as shown in Figure 7-12. It is important to remember that the script configures this rule through a GPO, so it will not be readily available.

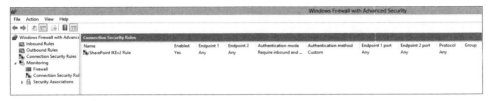

FIGURE 7-12 The Connection Security Rules.

Planning for and configuring SQL Server Transparent Data Encryption

To this point, you have learned how to encrypt network traffic between the servers in the farm and between the clients who use them. While this does offer a great deal of protection, the data in the farm can still be misused or stolen simply by restoring a copy of the database and attaching it to a SharePoint web application. One way to ensure that your data is not compromised is to encrypt it at rest with TDE.

> **Important** While TDE does encrypt the data at rest, the data is still available to SQL administrators through the use of SQL Queries or Windows PowerShell.

TDE performs real-time I/O encryption and decryption of both the data and the logs. The encryption uses a database encryption key (DEK), which is stored in the database boot record for availability during recovery. The DEK is a symmetric key secured by using a certificate store in the master database of the server or an asymmetric key protected by an EKM module. It is important to note that TDE does not provide encryption across communication channels, so use the previous section for that task. The encryption of the data is done at the page level. Pages are encrypted prior to the write and decrypted when read into memory; therefore, TDE will not increase the size of the database.

The TDE architecture comprises several different layers. The Windows Operating System Level Data Protection API (DPAPI) encrypts the Service Master Key. The Service Master Key is created at the instance level at the time of SQL Server setup. The Service Master Key encrypts the Database Master Key for the Master database. The Master Key of the Master database then creates a certificate in the Master database. The certificate is used to encrypt the database Encryption Key in the User database. And finally, the entire User database is secured by the DEK of the user database by using TDE. This is outlined in Figure 7-13.

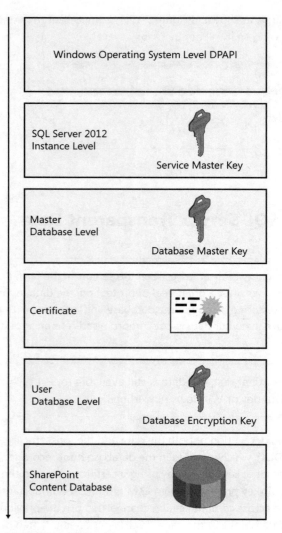

FIGURE 7-13 TDE architecture.

The primary steps to use TDE are:

1. Create a Master Key.

2. Create or obtain a certificate protect by the master key.

3. Create a DEK and protect it by the certificate.

4. Set the database to use encryption.

The SQL Server query in Listing 7-6 performs each of these steps on the *Contoso_Content_Team* database using the *Passw0rd1* password.

LISTING 7-6 TDE SQL Server query

```
USE master;
GO
-- Create DMK
CREATE MASTER KEY ENCRYPTION BY PASSWORD = 'PasswOrd1';
GO
-- Create DEK Certificate
CREATE CERTIFICATE TDECert WITH SUBJECT = 'SQL Server TDE Certificate'
GO
-- Backup the TDE Certificate
BACKUP CERTIFICATE TDECert TO FILE = 'C:\Certs\SQLTDECert.bak'
WITH PRIVATE KEY(
        FILE = 'C:\cert_privatekey.bak',
        ENCRYPTION BY PASSWORD = 'PasswOrd1'
        )
GO
-- Create the DEK encrypted w/ server certificate
USE Contoso_Content_Team
CREATE DATABASE ENCRYPTION KEY
        WITH
                ALGORITHM = AES_256
                ENCRYPTION BY SERVER CERTIFICATE TDECert
GO
ALTER DATABASE Contoso_Content_Team SET ENCRYPTION ON
GO
```

The processes to turn on TDE may take a while, so it is best to do it during a long maintenance window. To review the status of the encryption, execute the SQL Server query shown in Figure 7-14. You should see a similar result once the process is completed.

FIGURE 7-14 The TDE progress query.

Installing SharePoint using least privileges

Least privileges is a practice that gives the user or service account only the permissions they need to do their job and no more. Whether or not SharePoint 2013 fully supports a least privilege configuration is probably debatable, but there are certainly steps that you can take to limit the permissions that the user and service accounts have to only their job roles. The practice of least privileges and server hardening came from the early days of Novell and Windows NT 4, when the software was installed under the system account and everything worked. With the complexity of how current software products work, there are many moving parts and the ability to only give the appropriate access may get lost in the complexity of the software. If you were to research how to make your SharePoint installations fit into the least privileges bucket, you will unfortunately find conflicting thoughts and ideas. The problem is that what one person considers least privileged may actually put the product outside various support limits. This section will give you general guidance on what components should be considered and then let you take away what you need to create the appropriate solution for your organization. There is poor guidance everywhere and it is up to you to pick out what is most appropriate for your situation.

Application pools

As was the case in SharePoint 2010, the new product has a supportable limit of application pools that are allowed per web server. As of this time, it is currently limited to 10. The maximum number is determined by the hardware capabilities and is largely dependent upon the amount of memory allocated to the web servers. A highly active application pool can use 10 GB of RAM or more. So why is this important to understand in a conversation about least privileges? There are some SharePoint farms that have been built with an account for each service application and each SharePoint web application. While it may appear on the surface that the designer is following a least privilege design, he or she is actually consuming far too many resources. Every account that you use to configure a service account or application pool is taking away from the allowed number of application pools that are supported in your farm. You can go over 10 and the farm may work just fine. You will certainly need to have more RAM than the minimum requirements. To keep the application pools within friendly limits, consider using something similar to the recommendations in Table 7-1. Your organization may have security requirements that require more, but this should work for the vast majority of the organizations out there and will give you better use of the RAM on your servers.

TABLE 7-1 Recommended Application Pools

Application Pool	Account	Responsibilities
SharePoint Web Services Default	spServices	Hosts the SharePoint Service applications
SharePoint Web Content Default	spContent	Hosts the SharePoint content web applications
SharePoint Central Administration v4	spFarm	Hosts the Central Administration web application
SecurityTokenServiceApplicationPool	spFarm	Hosts the STS
SharePoint Secure Store	spSSS	Hosts the Secure Store Service
Expressed using a GUID for the name.	spFarm	Hosts the Topology Service

To review the latest software boundaries and limits for SharePoint 2013, read the Microsoft TechNet article located at http://technet.microsoft.com/en-us/library/cc262787.aspx.

User accounts

Designing your farm for least privileges happens before you install SharePoint and SQL Server. Some of the choices you make here can have huge impacts on the security of your farm. There is a running joke in the SharePoint Master community that in order to get SharePoint to work the way it is designed, you simply need to use a domain administrator account as the farm account. Unfortunately, there are farms out there that have been installed this way, and when the domain administrator password is changed, everything in SharePoint breaks. Your understanding of this content is the only way to get the farm back online. To be clear, you do not need to use the same account names here. This isn't a lesson on standards. It is only a general guide on mapping roles and responsibilities to Active Directory Users objects. The recommended user accounts by role can be seen in Table 7-2.

TABLE 7-2 Recommended User Accounts by Roles

Account	Purpose	Requirements
sqlInstall	Account used to install SQL Server	Local server administrator on the servers running SQL Server during the time of install.
sqlService	Account used for: ■ MSSQLSERVER ■ SQLSERVERAGENT	Permissions to external resources for backup and restore.
spInstall	Account used to perform: ■ Setup ■ SharePoint Product Configuration Wizard	Local server administrator where Setup is run during the installation process. SQL Server logon for the computer that runs SQL Server. Member of the SQL Roles: ■ *securityadmin* fixed server role ■ *dbcreator* fixed server role
spFarm	Account used to perform: ■ Acts as the application pool identity for the SharePoint Central Administration website ■ Runs the SharePoint Foundation Workflow Timer service	Permissions are automatically granted for the server farm account that is joined to the farm; the account is automatically added as a SQL Server logon for the computer that runs SQL Server. The account is added to the following: ■ *dbcreator* fixed server role ■ *securityadmin* fixed server role ■ *db_owner* fixed database role for all SharePoint databases in the server farm This account should not be used for farm administration! Never log on to the farm with this account.
spAdmin	Account used to configure and manage the server farm	Primary account for administration. Will need *SharePoint_Shell_Access* if Windows PowerShell Administration is needed. Local Administrator on servers running SharePoint.
spContent	Acts as the application pool identity for SharePoint Web Content	Automatically give the rights that it needs on the content databases: *spDataAccess*.
spServices	Acts as the application pool identity for SharePoint Service Applications	Automatically give the rights that it needs on the content databases: *spDataAccess*.
spC2WTs	The identity the C2WTs runs under	Local administrator rights on the server running the C2WTs and local security policies for: Act as part of the operating system, Impersonate a client after authentication, Log on as a service.
spUPS	The identity that is used during the User Profile Synchronization process	Active Directory Permission: Replication Directory Changes.

Account	Purpose	Requirements
spCrawl	The default content access account; used to crawl data for Search	Read Access to content to be searched.
spSSS	Acts as the application pool identity for the Secure Store Service	Automatically give the rights it needs on the content databases: *spDataAccess*.
spSuperUser	Account used for caching	Account has full access to Publishing web applications.
spSuperReader	Account used for caching	Account has full read access to Publishing web applications.
spUnattend	Account used for external data access	Access to external data.

Some of the accounts listed in Table 7-2 may not be needed in every farm. The Claims to Windows Token Services (C2WTs), introduced in Chapter 6, is typically only needed in business intelligence scenarios. None of the accounts listed in the table should be mapped to the DOMAIN\Administrator account. While this account may have access to SharePoint, it should not be a common credential. The level of access given to the person using this account exceeds any permissions needed in SharePoint. It is also worth noting that some organizations will want to have policies against the use of generic administration (*spAdmin*) accounts for auditing purposes.

The SharePoint Install account (*spInstall*) receives machine-level permissions that include:

- Membership in the WSS_ADMIN_WPG Windows security group

- Membership in the IIS_WPG role

After you run the configuration wizards, database permissions include:

- *db_owner* on the SharePoint server farm configuration database

- *db_owner* on the SharePoint Central Administration content database

The SharePoint Farm account (*spFarm*), which is also referred to as the *database access account,* is used as the application pool identity for Central Administration and as the process account for the SharePoint Foundation 2013 Timer service. The account must be a domain user. While this account receives the permissions that it needs automatically, after you run the SharePoint Configuration Wizard, it is granted machine-level permissions that include the following:

- Membership in the WSS_ADMIN_WPG Windows security group for the SharePoint Foundation 2013 Timer service

- Membership in WSS_RESTRICTED_WPG for the Central Administration and Timer service application pools

- Membership in WSS_WPG for the Central Administration application pool

After you run the configuration wizards, SQL Server and database permissions include the following:

- *dbcreator* fixed server role

- *securityadmin* fixed server role

- *db_owner* for all SharePoint databases except the *Farm_Config,* in which it receives *SP_DataAccess*

The account is also given membership in the WSS_CONTENT_APPLICATION_POOLS role for the SharePoint server farm configuration database and membership in the WSS_CONTENT_APPLICATION_POOLS role for the *SharePoint_Admin* content database.

The SharePoint Services account (*spServices*) is an application pool account that is used for application pool identity. The application pool account requires the following permission configuration settings:

- The following machine-level permission is configured automatically:
  - The application pool account is a member of WSS_WPG.

- The following SQL Server and database permissions for this account are configured automatically:
  - The application pool accounts for Web applications are assigned to the SP_DATA_ACCESS role for the content databases.
  - This account is assigned to the WSS_CONTENT_APPLICATION_POOLS role associated with the farm configuration database.
  - This account is assigned to the WSS_CONTENT_APPLICATION_POOLS role associated with the *SharePoint_Admin* content database.

The Default Content Access account (*spCrawl*) is used within the search service application to crawl content, unless a different authentication method is specified by a crawl rule for a URL or URL pattern. This account requires the following permission configuration settings:

- The default content access account must be a domain user account that has read access to external or secure content sources that you want to crawl by using this account.

- For SharePoint Server sites that are not part of the server farm, you have to grant this account full read permissions explicitly to the web applications that host the sites. This is most commonly a cross-farm or federated scenario.

- This account must not be a member of the Farm Administrators group.

The Unattended Service account (*spUnattend*) is used by several services to connect to external data sources that require a user name and password that are based on operating systems other than Windows for authentication. If this account is not configured, these services will not attempt to connect to these types of data sources. Although account credentials are used to connect to data sources of operating systems other than Windows, if the account is not a member of the domain, the services cannot access them. This account must be a domain user account. Examples of where this account may be used are with the Secure Store Service and PerformancePoint or with Microsoft Excel services.

SharePoint Managed Accounts

You should already have an understanding of how managed accounts work in SharePoint, so this section will serve as a brief reminder and highlight the accounts that should be managed accounts versus those that should not be.

You can register or delete SharePoint Managed Accounts either through Central Administration or Windows PowerShell *(*-SPManagedAccount)*. The thing to remember is that password management for SharePoint Managed Accounts should happen inside SharePoint and not through AD DS. The SharePoint Managed Account box shows the interface for password management (see Figure 7-15). Keep in mind that this is yet another area in the product that will send credentials in clear text, so you should have Central Administration running over SSL.

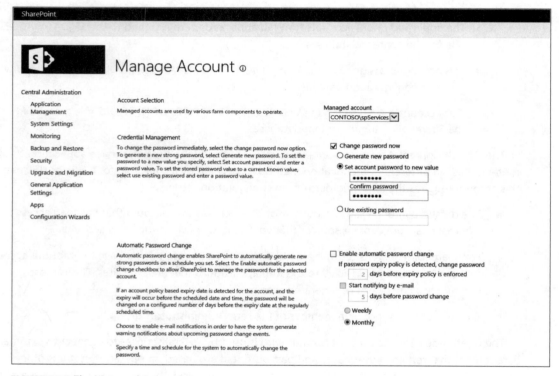

FIGURE 7-15 The Managed Account screen.

The Managed Account screen allows for either manual or automatic password management. The SharePoint Farm account (*spFarm*) will be added automatically to SharePoint as a managed account. You then are responsible for creating new managed accounts when you need them. This is typically for the Services (*spServices*) or Web Content (*spContent*) application pool accounts. The Default Content Access account (*spCrawl*) and the User Profile Synchronization account (*spUPS*) do not work as managed accounts. If the passwords are changed, you have to go to those areas manually to update those credentials. Any of the accounts that will be assigned to services using Configure

Service Accounts will also need to be a managed account. An example of this would be the Claims to Windows Token Service account (*spC2WTs*).

Some organizations have strict requirements that enforce password changes; an example of this would be to require password changes every 90 days. This can cause a great deal of issues in SharePoint if it is not planned properly. Whether or not policies like this should be enforced is a debate that will not happen here. Some experts have argued that automatically changing your passwords regularly after a certain number of days puts your system at more risk than using strong passwords would. In fact, once an account is configured as a managed account, the password is not required to be known. These passwords can contain a long string of characters that are difficult for anyone to remember. Make sure that your administrators know that managed accounts are to be modified in SharePoint and not Active Directory.

Understanding roles and group permissions

The accounts that you choose to operate your SharePoint farm with are assigned various roles and permissions. While these happen automatically, it is important to know their place in your security model. You will first learn about the various database roles and the improvements that Microsoft has made as far as giving accounts only the permissions they need. This section will then conclude with the group permissions that get assigned to the SharePoint accounts.

Roles

SharePoint 2013 has introduced a number of changes in the SharePoint database roles, which include WSS_CONTENT_APPLICATION_POOLS, WSS_SHELL_ACCESS, SP_READ_ONLY, and SP_DATA_ACCESS.

The WSS_CONTENT_APPLICATION_POOLS database role applies to the application pool account for each web application that is registered in the SharePoint farm. The role allows web applications to query and update the site map and have read-only access to other items in the configuration database. The role is assigned during the setup process and is applied to the *SharePoint_Config* and *SharePoint_AdminContent* databases. Members of the role will have execute permission for a subset of the stored procedures for the database. The role also provides select permission to the Versions table in the *SharePoint_AdminContent* database. You will also find that the *State Service* database takes advantage of this role.

The WSS_SHELL_ACCESS database role replaces the need to add an administrator account as a *db_owner* on the SharePoint configuration database. By default, the setup account (*spInstall*) is assigned to the WSS_SHELL_ACCESS role, which allows the account execute permission for all stored procedures for the database. In addition, members of this role have the read and write permissions on all the database tables. You can use Windows PowerShell cmdlets (*-SPShellAdmin*) to manage users in this role.

The SP_READ_ONLY database role replaces the need to use *sp_dboption*, which has been removed from SQL Server 2012, for setting a database in read-only mode. It should be used when only read access is required for data such as usage and telemetry data. The role will give its members *SELECT* capabilities on all stored procedures, functions, and SharePoint tables and *EXECUTE* capabilities on user-defined types where the schema is *dbo*.

The SP_DATA_ACCESS database role is the default role for database access and should be used for all object-model-level access to the database. SharePoint automatically adds an application pool account to this role during the upgrade or new deployments. The SP_DATA_ACCESS role replaces *db_owner*, but you will find that it has not yet been implemented across the board. Some of the databases that have implemented this role include the *App*, *State Service*, *Usage Services*, and the SharePoint *Configuration* and *Admin* databases.

Group permissions

During the installation process, SharePoint creates a number of groups that are important to the operation of the product. These groups include WSS_ADMIN_WPG, WSS_WPG, and WSS_RESTRICTED_WPG.

The WSS_ADMIN_WPG group has read and write access to local resources. The application pool accounts for the Central Administration and Timer service (*spFarm*) are in this role. The group is given full control over the directories that are vital to SharePoint, including all the SharePoint root, %windir%\System32\drivers\etc\HOSTS, and the IIS location of the Wss folder. You should monitor WSS_ADMIN_WPG with SCOM. The *Remove-SPShellAdmin* cmdlet will attempt to remove the account if it is not needed elsewhere.

The WSS_WPG group has read access to the local resources, and its members include all the application pools and service accounts. The group does have write access to the SharePoint log location but has only read access to the rest of the SharePoint root infrastructure.

The WSS_RESTRICTED_WPG can read the encrypted farm administration credential registry entry and is used only for the encryption and decryption of passwords that are stored in the configuration database. The group has full control over the registry entry that is used to store secrets in the configuration database. If the key is altered, service provisioning and other features will fail.

Putting it all together

Throughout this chapter, you have been presented a great deal of information on platform security. You have seen examples on preventing, tracking, and reporting on SharePoint installations in the enterprise. You then gained an understanding of how SharePoint communicates and learned the importance of using SSL in your SharePoint environment. Because SSL encrypts only communications and not the data at rest, the chapter then gave a working example on how to use SQL Server TDE to encrypt the data inside SQL Server. Finally, you were presented with the user accounts that would be needed to install SharePoint in a least privilege format, and then you examined the roles and group permissions that those accounts get associated with. One of the pieces of the puzzle that has not been made extremely clear yet is Central Administration over SSL. In a number of areas, the chapter highlighted many areas that would send the credentials in clear text, and you have undoubtedly seen the red warning messages throughout the product, as shown in Figure 7-16.

Register Managed Account ⓘ

al Administration

plication
anagement

stem Settings

onitoring

ckup and Restore

curity

Warning: this page is not encrypted for secure communication. User names, passwords, and any other information will be sent in clear text. For more information, contact your administrator.

Account Registration

Service accounts are used by various farm components to operate. The account password can be set to automatically change on a schedule and before any scheduled Active Directory enforced password change event.

Service account credentials

User name

Password

FIGURE 7-16 The Clear text warning message.

You have now been given the requirement to ensure that all Central Administration communications are encrypted. Because the farm is already built, your task is to convert the previously created website to use SSL. Whether you are converting an existing web application or creating a new one, the same general steps will apply. You can accomplish your task by doing the following:

1. Ensure that there is a Domain Naming Service (DNS) entry for *ca.contoso.local*.

2. Create an SSL certificate for the URL (*ca.contoso.local*).

3. Configure the Alternate Access Mappings (AAMs) for Central Administration.

4. Change the associated port.

5. Configure the IIS bindings.

The first step is to create a DNS entry for the URL you want to use. Central Administration is installed on a server with a high port, and you will be addressing it with a common name—for this example, it will be *ca.contoso.local*.

The next step is to create an SSL certificate. As mentioned earlier in the chapter, the best way to provide an SSL certificate to your organization for use over the corporate intranet is to use the Domain CA, as shown in Figure 7-17.

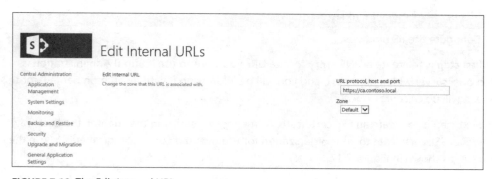

FIGURE 7-17 The Create Certificate dialog box.

Now that the certificate is created, you will need to change the associated AAM from the server name to the common name, as shown in Figure 7-18.

Edit Internal URLs

Central Administration

Application Management

System Settings

Monitoring

Backup and Restore

Security

Upgrade and Migration

General Application Settings

Edit Internal URL

Change the zone that this URL is associated with.

URL protocol, host and port
https://ca.contoso.local

Zone
Default

FIGURE 7-18 The Edit Internal URLs page.

For your next step, you need to change the associated port to Central Administration. If this was a new farm, you could simply use port 443 instead of the high port assignment. However, because you are converting an existing site in this exercise, you will use the *Set-SPCentralAdministion* cmdlet and set the port to 443, as shown in Listing 7-7.

LISTING 7-7 Change the port

```
Set-SPCentralAdministration -Port 443
```

The common name used to create the certificate will be used for the IIS bindings. This can be done either using the UI or with Windows PowerShell. For the sake of this demonstration, the UI will be used as shown in Figure 7-19.

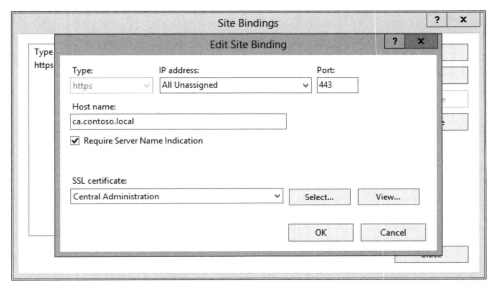

FIGURE 7-19 The Edit Site Binding dialog box.

Once you have completed the site bindings, you are ready to review Central Administration over SSL. If you navigate to the screens that gave you clear text warnings, you will find that the warnings have been removed from the screens (as shown in Figure 7-20).

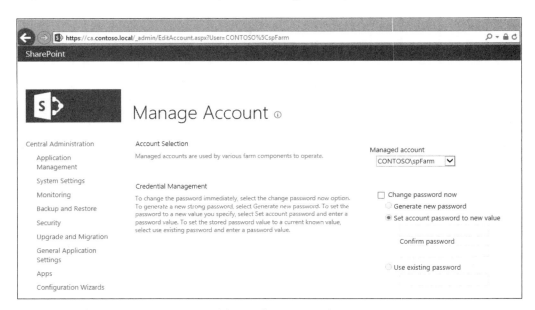

FIGURE 7-20 The Manage Account page without a clear text warning.

## CHAPTER 8

Upgrading your SharePoint 2010 environment

In this chapter, you will learn about:

- Determining which options are available for upgrade.

- Documenting your current Microsoft SharePoint Server 2010 environment.

- Testing the upgrade process.

- Minimizing and monitoring the upgrade process.

- Validating and troubleshooting upgrades.

Microsoft SharePoint 2013 has finally been released to manufacturing, and you want to bring your organization into the latest and greatest technology available. There are three ways to get the new product: new installations of SharePoint 2013, migrating content from a previous version of SharePoint to SharePoint 2013 (usually with a third-party tool), and upgrading from Microsoft SharePoint Server 2010 to SharePoint 2013. The latter two options will leave an organization at an important crossroad. Environments that lacked governance or structure may not be a strong candidate for the upgrade process and might use the migration process to help clean up and restructure themselves. It is difficult to upgrade an environment successfully when the previous one lacked any processes or rules. One of the greatest features of SharePoint is that it is highly customizable; on the flip side, one of the negative aspects of SharePoint is that it is highly customizable. If customizations aren't governed, understood, and documented, then they can turn a simple upgrade into an absolute nightmare.

One of the benefits of SharePoint 2013 is its architectural similarities with the 2010 product. The service application architecture that was outlined in Chapter 4, "Understanding the service application model," is relatively unchanged. While there are a couple of service applications that have been removed and a few others added, the basic architecture is the same. This makes for a much smoother upgrade compared to the Shared Service Provider upgrade from Microsoft Office SharePoint Server 2007 to SharePoint 2010.

One of the topics that will be discussed in more detail is that the upgrade process can only be accomplished from SharePoint 2010 to SharePoint 2013. If you were hoping to move directly from SharePoint Server 2007 to SharePoint 2013, the best approach will be to upgrade to SharePoint 2010, validate the design, and then move to SharePoint 2013. Many of you who find yourselves in this situation might want to consider the migration of content by using a third-party tool.

In this chapter, you will explore the options available in the upgrade cycle and then learn how to get the SharePoint 2010 environment ready for the move to SharePoint 2013. You certainly don't want to attempt your upgrade for the first time in production (and in fact, this option has been removed), so this chapter will also discuss creating a testing environment to validate the upgrade process and making sure everything is known prior to the actual production upgrade event. In an effort to keep the upgrade process as streamlined as possible, this chapter will explore ways to minimize and monitor the upgrade process, finishing with an overview of validating and troubleshooting your upgrade. Only the simplest environments upgrade without problems, so understanding how to mitigate issues during the testing phase will ensure a successful upgrade.

Introducing upgrades

Every release of SharePoint offers a new set of bells and whistles that makes the product more enticing; the one thing that never seems to get the spotlight is the changes that have been introduced in the upgrade processes. Back with the upgrade from Microsoft SharePoint Portal Server 2003 to SharePoint Server 2007, there were three choices for upgrade: gradual, in-place, and content database attach methods. When the upgrade path went from SharePoint Server 2007 to SharePoint Server 2010, the upgrade options were reduced to only two methods for upgrade: the in-place and content database attach methods. Now, with SharePoint 2013, there is only one method of upgrade available: the database attach upgrade method. This is a far safer approach than applying the new SharePoint parts on top of your production environment. One of the drawbacks of only being able to do a database attach upgrade is the inability to use your production hardware during the transition. However, because the minimum requirements for each version of SharePoint 2013 seem to require a few more resources, moving SharePoint to a virtual space is probably the most cost-effective move anyway.

There are two supported version-upgrade paths to SharePoint 2013:

- Microsoft SharePoint Foundation 2010

- SharePoint Server 2010

As previously mentioned, organizations that wish to upgrade previous products like SharePoint Server 2007 or Windows SharePoint Services 3.0 must either upgrade to SharePoint 2010 or migrate their content with a third-party tool. In truth, upgrading is a much easier move from SharePoint 2010 to SharePoint 2013 than it may be to move from SharePoint 2007 to SharePoint 2010. One point being that the architectures are similar and features have been provided in the new product to help make the move to SharePoint 2013 easier. One of these features includes the Feature Fallback behavior introduced in Chapter 1, "Understanding the Microsoft SharePoint 2013 architecture." The feature actually allows for SharePoint 2010 artifacts to be deployed to a scaled-down version of the SharePoint 2010 root folder that stands side by side with the SharePoint 2013 root folder. You may have also noticed that when creating a new SharePoint 2013 web application, there is a choice to use the SharePoint 2010 user experience. This is a fantastic way for organizations to adopt the new product without losing their customizations and branding after they have invested a great deal of time and money. Maintaining an environment with the SharePoint 2010 experience will also help user acceptance because users are already familiar with the product, and then the users' site collections can be upgraded after receiving the proper SharePoint 2013 training. While the deferred site collection may sound like the Visual Upgrade component that was introduced in SharePoint 2010, it is actually far better. The Visual Upgrade in SharePoint 2010 allowed you to keep the user experience for the pages you upgraded, but it was unsupported to use those master pages on sites created in SharePoint 2010. SharePoint 2013 allows organizations to not only keep their previous user experience, but create and maintain other sites as well.

Authentication upgrade

In order to understand how upgrading will affect a particular implementation, it is important to understand the core architecture changes made to the product. As you learned in Chapter 6, "Mapping authentication and authorization to requirements," when creating a new SharePoint 2013 web application, the option to create a Classic mode application no longer exists in the UI. While Classic mode web applications have been deprecated in the new version, they are still fully supported. A strong push toward using claims is underway; in fact, features like OAuth and S2S will not be available if your SharePoint Server 2010 web application is not migrated to claims-based authentication. You'll learn about the options for moving from Windows authentication to claims-based authentication later in this chapter. The good news is that if your SharePoint Server 2010 environment is already using claims-based authentication, there will be one less step required before you upgrade!

Database attach upgrade

Database attach upgrade is the only supported method for version-to-version (V2V) upgrades, such as SharePoint Server 2010 to SharePoint 2013. Database attach upgrades are supported for build-to-build (B2B) upgrades so long as the database being attached is from a version of SharePoint 2013 that is less than or equal to the current version of the consuming SharePoint 2013 farm. The length of time that it takes to upgrade a database is not based on the size of the database, but the complexity of the data within the database.

In-place upgrade

In-place upgrades are supported only for B2B upgrades. This would be an instance where you upgrade your environment by installing either a service pack or a cumulative upgrade (if required).

Supported databases

There were a lot of new capabilities added to SharePoint Server 2010 to allow for better management of your service applications. With new capabilities came new databases. In SharePoint 2013, you now have the ability to actually conduct a database attach for some of the service application databases. The supported databases that will upgrade using the database attach method are as follows:

- Content databases

- Search Admin database

- User Profile Service databases:

  - Profile database

  - Social database

  - Sync database

  The Social database and the Sync database are optional. If you do not upgrade these databases, new Social and Sync databases are created for you automatically.

- Secure Store database

  This will require you to remember your passphrase.

- Managed Metadata database

- Access databases

  This applies to SharePoint 2013 B2B upgrades only, since Access Services did not store the Access files in a SQL Server database in SharePoint Server 2010.

Unsupported databases

Here is a list of databases that are not supported for the database attach upgrade:

- Configuration database

  The Farm Configuration database is not supported for either V2V or B2B upgrades. It has never been supported for upgrade in any previous version (and most likely will never be supported in future versions).

- Search Index database

  The Search Index database is unsupported for V2V upgrades. Because search was rebuilt to incorporate FAST, this should not be much of a surprise.

Upgrade implementation improvements

Before getting into the specifics of performing an upgrade, let's first examine some of the investments Microsoft made in the upgrade arena. Upgrading from SharePoint 2007 to SharePoint 2010 offered few options that helped users evaluate SharePoint 2010. Eventually, users were forced to upgrade to the SharePoint 2010 UI, as it was unsupported to create new sites using the 2007 UI. In this section, you will learn about the upgrade capabilities in SharePoint 2013 that improved this scenario: the deferred site collection, feature fallback behavior, site collection health checks, upgrade evaluation site collections, upgrade throttling, new status bar notifications, and logging features.

Deferred site collection upgrade

There have been major strides taken to give you the ability to upgrade your environment successfully from SharePoint Server 2010 to SharePoint 2013. One of the new features is the deferred site collection upgrade, which replaces the SharePoint Server 2010 Visual upgrade. With the Visual upgrade in SharePoint Server 2010, the upgrade still happened during the database attach, and preserved only the old master pages, CSS files, and HTML files to make the pages look like SharePoint Server 2007. With the deferred site collection upgrade, you can continue to use the UI from SharePoint Server 2010. The master page, CSS, JScript, and SPFeatures will remain in what is now SP14 mode. One major difference between the Visual upgrade and the deferred site collection upgrade is that you can now upgrade per site collection (*SPSite*) instead of site (*SPWeb*). Users can now preview their site in the SharePoint 2013 UI before committing to the change. When you attach a SharePoint Server 2010 content database, the site collection will be run as a deferred site collection by default, and you cannot force the upgrade to SharePoint 2013 automatically. However, you can use Windows PowerShell to test, then mount, databases, followed by the upgrading the site collection.

Feature Fallback behavior

In SharePoint 2013, when you attach the content database, the database schema gets updated but the site collection content still runs in SharePoint Server 2010 mode. This gives SharePoint the ability to run SharePoint Server 2010 side by side with SharePoint 2013. SharePoint 2013 has all the required SharePoint Server 2010 files included to enable you to run SharePoint Server 2010 until you are ready to upgrade to the SharePoint 2013 experience. This means that your existing SharePoint Server 2010 customizations should work within SharePoint 2013 after you do your database attach. You can read more about how SharePoint Server 2010 and SharePoint 2013 can run side by side in Chapter 1.

Site Collection Health Check

Another fantastic new feature is the Site Collection Health Check, which allows you to run a "rules-based" health check to look for issues before upgrading your SharePoint Server 2010 site collection to SharePoint 2013. As shown in Figure 8-1, you can access the Health Check from the Site Settings page of the Site Collection. The Health Check will show you issues that will result in upgrade blocking, such as missing features or templates. The Health Check will also look for post-upgrade issues, such as unghosted files. There is a UI for the site collection administrators and there are Windows PowerShell cmdlets for the farm administrators. The Site Collection Health Check automatically runs for V2V upgrades and will prevent upgrades if issues are detected. However, the Site Collection Health Check does not run before B2B upgrades.

Site Collection Administration
Search Settings
Search scopes
Search keywords
Recycle bin
Site collection features
Site hierarchy
Site collection navigation
Site collection audit settings
Audit log reports
Portal site connection
Site collection policies
Storage Metrics
Site collection output cache
Content type publishing
Site collection object cache
Site collection cache profiles
Variations Settings
Variation labels
Translatable columns
Variation logs
Suggested Content Browser Locations
Help settings
Visual Upgrade
SharePoint Designer Settings
→ Site collection health checks
Site collection upgrade

FIGURE 8-1 The Site Collection Health Check location.

Upgrade Evaluation Site collections

SharePoint 2013 also gives you the ability to preview your SharePoint Server 2010 site collection as a SharePoint 2013 site collection before you finalize your upgrade. In other words, you can use the upgrade evaluation site collection to make a side-by-side copy of your existing SharePoint Server 2010 site collection in SharePoint 2013 mode. This is accomplished by creating and upgrading a temporary copy of your site collection instead of a preview in the existing instance of the site collection. As shown in Figure 8-2, you can access the Site Collection Upgrade link from the Site Setting page of the Site Collection. The reason for previewing a copy of the site collection is because of the complexity of what happens during site collection upgrade. Once a site collection is upgraded, it cannot be rolled back. Therefore, performing a preview would not be possible except in a copy of the site collection.

If you are using an Enterprise version or later of SQL Server, then the evaluation site collection will be created using the SQL Snapshot feature. If you are not using SQL Server Enterprise or higher, your SharePoint Server 2010 site collection will be put into a Read-only mode during the site collection backup process. You should consider emailing your users that the site collection could be in read-only mode for an extended period of time. Fortunately, when the copy and upgrade is complete, the requestor and site collection administrators will receive an upgrade completion email. If you start the creation of your evaluation site collection using Windows PowerShell, the receipt of an email is optional. The creation of the evaluation site collection is run from the Create Upgrade Evaluation Site Collections job timer job, which, by default, is scheduled to run daily between 1:00 A.M. and 1:30 A.M. (This means that if you request a site at 9:00 A.M., SharePoint will not start building your new site for 16 more hours.) Figure 8-3 shows the steps of creating an evaluation site collection using SQL snapshots.

Site Collection Administration
Search Settings
Search scopes
Search keywords
Recycle bin
Site collection features
Site hierarchy
Site collection navigation
Site collection audit settings
Audit log reports
Portal site connection
Site collection policies
Storage Metrics
Site collection output cache
Content type publishing
Site collection object cache
Site collection cache profiles
Variations Settings
Variation labels
Translatable columns
Variation logs
Suggested Content Browser Locations
Help settings
Visual Upgrade
SharePoint Designer Settings
Site collection health checks
→ Site collection upgrade

FIGURE 8-2 The Site Collection Upgrade location.

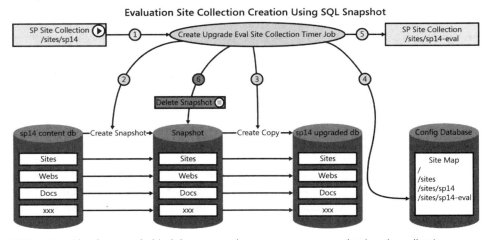

FIGURE 8-3 What happens behind the scenes when you request an evaluation site collection.

Site collection upgrade throttling

The horsepower required to upgrade a site collection is pretty outstanding. If you take a look at the message for creating an Upgrade Evaluation Site collection, as shown in Figure 8-4, it could take days to upgrade just one content database.

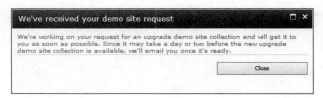

FIGURE 8-4 Modal dialog box after you have requested an evaluation site.

Well, what if you have several content databases and several site collections that need to be upgraded? How is this going to affect your farm? In SharePoint 2013, there is a new feature called Site Collection Upgrade Throttling to help keep your SharePoint 2013 environment running smoothly by preventing an overload scenario while all of the upgrades are happening in the background.

There are several throttle types in SharePoint 2013 that function together to help keep your farm running at peak performance and keep you from inadvertently upgrading all your databases and site collections all at once.

The first throttle is at the web-application level, and limits the number of concurrent site collection upgrades per application pool instance. By default you can upgrade five concurrent site collections per web application. This throttle is controlled by the web application instance property.

The next throttle is at the content-database level. This throttle limits the number of simultaneous site collections that can be upgraded at one time within a single content database. By default, you can upgrade 10 site collections concurrently within one content database. This throttle is controlled by the content database instance property.

The third throttle is at the content level. This throttle prevents self-service upgrades from happening within web applications with sites that have exceeded the default threshold. The default threshold for the site collection is < 10 MB and has fewer than 10 (< 10) subwebs.

If an upgrade is not possible to do without exceeding the limits of the throttle rules, your upgrade will get placed into the upgrade queue and will be processed by the Upgrade Site Collections Timer Job. Fortunately, this timer job is scheduled to run every minute. Throttling will be discussed in more detail later in the chapter.

System Status Bar and notifications

SharePoint now has the System Status Bar at the top of the site page to notify site collection administrators if there is an upgrade available (see Figure 8-5) to move from SharePoint Server 2010 to SharePoint 2013. The status bar can also be used to notify the users if there is an upgrade in progress (see Figure 8-6), if the site is in Read-only mode (see Figure 8-7), or if you are in an evaluation site collection (see Figure 8-8).

FIGURE 8-5 Upgrade Available status bar.

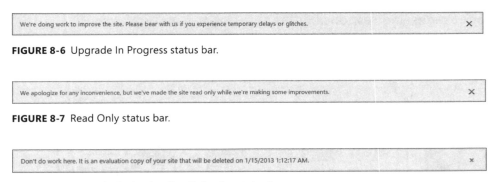

FIGURE 8-6 Upgrade In Progress status bar.

FIGURE 8-7 Read Only status bar.

FIGURE 8-8 Upgrade Evaluation Site Collection status bar.

Email notifications

Email notifications are now automatically sent out when starting an upgrade using the graphical user interface (GUI). Email will be sent out to the requestor and the site collection administrators. Email notifications about the upgrade will be sent when:

- The V2V upgrade has completed successfully.
- The V2V upgrade has completed with error(s).
- The Upgrade Evaluation Site has been requested.
- The Upgrade Evaluation Site has been created, but not upgraded.
- The Upgrade Evaluation Site has been created and upgraded.

Logging

SharePoint 2013 logs are now in the Unified Logging Service (ULS) format. That means that column data is tab separated, which will allow easier parsing of the data, as well as the ability to import the logs into Microsoft Excel. Log files are created for upgrades, upgrade errors, and site upgrades. They are created for both V2V and B2B upgrades. Logs are stored as content within the site collection that is being upgraded and is security trimmed for site collection administrators. Even as a site collection administrator, you cannot find the library that holds the documents easily; they are located at ../_catalogs/MaintenanceLogs.

These fantastic new features of SharePoint 2013 will help you get your SharePoint Server 2010 environment upgraded easily, reliably, and successfully.

Overview of upgrade process

For the successful completion of an upgrade, it is not good enough to know what has changed within the upgrade process compared to SharePoint Server 2010. It is best that you understand the sequence in which things happen so you know the proper order when the time comes to document your migration script. This section will go over the stages of a simple SharePoint Server 2010 farm upgrade and then through a bit more challenging Shared Services Farm upgrade.

Upgrade stages and responsibilities

Migrating over an entire SharePoint Server 2010 farm will take various stages of implementation and deployment. Figure 8-9 shows an overview of what is required to migrate existing content, and who is responsible for those actions.

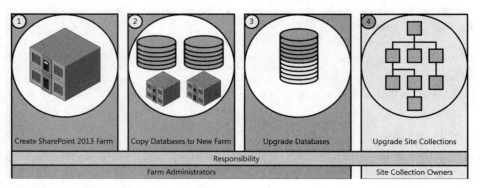

FIGURE 8-9 Upgrade order and responsibilities.

As shown in Figure 8-9, an upgrade involves four major steps:

1. Create, configure, and verify your SharePoint 2013 environment.

   a. Create and configure the service applications for your SharePoint 2013 farm.

   b. Create web applications for upgrade.

   c. Install, move, and, if required, create customizations.

2. Place your SharePoint Server 2010 content databases in Read-Only mode (optional, but highly recommended).

   Back up your SharePoint Server 2010 content and service application databases.

3. Restore all of your databases in the appropriate server running SQL Server in your new SharePoint 2013 environment.

   Upgrade service application databases.

4. Upgrade site collections.

For upgrading your SharePoint 2010 My Site site collections, the farm administrator will upgrade the My Site host first, which will allow the users to upgrade their My Site when they are ready. However, the farm administrator can upgrade all the My Sites using Windows PowerShell, which will be explained in the "Putting it all together" section later in this chapter.

Services upgrade and overview

In the "Supported databases" section earlier in this chapter, you learned which databases can be attached for upgrade to SharePoint 2013. It is imperative that you create your service applications on your new farm prior to upgrading the SharePoint Server 2010 content databases. Figure 8-10 shows a generalization of how to upgrade the service applications and proxies.

FIGURE 8-10 The upgrade order for service applications.

As shown in Figure 8-10, there are four basic steps to upgrade your service applications:

1. Verify that you have the appropriate permissions and that you are part of the Shell Admin group.

   Use Windows PowerShell cmdlet *Get-SPShellAdmin*.

2. Copy service application databases to the new farm.

3. Upgrade the service application.

   Use Windows PowerShell cmdlet *New-SPMetadataServiceApplication*.

4. Create a service application proxy.

   Use Windows PowerShell cmdlet *New-SPMetadataServiceApplicationProxy*.

There is an example of how to do the service application upgrade in the "Putting it all together" section later in this chapter.

Shared Services Farm

If you are running a Shared Services Farm, you will have a few extra steps to take when getting your SharePoint Server 2010 farm upgraded:

1. Create your new SharePoint 2013 services farm.

   a. Upgrade your Search service application.

   b. Upgrade the other cross-farm service applications.

2. Point service connections to the SharePoint Server 2010 content farm.

3. Upgrade the SharePoint Server 2010 content farm to SharePoint 2013.

4. Index the SharePoint 2013 farm.

   a. Point service connections to the SharePoint Server 2013 content farm.

   b. Repurpose SharePoint Server 2010 content and cross-farm servers.

Preparing your upgrade

"By failing to prepare, you are preparing to fail."

Benjamin Franklin

The preparation time for a single-server farm will usually be less than a large farm, but the information required to be documented will be the same. Taking the time to gather all the documentation of your existing farm will help you succeed in your SharePoint 2013 creation and upgrade. Unfortunately, in SharePoint Server 2010, you are not offered the luxury of running a command similar to the SharePoint 2007 (post-SP1) PreUpgradeCheck utility. However, you will be able to use Windows PowerShell cmdlets like *Test-SPContentDatabase* to help get your content ready to upgrade.

Cleaning up your content databases

To see what is happening within your content databases, run the *Test-SPContentDatabase* cmdlet to make sure that your content databases are going to upgrade successfully. The following script has an array (*$databases*) of all of the content database names on the "SQL-12" SQL Server (*$dbServer*) for the web application located at *http://projects.contoso.com* (*$webApp*). The script then takes the output information from the *Test-SPContentDatabase* cmdlet and saves the output as a text file to C:\scripts\ testlogs-Projects\ (*$outFileLocation*):

```
PS C:\> Add-PSSnapin Microsoft.SharePoint.PowerShell -EA 0
PS C:\> $databases = ("Content_AU","Content_NZ","Content_CA","Content_US","Content_Projects")
PS C:\> foreach ($db in $databases)
  {
    $dbServer = "SQL-12"
    $webApp = "http://projects.contoso.com"
    $outFileLocation = "c:\testLogs-Projects\" + $db + ".txt"
    Test-SPContentDatabase -name $db -webapplication $webApp -ServerInstance $dbServer
-ShowRowCounts | out-file $outFileLocation
  }
```

You can download the script from *http://sdrv.ms/UWT2tC*.

After the script has been run, you can go to the *$outFileLocation* and review the information about your content databases. It should look similar to Figure 8-11.

```
Category          : DatabaseStatistics
Error             : False
UpgradeBlocking   : False
Message           : Table [AllDocs] has [3988] rows.
Remedy            :

Category          : DatabaseStatistics
Error             : False
UpgradeBlocking   : False
Message           : Table [AllDocStreams] has [2922] rows.
Remedy            :

Category          : DatabaseStatistics
Error             : False
UpgradeBlocking   : False
Message           : Table [AllDocVersions] has [3119] rows.
Remedy            :

Category          : DatabaseStatistics
Error             : False
UpgradeBlocking   : False
Message           : Table [AllFileFragments] has [0] rows.
Remedy            :
```

FIGURE 8-11 Example output from running the *Test-SPContentDatabase* cmdlet.

You will need to be a bit more concerned if your output looks like Figure 8-12.

```
Category          : DatabaseStatistics
Error             : False
UpgradeBlocking   : False
Message           : Table [WorkflowAssociation] has [5] rows.
Remedy            :

Category          : SiteOrphan
Error             : True
UpgradeBlocking   : False
Message           : Database [Content-    -EmailHolding] contains a site (Id = [4a7b23ed-3cbd-4f04-9c01-693bbb1238eb], Url = [/sites/Offi
                    ce_Viewing_Service_Cache]) that is not found in the site map. Consider detach and reattach the database.
Remedy            : The orphaned sites could cause upgrade failures. Try detach and reattach the database which contains the orphaned sit
                    es. Restart upgrade if necessary.
```

FIGURE 8-12 Example of an error found after running the *Test-SPContentDatabase* cmdlet.

Luckily, in the Site Orphan category, Microsoft suggests a remedy to resolve the issue of having a site orphan. You will want to use the *Dismount-SPContentDatabase* cmdlet followed by a *Mount-SPContentDatabase* cmdlet, followed by a confirmation of repair by rerunning your *Test-SPContentDatabase* script.

Cleaning up your environment

When you are preparing to move into a new home, you do not want to pack up and move old, unused junk. The same holds true when it comes time to move from one SharePoint environment to another. The first step is to make sure that the web applications are all still being used. If you have a web application that is not being used, make a note not to move over the associated databases. Once you have determined which web applications that you are going to move across, you will want to determine which site collections are still being used. You will want to back up the unused site collections, have a discussion with the site collection owners, and then delete the site collections. The same stands true for your content. If you have old, outdated content, ask the content owners if *they* can delete the data, or if you can back it up for them and delete the data afterward. One last thing that you will want to address is code. Are you still using all of the deployed features and solutions? If not, disable them, retract them, and remove them from the farm. To double-check that the solution has been removed cleanly, you will want to go back to the site and verify that the solution gallery is cleaned out as well. You will also want to make sure that you are not trying to upgrade any features or elements that have been deprecated in

SharePoint 2013. For example, Web Analytics and SQL Server Search should both be turned off before attempting to upgrade them. For a list of changes from SharePoint Server 2010 to SharePoint 2013, review this page: *http://tinyurl.com/PCfromDC-Changes*.

Upgrade also offers you the opportunity to consolidate farms. If your organization is running multiple instances of SharePoint, now is a good time to look at upgrading your architecture and possibly taking all your SharePoint farms and consolidating them into one farm.

Documenting your environment

Now that your environment has been cleaned up, it is time to start documenting your environment. You will want to document everything that you want to move over into your SharePoint 2013 environment. Without the ability to run a PreUpgradeCheck, you are going to be creating several documents full of information about your environment. In the next section, you will learn which settings and environment information that is important to capture, and review how to get the information. You can download an existing Microsoft Upgrade worksheet that has been modified to help with your documentation of information from *http://sdrv.ms/VqNni7*.

Documenting current settings

Document the following settings so that you can build them into your new SharePoint 2013 environment before you attach your content databases:

- Alternate access mappings.

  Use the Windows PowerShell cmdlet *Get-SPAlternateUrl*.

- Authentication providers (see Figure 8-13).

  Use the Windows PowerShell cmdlet *Get-SPAuthenticationProvider*.

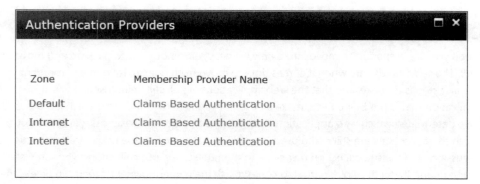

FIGURE 8-13 Authentication Providers dialog box for a specific web application.

- Authentication modes

  - Located in Central Administration | Manage Web Applications Authentication Providers

- Claims mode

- Classic mode

If your authentication mode looks like Figure 8-14, it is very important to note the web application.

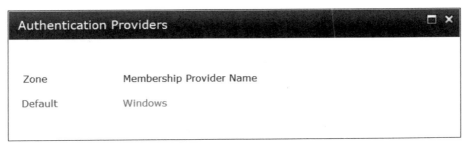

FIGURE 8-14 Authentication Providers dialog box showing the authentication type for a specific web application.

- Authentication types (see Figure 8-15).

    You must use the same names from your SharePoint Server 2010 farm.

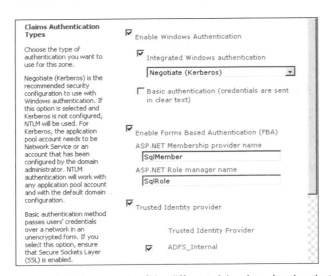

FIGURE 8-15 An example of the different claims-based authentication types.

Other items that you should document are certificates, such as Server certificates, Trusted Provider certificates, SSL certificates, and all Farm certificates. Don't forget to document Solutions (*Get-SPSolution*)—farm-based and sandboxed. Even though sandboxed solutions are housed within the site collection content database and will be moved over automatically when you move the database, it is good to have an inventory to keep track of things.

Make sure that you have documented your incoming and outgoing email settings, managed path information (*Get-SPManagedPath*), quota template settings, self-service site management settings, Web.config modifications, plus any and all customizations.

Documenting environment settings

The next step in preparing your SharePoint 2013 environment is to gather the following environment information to help make sure that you have moved over all your existing SharePoint Server 2010 content:

- Number of sites

  Use the Windows PowerShell cmdlet *Get-SPWeb* (don't forget to dispose of the web object).

- Number of databases

  Use the Windows PowerShell cmdlet *Get-SPContentDatabase*.

- Database names

  Use the Windows PowerShell cmdlet *Get-SPDatabase*.

- Number of users

  Use the Windows PowerShell cmdlet *Get-SPUser*.

- Any customizations

Documenting service settings

Another area to document involves how you managed your farm services. You will want to document the following items:

- Service names

- Service settings

- Database names

- Any customizations

This is a good opportunity to take the time to write a Windows PowerShell script that will pull back all the information about your environment and save the data into a *.csv* file. You should already have some type of script that you should be running on a weekly basis to compare how your farm is changing and to help keep up with the growth and changes of your environment. If you do not wish to create your own script, please feel free to grab the script from my blog, *http://tinyurl.com/PCfromDC-FarmInfo*, or just download it from *http://tinyurl.com/PCfromDC-FarmDownload*.

Customizations

It is important to generate a list of all of customizations that were created in your SharePoint Server 2010 environment. This would include all solutions, features, Web Parts, Web Pages, web templates, site definitions, event handlers, master pages, page layouts, themes, and CSS files. Other customizations might include web services, HTTP handlers, and HTTP modules. Now is also a good time to start thinking about how you are going to deal with the customizations. Are you going to keep them, upgrade them, or delete them?

Managing customizations

If you have left your SharePoint Server 2010 environment alone and have not added a single enhancement, then you do not have to worry about upgrading customizations. However, because most of you have been trying to use SharePoint to its fullest potential, the odds are good that there will be customizations to upgrade. If your SharePoint Server 2010 sites have been extensively customized, you will want to determine how you want to handle your customizations before your attempted upgrade to SharePoint 2013. Your approach to upgrading your customizations will vary based on the extent of the customizations, the kind of customizations, the complexity of your SharePoint Server 2010 site, and the other factors that determine a successful upgrade. As previously mentioned in the "Documenting your environment" section, it is very important that you identify the customizations, evaluate the customizations in your environment, and then determine whether you will upgrade those customizations. There are only three options when it comes to dealing with how to upgrade your customizations:

■ Keep the customizations; don't upgrade the sites.

You can continue to run your site in SharePoint Server 2010 mode in your new environment. You should use this approach only temporarily. This should be considered a temporary solution because eventually you will have to upgrade to the next version of SharePoint (vNext).

■ Replace or redo the customizations.

If you want to take full advantage of the new functionality of SharePoint 2013, or use this upgrade as an opportunity to "start over" with a new look and feel, then you will have to upgrade your customizations. How will the upgrade of your customizations affect the timeline to upgrade your site? Are you going to keep the site in SharePoint Server 2010 mode until the customizations are complete, or remove them and add them back at a later date?

■ Discard the customizations.

If you do not use the customization any longer, or if the customization is obsolete, it is a good time to delete it.

• Replace the customizations by using default functionality, such as replacing global navigation headers for the managed metadata navigation default functionality.

You can reset pages to the default site definitions and remove any Web Parts or features that you no longer wish to support. Remember that you can use SharePoint 2013 Site

Collection Health Check to find unghosted pages and you can reset the pages to their default versions to correct the ghosting issues.

- After discarding customizations, you should fix any issues that result from removing the customizations before the upgrade.

WSP files

You should have taken notes on the current customizations on your farm in the last section, but are you sure that you have the *.wsp* files that were used to having when deploying the solutions? Do you use a lot of third-party tools? Do you have a lot of solutions in your farm? Are you 100 percent sure that you have the correct *.wsp* files to deploy into your new SharePoint 2013 environment? If you cannot find all the farm solution *.wsp* files, there is a way to export them from your SharePoint Server 2010 environment. Luckily, Shane Young came up with a blog post on how to use Windows PowerShell to export your *.wsp* files from your farm. I have updated the Windows PowerShell script from his blog, and you can read about it at *http://tinyurl.com/PCfromDC-GetWSPs* or download it from *http://sdrv.ms/PwL6Oz*.

Remote BLOB Storage (RBS)

With the introduction of Shredded Storage in SharePoint 2013, the requirement for Remote BLOB Storage (RBS) is no longer needed. While there is always an exception to every rule, if you are using RBS, you should use this upgrade as an opportunity to stop using RBS. If you are using RBS through a third-party vendor, ask them how they recommend you bring your data back into the servers running SQL Server that are hosting your SharePoint 2010 environment. If you created the RBS yourself, there are plenty of blog posts available to help you with disabling RBS.

Third-party products

If you have installed products from third-party vendors, and they supplied you with an *.msi* file, then you will have to contact the vendor for their suggested upgrade path to SharePoint 2013. Granted that some vendors use the *.msi* file to deploy the *.wsp* files, but you really cannot be 100 percent sure what is happening behind the scenes, such as adding licensing information to the registry. One option to make sure that the *.msi* file did not make any other additions during deployment is by using tools like WinDiff.

Manually deployed code and updates

Running WinDiff will be very useful for those organizations that have allowed changes, features, or files to be deployed manually to their SharePoint Server 2010 farm. This also means that you will have to create a generic SharePoint Server 2010 farm to compare your modified farm against. It is imperative that the SharePoint farm for differencing matches your production version number exactly. You will have to copy each modified file from your SharePoint Server 2010 farm to the appropriate folder in your SharePoint 2013 environment. Manual updates or deployments should not be done on a production environment. You should use this upgrade as a talking point with your developers to try to get their code into a *.wsp* file or even built to deploy into the App Store.

You can read about how to use the Windiff.exe Utility program at *http://tinyurl.com/PCfromDC-WinDiff.*

Documenting other services

There are some services that will require a bit of extra work to get them migrated over to your new SharePoint 2013 environment.

InfoPath Forms Service

If you are using administrator-deployed Microsoft InfoPath (*.xsn*) forms, the forms will need to be extracted from your SharePoint 2010 environment and imported into your new SharePoint 2013 environment, as well as your managed data connection files. Because the InfoPath Forms Service is not created with the Farm Configuration Wizard, it will have to be configured manually by using the Configure InfoPath Forms Services link under the General Application Settings page in Central Administration (shown in Figure 8-16).

You can export your administrator deployed form templates (*.xsn* files) from your SharePoint 2010 environment by using the *Export-SPInfoPathAdministrationFiles* cmdlet.

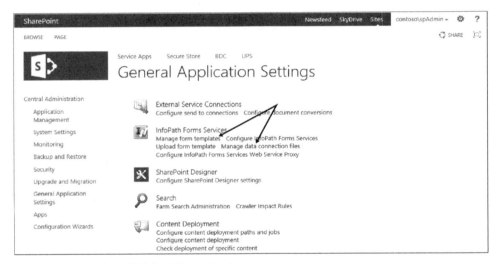

FIGURE 8-16 Location of InfoPath Forms Services.

Excel Services

Excel Services can be enabled through the Farm Configuration Wizard, but make sure to re-create all the trusted data connections, configuration settings, user-defined functions (UDFs), and trusted locations.

Microsoft Office Web Apps

As you know, Office Web Apps (OWA) has been moved to its own farm so OWA will not be available after you upgrade your environment to SharePoint 2013. You must deploy at least one OWA server and connect to your SharePoint 2013 environment after your content databases are upgraded. This does not mean that you have to wait for the site collection upgrade to happen, as the OWA farm can be utilized in both SharePoint Server 2010 and SharePoint 2013 modes within the SharePoint 2013 farm. It is important to know that your users will have to choose between the OWA version of Excel and Excel Services when clicking the items in a document library.

User Profile Service

Deploying User Profile Service (UPS) in SharePoint Server 2010 was not a lot of fun; in fact, it was nerve-racking to accomplish. Starting with the SharePoint Server 2010 RTM, UPS seemed to not only have issues with deployment, but it seemed that every time Microsoft pushed out a Cumulative Update (CU), UPS broke and had to be re-created from scratch. It was great to see the progress that was made with Microsoft Forefront Identity Manager (FIM) and UPS over time, even if the FIM version numbers went in the wrong direction. Now, with the advancements of UPS and FIM in SharePoint 2013, you need to look closely at your upgrade strategy for UPS. The answers to the following questions should determine whether you upgrade your current UPS or you start anew:

- Have you created any custom properties within UPS?

- How long would it take to document and rebuild your custom properties from scratch?

Basically, if you are running UPS out of the box, then do not worry about upgrading UPS from SharePoint Server 2010; just build it out in SharePoint 2013 from scratch. At RTM, the Sync Database upgrade is still having issues, which will cause the UPS Synchronization Service Instance to fail and get stuck on "Starting." Because this is the upgrade chapter, you will learn how to do the actual upgrade a bit later, in the "Putting it all together" section, but for now, let's review how Microsoft says to do the UPS upgrade.

Just like all of the other service application upgrades, the first step is to move and upgrade your *Social*, *Profile*, and *Sync* databases into your server running SQL Server and SharePoint 2013. Once your databases have been restored and upgraded, it is time to start the UPS instance, by going to Central Administration | Application Management | Service Applications | Manage Services On Server and clicking Start.

Once the service is up and running, log off the machine, and then log on as the Farm Service. You are then going to open Windows PowerShell as the administrator, and run the following command to get the application pool identity:

```
PS C:\> $appPool = Get-SPServiceApplicationPool -Identity "SharePoint Web Services Default"
```

To upgrade the UPS application, you are now going to run the following command:

```
PS C:\> $upa = New-SPProfileServiceApplication -Name "User Profile Service Application"
-ApplicationPool $appPool -ProfileDBName "Upgrade_UPS_Profile_DB" -SocialDBName "Upgrade_UPS_
Social_DB" -ProfileSyncDBName "Upgrade_UPS_Sync_DB"
```

You will want to use your database names for the *Profile*, *Social*, and *Sync* databases. Remember that the *Social* and *Sync* parameters are optional, and they will be created for you automatically if you do not already have them in SQL to upgrade. The databases will be named with parameters provided in the Windows PowerShell script.

Once the UPS has been provisioned, it is time to create the UPS Proxy. To create the proxy, you will run the following command:

```
PS C:\> New-SPProfileServiceApplicationProxy -Name "User Profile Service Application Proxy"
-ServiceApplication $upa -DefaultProxyGroup
```

Now comes the fun part. Because the user profile synchronization service utilizes FIM through the *Sync* database, you will have to import the Microsoft Identity Integration Server (MIIS) key from the server running SharePoint Server 2010 where you were running the UPS application. After exporting it from your SharePoint Server 2010 farm (see Figure 8-17), you will have to import it into your SharePoint 2013 server that is running your UPS application. You will need to be a local administrator on both farms to complete the export and import, and it is suggested that you log on as the service account that runs the UPS Service (which should be your farm account).

On your SharePoint Server 2010 UPS server, open the command prompt as administrator, go to %Program Files%\Microsoft Office Servers\14.0\Synchronization Service\Bin\, and run *miiskmu.exe /e <path>*. For example:

```
C:\Program Files\Microsoft Office Servers\14.0\Synchronization Service\Bin\> miiskmu.exe /e
c:\certs\export.bin
```

FIGURE 8-17 The commands and outcome of exporting the MIIS key.

Next, you will want to log on to your SharePoint 2013 User Profile Synchronization Server as your farm account, and move the Export.bin file from your server running SharePoint Server 2010 to your server running SharePoint 2013. You will want to have your UPS and User Profile Synchronization Service stopped before importing your *.bin* file.

To import the MIISKMU key (as shown in Figure 8-18), open the command prompt as dministrator, go to %Program Files%\Microsoft Office Servers\15.0\Synchronization Service\Bin\, and run *miiskmu.exe /I <path> {0E19E162-827E-4077-82D4-E6ABD531636E}*. For example:

```
C:\Program Files\Microsoft Office Servers\15.0\Synchronization Service\Bin> miiskmu.exe /i
c:\certs\export.bin {0E19E162-827E-4077-82D4-E6ABD531636E}
```

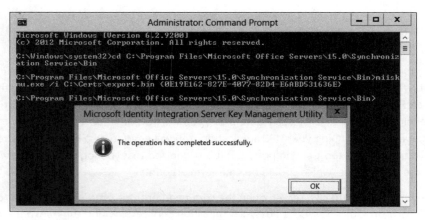

FIGURE 8-18 The commands and outcome of importing the MIIS KMU key.

When you are done with importing the certificate, you will need to restart the UPS and the User Profile Synchronization Service. (Remember that you should only start and stop your services through Windows PowerShell or through Central Administration.) While you are in Central Administration, and while you are still logged on as the farm account, now would be a good time to start your User Profile Synchronization Service instance. You will know if you have successfully provisioned everything correctly because your FIM service instances should look like Figure 8-19, and you will not be stuck on "Starting."

Extensible Authentication Protocol	The Extensi...		Manual	Local System
Forefront Identity Manager Service	Forefront Id...	Running	Automatic	CONTOSO\spFarm
Forefront Identity Manager Synchronization Service	Enables inte...	Running	Automatic	CONTOSO\spFarm
Function Discovery Provider Host	The FDPHO...		Manual	Local Service

FIGURE 8-19 Service instances showing that the FIM services have started using the farm account as the Log On As account.

Remember that at RTM, these steps will not work. There is an example of how to do a successful UPS upgrade implementation in the "Putting it all together" section later in this chapter.

Classic-mode authentication

While documenting your environment, did you run into a web application that was still in Classic mode (see Figure 8-20)?

FIGURE 8-20 An example of a SharePoint 2010 web application that is running Classic mode authentication.

You will want to change the web application to handle claims-based authentication before upgrading to SharePoint 2013. Now, that does not mean that you have to do it within your SharePoint Server 2010 production environment. You can actually do it within your SharePoint 2013 environment with a new Windows PowerShell cmdlet called *Convert-SPWebApplication*. You would do this by using Windows PowerShell to create a Classic mode authentication provider (*New-SPAuthenticationProvider*) and pushing that into your new SharePoint 2013 web application (*New-SPWebApplication*), then attach your content database, and finally run the *Convert-SPWebApplication* cmdlet. However, it might be easier to just upgrade your SharePoint Server 2010 environment to Claims mode authentication in your test environment and migrate the content database to your new SharePoint 2013 production environment after converting. Do not convert your SharePoint 2010 production web application on your live production farm! This should be done in your test environment as a step on the way to your new SharePoint 2013 farm.

Language packs

Are the required language packs available for your site collections? You must have the appropriate language packs installed to upgrade any sites based on the localized site definition. If you do not have the correct language pack installed prior to upgrade, the site will be unavailable. You should wait for the appropriate language pack to be released before trying to upgrade those sites that depend on language packs.

Limiting downtime

One of the reasons to upgrade from SharePoint Server 2010 to SharePoint 2013 is to enhance the user experience. You do not want to put a bad taste in your users' mouths by having their SharePoint Server 2010 farm down for an extended period of time. There are several options to help reduce the amount of downtime that your users will have to endure.

Read-Only mode

To help mitigate downtime and loss of data, you can put your SharePoint Server 2010 content databases into a Read-only mode. This will allow users to be able to access their data but not actually change anything, and still keep the migrated database the same as the SharePoint Server 2010 production content. You will not need to put your content databases into Read-only mode for test upgrades, but only for the final push into your production environment.

Parallel site upgrades

Another method for limiting downtime is to conduct parallel site collection upgrades. Parallel site collection upgrades are achieved by attaching your content databases and upgrading multiple site collections at the same time (see Figure 8-21). There is no maximum number of parallel upgrades that can be run simultaneously, but the number is limited by the server's hardware. Microsoft keeps you from shooting yourself in the foot by setting the default number of *SPSite* upgrades that can happen per web server to only five.

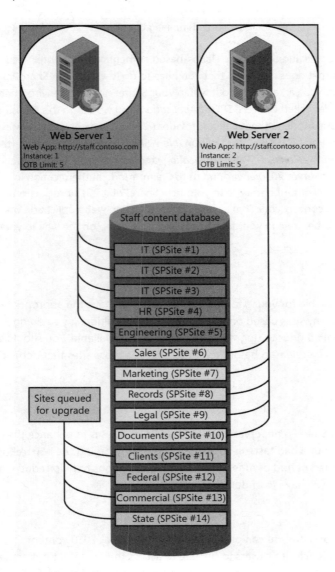

FIGURE 8-21 Parallel upgrade of content databases with more than one web server.

You can override the default throttle settings with the following Windows PowerShell script:

```
PS C:\> Add-PSSnapin Microsoft.SharePoint.PowerShell -EA 0
PS C:\> $webApp = "http://staff.contoso.com"
PS C:\> # Get Current Throttle Settings
PS C:\> $wa = Get-SPWebApplication $webApp
PS C:\> $wa.SiteUpgradeThrottleSettings
PS C:\> # Update Throttle Settings
PS C:\> $wa.SiteUpgradeThrottleSettings.AppPoolConcurrentUpgradeSessionLimit=10
PS C:\> $wa.SiteUpgradeThrottleSettings.UsageStorageLimit=15
PS C:\> $wa.SiteUpgradeThrottleSettings.SubwebCountLimit=15
PS C:\> # Verify Throttle Settings
PS C:\> $wa.SiteUpgradeThrottleSettings
```

You also have the ability to override the throttle settings when you do an upgrade to your site through Windows PowerShell by adding the *-Unthrottled* switch parameter, as follows:

```
Upgrade-SPSite [-Identity] <SPSitePipeBind> [-AssignmentCollection <SPAssignmentCollection>]
[-Confirm [<SwitchParameter>]] [-Email <SwitchParameter>] [-QueueOnly <SwitchParameter>]
[-Unthrottled <SwitchParameter>] [-VersionUpgrade <SwitchParameter>] [-WhatIf
[<SwitchParameter>]]
```

Testing your upgrade

Now that you have documented your entire existing SharePoint Server 2010 environment, it is time to start getting your hands dirty with testing. Testing is imperative to a successful production upgrade. Every step should be written down, and each time you do a test upgrade, your test script should be modified. The better you maintain your documentation, the better the chance for success at upgrading to your SharePoint 2013 production environment smoothly.

As with every kind of test, be it a SharePoint upgrade or theoretical physics, you should have goals outlined to determine whether your test was successful. What makes your upgrade successful? Is it 100 percent migration of data, with 75 percent migration of customizations, in less than 48 hours? Your opinion of what makes a successful upgrade might be different than that of your boss, and it will definitely be different than that of your boss's boss, so documentation and having the ability to justify your success criteria will be very important.

Upgrading your test farm

The following steps should be run again and again until you have met the criteria that determines a successful upgrade. You might find that as you go through your test procedures, you are changing your success criteria, and even your migration procedures. You will want to repeat these steps until you are happy (and your boss, and your boss's boss, are happy).

1. Set up your test farm.

   - This can be physical or virtual. If you are going the virtual route, please keep your SharePoint servers and SQL Server servers separate to mimic your production environment as much as possible.

- You will want to use your notes to build out your test environment to match your production environment's layout.

- You will want to use your hosts file to match URLs in your test environment for consistent naming so that you will not conflict with your production environment.

- Make sure your test environment is fully functional, and without error, before you upgrade testing.

2. Move customizations.

From your documentation, find all customizations and move/install them to the appropriate locations on your SharePoint 2013 farm.

3. Use real data.

- Prepare to move over *all* content and services databases.

- Test all your SharePoint 2010 content databases.

- Record the amount of time that it actually takes for each step.

4. Back up the content and services databases from your SharePoint Server 2010 farm.

Record the amount of time that it takes to back up each database, then move it to the appropriate server running SQL Server.

5. Test your content databases in your test farm.

Record the amount of time that it takes to test each content database.

6. Upgrade your content and services databases.

Record the amount of time that it takes to upgrade each content and services database.

7. Review database results and fix issues as necessary.

You will find your logs at %COMMONPROGRAMFILES%\Microsoft Shared\Web Server Extensions\15\LOGS.

8. Review your sites in SharePoint Server 2010 mode and verify that the site collections still work as expected.

9. Upgrade site collections and My Sites.

Record the amount of time that the upgrades take to complete.

10. Review the site upgrade log files located in your ../_catalogs/MaintenanceLogs document library.

After running through the first couple of test upgrades, you should have a good idea of how the upgrade process is going to work, and the estimated amount of downtime. Of course, the more you can do through the use of scripts to make your process more repeatable, the better. Your service application databases need to be installed in a proper order.

Validating your test upgrade

Moving your custom applications and databases is not enough to validate your upgrade. After getting your data and customizations moved into your test environment, you will want to get all your service applications running. You will want to make sure that you can crawl your farm, and that your Web Parts are working and in the correct place. Can you create a new site? Can you create a new page? Visual and behavioral issues will be the most obvious issues to find. You will want to leave the farm up and running for a day or two, then come back and review logs to help find the behind-the-scenes issues that might have arisen during upgrade or installation. You will want to run the same documentation scripts on your SharePoint 2013 environment and compare the output to the SharePoint Server 2010 documentation script output. You will also want to have your production environment available to compare Web Part functionality, branding, and load times (especially once you are in your production environment).

Learning from your deployment

Each time that you complete a test of your upgrade strategy, you should have learned and taken notes on what has failed, what has succeeded, and what was unexpected. You can then take your lessons learned and update your upgrade story to make your next attempt at an errorless upgrade to SharePoint 2013 more likely.

Implementing your upgrade

By now, you should have a solid understanding of how you are going to accomplish your upgrade to SharePoint 2013 and how long your upgrade is going to take. Having documented all your test data, you can finalize a Production Farm Upgrade Plan with a high degree of certainty for success.

Minimizing downtime

Because you want to keep your SharePoint Server 2010 farm and SharePoint 2013 farm with the same data, you will want to put your content databases into Read-only mode (as shown in Figure 8-22). Once the databases are in Read-only mode, you can back them up and start your upgrade process. Remember that once you restore the content databases to the servers running SQL Server in your new SharePoint 2013 farm, the databases will still be in Read-only mode.

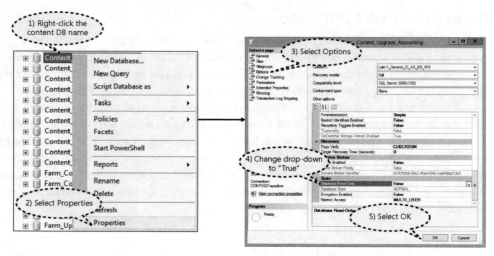

FIGURE 8-22 How to put your SQL Server databases into Read-only mode.

Upgrading your production farm

Your upgrade plan for the production farm should already be written out because you should have been able to upgrade your SharePoint 2010 farm repeatedly and successfully in your test environment. All your testing should be completed, and you should have a validated upgrade script to follow.

1. Set up your test farm.

   - You will want to use your notes from the creation of your test environment upgrade.

   - You will also want to verify that everything matches your SharePoint Server 2010 production environment layout.

   - Make sure your production farm is fully functional, and without error, before you upgrade.

2. Move your service application databases.

   Put the service application databases that you are moving into Read-only mode.

3. Upgrade and install all your service applications for your SharePoint 2013 farm.

   Verify that your services are functioning error free and your data has been moved across correctly.

4. Create SharePoint 2013 farm web applications, Alternate Access Mappings (AAMs), and other customization settings.

   - From your documentation, find all customizations and move or install them to the appropriate locations on your SharePoint 2013 farm.

   - Put your content databases into Read-only mode.

5. Move over all the required databases.

6. Test, mount, and upgrade your databases.

7. Review your logs at %COMMONPROGRAMFILES%\Microsoft Shared\Web Server Extensions\15\LOGS.

8. Review your sites in SharePoint Server 2010 mode, and verify that the site collections still work as expected.

9. Upgrade My Sites.

   Upgrade the site collections if you are responsible for that task.

10. Fix known issues according to your test scripts.

11. Review site collection results.

12. Review your site upgrade log files located in your ../_catalogs/MaintenanceLogs document library.

Monitoring progress

From Central Administration, you can monitor the upgrade process (see Figure 8-23). And just as in your test environment, you will want to audit your upgrade and ULS logs for errors.

FIGURE 8-23 This is where you go to monitor your upgrade progress.

Validating your upgrade

Because you have already perfected your upgrade scripts in your test environment, there should not be any surprises when you have finished going through your upgrade script.

Verifying your upgrade

The first thing that you will want to do is to review all logs after each upgrade. You will want to look for errors and warnings and address any issues that will cause problems for your farm later. Also, check the application event logs for errors and warnings. If you are having warnings or errors, then issues still exist. Either fix the issues while within SharePoint 2013 or fix the issue in SharePoint Server 2010 and start the upgrade process again. Remember that there is an ability to resume upgrades after the upgrade fails, but you really want to have your upgrades run smoothly by the time that you have to upgrade into your production environment.

Whether you are upgrading your company's environment or you are a consultant upgrading someone else's farm, if you run into issues in the SharePoint 2010 environment, they need to be documented. If the issues move from the SharePoint 2010 environment into the SharePoint Server 2013 environment, you do not want to be blamed as the implementer because the problem existed before the upgrade.

Troubleshooting your upgrade

If you are finding issues, you will want to start solving problems in the following order:

1. Authentication issues

   If you are having user or service accounts that cannot authenticate, then you will not be able to find any of the other issues to fix.

2. Missing files and customizations

3. Content-related issues

Remember to document your troubleshooting. Document each error that you find and what you did to find the error, as well as what you did to fix the error.

Putting it all together

Now that you have gone through how to put an upgrade strategy together, let's put what you have learned into a practical solution.

Scenario

Your chief information officer (CIO) returns from his annual golf outing with other industry-leading CIOs, and upon his return, he informs you and your team that he wants Contoso to be the first company of all his golfing friends to be on SharePoint 2013.

Current farm

Contoso has multiple SharePoint 2010 farms. They have a SharePoint 2010 Foundation farm exposed to the outside world that handles all their projects from around the world, located at *http://projects.contoso.com*. Contoso chose SharePoint 2010 Foundation to avoid having to pay the external connector fees associated with SharePoint Server 2010. Contoso also has an internal farm, at *http://staff.contoso.com*, which is a SharePoint 2010 Enterprise environment. To maintain a consistent search experience across both environments, Contoso also has a SharePoint 2010 Enterprise Search farm, at *http://search.contoso.com*. The existing SharePoint 2010 farms are shown in Figure 8-24.

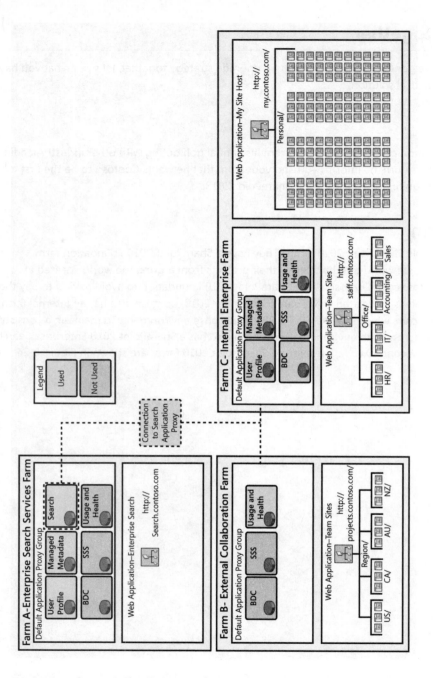

FIGURE 8-24 Contoso's SharePoint 2010 farm layout.

End goal

The final goal is to give Contoso users the best environment for the price. With the release of SharePoint 2013, there is no longer an external connector fee associated with exposing your environment to the Internet. Understanding that their environment is going to continue to grow, the business-savvy and shareholder-dollar-conscious group at Contoso has decided to keep the Internal farm web applications and Search farm in SharePoint 2013 Enterprise. The new environment should look like Figure 8-25.

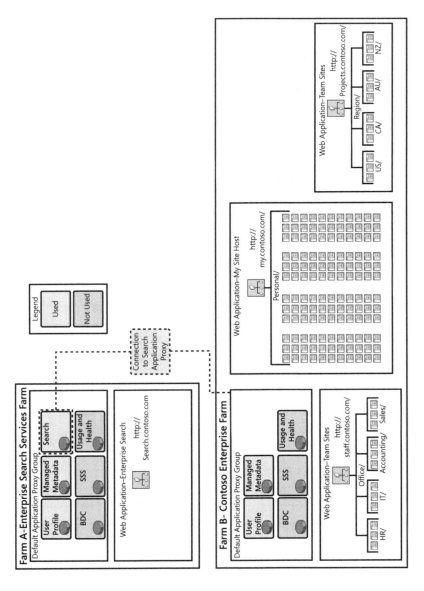

FIGURE 8-25 Contoso's SharePoint 2013 future farm layout.

By this point in the upgrade process, you should have already notified your users of the imminent upgrade to SharePoint 2013. This also should have started a process of cleaning house of old, nonpertinent data and sites. In the meantime, you should have wrapped up your documentation of your SharePoint Server 2010 environments, disabled and retracted any unused farm solutions, and even taken care of cleaning up unused sandbox solutions.

Now that everyone is busy cleaning up your old environment and your documentation is coming to a close, it is time to start building out Contoso's test environment.

Test environment

Because your goal is to have as pristine a production environment as possible, it is a good idea to build out a test environment that you can destroy and rebuild as much as needed. Once you are happy with your upgrade and migration story, then it will be time to build out your production environment. Even if you are short on resources, you can create your test environment, get your upgrade scripts perfected, destroy your test environment, and then create your production environment anew.

Because Contoso is running two separate farms in their SharePoint 2013 production environment, you are going to build out your test infrastructure to look like Figure 8-26.

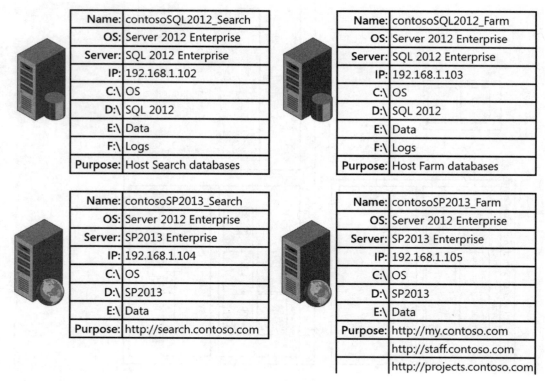

Name:	contosoSQL2012_Search
OS:	Server 2012 Enterprise
Server:	SQL 2012 Enterprise
IP:	192.168.1.102
C:\	OS
D:\	SQL 2012
E:\	Data
F:\	Logs
Purpose:	Host Search databases

Name:	contosoSQL2012_Farm
OS:	Server 2012 Enterprise
Server:	SQL 2012 Enterprise
IP:	192.168.1.103
C:\	OS
D:\	SQL 2012
E:\	Data
F:\	Logs
Purpose:	Host Farm databases

Name:	contosoSP2013_Search
OS:	Server 2012 Enterprise
Server:	SP2013 Enterprise
IP:	192.168.1.104
C:\	OS
D:\	SP2013
E:\	Data
Purpose:	http://search.contoso.com

Name:	contosoSP2013_Farm
OS:	Server 2012 Enterprise
Server:	SP2013 Enterprise
IP:	192.168.1.105
C:\	OS
D:\	SP2013
E:\	Data
Purpose:	http://my.contoso.com
	http://staff.contoso.com
	http://projects.contoso.com

FIGURE 8-26 Contoso's SharePoint 2013 future farm server layout.

Because we are talking about a test migration environment, it is acceptable to go ahead and put your data, logs, and indexes on the D:\ drive and everything else on your C:\ drive. However, your drive layout should mimic your future production environment as much as possible so that you can validate your installation and deployment scripts, as well as your migration scripts.

The first step to creating your migration strategy is to come up with the strategy and write it down someplace that is backed up. The last thing you want is to be 95 percent finished writing your migration story, only to find out that your local hard drive fried in the middle of the night. Because you are a SharePoint person, the odds are good that you will be creating an "Upgrade to 2013" site in your current 2010 environment to help you and your team stay organized and on task.

Test migration strategy

The first thing that you are going to do is create the SharePoint 2010 farm documentation. You are going to run Windows PowerShell and get as much information as possible about the current environment. You are also going to get all of the customizations annotated and create a list of any manual customization as necessary. You are going to take those several pages of notes that you have generated and put them into one master document. You are also going to start to accumulate all the *.wsp* files that will need to be installed so that you have an inventory of everything that will need to go onto your test environment servers. Do not put anything onto your test environment without having a copy of it in a folder in your "Upgrade to 2013" site, and do not move anything onto your test environment without documenting the move. While this does seem a bit excessive, you will be grateful after the first time you destroy your test environment without losing all your scripts and files.

Part of the migration strategy will be to determine which of the databases you wish to move and which ones you wish to rebuild from scratch. Your current Contoso environment has two (2) UPS instances and two (2) Managed Metadata Service (MMS) instances. To get the full functionality of Enterprise Search, UPS and MMS have to be provisioned on the Search farm. When Search for the SharePoint 2013 farm is created, you will have to re crawl the content of your environments to take advantage of the new features in SharePoint 2013 Search. This means that you will not have to move the Search farm UPS or MMS databases, but only the *Search Admin* database. The UPS and MMS will be migrated from the internal enterprise farm. Because you are running a Federated Services Search farm, you will create and upgrade Search first, then you will migrate all the content databases.

Building the test farm

You have documented all your install settings, or preferably, you have scripted out the entire installation process, so that when you go to install the production environment, you will have a proven and tested installation procedure. You have also documented everything that needs to be completed after installing the bits for SharePoint 2013 and SQL Server 2012. Remember to keep your scripts in your "Upgrade to 2013" site and update those scripts, and then copy them to your test environment before running them.

Upgrading the Search Service application

The first thing that you want to do is to move your databases from SharePoint Server 2010 to the SharePoint 2013 environment. You can either move just the service application databases, or grab all of the content databases as well. You are going to start by moving your *Search Admin* and *Content* databases from your Search farm SQL2008R2 server into your SharePoint 2013 Search farm SQL2012 server. As this is a test migration, there is no need to put any of your databases into Read-only mode. For the migration to production, you would want to put your databases into Read-only mode. After restoring your *Search Content* and *Admin* databases to your SQL2012 server, you are going to upgrade the databases (also known as *setting the compatibility level*) to SQL2012. You are going to run the following query on your server running SQL Server, where *Content_Search* is the name of the database to be altered:

```
USE master
GO
ALTER DATABASE Content_Search SET COMPATIBILITY_LEVEL = 110
GO
```

After upgrading the compatibility levels, you are going to create your service application pool account ("SharePoint Web Services Default" if you're using Windows PowerShell; otherwise, the Farm Configuration Wizard will create it), and then start the Search Service Instance:

```
PS C:\> # Get then Start Search Instance
PS C:\> $searchInstance = Get-SPEnterpriseSearchServiceInstance
PS C:\> Start-SPServiceInstance $searchInstance
```

Once the Search Service is started, you are going to mount the *Search Admin* database to SharePoint 2013:

```
PS C:\> $searchAppName = "Search Service Application"
PS C:\> $searchServiceAppDBName = "Farm_Search_Admin"
PS C:\> $databaseserver ="SQL-03"
PS C:\> $applicationPool = Get-SPServiceApplicationPool -Identity 'SharePoint Web Services Default'
PS C:\> $searchInst = Get-SPEnterpriseSearchServiceInstance -local
PS C:\> Restore-SPEnterpriseSearchServiceApplication -Name $searchAppName -applicationpool
$applicationPool '
    -databasename $searchServiceAppDBName '
    -databaseserver $databaseserver '
    -AdminSearchServiceInstance $searchInst
```

You will now have to create the Search service application proxy. You will do this by running the following script:

```
PS C:\> $searchServerName = "SP-04"
PS C:\> $serviceAppName = "Search Service Application"
PS C:\> # Start Search Service Instances
PS C:\> Write-Host "Starting Search Service Instances..."
PS C:\> Start-SPEnterpriseSearchServiceInstance $searchServerName
PS C:\> Start-SPEnterpriseSearchQueryAndSiteSettingsServiceInstance $searchServerName
PS C:\> # Create the Search Service Proxy
PS C:\> Write-Host "Creating Search Service Application and Proxy..."
PS C:\> $searchServiceApp = Get-SPEnterpriseSearchServiceApplication
```

```
PS C:\> $searchProxy = New-SPEnterpriseSearchServiceApplicationProxy -Name "$serviceAppName
Proxy" -SearchApplication $searchServiceApp
```

Once Search is online, you will want to verify your Upgrade Status to make sure that everything
went smoothly. You should also review the upgrade log file, as it too is very important to review, and
keep a copy for your records. You should create a library in your "Upgrade to 2013" site to hold your
test and production upgrade reports. Figure 8-27 shows an example of a successful Search service
application upgrade.

Selected upgrade session details	
Status	Succeeded
Server	SP-13
Start	12/12/2012 10:41:17 PM
Last Updated	12/12/2012 10:42:56 PM
Errors	0
Warnings	0
Starting object	SearchServiceApplication Name=Farm Search Service Application
Current object	
Current action	
Step within the action	0
Total steps in this action	0
Elapsed Time	00:01:39
Percentage completed	100.00%
Process Name	powershell_ise
Thread Id	3168
Process Id	4076
Command Line	C:\Windows\System32\WindowsPowerShell\v1.0\powershell_ise.exe
Log File	C:\Program Files\Common Files\Microsoft Shared\Web Server Extensions\15\LOGS\Upgrade-20121212-224117-948.log
Remedy	

FIGURE 8-27 Successful upgrade of Contoso's Search service application.

Upgrading the Search Center

To prepare for testing your content database and Search Center, you will start by modifying the hosts
file so that you can get to your Search Center URL without creating a conflict with Domain Name
System (DNS). You can find your hosts file at C:\Windows\System32\Drivers\etc\hosts.

You will be entering the IP address and URL of the Search Center.

Modifying the host file is a quick solution for testing with internal IT while getting ready for
upgrade testing. When it is time for user acceptance testing, you will want to make sure that you
have different URLs for the different stages of testing, such as *http://test.search.contoso.com* or
http://dev.projects.contoso.com.

Now that you have upgraded Search and updated your hosts file, it is time to upgrade your Search Center. If your Search Center is heavily customized, you will probably want to upgrade your content database. If you are using the out-of-the-box Search Center, then you will want to build your Search Center site from scratch, especially with the deprecation of Search Scopes. Search Scopes have been deprecated, but they are still usable from the upgrade (however, they are not modifiable). Because the Contoso Search Center is heavily customized, you will be upgrading the SharePoint Server 2010 Search Center. The first step will be to create a web application to hold your SharePoint Server 2010 Search Center content database. You will need to run the *Test-SPContentDatabase* cmdlet and fix any issues that were found with the Search Center. After fixing all pertinent issues returned, you will run the *Mount-SPContentDatabase* cmdlet, followed by checking the Upgrade Status in Central Administration.

Now you will take a look at your Search Center and make sure that you have traveled to the correct location by verifying that you now have the pink (salmon) System Status Bar on your home page. You will run your Site Collection Health Check and address any issues that have been pointed out.

You can now either request an evaluation site collection or go straight to the upgrade. Once you are happy that your Search Center is working correctly, you will go through getting Search federated to the SharePoint Server 2010 farms.

Federating the Search service

Basically, you will have to create the same trusts for the new SharePoint 2013 farm that you created for the SharePoint Server 2010 farm. You will start by exporting the certificates from both SharePoint Server 2010 farms. You will run the following Windows PowerShell cmdlet on both SharePoint Server 2010 farms and move the certificates to the SharePoint 2013 Search farm, changing the name of the file appropriately:

```
PS C:\> $rootCert = (Get-SPCertificateAuthority).RootCertificate
PS C:\> $rootCert.Export("Cert") | Set-Content "C:\Certs\SP2010-Search.cer" -Encoding byte
PS C:\> $stsCert = (Get-SPSecurityTokenServiceConfig).comLoginProvider.SigningCertificate
PS C:\> $stsCert.Export("Cert") | Set-Content "C:\Certs\SP2010-Search-STS.cer" -Encoding byte
```

After you have accumulated all four certificates, you will have to import them into the new SharePoint 2013 Search farm. You can accomplish this by running the following Windows PowerShell cmdlet on the SharePoint 2013 Search farm:

```
PS C:\> $trustCert = Get-PfxCertificate C:\Certs\StaffFarmRoot.cer
PS C:\> New-SPTrustedRootAuthority "StaffFarmRoot" -Certificate $trustCert
PS C:\> $stsCert = Get-PfxCertificate C:\Certs\StaffFarmSTS.cer
PS C:\> New-SPTrustedServiceTokenIssuer "StaffFarmRoot-STS" -Certificate $stsCert
```

You now need to export your root certificate from our SharePoint 2013 Search farm so that you can import it into your SharePoint Server 2010 farms. You can export your SharePoint 2013 certificate by running the following cmdlet:

```
PS C:\> $rootCert = (Get-SPCertificateAuthority).RootCertificate
PS C:\> $rootCert.Export("Cert") | Set-Content "C:\Certs\SearchFarmRoot-2013.cer" -Encoding byte
```

You will complete the trust relationship by importing the SharePoint 2013 root certificate to both SharePoint Server 2010 farms. You can accomplish this by running the following cmdlet on each farm:

```
PS C:\> $trustCert = Get-PfxCertificate C:\Certs\SearchFarmRoot-2013.cer
PS C:\> New-SPTrustedRootAuthority "SearchFarmRoot-2013" -Certificate $trustCert
```

Now that there is a trust between all the farms, and Search is up and running correctly, all that is left to do is change the IP address of the Host A Record for *search.contoso.com*. This change will allow you to go to the *staff.contoso.com* URL and search the farm using SharePoint 2013 Search.

Upgrading the remaining service applications

At this point, you will need to start moving the remaining service application databases to the enterprise farm. After you restore the SharePoint Server 2010 databases into the SQL2012 environment, you will upgrade them as well. Figure 8-28 shows a list of the service application databases that will be upgraded.

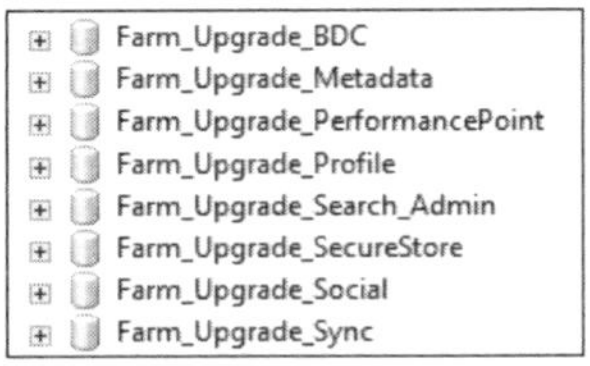

FIGURE 8-28 Contoso's service application databases that will be upgraded.

In the "Upgrading the Search Service application" section earlier in this chapter, you learned that you can run an Alter Database command to upgrade the SQL version of the database. As shown in Figure 8-29, another way to upgrade the database is to right-click the database | Properties | Options and change the Compatibility Level by selecting SQL Server 2012 (110) from the drop-down menu.

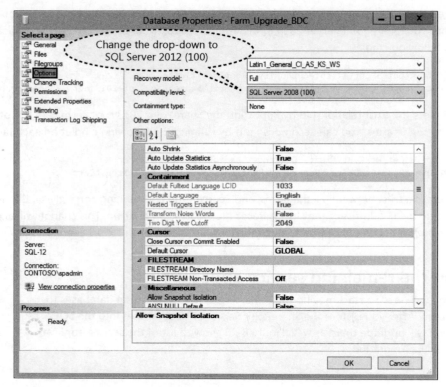

FIGURE 8-29 How to change the SQL Compatibility Level using the GUI.

Now that your databases have been restored and upgraded, it is time to create the service applications within SharePoint. After you have created your default service account, you will need to start the service instances by going to Central Administration | Application Management | Service Applications | Manage Services On Server and clicking Start next to the following services:

- Business Data Connectivity Service

- Managed Metadata Web Service

- PerformancePoint Service

- Secure Store Service

- User Profile Service

Now that all the services have been started, it is time to start creating the service applications and proxies. It is important that *you create the applications in the following order*:

Secure Store Service Application

```
PS C:\> $sssDBName = "Farm_Upgrade_SecureStore"
PS C:\> $sssKey = "Password1"
PS C:\> $appPool = Get-SPServiceApplicationPool -Identity "SharePoint Web Services Default"
PS C:\> # Upgrade Secure Store Service Application and Create Proxy
```

```
PS C:\> $sss = New-SPSecureStoreServiceApplication -Name "Farm Secure Store" -ApplicationPool
$appPool -DatabaseName $sssDBName -AuditingEnabled
PS C:\> $sssp = New-SPSecureStoreServiceApplicationProxy -Name "Farm Secure Store Proxy"
-ServiceApplication $sss -DefaultProxyGroup
PS C:\> # Upgrade Secure Store Key
PS C:\> Update-SPSecureStoreApplicationServerKey -Passphrase $sssKey -ServiceApplicationProxy $sssp
Business Data Connectivity Service Application
PS C:\> $bdcDBName = "Farm_Upgrade_BDC"
PS C:\> $appPool = Get-SPServiceApplicationPool -Identity "SharePoint Web Services Default"
PS C:\> # Upgrade Business Data Connectivity Service Application and Create Proxy
PS C:\> New-SPBusinessDataCatalogServiceApplication -Name "Farm Business Data Connectivity
Service" -ApplicationPool $appPool -DatabaseName $bdcDBName
```

Managed Metadata Service Application

```
PS C:\> $mmsDBName = "Farm_Upgrade_Metadata"
PS C:\> # Upgrade Managed Metadata Service Application and Create Proxy
PS C:\> # Get Application Pool Information
PS C:\> Write-Host ("Getting Application Pool Information")
PS C:\> $appPool = Get-SPServiceApplicationPool -Identity "SharePoint Web Services Default"
PS C:\> $mms = New-SPMetadataServiceApplication -Name "Farm Managed Metadata Service
Application" -ApplicationPool $appPool -DatabaseName $mmsDBName
PS C:\> $mmsp = New-SPMetadataServiceApplicationProxy -Name "Farm Managed Metadata Service
Application Proxy" -ServiceApplication $mms -DefaultProxyGroup
```

PerformancePoint Service Application

```
PS C:\> $ppsDBName = "Farm_Upgrade_PerformancePoint"
PS C:\> # Get Application Pool Information
PS C:\> Write-Host ("Getting Application Pool Information")
PS C:\> $appPool = Get-SPServiceApplicationPool -Identity "SharePoint Web Services Default"
PS C:\> $pps = New-SPPerformancePointServiceApplication -Name "Farm PerformancePoint Service
Application" -ApplicationPool $appPool -DatabaseName $ppsDBName
PS C:\> $ppsp = New-SPPerformancePointServiceApplicationProxy -Name "Farm PerformancePoint
Service Application Proxy" -ServiceApplication $pps -Default
```

You can download a copy of the upgrade script from *http://sdrv.ms/SCIEq9*.

UPS application

You are already aware that at RTM, the *Sync* database upgrade is not functioning correctly. To get around this problem, you are not going to upgrade the *Sync* database, only the *Profile* and *Social* databases. So when you restore the UPS databases, you are going to let the upgrade process create a new *Sync* database for you.

To upgrade UPS, you will need to be logged on as the farm account and open SharePoint Management Shell as an administrator. You are going to run the following script to upgrade the *Profile* and *Social* databases, create a new *Sync* database, and then create the UPS proxy:

```
PS C:\> $profileDBName = "Farm_Upgrade_UPS_Profile" # Should be in DB
PS C:\> $socialDBName = "Farm_Upgrade_UPS_Social" # Should be in DB
PS C:\> $syncDBName = "Farm_Upgrade_UPS_Sync" # Should NOT be in DB
# Get Application Pool Information
PS C:\> Write-Host ("Getting Application Pool Information")
PS C:\> $appPool = Get-SPServiceApplicationPool -Identity "SharePoint Web Services Default"
```

```
PS C:\> <# Upgrade User Profile Service Application and Create Proxy
 The SocialDBName and ProfileSyncDBName parameters are optional. If you do not specify these
parameters, new Social and Sync databases are created for you.
#>
PS C:\> Write-Host ("Upgrading User Profile Service Application and Create Proxy")
PS C:\> $upa = New-SPProfileServiceApplication -Name "Farm User Profile Service Application"
-ApplicationPool $appPool -ProfileDBName $profileDBName -SocialDBName $socialDBName
-ProfileSyncDBName $syncDBName
PS C:\> $upap = New-SPProfileServiceApplicationProxy -Name "Farm User Profile Service
Application Proxy" -ServiceApplication $upa -DefaultProxyGroup
```

After the successful running of the previous script, you will need to go into Central Administration, as the farm account, and start the User Profile Synchronization Service instance.

You can download the script from *http://sdrv.ms/Z6xtLr.*

Figure 8-30 shows a successful upgrade of the UPS.

Profiles	
Number of User Profiles	23,542
Number of User Properties	93
Number of Organization Profiles	1
Number of Organization Properties	15
Audiences	
Number of Audiences	1
Uncompiled Audiences	0
Audience Compilation Status	Idle
Audience Compilation Schedule	Every Saturday at 01:00 AM
Last Compilation Time	Ended at 12/1/2012 1:00 AM
Profile Synchronization Settings	
Synchronization Schedule (Incremental)	Disabled
Profile Synchronization Status	Idle

FIGURE 8-30 Successful import and upgrade of user profiles from Contoso's SharePoint 2010 environment.

Trust but verify

All our service applications that could be upgraded should now be up and running in the Default Application proxy group. You will want to verify that your service applications are in the correct location by running the following script:

```
PS C:\> # Verify Services are in the Default Application Proxy Group
PS C:\> $pg = Get-SPServiceApplicationProxyGroup
PS C:\> $pg.Proxies
```

You will also want to review the upgrade documentation and save copies of the log files for reference.

Service application creation

Because you have all your upgraded service applications created and verified, now would be the perfect time to build out the rest of the service applications that you and your organization plan on using. Please remember to test your applications, add documents to libraries, and make sure that your search is actually working. Your service applications should be working correctly before proceeding with your upgrade, as there is no reason to spend time upgrading content if you need to destroy your test farm due to a poor service application installation. It is much safer to start your installation over again than chase bugs and little oddities through out the life of your farm.

Customizations

You should now have the backbone of your SharePoint 2013 farm up and running without error. The next step is to create your web applications, AAMs, and customizations, and deploy any *.wsp* files and third-party tools that are going to be required for your successful upgrade. Because you are upgrading your My Sites, you will also need to verify your managed paths and Self-Service Site Creation settings. Ideally, this process should be scripted so that when it comes time to build out your next version of your test environment, or when it comes time to create your production environment, things will go smoothly and consistently. To be able to start testing your site customizations and your site collections without interrupting your production environment, you will want to modify the hosts file, as described in the "Upgrading the Search Center" section earlier in this chapter.

Upgrading the content databases

At this point, you have built out your service applications and your web applications, set your bindings in Internet Information Services (IIS), and modified your hosts file. You are finally ready to test and mount your content databases from your projects farm and from your staff farm into your SharePoint 2013 staff farm. You are going to follow the same procedure that you used to restore your service application databases in the "Upgrading the remaining service applications" section earlier in this chapter: restore the content databases and then change the compatibility level. You will now want to run the *Test-SPContentDatabase* cmdlet against the restored databases and address any issues that arise. As with every other phase of testing, documentation is very important. Having output files from your test is very important for keeping a record trail, and they also show the developers that the files that they have not upgraded are holding up your upgrade to SharePoint 2013.

After cleaning up any issues that made their way from your SharePoint Server 2010 environment, you will need to make sure that you have removed the content databases associated with your SharePoint 2013 web applications. To accomplish this, you would go to Central Administration | Application Management | Databases | Manage Content Databases, select your web application's content database, and then select Remove Content Database.

Next you are going to mount all your content databases using the *Mount-SPContentdatabase* cmdlet. The following script is used to mount the content databases to the Projects web application:

```
PS C:\> $databases = ("Content_Upgrade_AU","Content_Upgrade_NZ","Content_Upgrade_CA","Content_
Upgrade_US","Content_Upgrade_Projects")
PS C:\> foreach ($db in $databases)
  {
    $DbServer = "SQL-12"
    $webApp = "http://projects.contoso.com"
    Mount-SPContentDatabase -name $db -webapplication $webApp -DatabaseServer $DbServer
  }
You can download the script from http://sdrv.ms/W3abEp.
```

After your databases have been mounted, you will want to surf to your site collections and make sure that you can actually bring up your SharePoint Server 2010 sites in your SharePoint 2013 environment. You will also want to go to Central Administration | Check Upgrade Status, get the associated log files, and verify that the upgrade went according to plan.

You will now want to run the same cmdlets and follow the same procedures for the *Staff Web Application* database upgrades.

Upgrading My Site content

Upgrading My Sites is a bit different from upgrading a site collection database. Because you already have created the My Site web application, you will want to verify that you can actually create a My Site before trying to upgrade.

At this point, you should also have your User Profile Synchronization up and running and have tested your user profile source import. While you are within the Manage Profile Service page, verify your My Site settings by going to Setup My Sites. You will want to pay close attention to the Site Naming Format settings. The way that you come up with your My Site URL must be the same way that you provisioned in SharePoint Server 2010; otherwise, people will never get to their My Site. That means that if you had opted to "resolve conflicts by creating a domain_username" in SharePoint Server 2010, then you will want to change your option button selection to "do not resolve conflicts." Once you have successfully created your SharePoint 2013 My Site, and UPS is running, you will want to remove the content database from the My Site web application. From within the Manage Profile Service page, you should also review the Manage User Profiles to review the profile of the users to make sure that the personal site information is correct (see Figure 8-31).

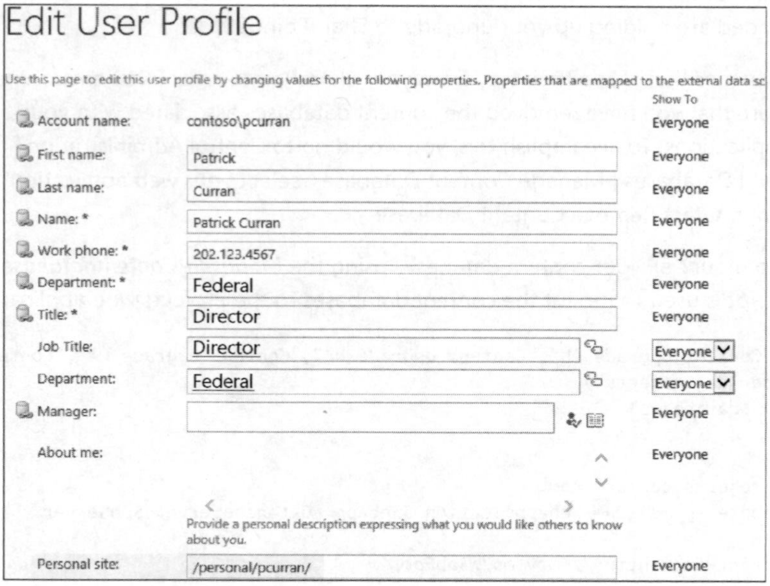

FIGURE 8-31 Verify that the Personal Site information is correct.

You will now want to run the *Test-SPContentDatabase* cmdlet, followed by the *Mount-SPContentDatabase* cmdlet, following the same logic that you used to test and mount the databases for the *projects.contoso.com* web application from the previous section. Figure 8-32 is an example of what your My Site looks like after you mount your *My Site* database (looks familiar, right?).

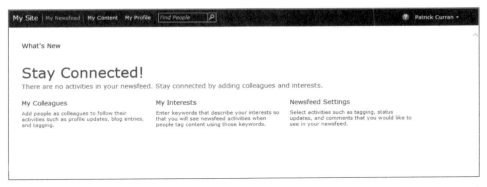

FIGURE 8-32 An example of what My Site looks like before the host site collection has been upgraded.

When it is time to start upgrading everyone's My Site, you will run the *Upgrade-SPSite* cmdlet for the host site collection first, and then let users decide when they want to upgrade their content to SharePoint 2013.

```
Upgrade-SPSite http://my.contoso.com -VersionUpgrade -Unthrottled
```

Once you upgrade the host, your My Site should look like Figure 8-33.

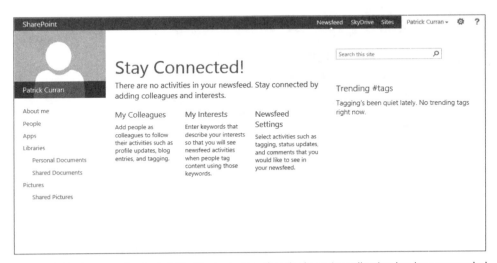

FIGURE 8-33 An example of what My Site looks like after the host site collection has been upgraded.

If you click Libraries, you will see a very familiar sight, as well as the pink System Notification bar letting your users know that they can upgrade their My Site, as shown in Figure 8-34.

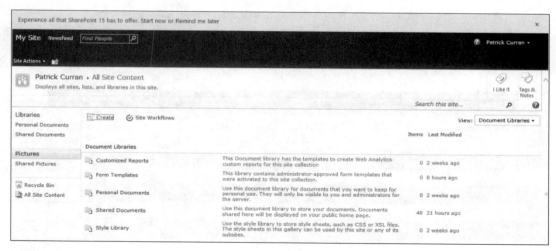

FIGURE 8-34 My Site before the site owner has started the My Site upgrade process.

Farm administrators have the option of running the *Upgrade-SPSite* cmdlet on any of the My Sites to push the upgrade manually. After the My Site has been upgraded, your users will be welcomed by the new pop-up window shown in Figure 8-35.

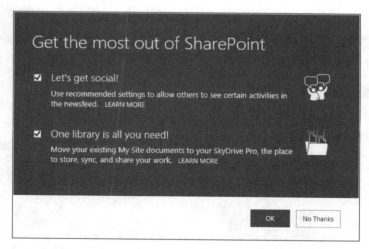

FIGURE 8-35 The new pop-up window that allows users to upgrade their settings.

Upgrading sites

At this point, it is time to go through your sites and verify that all your sites come up in SharePoint Server 2010 (SP14) mode. You will then run the Site Collection Health Check and fix any outstanding issues. Figure 8-36 shows you an example of the Results page after you run a Site Collection Health Check.

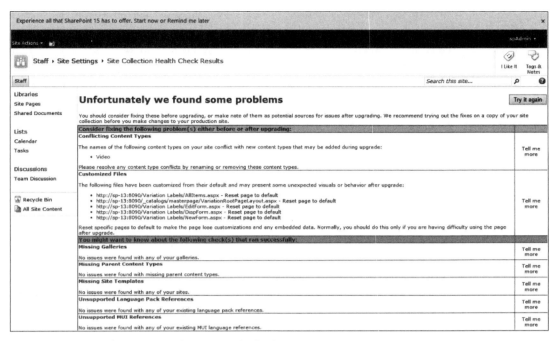

FIGURE 8-36 Results from a Site Collection Health Check.

If you run into a 404 error (site not found), verify that you have your hosts file set up correctly.

To get a list of all the site collections (including My Sites) and their compatibility levels, use the *Get-SPSite* cmdlet. However, to avoid creating a huge memory leak, get your *SPSite* information by running either of the following Windows PowerShell scripts:

```
PS C:\> $sites = Get-SPSite -Limit All; $sites; $sites.Dispose()
```

or

```
PS C:\> Start-SPAssignment -Global
PS C:\>    Get-SPSite -Limit All
PS C:\> Stop-SPAssignment -Global
```

To resolve the errors, Microsoft has been kind enough to give you guidance on how to fix your issues, and once the issues have been addressed, you will start your site collection upgrade process.

The purpose of your test environment is to get you comfortable with your upgrade story. By the time your upgrade story is completed, you will probably have upgraded your site collection dozens of times in your test environment, getting all the upgrade breaking issues resolved. This thorough testing will allow you skip the use of the new Request Evaluation Site Collection feature in your production environment. Remember that if you request the evaluation site collection, that the timer job goes off once a day and you will want to start the Create Upgrade Evaluation Site Collection job manually for the appropriate web application.

Theoretically, you would really only need to create an evaluation site collection in production to make sure that you are aware of all the headaches that are going to arise before your clients run into issues after the upgrade. This means the only reason that you would not be aware of all the issues for your sites and site collections that lay ahead would be because you skipped the test environment phase.

To upgrade a site collection, you are going to run the *Upgrade-SPSite* cmdlet, but because this is a test environment, you are going to upgrade them all at once using the following Windows PowerShell script:

```
PSC:\> $databases = ("Content_Upgrade_AU","Content_Upgrade_NZ","Content_Upgrade_CA","Content_
Upgrade_US","Content_Upgrade_Projects")
PSC:\> foreach ($db in $databases)
  {
    Get-SPSite -ContentDatabase $db -Limit All | Upgrade-SPSite -VersionUpgrade -QueueOnly
  }
```

The *-QueueOnly* parameter adds the site collections to the upgrade queue. This will allow the timer job to perform parallel upgrades when it is possible and can save time. The sites are upgraded in the order in which they are added to the queue. Depending on the number of CPU cores and RAM of your test environment, you may want to consider running a script to get your test upgrade accomplished quicker. You should try running both a throttled and an unthrottled site collection upgrade and tracking the upgrade completion times on your environment because putting the site collections into the queue might actually upgrade faster depending on the environment. To upgrade your sites without a throttle enabled, run the following Windows PowerShell script:

```
PS C:\> Get-SPSite -ContentDatabase $db -Limit All | Upgrade-SPSite -VersionUpgrade -
Unthrottled
```

You can download the script from *http://sdrv.ms/RueCa2*.

Once you have upgraded your site collections, you should review the upgrade logs. You can either surf to each site collection, go to ../_catalogs/MaintenanceLogs, and review the documents in place, or you can run a script that will grab all the upgrade documents and place them into a local folder for review. You can download that script from *http://sdrv.ms/WeE9ph*.

Back to Search

Now that your Contoso content is back up and has been successfully upgraded, you need to incorporate your federated Search farm. You are going to use the same steps that you used in incorporating the Search farm back into your SharePoint Server 2010 environment from the "Federating the Search service" section earlier in this chapter. You are going to exchange certificates to establish a trust between farms and add a sharing permission to the publishing farm for the Discovery and Load Balancer application (for Consuming Farm ID). You will then publish the Search Service application from the Search farm and put the published URL in the consuming farm.

Finally!

You have verified that everything works locally on your test environment, and the Contoso users would be able to work within your new SharePoint 2013 environment if you repointed your DNS to your test farm. At this point, there only a couple of steps left. You will want to go to each of your test servers and back up all your documentation, scripts, favorites, and anything else that you might have downloaded or referenced and move that information into your "Upgrade to 2013" site. Once you are satisfied that you have all your data safely backed up, it is time to destroy your test environment and rebuild it from scratch. Once you have the base operating system installed, you will want to try your upgrade script again to validate your success.

Now that you have successfully upgraded your SharePoint Server 2010 environment twice and verified that your upgrade script is correct, you can start your production upgrade. The only difference between the test and production upgrades is that at the end of your production upgrade, you will have to ask your network administrator to point your DNS entries to your new production servers.

## PART 3

Concepts for infrastructure reliability

CHAPTER 9

Maintaining and monitoring Microsoft SharePoint

In this chapter, you will learn about:

- Monitoring a SharePoint environment.

- Tuning and optimizing a SharePoint environment.

- Troubleshooting a SharePoint environment.

- Putting it all together.

Once you have designed and built the Microsoft SharePoint 2013 environment, you must then maintain it. The maintenance cycle, shown in Figure 9-1, contains three phases: monitoring, tuning and optimizing, and troubleshooting.

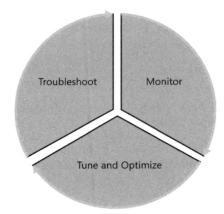

FIGURE 9-1 The maintenance cycle contains three phases.

The primary goal of the monitoring phase is to make sure that SharePoint is operating within the performance objectives that have been defined during the requirements gathering phase. Examples of such requirements may be short response times of HTTP requests, fast page loads, or ensuring that critical issues, like disk space, do not become factors. SharePoint 2013 can be monitored using SharePoint Central Administration, performance counters, System Center Management Pack for SharePoint Server 2013, and Windows PowerShell scripts. The SharePoint farm administrator or architect can then review the reports or logs from these tools and begin the tuning and optimizing phase of the maintenance cycle. This chapter will discuss configuring performance counters and examining page performance, which will help you identify any areas that may need attention.

The tuning and optimizing phase may require the SharePoint professional to perform a number of tasks. Some of these tasks may include reviewing Microsoft SQL Server for areas that can be optimized, ensuring that the software is running within its prescribed boundaries, configuring caching, or tuning the network. Most of the heath analyzer issues will have tips that will help you resolve them; other may require a little more troubleshooting.

The troubleshooting phase is often the most challenging phase of the maintenance cycle. There are a number of tools and techniques that you can use to isolate any issues that plague the system. Reviewing the Windows event logs, ULS logs, SQL Server logs, and security logs, as well as tracing events, can help lead you in the right direction. Furthermore, additional information may be obtained by using the throttle logging event severities or going through a troubleshooting triage to find out what has changed in the environment. Once the issue has been found and fixed, it is time to start the cycle of maintenance all over again.

Monitoring a SharePoint environment

One of the most critical components of the SharePoint cycle of maintenance is monitoring the health and performance of the SharePoint 2013 farm. Often, organizations learn that their environment is unhealthy when it goes down. When SharePoint goes down, it may be difficult to find the root cause in a timely manner, so monitoring the environment is important to the success of the implementation. Monitoring on a regular basis is also important as user adoption grows. SharePoint solutions that once worked within the acceptable boundaries may start to lag as more concurrent users are added.

Success in a SharePoint implementation can mean a number of things. In order to ensure that the stakeholders are happy with the design and performance of SharePoint, it is important to define monitoring requirements for both performance and reliability. The goal of defining monitoring requirements is to find bottlenecks or potential issues before they become critical.

Your goal is to provide the most responsive and reliable system. Nothing can be more frustrating to the information worker than the site taking too long to render its contents. After you have defined the rules in which the environment must run, you should turn your focus to capturing the data that you need in order to ensure a healthy environment.

SharePoint's Usage and Health Data Collection service application is built specifically for this purpose. When the Usage and Health Data Collection service application is provisioned, SharePoint 2013 writes usage and health data to the logging folder and to the logging database. You can use the SharePoint Central Administration website to configure health data collection settings. If properly used, this information can be used to safeguard the heath of the overall SharePoint farm. Later in this chapter you will gain an understanding of storage needs so you can ensure that your organization has enough space to collect critical data.

Understanding SharePoint monitoring requirements

SharePoint is built to be both scalable and resilient, but it depends on the architecture that supports it. After reviewing a number of failed SharePoint implementations, the issues all too often are a result of failure to plan, failure to monitor, and failure to understand the minimum requirements.

One of the first monitoring requirements that you must understand in order to have a successful SharePoint implementation is the Requests per Second (RPS). SharePoint can be built on a single server and can support 100,000 users so long as only a few users are accessing the system concurrently. You will explore this topic further in Chapter 11, "Validating your architecture." Next, you need to understand what the term *concurrently* means. Most SharePoint professionals know that SharePoint should be built to support a variable number of concurrent users, but ask the professional what defines a concurrent user and the time frame of the measurement, and you will most likely get a blank stare. To ensure that everyone is on the same page, the number of concurrent users is the number of unique users who are accessing the system within a given minute. You will learn how to validate your SharePoint farm design for concurrent users in Chapter 11.

As monitoring requirements are defined, it is important to specify who will perform the monitoring task and at what interval. Depending on the size of the SharePoint farm, there may be a number of team members who are responsible for the overall health and reliability of the environment. The monitoring requirements should be defined and then documented. As the needs of the organization change, the requirements should be updated to reflect those needs. Microsoft provides a number of tools that can be used for monitoring and troubleshooting the SharePoint environment, each covering various aspects of the environment. These tools include:

- **SharePoint Health Analyzer**   This feature is built into Central Administration. It's used to analyze and resolve problems in the following areas: security, performance, configuration, and availability. Health Analyzer rules are predefined and run at scheduled intervals, such as hourly, daily, weekly, and monthly. If an error is detected, the corresponding rule is triggered. Each rule has a brief explanation about why the error occurs and provides you with a link to a detailed article that contains step-by-step guidance to resolve the problem. When you take actions by following the guidance, you can rerun the rule to verify resolution. If the error does not appear in the list, the problem is resolved.

- **Timer jobs**   The Health Analysis job collects health data and then writes the data to the logging folder and logging database. The data is used in reports to display the farm's health status.

- **Reporting**   After configuring diagnostic logging and data collection, the farm administrator can view administrative and health reports. Due to some configurations will use up drive space and adversely affect system performance, you must carefully plan this configuration and which selected categories are important.

- **Windows PowerShell**   SharePoint contains a set of health-focused cmdlets that allows you to monitor SharePoint 2013 and view the logs.

- **System Center 2012 (SCOM)**   Operations Manager with System Center Management Pack for SharePoint Server 2013 can be used as an add-on to supplement System Center 2012. By using Operations Manager, you can view status, health, performance information, and alerts generated for availability, performance, configuration, and security situations. To use Operations Manager to monitor SharePoint products, you can install System Center Management Pack for SharePoint Server 2013 or configure the counters manually. You can use this tool to monitor events, collect SharePoint component-specific performance counters in one central location, and raise alerts for operator intervention as necessary.

- **Event viewer**   This lets you browse and manage event logs and is handy for troubleshooting problems. You can filter for specific events across multiple logs and reuse useful event filters as custom views.

- **SharePoint Developer Dashboard**   This utility provides diagnostic information that can help a developer or system administrator analyze performance of SharePoint webpages. For example, it can help if a page is loading slowly, a Web Part is not performing, or a database query on the page is not performing the way that it should.

- **Windows Management Instrumentation (WMI)**   This provides many classes that you can use to monitor the SharePoint 2013 environment. For each manageable resource, there is a corresponding WMI class. While SCOM provides a great solution, the WMI can be used to provide extensibility.

- **Microsoft SQL Server Reporting Services (SSRS)**   This helps you create, deploy, and manage reports for your organization.

In addition to defining and documenting who will be monitoring the environment and what tools will be used, a set of operational checklists should be defined, along with the frequency of when the tasks should be completed. There are some processes that should be performed on a daily basis, while others can be done on a weekly or monthly schedule. While the following lists may not answer every organization's needs, they should provide solid guidance for the vast majority of them. Once the maintenance requirements have been documented, they will be much easier to verify.

Daily processes

The following processes should be performed daily:

- Ensure that the daily backup completed successfully.

- Analyze and respond to backup warnings and errors.

- Perform a SharePoint farm backup and verify its completion.

- Follow the established procedures for backup rotation, labeling, and storage.

- Check if the trace logs are being backed up.

- Make sure the backups completed with the tolerance specified in the service level agreement (SLA).

- If custom solutions are part of the backup plan, verify that they completed.

- Review SharePoint audit logs.

- Review the scheduled and important timer jobs and verify that they are completed successfully.

- Check CPU and Memory Used.

- Examine the % Processor Time performance counter.

- Examine the Available MBs performance counter.

- Examine the % Committed Bytes In Use performance counter.

- Check against a performance baseline to determine the health of a server.

- Check Disk Use.

- Check disks with transaction log files.

- Check disks with trace log files.

- Check other farm server disks.

- Use server monitors to check free disk space.

- Check performance of disks.

- Check Disk Health (S.M.A.R.T.).

- Review the event logs.

- Check the trace logs.

- Review the security logs for any unauthorized activities or failures.

- Check the ULS logs.

- Respond to discovered failures and problems.

- Check IIS—IIS Logs and Performance.

- Review System Monitor for IIS performance and examine the output of performance counters.

- Verify that the application pools have enough memory and check if they are running correctly. Look for recycle events and memory leaks.

- Ensure that the application pools are recycled every day.

- Review the SharePoint Health Analyzer messages.

- Check the size of the site collections.

- Check the number of site collections per content database.

- Check the size of the content database.

- Check health reports.

- Check diagnostic logs.

- View the security event log and investigate unauthorized changes.

- Check security news for the latest viruses, worms, and vulnerabilities.

- Update and fix discovered security problems.

- Verify that Secure Sockets Layer (SSL) is functioning correctly.

- Confirm that the firewall is working as expected.

- Verify that SharePoint Server and the required Windows services have started correctly.

Weekly processes

The following processes should be performed weekly:

- Confirm that the backups can be successfully restored.

- Review and report uptime and availability.

- Review database sizes to ensure that they are in the expected ranges.

- Capacity reports.

- Queue use, size, and growth.

- Growth of SharePoint site collections being created.

- Incident reports.

- SharePoint database maintenance.

- Perform database consistency checks to ensure that your data and indexes are not corrupted. You can use the Database Console Command (*DBCC* (Database Console Command)) *CHECKDB* statement to perform an internal consistency check of the data and index pages and to repair errors.

- Measure and, if necessary, reduce database fragmentation. This is the result of many inserts, updates, or deletes to a table. When a table becomes fragmented, the indexes defined on the table also become fragmented, affecting performance.

- Check and compose IIS logs.

- Check and compose SharePoint ULS logs.

- Record, review, and compare the set of installed features with the previously recorded set. Confirm that all changes were authorized.

- Review, record, and compare SharePoint policies with the previous set. Confirm that all changes were authorized.

- Check to make sure the Farm Administrators group contains authorized personnel.

- Run a security report that outputs a full audit of the permissions assigned to sites.

- Create reports specifying your findings.

- Update virus definitions and scan for viruses.

Monthly processes

The following processes should be performed monthly:

- Review the capacity planning requirements and ensure that the farm is operating within the appropriate parameters.

- Check the computer's capacity and performance against SLA requirements.

- Review SLA requirements and capacity figures from the previous month.

- Hotfixes, service packs, update rollups, and security updates.

- Perform a disaster recovery test. Test one backup a month to restore.

Monitoring the health of SharePoint

SharePoint 2013 has a number of tools that are built into the product to help monitor the health of the environment. The first tool we will examine is the SharePoint Health Analyzer, which enables farm administrators to check automatically for potential configuration, performance, and usage problems within the SharePoint farm. The feature is dependent on a number of rules that range in severity, including: Error, Warning, Information, Success, and Rule Execution Failure. When one or more issues are found, the farm administrator is notified by an alert banner in the Central Administration home page, as shown in Figure 9-2.

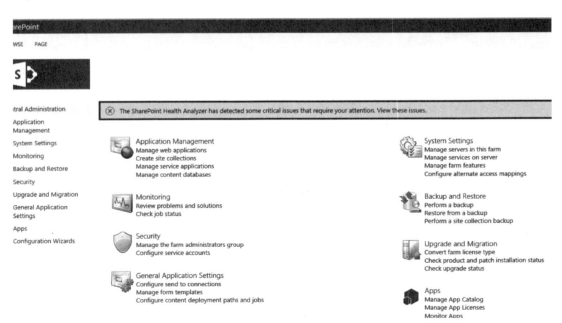

FIGURE 9-2 The Health Analyzer alerts of potential issues.

The farm administrator may click the highlighted link or review the issues by clicking Monitoring | Review Problems And Solutions With Central Administrator. The Review Problems And Solutions screen, shown in Figure 9-3, lists the issues by category and severity.

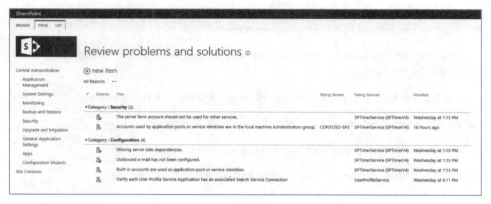

FIGURE 9-3 You can review problems within the SharePoint farm.

Each of the rules that support the Health Analyzer is customizable, and other rules can be added to the system. The built-in rules allow the farm administrator to schedule them hourly, daily, weekly, monthly, or on demand only. Each of the rules can be enabled or disabled depending on what needs to be monitored, and some of them have the ability to do automatic repairs. Each rule offers the farm administrator general guidance on how to correct the issue. Each option also has a Reanalyze Now feature that will rerun the rule to see if the problem still persists; this is available once you click the item in the problem list. Because these issues are presented in the form of a SharePoint list, administrators can take advantage of features like Alerts and RSS to stay on top of issues as they come in. To see a complete list of the rules that are configured for the given SharePoint farm, visit Monitoring | Review Rule Definitions.

It is important to not ignore problems when they arise. If the farm administrator are used to seeing the notification bar and not reviewing the issues they might miss critical issues when they are encountered.

Configuring usage and health provider settings

The Usage And Health Data Collection service application is one of the only SharePoint service applications that must be provisioned using Windows PowerShell; the others being the Subscription service and State service. In order to provision the service, use the *New-SPUsageApplication* cmdlet, as shown in Listing 9-1.

> Warning: Use of the SharePoint Farm Configuration Wizard will configure the services using the farm account and will not leave them in a desirable state. Using the configuration wizard is discouraged for production environments.

LISTING 9-1 Provision the Usage And Health Data Collection Service Application

```
PS C:\>$usageName = "Contoso Usage and Health Data Collection Service"
PS C:\>$usageDBName = "Contoso_Usage"
PS C:\>$serviceInstance = Get-SPUsageService
PS C:\>New-SPUsageApplication -Name $usageName -DatabaseName $usageDBName
-UsageService $serviceInstance
PS C:\>$UP = Get-SPServiceApplicationProxy | where {$_.TypeName -eq 'Usage and
Health Data Collection Proxy'}
PS C:\>$UP.Provision()
```

In addition to the *New-SPUsageApplication* cmdlet, Windows PowerShell can be used to review and modify the settings of the usage application. To review the settings or to get a reference to the object, use the *Get-SPUsageApplication* cmdlet. The *Set-SPUsageApplication* cmdlet, shown in Listing 9-2, can then be used to change settings related to the application to enable logging or change the database:

LISTING 9-2 Using Windows PowerShell to Modify the Usage Application

```
PS C:\>$ua = Get-SPUsageApplication
PS C:\>Set-SPUsageApplication -Identity $ua -EnableLogging
```

In addition to the *Set-SPUsageApplication* cmdlet, Windows PowerShell offers the cmdlets to review and modify the Usage service. To review the settings, use the *Get-SPUsageService* cmdlet. The *Set-SPUsageService* can then be used to modify the settings. Review Listing 9-3 to see how these two cmdlets work together.

LISTING 9-3 Using Windows PowerShell to Modify the Usage Service

```
PS C:\>$us = Get-SPUsageService
PS C:\>$logs = "D:\SharePoint\LOGS\"
PS C:\>$us | Set-SPUsageService -LoggingEnabled $true -UsageLogLocation $logs
```

The *Set-SPUsageService* cmdlet can be used to modify the location of the logs, the maximum drive space the logs will consume, and the cut time, along with a number of other things. It should be noted that the cmdlet does *not* validate the path of the usage log location.

Finally, Windows PowerShell offers cmdlets to review and modify the retention periods of the various usage providers, as shown in Listing 9-4.

LISTING 9-4 Using Windows PowerShell to Modify Usage Providers

```
PS C:\>$Set-SPUsageDefinition -Identity "Page Requests" -DaysRetained 31
PS C:\>$Set-SPUsageDefinition -Identity "SQL Exceptions Usage" -Enable
PS C:\>$Get-SPUsageDefinition
```

The usage providers are as follows:

Analytics Usage	App Monitoring	App Statistics
Bandwidth Monitoring	Content Export Usage	Content Import Usage
Usage fields for Education Telemetry	Usage fields for Microblog Telemetry	Usage fields for Service Calls
Usage fields for *SPDistrutedCache* Calls	Usage fields for workflow Telemetry	Feature Use
File IO	Page Requests	Rest and Client API Action Usage
Rest and Client API Request Usage	Sandbox Request Resource Measures	Sandbox Requests
SQL Exceptions Usage	SQL IO Usage	SQL Latency Usage
Task Usage	Tenant Logging	Timer Jobs
User Profile Active Directory Import Usage	User Profile to SharePoint Sync...	

The same settings that are available through the various Windows PowerShell cmdlets are also available through the UI. To view and configure the Usage And Health Data Collection service application settings, go to Central Administration | Monitoring | Configure Usage And Health Data Collection. The options shown in Figure 9-4 will be available.

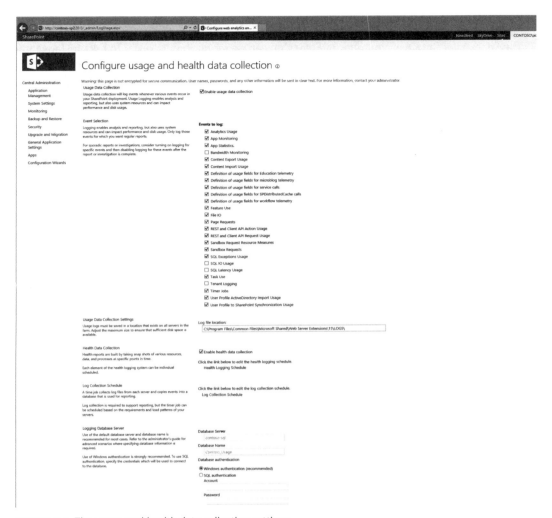

FIGURE 9-4 The usage and health data collection settings.

The user interface offers links to both the Heath Logging Schedule and the Log Collection Schedule. The Health Logging Schedule link will display the various job definitions and will allow the farm administrator allow the farm administrator to schedule, run, or toggle jobs on or off. The Log Collection Schedule will show job definitions for data importing and processing.

The data in the usage database can be viewed within the View Analytics reports option in the Monitoring section of Central Administration. Custom queries can also be generated to go directly against the usage database to give some very robust reporting capabilities. Each table in the database contains one day's worth of data. It can be tricky to find the data that you are looking for until all of the tables have collected data.

Monitoring performance counters

The SharePoint farm has a number of areas that can be monitored. In order to take full advantage of the tools that are available out of the box, the Usage And Health Data Collection service application should be providing data to the usage database. The usage database stores health monitoring and usage data temporarily and is also used for reporting and diagnostics. The usage database is the only SharePoint database that can be queried directly and have schema modified by either Microsoft or third-party applications. By default, the data from the SharePoint logs are aggregated into the database every 30 minutes—later in this chapter, we will discuss how to modify this value to help troubleshoot problems.

Some of the more generic performance counters that should be monitored on each server in the farm include:

- **Processor**   Should be below 80 percent during regular operations. If it is higher, the system may not be able to handle any sudden surges of activity. In the event of multiple servers that have the roles balanced, the average CPU across all servers should be under 60 percent so that if one fails, the other servers are able to handle the increased load.

- **Network Interface**   Shows the amount of data that is sent and received over the network interface card (NIC). This should remain below 50 percent of network capacity.

- **Disks and Cache**   The available disk space is critical for SharePoint. Not only is content stored in databases, but Search indexes and log files are stored on disks. The read and write operations should be reviewed to ensure optimum performance.

- **Memory and Paging File**   Shows how much physical memory is available for allocation. Insufficient memory will lead to excessive use of the page file and an increase in the number of page faults per second.

Once the usage database has been provisioned, SharePoint professionals are able to add various performance counters that can help monitor and evaluate the farm's overall performance. To review the performance counters that are configured in a SharePoint farm, use the *Get-SPDiagnosticPerformanceCounter* cmdlet. You can elect to only receive performance counters for either the *-DatabaseServer* or *-WebFrontEnd* server by using the corresponding parameters. An example of the cmdlet is shown in Listing 9-5. We will take a look at how to add performance counters using the *Add-SPDiagnosticsPerformanceCounter* later in this chapter.

LISTING 9-5 The *Get- SPDiagnosticsPerformanceCounter*

```
PS C:\> $counters = Get-SPDiagnosticsPerformanceCounter
PS C:\> $counters | Format-List
InstanceNames              : {*}
MonitorAllInstances        : True
CategoryName               : SharePoint Foundation
CounterNames               : {Global Heap Size, Native Heap Count, Process ID}
```

```
LocalizedCategoryName       : SharePoint Foundation
ProviderName                : job-diagnostics-performance-counter-wfe-provider
UpgradedPersistedProperties : {}
InstanceNames               : {OWSTIMER, W3WP, DISTRIBUTEDCACHESERVICE}
MonitorAllInstances         : False
CategoryName                : Process
CounterNames                : {Private Bytes, ID Process, Working Set}
LocalizedCategoryName       : Process
ProviderName                : job-diagnostics-performance-counter-wfe-provider
UpgradedPersistedProperties : {}
…
```

In addition to the generic counters listed above, there are a number of system counters that can be added to the usage database. Table 9-1 contains a partial list of important counters, along with recommended values.

TABLE 9-1 Performance objects and counters

Objects and Counters	Description
PROCESSOR	
% Processor Time	Shows processor usage over a period of time. Count "Total" in multiprocessor systems and ensure balanced performance between cores. If the counter is over 75 – 85 percent, consider upgrading the processor, increasing the number of processors, or adding additional servers.
DISK	
Avg. Disk Queue Length	Average number of read and write requests that were queued for the selected disk during the sample time. If the system is gradually increasing and not in a steady state, increase the number or speed of disks, change the disk array configuration, or move data to an alternate server.
% Idle Time	If the idle time is greater than 90 percent, increase the number of disks or move the data to an alternative disk or server. The percentage of idle time shows if disks are overloaded.
% Free Space	If the free space is less than 30 percent, increase the number of disks or move some of the data to an alternative disk or server. It is worth noting that the use of storage area network (SAN) storage is recommended over disk attached. This allows for dynamically sized volumes over Internet Small Computer System Interface \ Host Bus Adapter.
MEMORY	
Available Mbytes	The amount of physical memory available for allocation. Insufficient memory will lead to excessive use of the page file and increase the number of page faults per second. If less than 2 GB on a web server, add more memory.
Cache Faults/sec	The rate at which faults occur when a page is sought in the file system cache and is not found. If the value is greater than 1, add memory, increase cache speed or size, or move data to an alternative disk or server.
Pages/sec	The rate at which pages are read from or written to disk to resolve hard page faults. If this rises, it indicates systemwide performance problems. If the value is greater than 10, add more memory.
PAGING FILE	
% Used and % Used Peak	The server paging file, sometimes called the *swap file,* holds "virtual" memory addresses on disk. Page faults occur when a process has to stop and wait while required "virtual" resources are retrieved from disk into memory. These will be more frequent if the physical memory is inadequate. Add more memory.

Objects and Counters	Description
NIC	
Total Bytes/sec	The rate at which data is sent and received via the network interface card. You may need to investigate further if this rate is over 40–50 percent network capacity. To fine-tune your investigation, monitor Bytes Received/sec and Bytes Sent/sec. Monitor the bytes received/sec and bytes sent/sec, reassess the network interface card (NIC) speed, and check the number, size, and usage of memory buffers.
PROCESS	
Working Set	Indicates the current size (in bytes) of the working set for a given process. This memory is reserved for the process, even if it is not in use. If the value is greater than 80 percent of total memory, add more memory.
% Processor Time	Indicates the percentage of processor time that is used by a given process. If the value is over 75–85 percent, increase the number of processors or redistribute the workload to additional servers.
ASP.NET	
Application Pool Recycles	If several of these events are happening per day, this will cause intermittent slowness as the sites recompile. Make sure you have not implemented settings that automatically recycle the application pool unnecessarily.
Requests Queued	Microsoft SharePoint Foundation 2013 provides the building blocks for HTML pages that are rendered in the user browser over HTTP. This counter shows the number of requests waiting to be processed. If this number is hundreds per request or higher, add more web servers. The default maximum is 5,000 and can be modified in the Machine.config file.
Requests Wait Time	The number of milliseconds that the most recent request waited in the queue for processing. As the number of wait events increases, users will experience degraded page-rendering performance. As the number of waits increase, so will the users' wait time for page rendering. Add more web servers.
Requests Rejected	The total number of requests that were not executed because of insufficient server resources to process them. This counter represents the number of requests that return a 503 HTTP status code, indicating that the server is too busy. If the number is greater than zero, add more web servers.

There are additional counters in each of the above categories along with a number that are specific to SQL Server and Microsoft Office Web Apps (OWA). Review Microsoft TechNet for the latest list of counters. Once you know which counters you wish to monitor, you can use the *Add-SPDiagnosticsPerformanceCounter* cmdlet to add the counter to the usage database. Listing 9-6 adds the Requests Queued, Avg. Disk Queue Length, and the _Total Instance counter of the % Processor Time.

LISTING 9-6 The *Add-SPDiagnosticsPerformanceCounter*

```
C:\PS>Add-SPDiagnosticsPerformanceCounter -category ASP.NET -Counter "Requests
Queued"
C:\PS>Add-SPDiagnosticsPerformanceCounter -category PhysicalDisk -counter "Avg.
Disk Queue Length" -allinstances
C:\PS>Add-SPDiagnosticsPerformanceCounter -category Processor -counter "%
Processor Time" -instance "_Total" -databaseserver
```

> **More Info** For more information on this topic, refer to "Monitoring and Maintaining SharePoint Server 2013," at *http://technet.microsoft.com/en-us/library/ff758658.aspx.*

Once you no longer need a specific counter, it can be removed using the *Remove-SPDiagnostic-sCounter* cmdlet, as shown in Listing 9-7.

LISTING 9-7 *Remove-SPDiagnosticsCounter*

```
Remove-SPDiagnosticsPerformanceCounter -category ASP.NET -Counter "Requests
Queued"
```

Performance counters can also be used to examine the health of the system using System Center 2010 with the SharePoint 2013 Management Pack. In addition, Microsoft Visual Studio may be used, which will be discussed in Chapter 11.

Monitoring page performance

Often, performance issues may be specific to a particular page. These issues can be caused by a number of factors, which may include poorly designed pages that contain a large number of Web Parts, Web Parts that send a large number of server requests, or utilize extensive custom code. SharePoint offers the Slowest Pages report to the SharePoint farm administrator that will identify pages that may need to be examined. This report is part of the monitoring options available through Central Administration. To run a Slowest Pages report from Central Administration, select Monitoring | View Health Reports, and then click Go (see Figure 9-5).

FIGURE 9-5 The Slowest Pages report is available through Central Administration.

The report is made available through the Usage And Health Data Collection service application. If you try to access the View Health reports prior to provisioning and configuring the service application, you will receive a message stating that the usage processing may be disabled on the server. Once you have the service provisioned, you will also need to enable the Microsoft SharePoint Foundation Usage Data Processing timer job. The Slowest Pages report may identify a number of pages with performance issues, which may be a result of high-bandwidth or low-latency connections. If the issues are restricted to a small number of pages, SharePoint offers the newly redesigned Developer Dashboard. The Developer Dashboard will provide insight of customizations and execution of code on the individual pages and help identify any problematic areas on the page.

The Developer Dashboard was first introduced into the SharePoint 2010 product, but it has been redesigned for the 2013 release and provides even more information. The dashboard now uses a dedicated Windows Communications Foundation (WCF) service (*diagnosticsdata.svc*) to provide tracing information. The new design runs in a separate window to avoid affecting the rendering of the actual page. The addition of the Developer Dashboard rendering in a separate window is a huge advantage over the previous version. Previously, master page designers had to account for an area in the master page to render the dashboard. With the new product they no longer have to worry about this in their designs.

The Developer Dashboard also has a new ULS Log tab that displays the ULS Log entries for the particular page. There is also additional detailed information included for request analyzing.

To enable the Developer Dashboard in SharePoint 2013, use the Windows PowerShell script shown in Listing 9-8.

LISTING 9-8 Enable the Developer Dashboard

```
$content = ([Microsoft.SharePoint.Administration.SPWebService]::ContentService)
$appsetting =$content.DeveloperDashboardSettings
$appsetting.DisplayLevel = [Microsoft.SharePoint.Administration.
SPDeveloperDashboardLevel]::On
$appsetting.Update()
```

In SharePoint 2010, the OnDemand option was used to open the dashboard when needed. Because it now opens in the context of another window, the OnDemand option is no longer used. Setting the dashboard to On will display the dashboard icon, as shown in Figure 9-6. To disable the dashboard, set DisplayLevel to Off.

FIGURE 9-6 The location of the Developer Dashboard option.

Monitoring SharePoint storage

With the databases being one of the most critical aspects of SharePoint 2013, there are a number of storage needs that must be examined, but the databases aren't the only components that need storage. Some of the other components of SharePoint that require storage include the binary large object (BLOB) cache on each web server, the search index, and the SharePoint logs.

We examined storage needs in great detail in Chapter 5, "Designing for SharePoint storage requirements." Here, we will highlight a couple of the monitoring features that are available for monitoring that storage. The Health Analyzer, which we discussed earlier in this chapter, has a couple of rule definitions designed to monitor disk space. By default, they run every hour. In most cases, the SharePoint farm administrator should find storage issues while performing the farm reviews discussed earlier in the monitoring requirements section, so by the time SharePoint reports them, the issues should be no surprise. Once you know that space is critical, a number of steps can be performed. These will be highlighted later in the chapter, when we discuss troubleshooting.

Site collection administrators can view how their sites are being used and how much content is being stored. The Site Settings Storage Metrics report, available under the Site Collection Administration options within each site, gives a detailed breakdown of the amount of space used by each component, as shown in Figure 9-7.

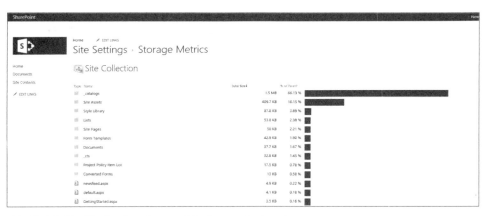

FIGURE 9-7 The Site Settings Storage Metrics are displayed.

Tuning and optimizing a SharePoint environment

Once you have your monitoring plan in place to maintain SharePoint, it is time to focus some attention on tuning and optimizing SharePoint to ensure that it is running as efficiently as possible. Prior to planning and building out the farm, it is highly recommended that both the SharePoint architect and farm administrator review the capacity software boundaries on TechNet to ensure that the farm is built and running with the latest guidance for your version of SharePoint 2013. New guidance becomes available as new scenarios are tested and limits are defined. In this section, we will examine the resource throttling options available in SharePoint, then examine techniques that can be used to optimize the SQL Server instances that are supporting SharePoint, and the networks that support the farm. Additionally, SharePoint 2013 has a number of caching capabilities that can be implemented—each of these will be explained to help you gain an understanding of what they offer and how to configure them. Finally, we will examine the new Request Management feature.

Resource throttling

Resource throttling provides options for monitoring and throttling server resources and large lists at the SharePoint web application level. These can be configured globally, or locally on a list by list basis. The settings are available globally through the General Settings in Central Administration, the feature enables the farm administrator to control resource utilization peak usage and prevents user activities from negatively affecting the performance of the farm. You can disable or enable throttling locally at the list level at the list level through the object model. This allows for resource utilization on known large lists that may need additional resources without including any new ones that may be created.

Resource throttling can be used to prevent a number of resources, including CPU, Memory, and Wait Time, from using too many resources and does so at an interval every five seconds. Throttling will begin after three unsuccessful checks of a particular resource and will remain throttled until the resource is successfully contacted. During periods of throttling, *HTTP GET* requests and Search Robot requests will generate a 503 error and an event will be logged in the Event Viewer. During this time, no new jobs will begin. You can review the options available through the Resource Throttling feature in Table 9-2.

TABLE 9-2 Options available through the Resource Throttling feature

Resource	Description
List View Threshold	Specify the maximum number of items that a database operation can involve at one time. Operations that exceed this limit are prohibited.
Object Model Override	If you choose to allow Object Model Override, users can override the List View Threshold programmatically for particular queries.
List View Threshold for Auditors and Administrators	Specify the maximum number of items that an object model database query can involve at one time for auditors or administrators through Security Policy.
List View Lookup Threshold	Specify the maximum number of Lookup, Person/Group, or workflow status fields that a database query can involve at one time.
Daily Time Window for Large Queries	Specify a daily time window when large queries can be executed. Specify a time outside of working hours for this window because large queries may cause excessive server load.
List Unique Permissions Threshold	Specify the maximum number of unique permissions that a list can have at one time.
Backward-Compatible Event Handlers	Turn on or off backward-compatible event handlers for this web application. If this is turned off, users cannot bind document libraries to backward-compatible event handlers.
HTTP Request Monitoring and Throttling	Turn on or off the HTTP request throttling job. This job monitors front-end web server performance, and in the event of HTTP request overload, rejects (throttles) low-priority requests. You can turn request throttling off to allow services such as Search to run uninterrupted on the farm; however, in an unthrottled farm experiencing overload, front-end web servers become less responsive, and may stop working.
Change Log	Specify how long entries are kept in the change log.

While many of these Resource Throttling settings can be customized, it is important to note that doing so may require additional server resources, or other operations may be degraded when performing intensive operations such as querying or deleting large lists.

SQL optimization

In most SharePoint 2013 environments, the primary limitation on speed falls on the I/O operations of SQL Server. This is because the majority of the data that SharePoint needs is stored within a variety of databases. We outlined the databases that support SharePoint 2013 in Chapter 1, "Understanding the Microsoft SharePoint 2013 architecture," and discussed storage in great detail in Chapter 5. In this section, we will discuss benchmarking the I/O subsystem, the max degree of parallelism (MAXDOP), and Auto Create/Update Stats, min and max memory, and autogrowing the SQL Server databases.

It is a good practice to benchmark the I/O subsystem using an I/O stress tool to determine the hardware's capacity and ensure that the system is tuned for optimal performance before deploying SQL Server. Doing this initial testing helps to identify any hardware- or driver-related performance issues early, before the complexity of SQL Server is introduced. Microsoft provides a free tool to help gather these metrics; it is called the SQLIO Disk Subsystem Benchmark tool, or SQLIO. Once the I/O capacity for a given I/O configuration is known, the system can be configured to ensure the best performance. The SQLIO tool, in conjunction with Performance Monitor (PerfMon), will give an accurate picture of the I/O subsystem's current performance. It will not, however, be able to give detailed information at the SAN layer, so it is recommended that you become familiar with the monitoring capabilities of the specific SAN in use. The areas to focus on would be the utilization of port(s), write pending levels, % cache utilization, internal processor utilization, LUN activity, and physical spindle activity are all points of interest that can be potential bottlenecks for performance.

SharePoint has always had a strong dependency on SQL Server; to ensure optimal performance for SharePoint operations, SQL Server should be installed on a dedicated server that is not running any other farm roles and is not hosting databases for any other applications. The only exception is if you are deploying SharePoint on a stand-alone server, which is not recommended for production environments.

Prior to deploying SharePoint, it is recommended that SQL Server be configured to not enable autocreate statistics and that MAXDOP be set to *1* to ensure that each request is served by a single SQL Server process.

When SQL Server starts, it typically continues to steadily increase the amount of memory that it uses. The min server memory and max server memory configuration options establish upper and lower limits to the amount of memory used by the buffer pool of the SQL Server Database Engine. The buffer pool does not immediately start with the memory specified in the min server memory. The buffer pool starts with only the memory required to initialize. As the Database Engine workload increases, it keeps acquiring the memory required to support the workload. The buffer pool does not free any of the acquired memory until it reaches the amount specified in the min server memory. Once min server memory is reached, the buffer pool then uses the standard algorithm to acquire and free memory as needed.

In past experience, we have seen computers running SQL Server that have only been given the RAM specified by the minimum SharePoint requirements use enough RAM that the hosting operating system didn't have enough for general operations. This caused slow performance throughout the entire SharePoint farm. By setting limits to the max server memory, the hosting operating system was guaranteed enough RAM. In cases such as these, the amount of RAM given to the hosting server should be evaluated. SQL Server, as a process, acquires more memory than specified by the max server memory option. Both internal and external components can allocate memory outside the buffer pool, which consumes additional memory, but the memory allocated to the buffer pool usually represents the largest portion of memory consumed by SQL Server.

To configure the minimum and maximum server memory, open the properties of the SQL Server instance (Contoso-SQL1), as shown in Figure 9-8. Then select the Memory page. In the example shown, the minimum memory is set to 16 GB and the maximum memory is set to 20 GB. The administrator would then ensure that the system would have enough memory added to 20 GB that would support the functioning of the operating system and any operations outside the SQL Server buffer pool. This amount will depend on the actual workload of the system. In the system shown, the amount of memory given to the server hosting SQL Server is 24 GB.

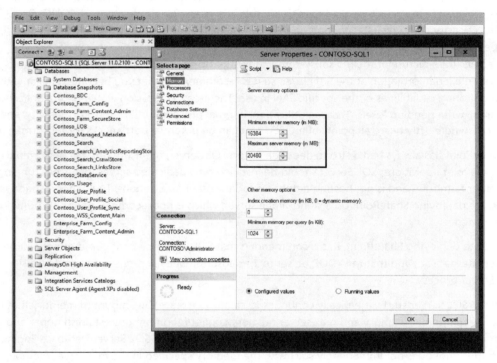

FIGURE 9-8 You configure the minimum and maximum server memory in the Server Properties window.

On servers that are hosting multiple instances of SQL Server, each instance should be limited to ensure that they will have adequate memory and do not attempt to use more memory than the system actually has.

As the user adoption of SharePoint increases, so will the size of its databases. One of the important aspects of the default configurations of the databases to note is that the autogrowth for the primary database is set to 1 MB, as shown in Figure 9-9. As databases reach their maximum size, each row added or modified with large data can potentially put extra and unnecessary load on the SQL Server as it grows the database. It is critical that you do not rely on the default settings for autogrowth; the values should be configured as a percentage instead of a fixed number of megabytes.

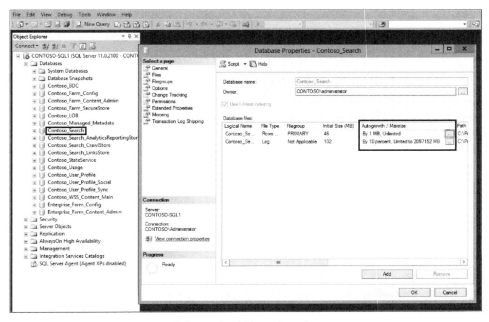

FIGURE 9-9 The default Autogrowth factor should be reviewed.

The bigger the database, the bigger the growth increment should be. For a production system, consider autogrow to be merely a contingency for unexpected growth. Do not manage the data and log growth on a day-to-day basis using the autogrowth option.

The job of the farm or SQL Server administrator who supports the SharePoint implementation is never-ending. The SQL Server storage and performance should be monitored continuously to ensure that the production database server is handling the load put on adequately it. Additionally, continuous monitoring enables the administrator to establish benchmarks that can be used for resource planning.

When monitoring SQL Server, it is important not to limit monitoring to resources that are specific to SQL Server; other factors such as CPU, memory, cache/hit ratios, and the I/O subsystem must also be monitored constantly.

Defining and executing a database maintenance plan

Once SQL Server has been optimized, the next step is to define and execute database maintenance rules to ensure that the SQL Server databases are maintained properly. When you're creating maintenance rules, consider the following operations in your maintenance plan:

- Reviewing the Database Health Analyzer rules

- Checking the database for consistency errors using *DBCC CheckDB*

- Measuring and reducing index fragmentation

- Fine-tuning index performance by setting a fill factor

- Shrinking data files

- Creating SQL Server maintenance plans

Reviewing the database Health Analyzer rules

There are a number of Health Analyzer rules (mentioned earlier in this chapter) that are specific to the database. Table 9-3 lists these rules, their schedules, and whether or not they can be repaired automatically.

TABLE 9-3 Database Health Analyzer rules

Rule	Schedule	Repair Automatically?
Databases used by SharePoint have fragmented indices.	Daily	Yes
Databases exist on servers running SharePoint Foundation.	Weekly	No
Databases used by SharePoint have outdated index statistics.	Daily	Yes
Search—One or more crawl databases may have fragmented indices.	Daily	Yes
Databases require upgrade or not supported.	Daily	No
Databases running in compatibility range; upgrade recommended.	Daily	No
Content databases contain orphaned items\apps.	Monthly	No
Some content databases are growing too large.	Hourly	No
Database has large amounts of unused space.	Weekly	No
Drives used for SQL Server databases are running out of free space.	Hourly	No

Checking the database for consistency errors using *DBCC CheckDB*

One of the first things a SQL administrator should do is ensure that the data and indexes are not corrupted. The *DBCC CHECKDB* statement is used to perform internal consistency checks of the data and index pages. The statement checks the logical and physical integrity of all the objects in the specified database by performing equivalent operations to the *DBCC CHECKALL, DBCC CHECK-TABLE,* and *DBCC CHECKCATALOG*, which means that these statements do not need to be executed independently. The *DBCC CHECKDB* is very resource-intensive in terms of memory, I/O, and CPU, so it should be executed during low-productivity hours if possible. If the *DBCC CHECKDB* finds errors, it is recommended that the affected database be restored using the most recent backup.

It is important to note that the *DBCC CHECKDB WITH REPAIR_ALL_DATA_LOSS* is not supported; however, running *DBCC_CHECKDB WITH REPAIR_FAST* and *REPAIR_REBUILD* is supported because these commands only update the indexes of the associated database.

When executing the *DBCC CHECKDB* statement, it is recommended that you use the *WITH PHYSICAL_ONLY* option to reduce the CPU and memory usage; alternatively, you can elect to restore a database backup on a separate SQL Server server and run consistency checks on the restored copy of the database.

Measuring and reducing index fragmentation

Index fragmentation occurs when the logical order of pages in a table or index is not the same as the physical order of the pages in the data file. It can also be an indication that the data density on data file pages is low, resulting in wasted disk space, memory, and I/Os and can be a result of many inserts, updates, or deletes to a table.

Index fragmentation can result in performance degradation and inefficient space utilization with indexes becoming quickly fragmented on even moderately used databases. Before implementing an index fragmentation maintenance plan, find the tables and indexes that are the most fragmented and then create a plan to rebuild or reorganize those indexes. The Health Analyzer has automatic operations that can correct this issue.

Fine-tuning index performance by setting a fill factor

The fill factor setting can be used to improve index data storage and performance. When indexes are created or rebuilt, the fill factor (1-100) determines the percentage of space on each leaf page that can be filled with data. The remaining space is reserved for future growth. While a fill-factor level of zero is optimal for many databases that are READ ONLY, it is recommended that the serverwide setting for SharePoint be set to 80.

Shrinking data files

SQL Server offers the ability to compact or shrink the database and remove unused pages and recover disk space. SharePoint does not automatically shrink data files, all though many operations can create unused space in the database like the *Move-SPSite* cmdlet that moves data from one database to another. The deletion of large lists will also leave unused space. The shrink operation should only be executed after executing an operation that removes a very large quantity of data from a database. The shrink operation causes heavy index fragmentation and is extremely resource intensive. Use the following guidelines for considering shrinking databases:

- Shrink a database only when 50 percent or more of the content in the database has been removed and it is not anticipated that the unused space will be reused by more data.

- Do not autoshrink databases.

Creating a SQL Server maintenance plan

In SQL Server, maintenance plans can be created and executed by a SQL Server Agent job and can be run manually or at scheduled instances; furthermore, Microsoft offers the Maintenance Plan Wizard for both SQL Server 2008 and SQL Server 2012 to help in the automation and scheduling of essential tasks to protect the data.

The Maintenance Plan Wizard can be configured to take care of many of the operations listed previously. For an example of the wizard tasks, see Figure 9-10.

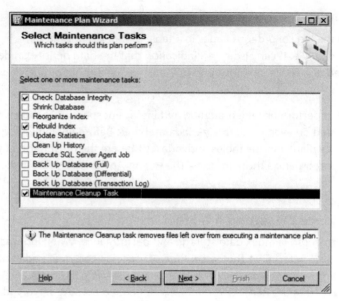

FIGURE 9-10 An example of tasks that are available through the Maintenance Plan Wizard.

In the next section, we will take our survey of performance issues to the network layer.

Fine-tuning network performance

There are a number of issues that can plague a SharePoint environment. Up until this point, the primary focus has been outlining the basics of resource throttling and tips for improving SQL Server performance. Another area that may need to be examined is the network. The network can come into play in several areas. The method of authentication chosen for the SharePoint web application can put an additional load on the Active Directory server. The network infrastructure may also be hindered with hardware issues such as NICs, switches, routers, domain controllers, and the configuration of the virtual environments. One tool that may help in locating many of these issues is WireShark, because it captures packets from TCP/IP conversations. WireShark is a free, open-source packet analyzer that is used for analyzing network packets or simply the activity inside the network cable. It can be used to troubleshoot network problems, examine security problems, or debug protocol implementations.

Authentication

We reviewed the various types of authentication available to SharePoint 2013 in Chapter 6, "Mapping authentication and authorization to requirements." The choice of authentication may put additional load on the both the network and domain controllers. When using Windows NT LAN Manager (NTLM), each user request must be authenticated against the domain controller. Not only does NTLM not perform well, but it doesn't scale well. The alternative is to use Negotiation, which is a security support provider that analyzes the HTTP request and uses the best form of authentication possible. This means that if only NTLM is available or Kerberos isn't configured correctly, NTLM is used. If Kerberos is available, then Negotiate will use it. Kerberos can be much faster than NTLM, and in most cases, it is second only to Anonymous Access, which doesn't perform any validations at all. Keep in mind that the number of web servers in the farm increases the load on the domain controller when using NTLM.

Kerberos is a ticket-based protocol. Tickets are obtained from the Kerberos Key Distribution Center (KDC), which is typically a domain controller, and are presented to servers when connections are established. The Kerberos ticket is sent in place of the user's credentials, and thus it is more secure. The use of the Kerberos ticket reduces traffic as because it only needs to authenticate when the ticket expires, as opposed to at every request.

NIC

The network supporting the SharePoint farm should always use Gigabit network cards. In some cases, the NIC may have self-switching, which toggles between 100 MB and 1 GB; in this case, the NIC should be set to use the 1 Gigabit override. For high-traffic scenarios, it is recommended to have separate NICs to handle inbound and outbound traffic. For iSCSI attached storage, it is recommended to have 10Gb NICs.

Switches and routers

Like the NIC, if switches are used to support the SharePoint farm, ensure that the network is using a GB switch with the same number of inbound and outbound channels. Routers should also be configured on a GB infrastructure.

Virtual servers

The use of virtual servers is growing within the typical SharePoint farm. Here is a general list of "gotchas" that may exist in an environment:

- Do not oversubscribe the cores; running more cores than are physically available will have a negative effect on performance due to contention for CPU resources.

- Examine the use of NUMA nodes. A CPU can access its local NUMA node (the memory directly assigned to the CPU) more quickly than it can access a nonlocal NUMA node. In Microsoft testing, it has been found that there is approximately an 8 percent hit on performance when exceeding a NUMA boundary. For example, if the virtual machine (VM) host has 8 sockets and 64 GB of RAM, the guest memory should be 8 GB or 16 GB in order to minimize the number of split boundaries.

- Scaling out VMs as web servers on a single host produces diminishing returns. It also fails to offer redundancy if the host fails.

- Do not take snapshot of a running production VM.

- Avoid using differencing disks.

- The host root partition should only have the operating system and Hyper-V roles installed on it.

- Use virtual SCSI disks for all data disks, but not the guest operating system.

- Use a private virtual network for all the servers in the farm to communicate with each other.

- Make sure the SharePoint redundancy crosses host machines. This will ensure that if one host server goes down, you don't have a loss of service.

- Try to use pass-through disks for the best performance.

Planning and configuring caching

SharePoint 2013 has a number of caching features that optimize the performance of the SharePoint implementation. SharePoint offers systemwide caching that improves authentication, newsfeeds, OneNote client access, security trimming, and page load performance (Distributed Cache); caching at the page level (Output Cache); caching individual objects, like web parts, navigation, and site map provision (Object Cache); and a disk-based cache to reduce latency and improve rendering times for image, sound files and custom code (BLOB Cache). In this section, you will explore each of these and learn the benefits of each.

Distributed Cache service

The Distributed Cache service in SharePoint 2013 enables in-memory caching for many features within the product, including newsfeeds, authentication, OneNote client access, security trimming, and page load performance. Because the Distributed Cache service uses in-memory caching, it does not have a dependency on databases, although it is worth noting that some features that use the Distributed Cache service may also store data within databases. The service that supports the Distributed Cache is the AppFabric component, which is installed during the SharePoint prerequisites install. The Distributed Cache service may be turned on automatically in the farm, depending on how the farm was built, and it is important to understand the impact of these services; this will be discussed further in a moment. It is recommended that the Distributed Cache service be hosted on a dedicated server or Distributed Cache cluster to gain the performance improvements due to the fact that 8 GB of memory is the minimum recommendation for the cache size for the service. The maximum size that is recommended is 16 GB. It is important to note that the memory allocation of the cache size must be less than or equal to 40 percent of the total memory on the server.

During the installation of SharePoint 2013, if either *PSConfig.exe* or the Windows PowerShell SharePoint cmdlets are used without the */skipRegisterAsDistributedCachehost* flag, all the servers in the farm will have a machine instance of the service running. This may be an issue when using scripts from SharePoint 2010 to build a SharePoint 2013 farm. It is recommended that the */skipRegisterAsDistributedCachehost* flag be used to ensure that the service is not started automatically on every server. During the installation of SharePoint 2013, 10 percent of the server memory is automatically allocated to the Distributed Cache service's cache size. The maximum amount of memory that can be allocated to the Distributed Cache service's cache size is 16 GB per cache host in the server farm.

When installing the Distributed Cache service on a server with 320 GB of memory, the default memory assignment for the Distributed Cache service's cache size is automatically set to 16 GB. For servers with memory greater than 320 GB, the farm administrator must reconfigure the memory allocation of the service's cache size because the limit of 16 GB is not enforced. Allocating more than 16 GB of memory to the Distributed Cache service may cause the server to stop responding unexpectedly. 8 GB is the minimum recommended cache size of the Distributed Cache service.

As the SharePoint 2013 farm grows, additional servers that host the Distributed Cache service may be required. When adding more servers, ensure that the memory allocation for the Distributed Cache service's cache size on each host is set to the same value and that the amount of memory. The farm administrator has two choices when adding more cache servers. The first is to add a new server to the farm and cache cluster using either the Windows PowerShell SharePoint cmdlets or *PSConfig.exe* without the flag, as mentioned earlier, or by taking a server that is part of the farm and changing it from a non-caching host to a caching host; this can be done using the *Add-SPDistributedCacheServiceInstance* cmdlet. To remove a particular server from the cache cluster, the *Remove-SPDistributedCacheServiceInstance* cmdlet can be used. Once the service has been removed, it will no longer show up in the list of services in Central Administration. Both of the previously mentioned cmdlets must be executed on the server that they pertain to, as there is no -*server* parameter available to specify the server.

At times, the Distributed Cache service may enter a nonfunctioning state. This most often occurs during installations, configuration changes, or maintenance activities. This issue will surface in the Health Rules in Central Administration or when users use features in SharePoint 2013 that rely on the Distributed Cache, like newsfeeds. The Distributed Cache service uses TCP port 22236. In some cases, when attempting to add the service to a new server, the system may report that TCP port 22236 is already in use. If this is the case, the service will be added but will be disabled. If the *Remove-SPDistributedCacheServiceInstance* cmdlet is executed, it will fail to remove the service instance and inform the administrator that the *cacheHostInfo* is null. In this case, use the code in Listing 9-9 to remove a particular instance.

LISTING 9-9 Repairing a Cache Host

```
PS C:\ > $svc = Get-SPServiceInstance | where {$_.TypeName -eq "Distributed Cache"}
PS C:\> $svc
TypeName                          Status    Id
--------                          ------    --
Distributed Cache                 Online    3eb54138-79ae-4291-9454-5f16846f995d
Distributed Cache                 Disabled  a06ab8b7-f0c7-4eb5-962e-69834f28b845
PS C:\> $svc1 = Get-SPServiceInstance | where {$_.Id -eq "a06ab8b7-f0c7-4eb5-
962e-69834f28b845"}
$svc1.Delete()
```

When the Distributed Cache service is first provisioned, it will assign 10 percent of the memory of the server to the service. While there is no way to review or verify how much RAM has been assigned to the service, you can use the *Update-SPDistributedCacheSize* cmdlet to set the size. This is not only helpful after the initial configuration, but it may also be used if the overall memory of the server has been changed and you wish to reconfigure the memory assigned to the service. Listing 9-10 shows an example of how to configure the memory allocation to 8 GB.

LISTING 9-10 Reconfiguring the Memory Allocation

```
Update-SPDistributedCacheSize -CacheSizeInMB 8196
```

If you would like to remove all the Distributed Cache services in the cluster at one time, review Listing 9-11.

LISTING 9-11 Repair a Caching Cluster

```
PS C:\> $svc = Get-SPServiceInstance | where {$_.TypeName -eq "Distributed
Cache"}
PS C:\> $svc.Delete()
```

Once the Distributed Cache service is configured, you will want to change the service account associated with it. By default, the account uses the farm account and therefore will violate a Health Analyzer rule. The account for the Distributed Cache can be modified only via Windows PowerShell; while it appears to be editable in the UI, it will throw an exception. An example of what this would look like is provided in Listing 9-12.

LISTING 9-12 Change the Service Account

```
PS C:\> $farm = Get-SPFarm
PS C:\> $cacheService = $farm.Services | where {$_.Name -eq
"AppFabricCachingService"}
PS C:\> $accnt = Get-SPManagedAccount -Identity "CONTOSO\spServices"
PS C:\> $cacheService.ProcessIdentity.CurrentIdentityType = "SpecificUser"
PS C:\> $cacheService.ProcessIdentity.ManagedAccount = $accnt
PS C:\> $cacheService.ProcessIdentity.Update()
PS C:\> $cacheService.ProcessIdentity.Deploy()
```

The Distributed Cache service is utilized by a number of cache objects, which include the Login Token Cache, Feed Cache, Last Modified Time Cache, OneNote Throttling, Access Cache, Search Query Web Part, Security Trimming Cache, App Token Cache, View State Cache, and Default Cache. To clear the Distributed Cache, Microsoft provides the *Clear-SPDistributedCacheItem* cmdlet.

While the Distributed Cache service does offer some great caching functionality, it does not replace the use of the Output, Object, and BLOB Caches that still exist in the product.

Output Cache

The Page Output Cache in SharePoint 2013 uses the output caching technology native to ASP.NET and is responsible for storing the output of a SharePoint page. The Page Output Cache feature is only available to sites that have the publishing features enabled. It has the capability to store various versions of the same page based on parameters. Like the other caching options, Output Cache can improve the overall performance of your SharePoint implementation by eliminating the most expensive part of the request: the content database. Review the "Putting it all together" section in Chapter 1 for more details on the HTTP request. If you examine the steps, you will notice that having the Output Cache enabled cuts out the majority of the work. Although the Output Cache can help in many areas, it is extremely powerful when it comes to publishing pages where anonymous access is enabled. In the world of content publishing, you don't want to serve cached content to the contributors because they should be able to review the latest content. When it comes to anonymous users, it's an entirely different story. Output Cache stores the pages in RAM, so after the page is requested the first time, it is ready to be served up quickly. One of the features of SharePoint's output caching is that is offers caching profiles so that the Page Output Cache can be configured based on who is visiting the site. The Output Cache settings are site collection wide. A cache profile specifies how long items should be held in the cache and will serve up the same element to different users that match the profile, which are typically either anonymous or authenticated, as shown in Figure 9-11.

FIGURE 9-11 The Output Cache Settings page allows you to change configurations.

The settings allow further configuration if you wish to have the profiles of other individuals, such as administrators and page layout designers, separate from the authenticated cache profiles. By default, SharePoint 2013 offers four profiles out of the box: Disabled, Public Internet, Extranet, and Intranet. Within the Site Collection options, the SharePoint administrator may elect to modify the existing profiles or create new ones. The configuration settings allow each profile to be set up in various configurations, with the following properties:

- Title

- Display Name

- Display Description

- Perform ACL Checks

- Enabled, Duration

- Check For Changes

- Vary By Customer Parameter

- Vary By HTTP Header

- Vary By Query String Parameters

- Vary By User Rights, Cacheability

- Safe For Authenticate Use

- Allow Writers To View Cached Content

The Debug Cache Information option enables the display of cache information on publishing pages. It can be used to determine how caching is being used for the given page, as shown in Figure 9-12.

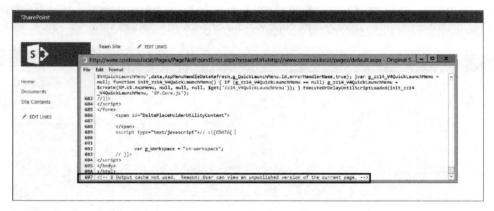

FIGURE 9-12 The Debug Cache Information displays information from a publishing page.

Object Cache

Like the Output Cache, the Object Cache is also a publishing feature, and it reduces the amount of traffic between the web server and the SQL Server database by storing objects such as lists and libraries, site settings, and page layouts in memory on the web server. This allows the pages that require these items to be rendered with greater efficiency. The Object Cache is configured at two layers: web application and site collection. The configuration at the web application level is done using the *web.config* file and sets the maximum number of megabytes that the object cache can use. The setting can be found by searching for the ObjectCache maxSize. By default, this is set to 100 MB. The configuration at the site collection level specifies the maximum cache size that can be used at the individual site collection but it will not exceed the amount set in the Web.config file. If you are using the default configuration and would like to increase the amount of RAM available for the Object Cache at the site collection, you will need to also increase it inside the Web.config file. Furthermore, it is important to configure the cache super-user and super-reader accounts at the web application level in order for the object cache to function properly.

Within the site collection settings, the administrator has the ability to set the maximum cache size, reset the Object Cache, configure the Cross-list Query Cache, and configure the cross-list query results multiplier.

Cross-list queries initiated by the Content Query Web Part or other custom implementations can use up server resources. Specifying an amount of time to cache the results of a cross-list query can positively affect cross-list query performance but may display results that do not reflect the most recent changes to the items returned by the query. Checking the server each time a cross-list query runs will produce the most accurate results, but at the possible cost of slower performance across the site.

The cross-list query results multiplier allows for the configuration of cross-list queries. Each cross-list query might retrieve results for a variety of users. To ensure after security trimming that all users will see a valid set of results, the cross-list query cache must pull more results than originally requested. Specifying a larger number will retrieve more data from the server and is ideal for site collections that have unique security applied on many lists and sites. Specifying a smaller number will consume less memory per cross-list query and is ideally suited for site collections that do not have unique security on each list or site.

BLOB Cache

As with Page Output Cache and Object Cache, BLOB Cache is also a feature of the publishing infrastructure. BLOB Cache has been with SharePoint for several versions now and is ideal for publishing sites that serve up items that are static in nature, such as image, sound, video files, and code fragments such as JavaScript files. Only files that are stored in SharePoint libraries are eligible for caching. By default, BLOB Cache is turned off and can be turned on by modifying the Web.config file for the web application. The entry that controls the BLOB Cache resembles the following:

```
<BlobCache location="C:\BlobCache\14" path="\.(gif|jpg|jpeg|jpe|jfif|bmp|dib|tif|tiff|themedbmp|
themedcss|themedgif|themedjpg|
    themedpng|ico|png|wdp|hdp|css|js|asf|avi|flv|m4v|mov|mp3|mp4|mpeg|mpg|rm|rmvb|wma|wmv|ogg|
ogv|oga|webm|xap)$" maxSize="10" enabled="false" />
```

BLOB Cache is a disk-based caching control that stores items at the location specified in the Web.config file on each web server that serves the particular web application. The Web.config file must be configured manually on each server hosting the web role. The file types can be configured by simply adding or removing them from the path string using the pipe as a delimiter. The *maxSize* is the maximum allowable size of the disk-based cache in gigabytes. Remember that this is web application–specific, so if each web application specifies 10 GB and the server has a large number of Internet Information Services (IIS) web applications, space can be come limited quickly. It is also important to remember that as web applications are extended to use additional zones, new IIS web applications are created and can consume additional space. Each zone will need the Web.config file manually configured; this helps by having different caching profiles for web applications that host various audiences such as corporate intranets or anonymous content. The max-age parameter, which is not in the BlobCache entry by default, specifies the maximum amount of time (in seconds) that the client browser caches BLOBs downloaded to the client computer. If the downloaded items have not expired since the last download, the cached items are not requested with the page and will not be rendered. The max-age attribute is set by default to 86,400 seconds, which translates to 24 hours, but it can be set to a timer period of 0 or greater. Furthermore, the attribute doesn't affect server-side operations at all; it controls client-side cacheability. That means that if the file is located on the client, a request to the web server is never made. The file gets served directly from the local browser cache, helping to reduce traffic between the client and the server. In most cases, these BLOBs are larger than most files, so the reduced requests greatly benefit performance. On the negative side, large max-age settings could leave a client with stale content, so it is important to know how and when these files are being cached.

The enabled parameter, which is set to *false* by default, is the Boolean indicator that specifies if the web application will use BLOB Cache on that particular server. Because both the Page Output Cache and BLOB Cache use the individual web servers, they are not implementing the Distributed Cache feature.

Once BLOB Cache has been configured, saving the Web.config file should trigger an *IISReset* that should create the BlobCache folder when the site collection is accessed. You will notice that the web application ID in IIS is used as a root folder and several files are created: Change.bin, Dump.bin, Filestodelete.bin, Flushcount.bin, Inprogreedump.bin, and Oldcachefolders.bin. It should be noted that manually manipulating files or folder structures within the BLOB Cache is unsupported and can corrupt the cache. Every time a file is accessed, the cache index (.bin files) get updated. Every request from the client will check the index file first for whether the file is in the index and not the folder that contains the file. This means that if the file is deleted, the cache will believe that the file is available, and it will not present the item correctly. If the index does not have an entry for the file, then the request is served from the content database. A copy of the file is then stored in the disk cache and the index is updated. The file is stored with an identical name as a prefix, as shown in Figure 9-13.

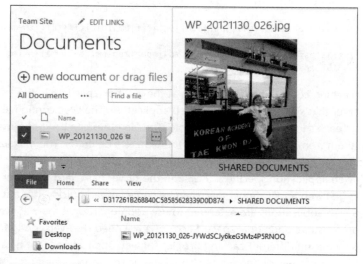

FIGURE 9-13 The document library contains the BLOB Cache.

One of the biggest downfalls of BLOB Cache is that it is possible for multiple web servers to be showing inconsistent files because each server hosts its own version of the file.

Introducing Request Management

SharePoint 2013 introduces the Request Management service, which helps manage incoming requests by evaluating them against a set of rules and then determining if a SharePoint farm will accept requests and, if so, how the requests will be handled. The SharePoint servers that are eligible for this service are those running the SharePoint Foundation Web Application (SPFWA) service. The SPFWA service is responsible for ensuring that the SharePoint content web applications are provisioned on the server and that IIS is prepared for handing requests. The Request Manager is built into the SharePoint 2013 IIS module so it affects only the requests of SharePoint applications that IIS hosts. With the Request Manager, there are three major functional components: Request Routing, Request Throttling and Prioritizing, and Request Load Balancing.

The Request Management service is designed to be configured in one of two ways: dedicated mode or integrated mode.

The dedicated mode configuration is a dedicated farm of web servers that sit between the hardware load balancers and SharePoint farms, as shown in Figure 9-14. The load balancers send all requests to the web servers in the Request Management farm, which then process the requests and determine how they should be routed; some requests may be ignored depending on the routing and throttling rules. The web servers that receive the final requests then process them and send the responses back through the web servers in the Request Manager farm, which then respond to the clients.

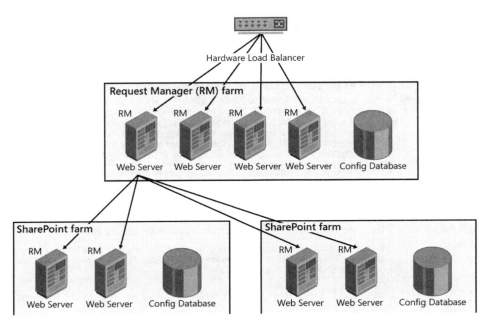

FIGURE 9-14 The dedicated-mode Request Manager farm sits between the hardware load balancer and SharePoint farms.

The dedicated-mode Request Manager farm provides two benefits: Request Manager and SharePoint processes do not compete for resources, and you can scale out one without having to scale out the other, thus giving you more control over the performance of each role.

The integrated mode configuration is intended for smaller deployments. The hardware load balancers send requests directly to the intended SharePoint farm's web servers, as shown in Figure 9-15. When the web server receives the request, the Request Manager makes the decision to allow it to be processed locally, route it to a different web server, or deny the request entirely.

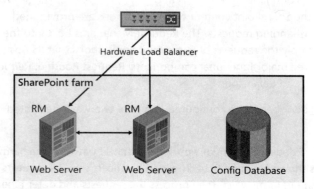

FIGURE 9-15 The integrated-mode Request Manager shares resources with the SharePoint farm.

While the SharePoint administrator is able to start the Request Management service in Central Administration, there is no UI available for the actual configuration. The Request Manager configuration is comprised of five elements: Routing Targets, Machine Pool, Routing Rules, Throttling Rules, and Execution Groups. Table 9-4 describes each of these elements.

TABLE 9-4 Request Manager configuration elements

Element	Description
Routing Targets (Servers)	Routing Targets, also known as Routing Machines, are the servers in a SharePoint farm that are running the Microsoft SharePoint Foundation Web Application service; by default, all servers that are running the SPWAS service are included in the Routing Targets. Each Routing Target has both a Static Weighting and Health Weighting. While the Static Weighting can be configured by an administrator to specify the strength of a web server, the Health Weighting cannot. It derives its score (0 to 10) from the Health Analysis.
Machine Pool	Machine Pools are a collection of Routing Targets that are contained in the *MachineTargets* property. The Machine Pool is then used as a target for one or more routing rules.
Routing Rules	Routing Rules define the criteria of requests prior to routing them.
Throttling Rules	Throttling Rules define the criteria of requests prior to refusing them.
Execution Groups	Execution Groups are collections of Routing Rules that allow rules to be prioritized and managed in batches. There are three execution groups (0,1 & 2), which are evaluated in order. Execution group 0 is the default.

Figure 9-16 demonstrates how the elements listed in Table 9-4 work to provide the Request Management service.

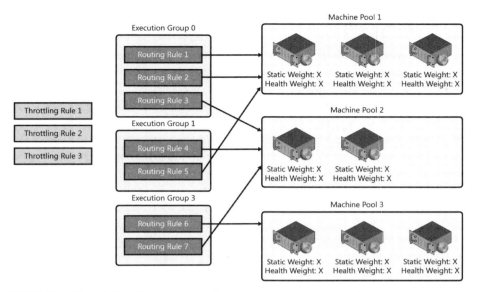

FIGURE 9-16 The relationships among the Request Management elements are shown.

As you examine the Request Management feature, keep the following in mind:

1. As requests are received, they are evaluated against the Throttling Rules, and if the incoming requests match the criteria of one of these rules, they are refused.

2. Once the Throttling Rules have been evaluated, the Execution Groups are evaluated. These are done in the order of Execution Group 0, Execution Group 1, and Execution Group 2. If an incoming request matches one of the rule criteria, the request is prioritized and routed to a Routing Target within a Machine Pool. Once a rule is matched to an Execution Group, no other Execution Groups are evaluated. If an incoming request matches Routing Rule #2 in Execution Group 0, then Execution Group 1 and 2 will not be reviewed. This will require sufficient planning when associating Routing Rules with Execution Groups.

If requests do not have a corresponding routing rule, the requests are sent to all the available Routing Targets. Take a look at configuring the service.

Microsoft provides the *Set-SPRequestManagementSettings* cmdlet, which allows the administrator to set the appropriate values for the *-RoutingEnabled* or *-ThrottlingEnabled* parameters. By default, the *RoutingRules, ThrottlingRules*, and *MachinePools* properties are empty and the *RoutingTargets* property includes every machine in the farm that is running the SPFWA service. Spence Harbar has provided detailed step-by-step instructions for configuring the Request Management service in his blog post, "Request Management in SharePoint Server 2013, Part Two: Example Scenario and Configuration Step by Step," which can be found at *http://www.harbar.net/articles/sp2013rm2.aspx*.

Troubleshooting a SharePoint environment

By using the maintenance schedule discussed at the beginning of this chapter, a large majority of critical issues will be revealed before they cause major farm issues. One of the toughest issues to troubleshoot is one of the easiest to avoid—running out of disk space. SharePoint reports a wide variety of issues when it can no longer write to the database, logs, or other critical storage locations. Many organizations ignore the warnings until their farm becomes unresponsive at which point the errors do not indicate the root cause of the problem. Luckily, the Health Analyzer gives us over 60 predefined rules that help keep our system in check. In addition to reviewing the Health Analyzer, regularly scheduled reviews of the Windows event log, SharePoint ULS logs, SQL Server logs, security logs, and system resources will help keep our systems healthy and available. However not every system is bulletproof. It is inevitable that errors will creep up and users will find problems. The most important part of troubleshooting a SharePoint environment is gaining an understanding of the issue so that the appropriate tools can be used to determine the root cause. Only by finding the root cause will the issue be resolved correctly.

Understanding the issues through logs

Problems will surface in a number of ways, which include user-reported errors, system-reported errors, reduced functionality, or reduced availability. Each of these issues has several different escalations depending on their nature and how they affect the underlining business of the company. As these issues arise, it is important to get a clear picture of the issues at hand. Consider the following questions when trying to learn more about the issues from the information worker:

- What is the error? Does the information worker see an error message or a correlation ID or is it missing functionality?

- Is the issue isolated to a particular person or group? Is it systemwide, web application wide, site–wide, or restricted to a particular web?

- When does the error occur? Does it appear to be random, intermittent, or consistent?

- What browser is the information worker using?

Critical errors are typically a result of some change. If we apply Newton's laws of motion to our SharePoint environment, things generally keep working until something changes. A good practice that is often overlooked is the change log. If administrators record the changes they make to the system, it is often easy to isolate root causes that may not be so obvious. A difficult error to track down would be the configuration of the cache super-user and cache super-reader account. Both accounts needs web policy permissions. If these are not set up correctly, every account (even administrators) will not be able to access a SharePoint web application. If such an event is not tracked in a change log, it may take quite some time to realize what has happened.

Additionally, prior to troubleshooting, verify the service pack and cumulative update (CU) of the product. In the past, some service packs have required CU updates, and if they aren't applied, some features fail to work. Once the issue is understood, it is important to replicate it using a series of accounts. Some issues simply fall into security constraints, like a password could have expired or been changed. Once the troubleshooter is able to verify the issue, record the time that it happened. This will help focus only on issues in the logs that may pertain to the current issue. Keep in mind that these issues may be the result of an entirely different process, so it may be required to comb through all the logs. Some errors may be outside the boundaries of the SharePoint farm and may be related to the Domain Name Service (DNS) or Active Directory. Several scenarios will be presented in the final section of this chapter.

In addition to using the tools mentioned earlier, there are a number of other tools that you may find useful, which include the SharePoint ULS Log Viewer, Log Parser, and additional Windows PowerShell cmdlets. The SharePoint ULS Log Viewer, available on CodePlex, offers a great way to traverse the ULS logs. Log Parser is able to provide query access to log files, XML files, and CSV files, as well as Windows operating system files, such as the event log and IIS logs. Additionally, Microsoft provides a PowerShell cmdlet, *Get-SPLogEvent*, that retrieves log data from the SharePoint ULS logs, as shown in Listing 9-13. The cmdlet allows for a number of parameters to help limit the amount of data coming back. In the example, only the data from the date specified with a critical level was retrieved.

LISTING 9-13 The *Get-SPLogEvent* Cmdlet

```
PS C:\>$today = "12/16/2012"
PS C:\>Get-SPLogEvent -StartTime $today | where {$_.Level -eq "Critical"} |
Select Message
Message    : The Execute method of job definition Microsoft.Office.Server.
UserProfiles.LMTRepopulationJob threw an exception. More information is included
below.  Unexpected exception in FeedCacheService.IsRepopulationNeeded: Unable to
create a DataCache. SPDistributedCache is probably down.
Message    : The SharePoint Health Analyzer detected an error.  Distributed cache
service is not enabled in this deployment. Distributed cache service is not
running in this deployment.  Turn on the Distributed cache service.
```

Once the error(s) have been identified, finding the correct resolution may be the next tricky task. The issues in the Health Analyzer have resolutions available, but when you find other errors in the logs, they may not be so obvious. Case in point: the errors mentioned previously specify that they may be resolved by turning on the Distributed Cache service. As you will find out in the final section, this is an incorrect diagnosis, and the issue is actually tied to another problem.

In reality, troubleshooting SharePoint is something that one learns over time. Experience is the best teacher. It is important to use the tools that are available to you, like reviewing blog posts, asking questions on TechNet forums, or escalating the issue to Microsoft. No matter what you decide, it is absolutely vital that you fully understand the remedies that are being offered. Blindly accepting advice may put you in a bigger jam.

Putting it all together

In this chapter, we discussed the importance of monitoring, tuning and optimizing, and troubleshooting a SharePoint environment. The most proactive task that a SharePoint professional should perform is defining and following the monitoring requirements. Each organization will have different toolsets at their disposal, but the one thing each of them will have is the set of built-in tools provided by the SharePoint platform. In this final section, we will continue to build on the lessons learned by examining the Health Analyzer, Windows event logs, and ULS logs using the Windows Server tools, the SharePoint ULS Log Viewer, and Windows PowerShell.

To start our example, we will first review the Health Analyzer results of the Contoso farm, as shown in Figure 9-17.

FIGURE 9-17 An example of where to review problems and solutions.

The farm has a number of issues. We will map some of the issues to problems in the system and identify some of the related logs in both the Windows event log and ULS logs. The issues that will be discussed in this section include:

- The server farm account should not be used for other services.

- Accounts used by application pools or service identities are in the local machine Administrators group.

- Missing server-side dependencies.

- Outbound email has not been configured.

- Built-in accounts are used as application pool or service identities.

- Verify that each User Profile service application has an associated Search Service connection.

Each of these issues has a fairly simple fix, but the last one pertaining to the User Profile service has surfaced in a number of ways, some not so obvious. We will assume that when an administrator was attempting to manage the User Profile synchronization connections, he or she saw the message: An error has occurred while accessing the SQL Server database or the SharePoint Server service, as shown in Figure 9-18.

Synchronization Connections

Use this page to manage the list of connections to import sources such as Active Directory, LDAP Directory and Business Data Connectivity. User information will be imported from these sources.

■ Create New Connection

Name	Type	Source
An error has occurred while accessing the SQL Server database or the SharePoint Server Search service. If this is the first time you have seen this message, try again later. If this problem persists, contact your administrator.		

FIGURE 9-18 Synchronization Connections displays the synchronization errors.

Upon investigation of the Windows event log, the administrator finds a number of repeating Windows event logs with the Event ID of 6398, as shown in Figure 9-19. The general error message states: "The Execute method of job definition Microsoft.Office.Server.UserProfiles.UserProfileImport threw an exception."

Level	Date and Time	Source	Event ID	Task Category
Critical	12/16/2012 12:14:20 PM	SharePoint Foundation	6398	Timer
Critical	12/16/2012 12:13:20 PM	SharePoint Foundation	6398	Timer
Information	12/16/2012 12:12:21 PM	AppFabricCachingService	0	None
Critical	12/16/2012 12:12:19 PM	SharePoint Foundation	6398	Timer
Critical	12/16/2012 12:11:19 PM	SharePoint Foundation	6398	Timer
Critical	12/16/2012 12:10:19 PM	SharePoint Foundation	6398	Timer
Critical	12/16/2012 12:10:06 PM	SharePoint Foundation	6398	Timer
Critical	12/16/2012 12:09:19 PM	SharePoint Foundation	6398	Timer
Critical	12/16/2012 12:08:19 PM	SharePoint Foundation	6398	Timer
Critical	12/16/2012 12:07:20 PM	SharePoint Foundation	6398	Timer
Critical	12/16/2012 12:06:19 PM	SharePoint Foundation	6398	Timer
Critical	12/16/2012 12:05:19 PM	SharePoint Foundation	6398	Timer
Critical	12/16/2012 12:05:06 PM	SharePoint Foundation	6398	Timer
Critical	12/16/2012 12:04:19 PM	SharePoint Foundation	6398	Timer

Event 6398, SharePoint Foundation

| General | Details |

The Execute method of job definition Microsoft.Office.Server.UserProfiles.UserProfileImportJob (ID 6b97b22f-63fd-4801-bdb7-84c3c01719cd) threw an exception. More information is included below.

There was no endpoint listening at http://contoso-sp2:5725/ResourceManagementService/MEX that could accept the message. This is often caused by an incorrect address or SOAP action. See InnerException, if present

FIGURE 9-19 The Windows event log shows the list of errors.

In reviewing the ULS log using the ULS Log Viewer, the same message is revealed, as shown in Figure 9-20.

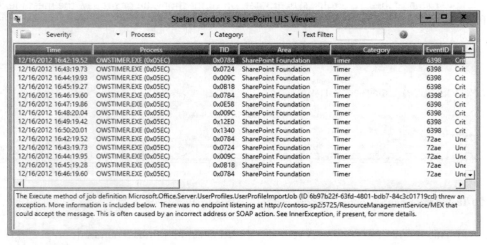

FIGURE 9-20 The SharePoint ULS Log Viewer shows errors.

In reviewing all the information, we will find that the most informative piece of information is presented in the Health Analyzer report. In this particular case, the Search service was removed from the farm and is needed by the User Profile service. The explanation given in the Health Analyzer is:

> *In places such as "What's happening with my network?" web part and tag profile pages, User Profile Service presents a set of URLs to end users. These URLs are trimmed for security to make sure that a user does not see URL to which he does not have access to. User Profile Service uses Search Service to perform this trimming of URLs for security. If there is no Search Service associated with the User Profile Service, this trimming of URLs will not work, and hence all URLs will be visible to everyone. Of course, when a user clicks on a URL to which he does not have access, he will still be denied access.*

With this information, you simply need to create a Search Service application and rerun the rule. The remaining issues are fairly common, so you will probably see these in most newly created farms.

Issue: The server farm account should not be used for other services.

Explanation: CONTOSO\spfarm, the account used for the SharePoint timer service and the Central Administration site, is highly privileged and should not be used for any other services on any machines in the server farm. The following services were found to use this account: User Profile Synchronization service (Windows Service).

Resolution: Change the service account associated to the User Profile Synchronization service to use CONTOSO\spServices instead of CONTOSO\spFarm. The farm account is automatically assigned when the User Profile Synchronization (UPS) service is provisioned. This is common among many of the services.

Issue: Accounts used by application pools or service identities are in the local machine Administrators group.

Explanation: Using highly privileged accounts application pool or service identities poses a security risk to the farm and could allow malicious code to execute. The following services are currently running as accounts in the machine Administrators group.

Resolution: The UPS requires that the farm account (CONTOSO\spFarm) be in the local Administrators group during the provisioning of the service. After that, it is no longer required and should be removed. From time to time, you may need to provision UPS again; this may be a result of changing sync settings or applying patches. When this is needed, you will need to put the farm account back into the Administrators group until the service is running again.

Issue: Missing server-side dependencies.

Explanation: [MissingWebPart] WebPart class [28c23aec-2537-68b3-43b6-845b13cea19f] is referenced [5] times in the database [Contoso_Farm_Content_Admin], but is not installed on the current farm. Please install any feature/solution which contains this Web Part. One or more Web Parts are referenced in the database [Contoso_Farm_Content_Admin], but are not installed on the current farm. Please install any feature or solution which contains these Web Parts

Resolution: This issue was a little tougher. The explanation points to my Central Administration content database and is typically an indicator that customizations weren't brought into the new farm. Since this was a clean build, I knew that wasn't the case. I executed the SQL query in Listing 9-13 and it returned the *SearchFarmDashBoard.aspx* page. The GUID ties to a Search Web Part that was not located on the page, but once I visited the page, the dependency error disappeared.

LISTING 9-13 Query to Find Web Parts

```
SELECT DISTINCT DirName, LeafName FROM AllDocs
Inner join AllWebParts
On AllDocs.Id = AllWebParts.tp_PageUrlID
WHERE tp_WebPartTypeId in (
'28c23aec-2537-68b3-43b6-845b13cea19f'
)
```

Issue: Outbound email has not been configured.

Explanation: A default Simple Mail Transfer Protocol (SMTP) server has not been configured. One or more web applications do not have SMTP servers configured. Because of this, features such as alerts will not function properly.

Resolution: This one is quite simple to solve. Configure the outgoing email settings and rerun the analyzer.

Issue: Alternate access URLs have not been configured.

Explanation: A default zone URL is pointing to the machine name of a web front end. Because this installation has more than one web front end, this can result in a variety of errors, including incorrect links and failed operations.

Resolution: This is simply an issue with how I set up my demo environment to have my web application using a server name instead of the host header. This is a combination of creating site collection host headers and configuring the Request Manager on another server. I would need to change the server name to use a host header, configure AAM to use both servers or turn off the SPWAS service on Contoso-SP1, which serves as my Distributed Cache server.

Issue   Built-in accounts are used as application pool or service identities.

Explanation: Using built-in accounts like Network Service or Local System as application pool or service identities is not supported in a farm configuration. The following services are currently running as built-in identities on one or more servers: OSearch15 (Windows Service).

Resolution: This is similar to the UPS issue that we encountered earlier. I need to configure the Search Host Controller service to use the CONTOSO\spServices account instead of the farm account.

Once all the issues have been resolved, the Health Analyzer results should look like Figure 9-21.

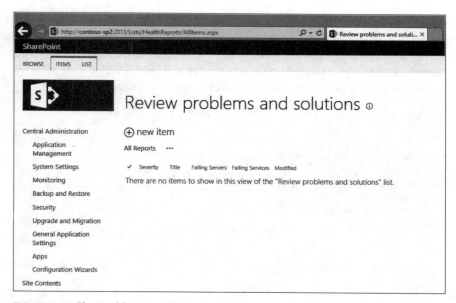

FIGURE 9-21 The Health Report displays no issues.

Once the items are clear, it will be much easier to check the page on a daily basis and tackle any issues that come up. The timer jobs that examine the farm for issues are on various schedules, so an issue may take over a week to surface.

## CHAPTER 10

Planning your business continuity strategy

In this chapter, you will learn about:

- Planning for your business continuity needs.

- Exploring the features native to SharePoint.

- Avoiding service disruptions.

- Implementing various business continuity techniques.

- Implementing network load balancing.

There are many factors that must be evaluated during the planning phase of your Microsoft SharePoint 2013 farm, and one of the most crucial aspects is ensuring that the implementation continues to operate when unforeseen issues plague the environment. Up until this point, you may have started to formulate a design of how everything should be structured, but does your design include protecting your investment?

Protecting SharePoint is often overlooked. One possible reason for this may be that there isn't a feature in SharePoint that you can enable that automatically protects your implementation. You can visit Central Administration and perform full-farm or granular-level backups, but these features don't promote the continuity of business. They are more or less an option for disaster recovery.

Disaster recovery (DR) certainly has its place within how you are going to plan your SharePoint environments, and this chapter will focus on some of the features throughout. A DR plan is great for when you need to recover a deleted item within SharePoint, but it doesn't help keep SharePoint from service disruptions. First, how does SharePoint fit into your organization? More specifically:

- What is the role of SharePoint in your organization?

- Do you have plans to integrate it with your accounting software or other aspects of your business?

- Do you consider SharePoint to be mission critical?

- Have you performed a business impact analysis (BIA) on your environment?

In this chapter, you'll learn what needs to be protected and how to plan for this, as well as what the business continuity management (BCM) objectives are and how they might define an organization's tolerance toward data or service loss. You'll then use that information to explore options for mitigating risk.

Planning for your business continuity needs

The only sure way to be successful in protecting your data is to properly plan what you are going to protect and then how you are going to protect it. The first step is to perform a BIA to determine which business processes are critical to your business and then identify the core components that those business systems rely on. In SharePoint, everything comes down to one piece: the data. This could simply be the database, but in some cases it may include Remote BLOB Storage (RBS) shares.

Understanding what to protect

The databases in SharePoint are the most common protection points and are considered the principal vehicles for service and recovery of service. If you lose a SharePoint server that is servicing the Web role, rebuilding your farm may be difficult if you have custom solutions improperly applied to the farm or have custom *web.config* files in your web applications, but overall, the data is still available and the farm can be rebuilt. Your objective here is to think outside of the single-server environment to ensure that your system can withstand a failure and that you stay within your BCM objectives.

Applying BCM objectives

BCM objectives are the ultimate requirements guide for how the SharePoint implementation should be built, but they may be difficult to obtain and stay within budget. As you'll see later in this chapter, each layer of protection comes at a cost. It is up to you to know what the technologies are and how they work; but ultimately, it is up to the business to decide if what they are asking for is worth it. Once the business has dictated their needs, a service-level agreement (SLA) can be created and then honored. An SLA is a negotiated agreement between a service provider and a customer. Often, the service provider may actually be an internal IT group and the customers will be various lines of businesses.

While the SLA may specify several topics, the focus of this chapter is on the tolerable amount of service loss and the tolerable amount of data loss. These are often referred to as Recovery Time Objectives (RTO) and Recovery Point Objectives (RPO). To simply these terms even further, examine the following:

- **RTO** This specifies the acceptable amount of time that the organization can be without the system. This can range from seconds to days. For many small organizations, this is 8 hours.

- **RPO** This specifies the acceptable amount of data that the organization can lose. For many small organizations, this may be 24 hours.

When stakeholders determine the value that is to be associated with both the RTO and RPO, they are naturally going to determine that zero is the best value. In their mind, they should never lose any data, and it should always be accessible. The problem is that this is an unachievable metric, and the closer you can get to zero, the more expensive it will be.

As you progress through this chapter, you will learn why these zero value-based objectives are unachievable as you gain a greater understanding of each technology. Your task is then to select the technologies that will get you as close as possible to the expectations and still keep the solution within budget. Once the stakeholders understand the costs involved, a few minutes of downtime may be acceptable.

In your requirements documentation, you will want to capture what the goal is. It could be something as simple as, "I can lose 10 minutes worth of data, and all of my data can be inaccessible for 60 minutes."

Keep in mind that your RTOs and RPOs need to be realistic and potential service disruptions will happen causing a break in availability. Availability is defined with five classes, as shown in Table 10-1.

TABLE 10-1 Five classes

Availability	Uptime	Downtime
Mission Critical	99.999%	5 minutes per year
Business Vital	99.99%	53 minutes per year
Mission Important	99.9%	9 hours per year
Data Important	99%	3.6 days per year
Data Not Important	90%	36 days per year

If you are building a Mission Critical environment, you have 5 minutes of allowable downtime per year. This doesn't leave any time for administering the system with patches or upgrades; even database snapshots will bring you over the 5 minutes if not properly discussed in the plan.

You should also keep in mind the amount of time it takes to replace a SAN/RAID, perform a database backup, or even some of the BCM methodologies that will be discussed shortly. Your job is to keep the agreed uptime as low as possible, while the client's job is to have it as high as possible. Can you really afford to offer 99.999 percent?

Exploring the features native to SharePoint

SharePoint 2013 provides you with several backup and restore options, as shown in Figure 10-1.

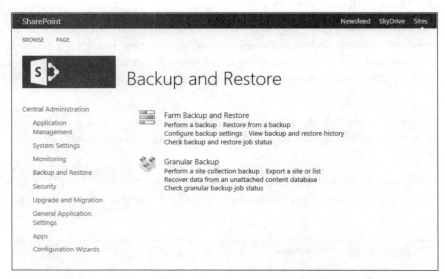

FIGURE 10-1 The backup and restore options available through Central Administration.

In this section, you'll learn about the backup and restore features that are native to SharePoint 2013, including the following:

- **Native backup and restore**   Provides for full and differential backups

- **Site-collection backup**   Provides the ability to back up a specific site collection

- **Exporting a site or list**   Provides the ability to export a site or list

- **Recovering data from an unattached content database**   Allows for the recovery of data from a SharePoint content database without having to attach the content to a web application

- **Recycle Bin**   Provides an easy way for users and site collection administrators to recover recently deleted items

- **Read-only improvements**   Provides a better experience to the user while the site is in read-only mode

The features in this section are targeted more towards DR, meaning that they help you recover lost data.

Native backup and restore

On the surface, there aren't any apparent changes to the native backup and restore functionality that is included in the product, but they have made some internal improvements. The farm backup supports both a full and differential backup. The biggest selling point, and what makes it unique, is the ability to back up the configuration, SQL Servers databases, the file system hierarchy, and the state of the search index simultaneously.

Backup

To perform a backup through the UI, click Backup And Restore | Perform A Backup. This will allow you to select the components that you wish to back up, as shown in Figure 10-2.

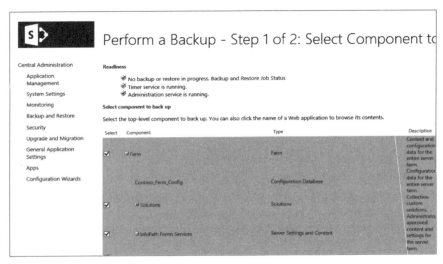

FIGURE 10-2 The full farm backup option gives you the ability to select components granularly.

Once you select the components that you wish to back up, click OK. You will now be presented, as shown in Figure 10-3, with the Backup Type options (full or differential), Back Up Only Configuration Settings, and the location where your backup file will be stored.

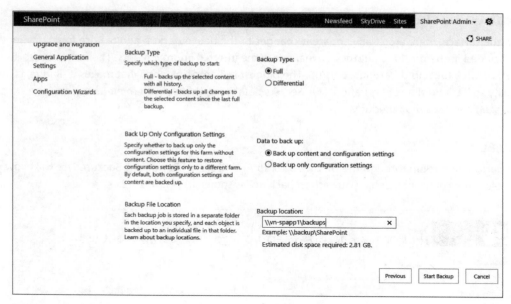

FIGURE 10-3 The second step allows you to save to a specified location.

Note The farm account will need to have access to the backup location.

If you prefer to use Windows PowerShell, the backup farm cmdlet would look like the following:

```
C:\PS>Backup-SPFarm -Directory \\file_server\share\Backup -BackupMethod full
```

You may also add the *-ConfigurationOnly* parameter to back up only the configuration database, but this parameter is intended for inactive farms. If you would like to take a backup of only the configuration data from the active farm, you should use the *Backup-SPConfigurationDatabase* cmdlet.

You can use the *Backup and Restore Job Status* link to check in on the progress. Once it is complete, you will then be able to verify the files in your specific backup location. You will need to ensure that you have enough disk space for your backups, so incorporate this into your file system or storage area network (SAN) plans. It is worth noting that SharePoint doesn't provide a way to schedule backup jobs, but you can use the Windows Task Scheduler to call Windows PowerShell scripts. Any users that plan on using the Windows PowerShell cmdlets for backing up or restoring farm components must be added to the SharePoint_Shell_Access role for the specified database.

Note The *Backup-SPFarm* cmdlet may appear to complete without issues, but this does not mean that the backup itself was successful. You should always view the *spbrtoc.xml* file located in the specified backup directory for any possible errors.

Restore

Once a backup is performed, a restore follows a similar path. To perform a restore through the UI, click Backup And Restore | Perform A Restore (see Figure 10-4).

FIGURE 10-4 The restore feature allows you to select from a specified location.

Site-collection backup

The backup and restore functionality at the site-collection level gives you a little more granular control over your operations. Besides being a great way to restore content, these operations allow for content migration. You can access the Site-collection Backup feature by clicking Backup And Restore | Perform A Site Collection Backup. This will give you the option to select the site collection to back up along with the storage location of the file, as shown in Figure 10-5. This feature only takes backups and does not offer a UI for restores. In order to restore a backup, you will need to use the *Restore-SPSite* cmdlet.

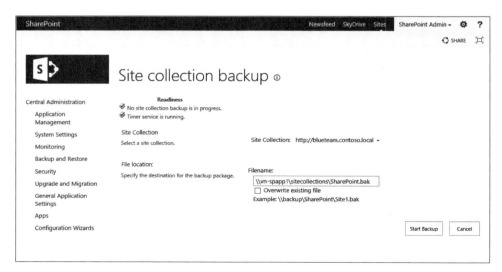

FIGURE 10-5 The Site-collection backup does not have a UI for restores.

Note The farm account will need to have access to the backup location.

As with many features in SharePoint 2013, there are ways to achieve the same tasks through Windows PowerShell. In the case of backup and restore, there are two important cmdlets: *Backup-SPSite* and *Restore-SPSite*.

Backup-SPSite

The *Backup-SPSite* cmdlet allows you to granularly back up a site collection to a specific path. In the following example, the cmdlet is backing up a site collection located at *http://server_name/sites/site_name* to the *C:\Backup\site_name.bak* file:

```
C:\PS>Backup-SPSite http://server_name/sites/site_name -Path C:\Backup\site_name.bak
```

Restore-SPSite

The *Restore-SPSite* cmdlet is the only way to restore a site collection, regardless of whether it was done through the UI or using the *Backup-SPSite* cmdlet. In the following example, the cmdlet is restoring a site collection located at *http://server_name/sites/site_name* using the *C:\Backup\site_name.bak* file:

```
C:\PS>Restore-SPSite http://server_name/sites/site_name -Path C:\Backup\site_name.bak
```

Exporting a site or list

Now that you have the ability to back up and restore content, it is now time to review exporting and importing data. You may have noticed the wording has changed for these operations. In the previous sections, you were backing up and restoring the farm or site collection, but in this section, you're going to be exporting and importing. Although this may seem like a small wording difference, there are significant implications. Specifically, the difference is all about fidelity. There are several things that are not exported, and thus are not available for import. These settings include workflows, alerts, audit logs, personalization settings, and recycle bin items. Other things that may cause issue are dependencies on other lists, so keep this in mind as you're moving content around.

To export a site or list, click Backup And Restore | Export A Site Or List. The UI should resemble Figure 10-6. You will have the option to select the site or list, with the following results:

- If you select a site, you will be able to select whether to include security for that site.

- If you select a list, you will also be able to select the type of versions you would like to export.

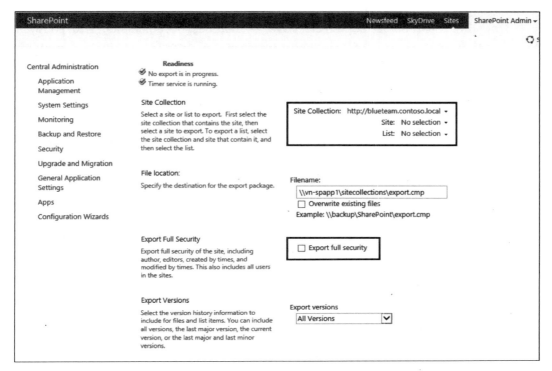

FIGURE 10-6 The Export A Site Or List functionality allows you to export security.

You can export a site or list through the UI, but you must use the *Import-SPWeb* cmdlet for the import.

Export-SPWeb

If you wish to export a site or a list, you have the option to use Central Administration or the *Export-SPWeb* cmdlet. The following example will export a site at *http://site* to a file located at *C:\backups\export.cmp*:

```
C:\PS>Export-SPWeb -Identity http://site -Path "C:\backups\export.cmp"
```

Import-SPWeb

To import a site or list, you must use the *Import-SPWeb* cmdlet. The following example will import a site to *http://site* from a file located at *C:\backups\export.cmp*:

```
C:\PS>Import-SPWeb http://site -Path C:\backups\export.cmp -UpdateVersions -Overwrite
```

Note The *Import-SPWeb* and *Export-SPWeb* cmdlets help documentation erroneously makes references to "Web Application," suggesting that these cmdlets support an entire web application. This is not correct. These cmdlets support only the export and import of sites and lists.

Recovering data from an unattached content database

In Microsoft Office SharePoint Server (MOSS) 2007, when users needed to grab content out of a copy of a SharePoint content database, they had to create a new web application, attach a database to it, and then browse for the content. In SharePoint 2010, recovering data from an unattached content database was introduced. This feature allows you to point to a content database and then extract what you need without all of the hassle. In Figure 10-7, you can see that you have the ability to select the database and then browse for content, back up a site collection, or export a site or list.

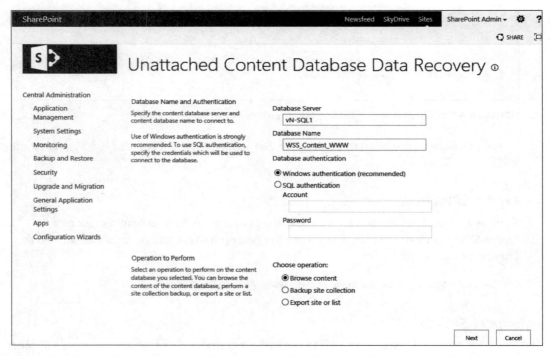

FIGURE 10-7 Recovering data from an unattached content database allows for easy access to old data.

Restoring data using the Recycle Bin

The Recycle Bin feature provides a safety net for when items are deleted from SharePoint. The Recycle Bin feature is configurable at the SharePoint web application layer and is available via the UI, Windows PowerShell, or the application programming interface (API). The Recycle Bin feature is comprised of two locations: the Recycle Bin and the Site Collection Recycle Bin. It is important to know how each of these come into play. For most deleted objects (documents, list items, lists, folders, and files), they will be placed into the Recycle Bin; this area is available to the information worker and they can recover items here without assistance from the site collection administrator. By default, items that are placed in the Recycle Bin are kept there for 30 days. This value is configurable in Central Administration at the web application level, as shown in Figure 10-8. The item will remain in the Recycle Bin until either the item expires, the item is restored, or the user deletes the file. If the user deletes the file, it will then be placed in the site collection administrator Recycle Bin, where it will remain until the end of the expiration period.

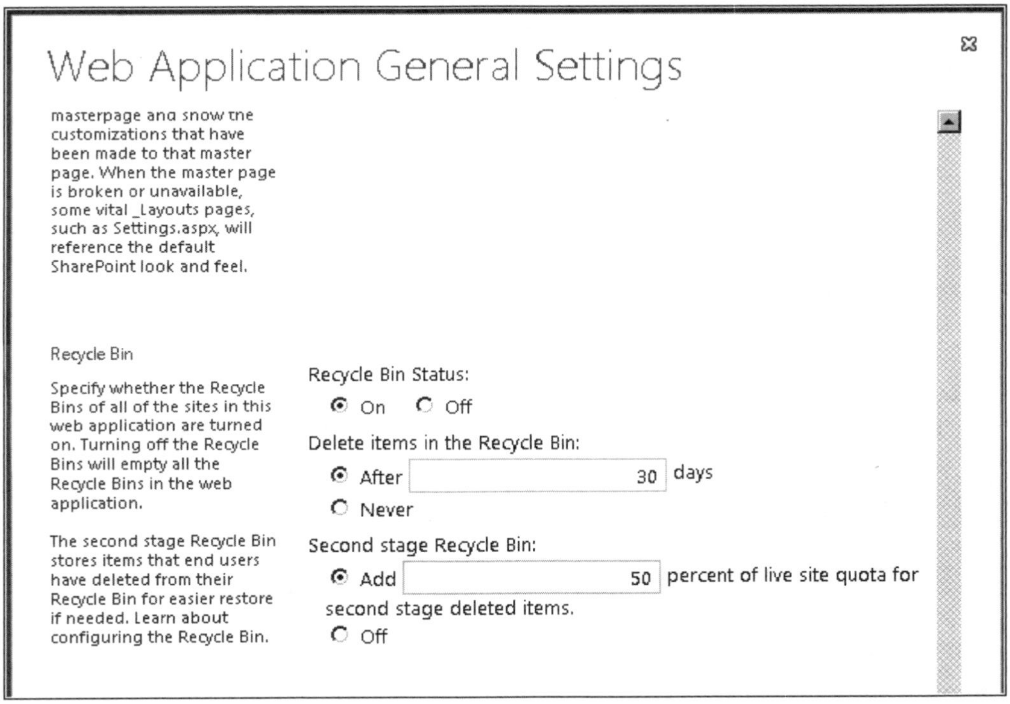

FIGURE 10-8 The Recycle Bin is configurable for each web application.

If a SharePoint website is deleted, it will go directly to the site collection administrator's Recycle Bin, where only someone with site collection administrator rights can restore the item. The items will remain there until the item is restored, manually deleted, the item expires or the quota limit is reached. These items are now permanently deleted.

The Recycle Bin feature is often referred to as *stages,* and this is true in the UI as well. This can be a bit misleading, as items do not have to pass through both areas. Items that are deleted by the user and complete their expiration period in the Recycle Bin will not be moved to the Site Collection Recycle Bin. SharePoint websites go directly to the Site Collection Recycle Bin and a confirmation message is shown to the user, as shown in Figure 10-9. If a Site Collection is deleted, there is no Recycle Bin to move the item into, but they can be recovered using the *Restore-SPDeletedSite* cmdlet.

FIGURE 10-9 The Recycle Bin sends sites to the Site Collection Recycle Bin.

Note The Gradual Site Delete timer job is used to gradually remove content from a site to ensure there are no SQL locks from an instant delete. This has no effect on the site until it leaves the Recycle Bin.

Read-only improvements

SharePoint 2010 introduced improvements on the information worker's experience with read-only sites but the read-only state was not obvious. The write features that were available to Site Owners and Members would be removed, and they would have similar experiences to those who had strictly read permissions. For users who expect the ability to save data to the database, they may be left wondering why the system no longer allows them to do so. SharePoint 2013 has expanded on the read-only feature by showing a message bar stating: "We apologize for any inconvenience, but we've made the site read-only while making some improvements," as shown in Figure 10-10.

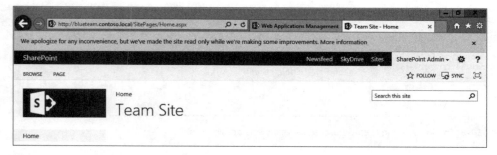

FIGURE 10-10 SharePoint 2013 has a read-only status message.

Further information may be given to the user by setting the *ReadOnlyMaintenanceLink* property that is available through the web application object. This property can be configured either by using the SharePoint API or through Windows PowerShell. The *ReadOnlyMaintenanceLink* property can be set to any working webpage. If the page is local within SharePoint, only the relative URL is required, as shown in Listing 10-1.

LISTING 10-1 Configure the *ReadOnlyMaintenanceLink*

```
C:\PS>Add-PSSnapin "Microsoft.SharePoint.PowerShell" -EA 0
C:\PS>$webApp = Get-SPWebApplication -Identity http://www.contoso.local
C:\PS>$webApp.ReadOnlyMaintenanceLink = "/SitePages/ReadOnly.aspx"
C:\PS>$webApp.Update()
```

Once the *ReadOnlyMaintenanceLink* property has been set, a "More information" link will be appended to the read-only status message that will send the user to a page that may have detailed information about the maintenance operation, as shown in Figure 10-11.

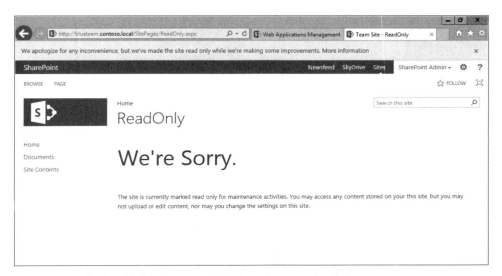

FIGURE 10-11 The ReadOnlyMaintenanceLink allows for more detailed messages.

If the "More Information" link is no longer required, simply setting the property to an empty string will put the status message back to its original format:

```
C:\PS>$webApp = Get-SPWebApplication -Identity http://www.contoso.local
C:\PS>$webApp.ReadOnlyMaintenanceLink = "/SitePages/ReadOnly.aspx"
C:\PS>$webApp.Update()
```

Avoiding service disruptions

Now that the RPOs and RTOs have been defined, it is time to plan the level at which you will protect your implementation from service disruption. The options in protecting your data are endless. People plan out everything from stretched farms to a Microsoft SQL Server backup. This section highlights the pros and cons of several options, but first, you will learn more about fault domains at an abstract level.

What do you plan to protect against? You can scale out the best SharePoint farm in the world, with multiple servers hosting your environment so that if one server goes down service continues, but if all of your servers are on the same rack, you can easily have a service disruption when you lose power or network connectivity to the rack. So now we add a second rack, as shown in Figure 10-12. Let's think outside of the rack for a minute, because you can easily have a power outage that affect the entire building, or even an entire city. If this happens, is this acceptable? It may very well be.

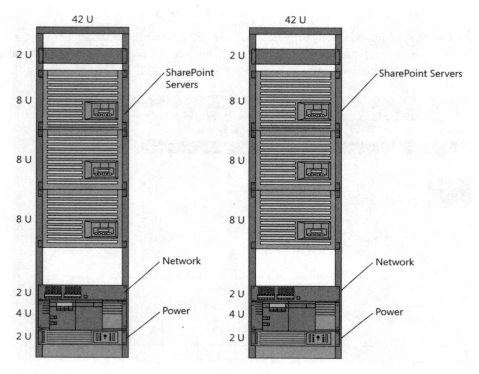

FIGURE 10-12 SharePoint server components should span multiple racks to allow for fault tolerance at the rack level.

If you are powering an intranet for a small organization and you lose power to the building, it is safe to say that everyone loses power and everyone walks outside and hangs out while waiting for power to be restored. In this day and age, the small organization where everyone is on site is quickly going away. More and more companies are starting to support remote access, so the same power disruption can now affect more people than just those inside the building. Will the same levels of tolerance be acceptable for a large Internet company? Think about the revenue that could potentially be lost if a large online company lost power to their data center for even a few hours.

What about natural and artificial disasters? If a primary data center is in California and they have an earthquake, how long can your system be down before it causes a problem? Do you then plan to have multiple data centers? If so, what risks are you mitigating?

Review Figure 10-13. If California has an earthquake, it is probably safe to say that it will not affect Colorado. If the data center in Colorado gets hits by a tornado at the same time as your earthquake in California, you are having a bad day—but a third data center in Minnesota might do the trick. At this point, you must ask yourself if data center redundancy is going to the extreme. How often do people lose entire data centers? Are the benefits worth the cost? What fault domains are most vital to your implementation?

FIGURE 10-13 In order to protect against large-scale disasters, it may be necessary to have multiple data centers.

Without the database, there is no SharePoint farm. If you can protect the databases, the argument can be made that your farm can be recoverable. If you lose your data, no trick in the world will help restore your farm. If you lose a server that is hosting SharePoint, it may be painful to reconfigure some of the web applications, but the data is still intact.

With this in mind, the most common protection point would be the databases. In the next section, you will investigate the options you have to protect your databases.

Implementing various business continuity techniques

How do you take what you've learned so far and put those ideas into action? Some of the requirements for SharePoint 2013 that have changed from the infrastructure perspective are the supported operating systems and SQL Server machines. Here are the minimum versions that are supported for the new version of SharePoint:

- Windows Server 2008 R2 with SP1

- Window 8 Server RTM

- SQL Server 2008 R2 SP1

- SQL Server 2012

Note Prior to choosing the version of SQL Server, be aware that some features may only work with SQL Server 2012.

Microsoft offers several technologies to help you protect your databases. In this section, you will learn about failover clustering, database mirroring, log shipping, and AlwaysOn Availability groups.

The first three may be familiar to you, at least at a high level, but the SQL Server team has delivered new features in SQL Server 2012 that are beneficial in this space. Each of these concepts should be in your mind as you are trying to find the right solution.

Failover clustering

Failover clustering is a software-based solution that was introduced in the days of Microsoft Windows NT Server 4.0 and SQL Server 6.5 Enterprise edition. Since then, that technology has been given the opportunity to mature and is now a proven method of handling hardware issues. The RPO and RTO are extremely low, but is technically not zero. While the data that is stored on the shared storage device will remain intact, the in-flight transaction will be lost. There will be a small disruption in service while the failover occurs from one node to the next, which may average between 30 seconds and 2 minutes.

Failover clustering consists of a series of nodes (computers) that protect a system from hardware failure. In Windows Server 2008 Enterprise edition, you can support up to 16 nodes. This has been dramatically increased to 63 nodes in Windows Server 2012. To cluster SQL Server, you must cluster both the server operating system and SQL Server. The nodes monitor the health of the system and can step in when issues are detected; more about this shortly.

Note SQL Server Standard edition supports two nodes for failover clustering.

Failover clustering is typically done with a SAN, but keep in mind that the SAN may be a single point of failure.

Now you can get around this scenario by configuring a multisite cluster (also known as a *geocluster*). SQL Server 2012 Enterprise has been released with enhancements for geoclusters, but it should be noted that SharePoint has some strict support requirements between the communications between the SharePoint servers and the SQL Server machines, so if there is any measureable distance between the geoclusters, it may not be supported. You will learn about this further in the next section when you approach the topic of stretched farms.

How it works

Let's go back and visit how the cluster works. As discussed previously, a failover cluster is a set of independent computers or nodes that increase the availability of software, which in this case is SQL Server. Each node in the cluster has the ability to cast one vote to determine how the cluster will run. The voting components, which may or may not be restricted to nodes, use a voting algorithm that determines the health of the system; this is referred to as a *quorum*. There are a few variations on how the quorum works: node majority, node + disk majority, node + file share majority, and no majority.

- **Node majority**   In this configuration, each node is a voting member and the server cluster functions with the majority vote. This is preferable with an odd number of nodes.

- **Node + disk majority**   In this configuration, each node is a voting member as in node majority, but a disk-based witness also has a vote. The cluster functions with the majority vote. This is preferable for single-site clusters with an even number of nodes. The disk majority witness is included to break a possible tie.

- **Node + file share majority**   This configuration is similar to the disk majority in that each node has a vote and it uses a disk-based witness. This is the preferred configuration for geoclusters with an even number of nodes. The disk majority is included to break the tie.

- **No majority**   This configuration functions with a single node and a quorum disk. The nodes that communicate with the quorum disks are voting members. This configuration is one of the most common for SQL Server implementations.

If a quorum detects a communication issue, failover will occur and another node will step in.

 Note For more information on how a quorum works, see *http://technet.microsoft.com/en-us/library/cc730649(v=ws.10).aspx*.

The failover cluster can be configured in a wide variety of ways. For the purpose of this discussion, you will focus on the following configurations: Active-Passive, Active-Active, and Active-Passive-Active.

Active-Passive

In the Active-Passive configuration, one node is active, while the second one is passive or inactive. The biggest complaint about this type of configuration is that the inactive node is idle—in other words, it's not performing any work. If the active server should fail, failover would occur, making the second server active and the first server inactive. At any given moment, only one server is available for activity.

Active-Active

In the Active-Active configuration, both nodes are active and are available for activity. The issue with this type of configuration is that in the event of a node failure, the surviving node must have enough resources to handle the load of both servers. This may leave the environment in a reduced capacity.

Active-Passive-Active

The Active-Passive-Active configuration is a solid plan over the two previous designs. In Active-Passive, 50 percent of the hardware is idle and is perceived to be "wasted." In Active-Active, both servers are working, but if a failure happens, a reduced workload is probable. In Active-Passive-Active, or additional variations, a smaller percentage of the servers are idle. This configuration could have any number of active servers that are supported by any number of inactive ones. If you have a single inactive node and two active nodes fail, a reduced workload is probable.

Disadvantages

Now that we have highlighted the advantages of failover clustering and how it works, it is time to discuss some of the disadvantages of the technology. You may have already realized this, but failover clustering only solves the high availability of your data and doesn't give you a way to recover data in case of a cluster failure. You will need to look at other technologies for DR.

Another disadvantage is that all of the drivers, firmware, and BIOS versions must match on each of the nodes in the cluster.

Finally, while there are a lot of resources on Microsoft TechNet that can guide you through the process, configuring failover clustering can still offer challenges.

Database mirroring

Database mirroring is a software-based solution that enables you to add a layer of resiliency to highly available architectures—at a granular level not available to failover clustering. While failover clustering is configured at the SQL instance layer, database mirroring is a solution that is configured at the database level.

Database mirroring has been achievable for several products now, but it wasn't until SharePoint Server 2010 that it was integrated into the product. In MOSS 2007, database mirroring required database connection strings in both an unmanaged SQL layer and in managed code. The administrator was required to use SQL Aliases across the SharePoint servers and required the database principal to maintain node majority, meaning all of the principal databases were on the same instance and had to fail over together. Now with database mirroring as part of the product, the failover database is specified when the SharePoint content web application is being created, and the complexity of the configuration has been diminished. The following Windows PowerShell script demonstrates how to set the failover service instance:

```
$server = "Contoso_SQL_1"
$databaseName = "WSS_Content_Contoso"
$db = get-spdatabase | where {$_.Name -eq $database}
$db.AddFailoverServiceInstance($server)
$db.Update()
```

Similar to failover clustering, database mirroring will ensure no stored data loss, but it has many advantages over failover clustering. The first is the perceived hardware under usage. As previously discussed, in a failover cluster, you generally have an inactive node. If you do not, then the active nodes will need to support the addition load, in which case a performance hit would be expected. In database mirroring, a given server may host the principal for one database and a mirror for another. This allows a configuration to use the hardware without having to fail over to it.

Database mirroring also makes use of a redundant I/O path, where as the failover cluster does not. What this means is that if a dirty write affects the principal, it will not affect the mirror—more about this in the next section. Furthermore, when the primary server detects a corrupt page on disk, the mirror can be used to repair it automatically without any intervention. Finally, database mirroring is not dependent on shared storage, so it is not suspect to the same single point of failure as the failover cluster is.

The hardware on the failover clusters must also maintain the same drivers, firmware, and BIOS versions, whereas database mirroring is not dependent on the server binaries to be in sync. Database mirroring also supports sequential upgrade of the instances that are participating in the mirroring session.

How it works

Database mirroring maintains two copies of a single database on separate SQL Server instances. A transaction is applied to the primary or principal instance and then replayed on the mirror. This relationship is known as a *database-mirroring session*. Since these are using two distinct I/O paths, dirty writes or torn pages that affect one instance will not affect the other.

Note Database mirroring is only supported in Full recovery mode.

The principal instance is responsible for handling requests to the client, while the mirror acts as a hot or warm standby server.

- **Hot standby**   A method of redundancy in which the principal server and mirror server run simultaneously and the data is identical on both systems.

- **Warm standby**   A method of redundancy in which the mirror server runs in the background of the principal server. The mirror server is updated at regular intervals, which means that there are times when the data is not identical on both systems. There is a possibility of data loss while using this method.

Database mirroring works at the physical log record, which means that for every insert, update, or delete operation on the principal, the same operation is executed against the mirror. These transactions will run with either asynchronous or synchronous operations, as described next:

- **Asynchronous**   Transactions on the principal commit without waiting for the mirror server to write the transactions to disk. Since the principal does not wait, this operation maximizes performance.

- **Synchronous**   Transactions occur on both the principal and mirror. There is longer transaction latency under this operation, but it ensures data consistency.

Database mirroring supports both manual and automatic failover. In order to take advantage of the automatic failover functionality, a witness server must be in place. The witness server can be any instance of SQL Server, including SQL Express, since it does not serve any of the databases. An example of this is shown in Figure 10-14. This same witness can reside over multiple mirroring sessions and acts as part of the quorum for the mirror. The witness is not a single point of failure, as the principal and mirror participate in the quorum as well. In order for the mirror to become the principal, it must be able to communicate with one other server.

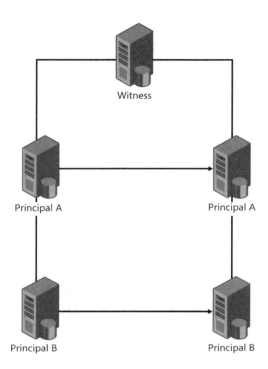

Witness

Principal A   Principal A

Principal B   Principal B

FIGURE 10-14 A witness server can preside over multiple mirroring sessions.

There are three mirroring operation modes: high-availability mode, high-safety mode, and high-performance mode. These modes operate as follows:

- **High-availability mode runs synchronously.** This requires a witness, and the database is available whenever a quorum exists and will provide automatic failover.

- **High-safety mode runs synchronously.** This ensures data consistency, but at the risk of hurting performance. With respect to the SharePoint server, when the primary database instance sends the transaction to the mirror, it will want to send the confirmation back to the SharePoint server until the mirror confirms the transaction. To see an overview of the process flow, refer to Figure 10-15.

- **High-performance mode runs asynchronously.** Since the transaction does not wait for the mirror to commit the log, it is faster but is also at risk for data loss. With respect to the SharePoint server, when the primary database instance sends the transaction to the mirror, it also sends a confirmation to the SharePoint server and is not delayed by the additional write.

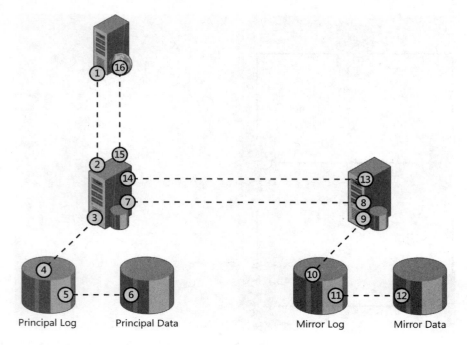

FIGURE 10-15 Diagram of data flow for database mirroring.

In high-safety mode   The client writes data to the principal SQL Server database (steps 1 and 2). The principal writes the data to the transaction log and the data is committed (steps 3 to 6). The principal sends the transaction to the mirror (steps 7 and 8) and waits for the mirror instance to commit. The mirror instance write the data to the transaction log and the data are committed (steps 9 to 12) and the mirror confirms with the principal (steps 13 and 14). The principal confirms the transaction back to the client (steps 15 and 16).

In high-availability mode   The client writes data to the principal SQL Server database (steps 1 and 2). The principal writes the data to the transaction log and the data is committed (steps 3 to 6). The principal sends the transaction to the mirror (steps 7 and 8). The principal confirms the transaction back to the client (steps 15 and 16). The mirror instance write the data to the transaction log and the data are committed (steps 9 to 12) and the mirror confirms with the principal (steps 13 and 14).

Note   The mirror database is in a recovery mode and is not accessible by anything but SQL Server. Therefore, you cannot do reporting operations on the mirror. If you require this type of functionality, review the "Log shipping" section later in this chapter.

Disadvantages

Now that you have encountered the advantages of database mirroring and how it works, it is time to discuss some of the disadvantages of the technology. Database mirroring is not supported by all SharePoint databases. This is constantly evolving, so check the latest guidance to find out which databases are supported.

There are many practices that change the recovery mode on their databases to Simple. This is primarily done to restrict the logs from accumulating on the server when other backup methodologies are used. Database mirroring requires Full recovery and therefore will not work in this mode. Some databases, like the *Usage And Health Service* database, may be in Simple recovery mode for performance, as shown in Figure 10-16.

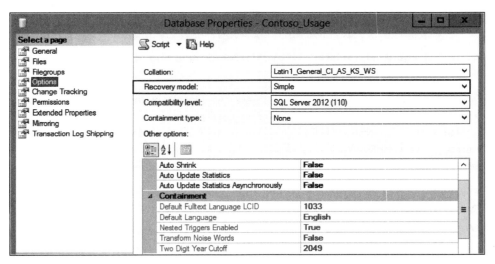

FIGURE 10-16 The *Usage And Health* database utilizes the simple recovery model by default.

Log shipping

Log shipping is a software-based solution that increases database availability. Similarly to database mirroring, log shipping is implemented on a per-database level. Log shipping offers several benefits over database mirroring. In database mirroring, there is only one mirror or secondary storage. In log shipping, the primary database sends backups of the transaction log to any number of secondary databases. You may also remember that in database-mirror sessions, the mirror database is not readable. Log shipping supports read-only secondary copies that are suitable for reporting.

Finally, one of the greatest benefits of log shipping is that geographic redundancy is approachable. Geographic redundancy and the concept of stretched farms will be discussed in a little more detail in the "Putting it all together" section at the end of the chapter.

How it works

Log shipping is nothing more than a backup, copy, and restore of the SQL transaction logs from one server to another. The steps include:

1. Back up transaction log from the primary database.

2. Copy the transaction log to the secondary server(s).

3. Restore the transaction log on the secondary server(s)

All three of these operations run at specified intervals. It is important to note that in order for the transaction logs to be restored to the secondary server(s), all users must exit so that database transactions can accumulate while the database is in use. Because of this, log shipping is used more for disaster recovery, as opposed to high availability.

> **Note** The SQL agent service has to be running for log shipping to work.

The history and status of the log shipping jobs are saved locally by the log shipping jobs. The primary server will keep the history and status of the backup operation, while the history and status of the copy and restore operations will be stored on each of the secondary servers. Once log shipping is configured, you can implement a monitor server that will consolidate the history and status of all of the servers and give you a single location to review them. Review Figure 10-17 for the data flow.

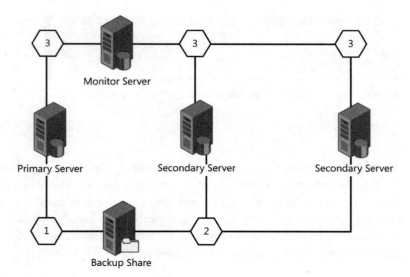

FIGURE 10-17 The monitor server consolidates the history and status from the other servers.

The log shipping data flow in Figure 10-17 demonstrates the following:

1. The backup job runs on the primary server and stores the files on the backup share.

2. The copy jobs runs on the secondary server(s) and the restore jobs run.

3. The monitor server consolidates the history and status from the other servers.

Disadvantages

Now that you have seen the advantages of log shipping and how it works, it is time to discuss some of the disadvantages of the technology. Log shipping does not support automatic failover from the primary server to the secondary server. The data on the secondary server(s) may not be up to date, depending on the last time the transactions were restored. Log shipping is not a methodology for high availability and has a much higher RTO/RPO than database mirroring and failover clustering.

AlwaysOn Availability

HADRON (High Availability Disaster Recovery—AlwaysOn) or AlwaysOn Availability is a feature of SQL Server 2012. It is considered to be the next generation of high-availability solutions. While AlwaysOn Availability may have similarities with other technologies, it isn't built on any existing technologies and was designed from the ground up.

At first glance, you will undoubtedly see similarities with the previously mentioned technologies. It offers the high availability of database mirroring, along with the power of geoclustering of log shipping.

How it works

The first thing to take into account is that AlwaysOn Availability does require nodes to be configured using Windows Failover Clustering, which is a feature of Windows Server (review Figure 10-18). This may give you the impression that configuring AlwaysOn Availability may be complicated, but it is rather straightforward and the wizards that are included at both the clustering aspects of Windows Server and HADRON make it very easy to set up. While clustering is required at the server level, SQL Server 2012 itself is not configured for clustering.

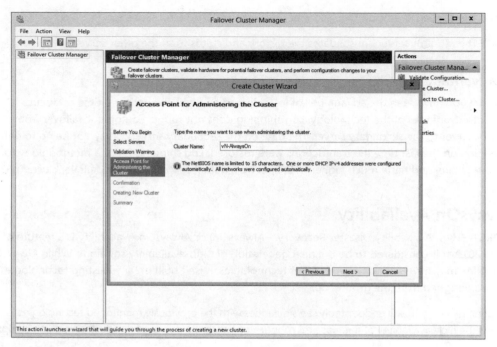

FIGURE 10-18 HADRON requires failover clustering at the Windows Server level.

Once Windows Failover Clustering is configured, SQL Server 2012 will have new AlwaysOn options available from the SQL Server Instance properties windows, as shown in Figure 10-19. Simply select Enable AlwaysOn Availability Groups and click OK.

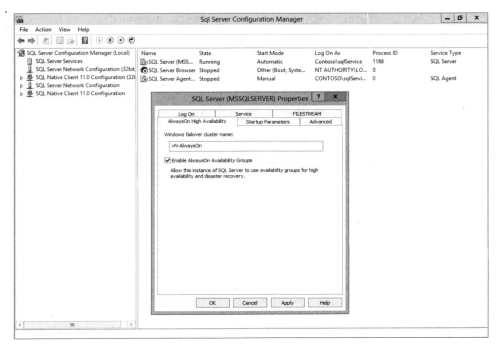

FIGURE 10-19 Select AlwaysOn Availability Groups from the SQL Server Configuration Manager.

Enabling AlwaysOn Availability Groups creates an AlwaysOn High Availability folder under the SQL Server instance that allows for the management of Availability Groups. Availability Groups are collections of SQL Server instances that are available for database operations by only specifying the Availability Group Listener. Availability Group Listeners will be discussed shortly.

To create a new Availability Group, you have the option of creating one manually or by using a wizard. The wizard will display all of the databases that exist in the instance but only allow you to select the ones that meet the prerequisites, as shown in Figure 10-20. It will then allow you to specify replicas for the databases. Replicas are basically the various nodes that were included in the Windows Failover Cluster, but are individual SQL Server instances. These replicas may be configured for automatic failover, synchronous or asynchronous operations, or even a readable secondary database. If you remember from the previous section, database mirroring did not support readable secondary databases; so this is a huge advantage over database mirroring.

Note Database mirroring has been marked as deprecated in SQL Server 2012, which means that while it is supported in SQL Server 2012, it may not be a feature in the next version of SQL Server.

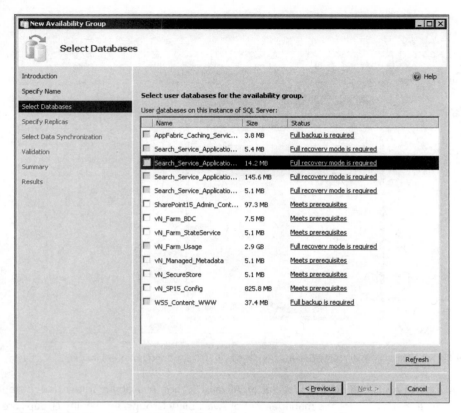

FIGURE 10-20 You can select only databases that meet the prerequisites.

The replicas are accessed by the Availability Group via the Availability Group Listener. The listener is configured in SQL Server and is a virtual network name that points to the active node in the Availability Group for that particular database. Once the Availability Group Listener has been specified, the following data synchronization options will be available:

- **Full** Starts data synchronization by performing full database and log backups for each selected database. These databases are restored to each secondary and joined to the Availability Group.

- **Join only** Starts data synchronization where you have already restored database and log backups to the database. These databases are restored to each secondary and joined to the availability group.

- **Skip initial data synchronization** Choose this option if you want to perform your own database and log backups of each primary database.

If database mirroring hasn't been previously configured, select the Full option. This greatly reduces the amount of work to configure AlwaysOn Availability. Once the wizard completes the data synchronization, one database will be synchronized while the secondary is restoring. It is possible to have other states, depending on how the replicas have been configured, as shown in Figure 10-21.

FIGURE 10-21 One database will be synchronized while the secondary database will be restoring.

If you are familiar with database mirroring in SharePoint, you'll notice that the configuration of AlwaysOn Availability is simpler since you specify the AlwaysOn Availability Group as the main database and the failover database is not needed.

Note SQL Server aliases should be used in your configurations. This reduces the overhead of converting your hardware availability to AlwaysOn.

One of the key advantages of AlwaysOn Availability is the lack of dependency on shared storage. It also utilizes a separate I/O path so each database has the benefit of torn page detection. AlwaysOn also provides the benefits of log shipping and allows for geoclustering and multi-subnet clustering.

If your implementation has database mirroring configured, it is easy to convert to AlwaysOn Availability by following these steps:

1. Remove or break the mirror at the SQL Server instance level.

2. Create an Availability Group.

3. Create an Availability Group Listener.

4. Select the synchronization preferences.

5. Change the aliases on the SharePoint boxes to point to the Availability Group Listener instead of the principal database server.

Disadvantages

The configuration of AlwaysOn Availability is easier than SQL failover clustering, database mirroring, and log shipping and offers all of the positives of each of the technologies. The disadvantage of the technology is that it requires SQL Server 2012 Enterprise. While database mirroring is available in SQL Server 2012 Standard, the technology has been depreciated in SQL Server 2012 and may not be carried forward into the next version.

Implementing network load balancing

There are many network load balancing options available, most of which come at a cost. Microsoft introduced a free IP load balancer with Windows NT Server 4.0, Enterprise edition, and it continues to exist in the server operating systems that support SharePoint 15.

The network load balancer (NLB) that comes with Windows Server is a feature that can be turned on to allow requests to be directed at a series of nodes. In the SharePoint world, this is done on the SharePoint servers that are being used to support web requests from the users. If one of the servers in the NLB cluster goes down, the requests will be directed at the next available server in the cluster.

When you create a new cluster, you will specify a virtual cluster IP address, subnet mask, and a cluster mode, as shown in Figure 10-22.

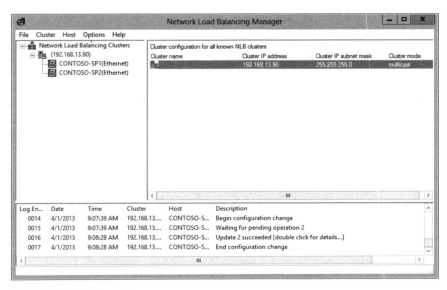

FIGURE 10-22 Cluster settings.

The cluster mode supports the following unicast and multicast methods:

- **Unicast** The cluster adapter for the hosts are assigned the same unicast media access control (MAC) address. This requires an additional adapter to be installed for non-NLB communications between the cluster hosts. A second network adapter is required for peer-to-peer communications. There is also a possibility of switch flooding if the cluster is connected to a switch because all of the incoming packets are sent to all of the ports on the switch.

- **Multicast** The cluster adapter for the hosts retain their individual unicast MAC addresses, and they are all assigned a multicast MAC address. Unlike the unicast method, communications between the cluster hosts are not affected because each cluster retains a unique MAC address.

Once the cluster has been created, server nodes are added and will be assigned a host priority, as seen in Figure 10-23. The host priority specifies the node that will handle cluster traffic that is not governed by port rules. If this node fails or goes offline, traffic will then be handled by the server with the next lowest priority. In an active/passive mode (single host mode), the server with priority 1 is the active node.

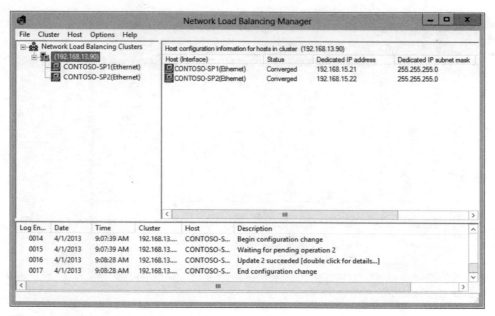

FIGURE 10-23 Network Load Balancing Manager.

Putting it all together

In this chapter, you were introduced to several major topics that all begin with understanding one thing: SLAs. All too often, companies try to incorporate BCM methodologies without understanding what their users both expect and require. Prior to implementing a strategy, one should make sure that there is a mutual understanding between the stakeholders, users, and infrastructure teams of what needs to be protected, how it is going to be protected, who is responsible for putting those measures in place, and who is responsible for testing them. In this section, you are going to expand the focus on what you have learned by creating a HA/DR plan for Contoso.

Contoso requirements

Contoso has a new chief technology officer (CTO) and has decided that its SharePoint 2013 farm should be classified as "business vital." (Review the classifications mentioned earlier in the chapter to see how this relates to uptime.) The SharePoint implementation is surfacing LOB data using Business Data Connectivity Services (BCS), Secure Store Service (SSS), and Enterprise Search. While the CTO understands that it will be difficult and expensive to build a solution that provides five nines of support, he wants it to be as close as possible. The Enterprise Search service is absolutely critical, as is the LOB system; furthermore, it would be ideal if the databases that weren't being used to support SharePoint actively could be used for other operations. Consultants need this data to perform their jobs and if SharePoint goes down, the company is crippled. Since the data is critical, it is imperative that no saved data is lost; furthermore, the data should have redundant I/O paths in case of corrupted data. The CTO heard that SQL Server 2012 has improved support for geoclustering, and he wants to leverage as much as possible from the product. Contoso has a worldwide presence and needs to operate in the unlikely event of a national disaster; the company has data centers in San Diego, California, and Denver, Colorado. If something should happen to the San Diego office, Denver is to be used to support the SharePoint implementation.

The SharePoint implementation will be supporting up to 500 concurrent users, and a single hardware failure should not cause a discontinuation of service. In the event of a local disruption in California, the CTO expects the Denver infrastructure to be available for requests within 30 minutes. SharePoint patches and upgrades should not cause a disruption of services from Sunday night through Friday night; the company has planned outage periods when these services should be performed. During these patches, a status message should inform the users of when they can expect full access to the system.

SharePoint items should be able to be recovered by the site collection administrator for 45 days, and in the event that this time expires, the item should be recoverable for up to 6 months by the SharePoint farm administrator. All SharePoint backups will be done by the spAdmin account, and they will be stored in a network share directory. It would be nice if there was a way to automate farm backups.

Key factors

Based on the requirements in the previous section, what factors do you see that give shape to a solution? While there may be more than one solution, here are the key concepts that you will need to plan for to have a successful implementation:

- Contoso has a worldwide presence and needs to operate in the unlikely event of a national disaster; there are data centers in San Diego, California, and Denver, Colorado. The latency between San Diego and Denver exceeds the 2-millisecond round trip.

- Contoso cannot lose any saved data, and all of its data can be inaccessible for 30 minutes.

- The data should have redundant I/O paths in case of corrupted data.

- The user accounts that need to perform backup and restore operations will require the SharePoint_Shell_Access role for each database that will be part of the job.

- A landing page for site maintenance will need to be created to give the information workers details about the maintenance period.

- The *ReadOnlyMaintenanceLink* for each web application will need to be configured.

- The system should support up to 500 concurrent users, and a single hardware failure should not cause a discontinuation of service.

- The Enterprise Search service is absolutely critical, as are the LOB systems.

- The Recycle Bin will need to be modified slightly to support the 45-day item restore.

Solution

The CTO has made it clear that he would like to have a geoclustered (stretched-farm) environment and that there are two data centers: one in San Diego and one in Denver. The biggest issue is that the latency between these two cities exceeds the Microsoft support limit of 2 milliseconds. This does not mean that both data centers can't be utilized; it just means that in case of a local disruption, all of the servers must switch over. So long as the SharePoint servers are in close proximity to the SQL Server servers, then having multiple data centers will fit into the equation. Contoso will use DNS to switch between the Primary and DR farms. This will have to be continuously monitored, as the switch needs to happen within 30 minutes to stay within the constraints of the SLA. Due to the need for the second farm to handle 500 concurrent users, a hardware or software load balancer will be needed. In a mission-critical environment, it is recommended that a hardware load balancer be used, but in situations where this may have a budget constraint, the use of Windows NLB will satisfy the requirement. An example of the proposed solution is illustrated in Figure 10-24.

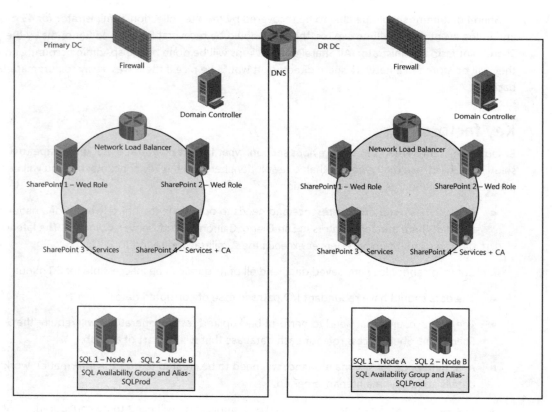

FIGURE 10-24 A high-availability network with a secondary location.

Contoso does not want to lose any saved data. This automatically brings to mind Windows failover clustering, database mirroring, or HADRON as a solution. Due to the need to have redundant I/O paths, this would eliminate failover clustering, as this is only a feature of database mirroring and HADRON. The need to duplicate data from one environment (San Diego) to another (Denver) either calls for an implementation of log shipping or the use of HADRON. In this case, the CTO is on board with SQL Server 2012, so HADRON offers a great solution. If this was a budget-constrained environment, the combination of database mirroring and log shipping may be more appropriate.

There is only one user that will be performing SharePoint Farm backups. This user will need to be added to the SharePoint_Shell_Access role by using the *Add-SPShellAdmin* cmdlet. The network share directory will need to give both the SharePoint timer job account (Farm Account) and the SQL Server service account full access to this location. The spAdmin user account will not need permission, as this job happens under the context of the other two accounts.

A landing page will need to be created that updates the information workers on the status of any service disruptions. This can be done within the Site Pages library of SharePoint, as shown in Figure 10-11. Windows PowerShell will then be used to set the *ReadOnlyMaintenanceLink* property.

The high impact of several of the SharePoint service applications would require that these services are running on more than one farm. Depending on the service and how it taxes the host server, it may be appropriate to have the services running on all four SharePoint servers. The Enterprise Search service application should be running in some form or another on each of the servers. There are multiple components that will need to be planned for.

To complete the solution, a working knowledge of the Recycle Bin and SharePoint cmdlets will be important. The default setting of the Recycle Bin's first stage is 30 days. This will need to be changed to 45 days, after which the item is no longer retrievable without going to an unattached copy of the database or other granular copy. The SharePoint backup cmdlets can be used to create a Windows PowerShell script file (*.ps1*) hat can be executed via a Windows Scheduled Task. This would allow for farm backups that are capable of protecting much more than the databases.

There are some additional benefits to this particular implementation. The second farm could be used as a testing area for upgrades, but this would put the company's SLAs at risk should a fault domain failure require the secondary farm to spring into action.

As you can see, there are many different options to weigh when trying to determine the best solution. The most important factor is to get an SLA that is achievable and then use the advantages and disadvantages of the various technologies to help identify the solution that is right for you.

## CHAPTER 11

Validating your architecture

In this chapter, you will learn about:

- Verifying server happiness through the use of Unified Logging System (ULS) verification.

- Verifying port allocation and web requests.

- Verifying Kerberos.

- Utilizing tools for network sniffing and packet tracing.

- Stress testing various environments.

You have finally installed and started to set up your Microsoft SharePoint Server 2013 environment, but is it set up correctly? Is your farm functioning within your expectations? Are there hiccups in your network infrastructure? This chapter is about different methods for monitoring and stress-testing your SharePoint 2013 environment(s).

You want to make sure that your environment is ready to handle more than the group of test users and administrators by really taxing your environment and making sure that your SharePoint Server 2013 environment and applications are running on the correct ports. SharePoint is a very robust tool; it can handle a couple of hundred users without slowing down; the problem is that SharePoint can handle that workload even with imperfections on the back end. However, if you start increasing your farm utilization, the imperfections will start to have dire consequences on your farm, as your performance will decrease and potentially crash your environment. This chapter will help you find those issues before they happen and verify your architecture and your installation.

If you are upgrading from SharePoint Server 2010 to SharePoint Server 2013, you should have a spot-on idea of your farm load, and if you are doing a fresh installation of SharePoint Server 2013, you should have a rough idea of your user utilization. In your capacity planning, you should already have come up with the values for your farm metrics; if not, spend some time researching so that you have an idea of the values for your user utilization metrics before testing your environment. This chapter assumes that your Active Directory (AD) and ability to log on can handle your SharePoint traffic and is robust enough to handle the load and stress testing described in this chapter.

Verify farm contentment

You have installed SharePoint, opened up Central Administration, and created the required service applications. Everything seems to be working okay through the browser, but how can you be sure that everything is working behind the scenes? As discussed in Chapter 8, "Planning an upgrade strategy," SharePoint Server 2013 outputs in a Unified Logging System (ULS) standardized format, which means that you can now use different methods to monitor your environment. In Chapter 9, "Maintaining and monitoring Microsoft SharePoint," you learned what to monitor on a daily basis to maintain a healthy farm, and that keeping up to date with your logs will help you achieve the goal of a happy and healthy farm. There are many ULS viewers available; this section explores one viewer to monitor your farm and one viewer to monitor your webpages.

Microsoft ULS Viewer

With the amount of data that gets written by SharePoint into its ULS logs, it is easy to miss errors, especially if you are running more than one SharePoint server. Try to minimize the amount of errors that you are receiving before putting your farm into production, and once your farm is in production, make sure that you stay ahead of the errors by monitoring your farm logs. The best way to validate that your farm is not outputting any errors is to review your farm's ULS logs. One way to track errors in the ULS logs is to use Microsoft ULS Viewer (*http://tinyurl.com/PCfromDC-ULS*). ULS Viewer will allow you to do things like sort, filter, and highlight log entries based on what you are trying to accomplish. The added bonus is that you can monitor remote machines' logs and open log files from multiple machines at the same time. To monitor log files from a remote machine, create a share for the root LOGS folder. The default folder location is located at

```
C:\Program Files\Common Files\microsoft shared\Web Server Extensions\15\LOGS
```

Set the folder share for either the SharePoint Administrator account (*spAdmin*) or a specific security group (*spAdmins*) and assign the group read permissions. Do not share the folder with Everyone because you do not want to grant everyone access to your SharePoint servers. Remember to write down the share name, as it will be needed to set up the ULS Runtime Feed.

Another server that you can grab the ULS log files from would be your Microsoft Office Web Application Server 2012 (WAC server, formerly known as OWA). Enable sharing of the Logs folder as well, and its default folder location is

```
C:\ProgramData\Microsoft\OfficeWebApps\Data\Logs
```

Remember that the ProgramData folder is a hidden folder. In Windows Server 2012, enable viewing of hidden files and folders by going into File Explorer (formerly known as Windows Explorer), selecting View on the ribbon, and selecting Hidden Items from the Show/Hide section. Write down the share name, as it will be needed to set up the ULS Runtime Feed.

Setting up ULS Viewer

There are two options when it comes to where to install your ULS Viewer: locally on your client or somewhere on your server farm. You should install the ULS Viewer on your local client, not on any of your SharePoint farm servers. There is no reason to be logged on to your production environment if you do not have to be there.

This demonstration sets up the ULS Viewer in a Windows 8 Enterprise (x64) environment. ULS Viewer requires the ".NET Framework (includes .NET 2.0 and 3.0)" Windows feature to run. After granting read access to the ULS LOGS folders for your environment(s), and after installing the ULS Viewer, point the ULS Viewer at all the LOGS folders for your farm.

Start by Shift + right-clicking the ULS View icon and selecting Run As Different User (see Figure 11-1). Start the program as the user (hopefully the SharePoint Admin Account) that you gave the read-only permissions for the LOGS folders.

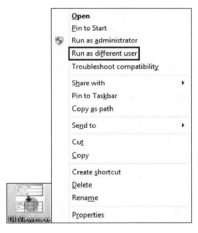

FIGURE 11-1 Run the ULS Viewer as the farm administrator.

You are then going to start adding the ULS LOGS folder locations that you want to monitor (see Figure 11-2).

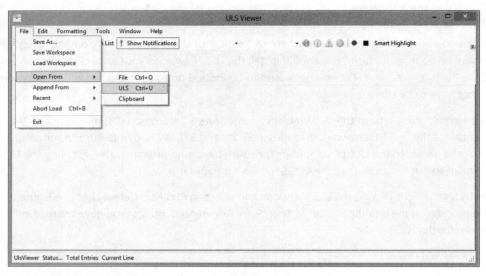

FIGURE 11-2 Adding the ULS LOGS folders to the ULS Viewer.

Put in the location of the LOGS folder into the Log File Location text box, as shown in Figure 11-3.

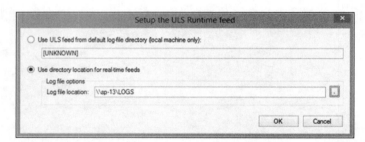

FIGURE 11-3 Enter the location of the LOGS share folder in the Log File Location box.

You should have one tab for each log file location entered.

As shown in Figure 11-4, select the level of severity of the messages that you wish to see for each server, enable the correlation tree, verify that you have the Show Notifications option turned on, and then save your workspace.

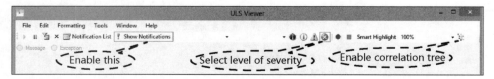

FIGURE 11-4 The settings for the common features of the ULS Viewer.

You can create several versions of workspaces to make it easier to track what is important to get your task completed.

The ULS Viewer from Microsoft is a fantastic tool to start the validation process of your installation through the tracking of critical errors. While some might be tempted to leave the viewer running all the time to find critical errors, it is best to just use the tool when needed.

Developer Dashboard

In SharePoint Server 2013, you now have the ability to monitor page load issues found within the ULS files through the use of the Developer Dashboard. The improved Developer Dashboard in SharePoint Server 2013 is a fantastic tool that now has several troubleshooting tabs on one page. As stated back in Chapter 9, the ULS Log tab displays the ULS log entries for the particular page, but there is also a SQL tab that shows you the SQL queries that SharePoint has performed for that request. If you are having page-loading issues, the Developer Dashboard is a great starting place for troubleshooting. Just make sure that you have the Usage And Health Data Collection Service application created. Once your farm is up and running, it is a good idea to enable your Developer Dashboard and log your baseline page load and SQL execution times. Over time, as your farm grows and as you customize your pages, you will need to know the impact that the new features added to your farm. Without baseline numbers, you will not have any clue as to what your branding has done to your page load times or what that change to SQL has affected. Let's take a look at Figure 11-5 and Figure 11-6 and review some of the data returned.

FIGURE 11-5 This screen shows the page load information from the SP-15 server.

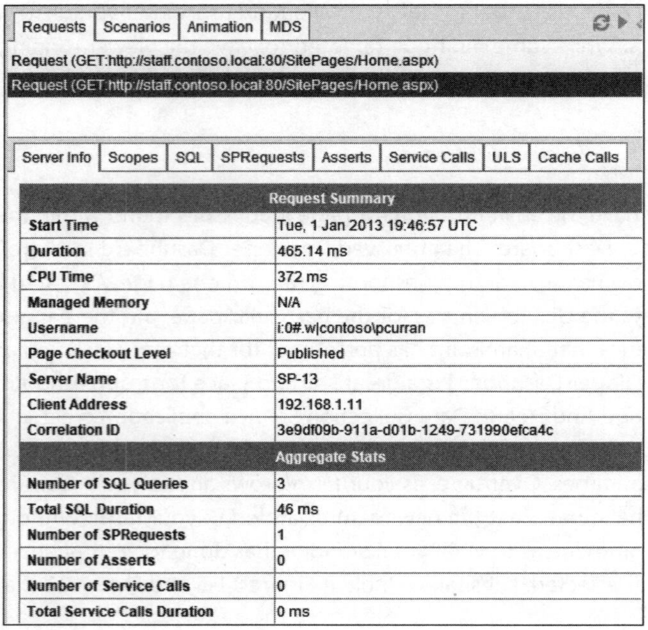

| Requests | Scenarios | Animation | MDS | | | | | ⟳ ▶ |

Request (GET:http://staff.contoso.local:80/SitePages/Home.aspx)

Request (GET:http://staff.contoso.local:80/SitePages/Home.aspx)

| Server Info | Scopes | SQL | SPRequests | Asserts | Service Calls | ULS | Cache Calls |

Request Summary	
Start Time	Tue, 1 Jan 2013 19:46:57 UTC
Duration	465.14 ms
CPU Time	372 ms
Managed Memory	N/A
Username	i:0#.w|contoso\pcurran
Page Checkout Level	Published
Server Name	SP-13
Client Address	192.168.1.11
Correlation ID	3e9df09b-911a-d01b-1249-731990efca4c
Aggregate Stats	
Number of SQL Queries	3
Total SQL Duration	46 ms
Number of SPRequests	1
Number of Asserts	0
Number of Service Calls	0
Total Service Calls Duration	0 ms

FIGURE 11-6 This screen shows the page load information from the SP-13 server.

As you can see, the Requests tab in both Figure 11-5 and Figure 11-6 is requesting the same page. However, the page load times are different. Reading through the dashboard a bit more, notice that the pages are coming back from different servers. Even if these screenshots were from the same server, the timed duration would not be identical, so it is best to refresh the page 12 times or more to get a good average before you determine your estimated page load time. If these numbers were indicative of the mean page load time, then you would have a good starting location for troubleshooting why one server takes four times longer to load than the other.

Another thing that you should be aware of is that the times returned are measured in milliseconds (ms), which is equal to 1/1000 of a second (that is, .001 of 1 second). Before spending too much time on troubleshooting the issue of one server loading four times slower than another, you might want to justify why you are trying to solve a 3/10 of a second page load issue. Developer Dashboard will also help with the issue of users telling you that a page is "slow to load." "Slow" is a subjective term, so the best way to determine the truth is to compare the actual page load measurements of the "slow" page to the baseline numbers that were first recorded when you stood up the farm.

Verifying port allocation and web requests

The ability to monitor your farm is important, but making sure that your web requests are going to the correct place on the correct port is just as crucial. For example, if one of the custom applications from the SharePoint App Store is not returning data or if you just want to verify that feeds within your webpage are accessing the data from the correct URL, then you will need a tool to capture your network traffic.

Fiddler

Having the ability to look at the captured HTTP(S) protocol is very important when trying to debug or troubleshoot SharePoint, as not everything is written into the ULS logs. One of the industry-standard tools is Fiddler (*http://www.fiddler2.com*), which is used to capture HTTP and HTTPS traffic and allows the user to review and even "fiddle" with the HTTP traffic as it is being sent. Fiddler currently has two versions. The first version, Fiddler2, is for machines that use .NET 2.*x*, and the second version, Fiddler4, is for machines that use .NET 4.*x*. The version that you download depends on the .NET version you have running on the machine that will be running Fiddler, not what .NET version SharePoint is running. You should not need to install this on a production server, but on your local client or on a server in your test farm.

Setting up Fiddler

If you are installing Fiddler on a Windows 8 client, you should download Fiddler4 from *http://tinyurl .com/PCfromDC-Fiddler4*. After downloading the program, run the installer as the Administrator, click Next a couple of times, and finally close out the installer; your default browser should pop up and tell you that your installation was successful.

There are add-ons that you can install for Fiddler to help with a variety of tasks. You can review the add-ons at *http://tinyurl.com/PCfromDC-Extensions*. With Windows 8, you have the ability to capture the app traffic as well, so make sure that if you are using Fiddler for only capturing your SharePoint HTTP traffic, keep the tracking of Windows 8 apps functionality disabled to keep your web session traffic capture as clean as possible.

Internet Explorer Developer Tools

Like Fiddler, Windows Internet Explorer Developer Tools (IE Dev Tools) is used to help debug webpages. With IE Dev Tools, you have the ability to read through, and even modify, the HTML and Cascading Style Sheets (CSS) of the page. While Fiddler is known for its network capturing ability, IE Dev Tools also has that ability.

From within Internet Explorer versions 8, 9, and 10, you can access IE Dev Tools by pressing F12. If you are still running earlier versions of Internet Explorer (either Internet Explorer 6 or Internet Explorer 7), you can download the IE Developer Toolbar from *http://tinyurl.com/PCfromDC-DevToolBar*.

You'll learn more about how to utilize some of the functionality of IE Dev Tools in the "Performance-testing your environment" section later in this chapter.

Verifying Kerberos with Klist

You may believe that you have set up your delegation of authentication correctly, but because authentication happens behind the scenes, how can you be sure? With the release of Windows Server 2003, you had the ability to use a product named Kerbtray to help troubleshoot Kerberos tickets. Since Windows Server 2008, there is now the ability to use a built-in tool called Klist, and you can even access Klist from the command prompt in Windows 8. Klist is used to help manage the Kerberos ticket cache and will allow you to view and even delete (purge) all the Kerberos tickets for the specified logon session. You can read about Klist and its parameters at *http://tinyurl.com/PCfromDC-Klist*.

Klist will be utilized to help validate a Kerberos implementation in the "Putting it all together" section at the end of this chapter.

Inspecting your network packets

Why in the world would there be a section about network troubleshooting in a SharePoint book? The servers are talking, and the service accounts are authenticating, so it all must be working correctly, right? While SharePoint is a reliable product, there are standards that need to be met to make sure that your environment is running correctly. SharePoint requires a fast network, and your fast network will give a distributed SharePoint farm faster inter-server communications. This faster inter-server communication means that your clients have the ability to access their data faster. The speed of communication and return of data are especially important when you distribute your services across multiple servers or federate services from other farms. The network round trip between the client and server(s) has the single biggest impact on webpage performance and can have a larger impact than server response time.

There is significant traffic in a SharePoint farm across the web server tier, the application server tier, and the database server tier, and your network can easily become a bottleneck under heavy loads, especially if you are dealing with large files. Web servers and application servers should be configured to use at least two network interface cards (NICs)—using one NIC to handle user traffic and the other to handle the inter-server communications. Network latency between servers can have a significant effect on performance. Therefore, it is important to maintain a network latency that is equal to or less than 1 millisecond between the web server and the SQL Server–based computers hosting the content databases. Not only is it important, it is a requirement! The SQL Server-based computers that host each service application database should be as close as possible to the consuming application server, and don't forget that there should be less than a 20-millisecond latency for your SQL Read/Write. The network between farm servers also requires that you use at least 1 Gbps of bandwidth for your NICs. The validation of 1-Gbps NICs, switches, and cable is pretty simple, but how can you be sure that the electrons are flowing fast enough? How can you be sure that the latency of your network is within specifications? It might not even be possible for you to have a latency of less than 1 millisecond or even ping other servers based on your switch configuration. Once you have exhausted the use of Fiddler, there are a couple of options to help you dive deeper into inspecting your network, as described in the following subsections.

Microsoft Network Monitor

One of the tools created by Microsoft to help you determine the health and speed of your network is called Microsoft Network Monitor (Netmon). The current version is 3.4 and was last published back in 2010. You can download version 3.4.2350 from *http://tinyurl.com/PCfromDC-Netmon*. There are add-ons available for Netmon, including Parser Profiles. Parser Profiles provide even more useful information about every packet because they are prebuilt profiles to help you set up Netmon for what you are trying to monitor. For example, you can download the Office and SharePoint Products Network Monitor Parsers to extend the functionality of Netmon by filtering packets based on the rules defined within the parser for Office and SharePoint. You can download the parser from *http://tinyurl.com/PCfromDC-SPParser*. Another fun add-on for Netmon is TCP Analyzer (*http://tinyurl.com/PCfromDC-Analyzer*), and for tracking heavy network traffic culprits there is Top Users Expert for Network Monitor (*http://tinyurl.com/PCfromDC-TopUsers*).

After you install Netmon, log off the machine and then log on again before you try to start capturing network packets using Netmon.

Microsoft Message Analyzer

Microsoft Message Analyzer (MMA) is the successor to Netmon. At the time this chapter was written, MMA was still in beta, and the Test Suite was at Beta 4.0.5494.0. You can download MMA from *http://tinyurl.com/PCfromDC-MMA*. MMA is a fantastic troubleshooting tool, not just for network traffic but for any kind of communication such as USB, Bluetooth, and wireless local area networks (LANs). Out of the box, you have the ability to monitor all network LAN traffic on your client or select the Web Proxy trace scenario and monitor only the web traffic.

Just like Netmon, after installing MMA, log off the machine and then log on again before attempting to start capturing packets.

Testing your environments

You have your farm set up, the user acceptance testing has gone swimmingly, and all that is left is for the Domain Name System (DNS) team to update the Host-A record to open your site to the world. Unfortunately, the marketing team put out a press release telling the world about your new site and offering a free $200 gift card to the first 100,000 visitors! Nobody likes to be caught off guard, especially by a phone call from the boss asking why, when he browses to his brand-new SharePoint environment, he keeps getting an error message that tells him that the server is busy and that he should try his request again later.

The servers that host your SharePoint farm are tools, and it is important to know the limitations of your tools so they don't break when you need them the most. Maybe you have a service-level agreement (SLA) that requires your farm to handle 100,000 users simultaneously with a maximum page load time of 1 second or that the CPU percentage and RAM utilization is less than 85 percent when under maximum load. If you do not load-test your environment before going live, you have the potential to run into server failure issues without fully understanding why. Knowing that your farm can handle your day-to-day workload is not enough; you want to see what your environment can handle so that when you start to reach the threshold of your farm, you can add, expand, or upgrade hardware to handle the growth. You need to know the limitations of your environment because telling your boss, "Theoretically, the farm should be able to handle 200,000 simultaneous users," should not be an acceptable statement at any organization. Having the ability to tell your boss, "Currently, the farm can handle 200,000 simultaneous users," is great, and it's even better if you know that you only have 10,000 people that hit your farm simultaneously. On the flip side, it is great to have that level of detailed farm knowledge, especially if you are expecting 500,000 simultaneous users, because you caught it before going live (however, you should probably review Chapter 3, "Gathering requirements").

Inspecting your IIS logs

Knowing where you have been is critical to the understanding of where you are going. By looking through your existing Internet Information Service (IIS) logs (SharePoint or not), you can gather a lot of information required for testing your new environment (SharePoint or not). If you have logging enabled within IIS, then you will be able to come up with actual numbers for your load- and stress-testing scenarios. As shown in Figure 11-7, you can validate IIS logging or start your IIS logging by going to the web server that is hosting IIS, selecting the server name from the connections section, and selecting Logging under the IIS features.

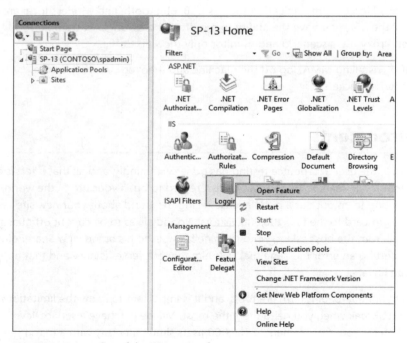

FIGURE 11-7 Location of the IIS Logging feature.

If you have had your logging disabled, try to start collecting data for at least two weeks so that you can get a minimum set of site utilization statistics. Also, you might want to start researching why logging was turned off before you re-enable it. If IIS is handling a lot of traffic, your log storage might exceed your hard drive free space and cause other issues (possibly to the extent of taking down the server). Please use extreme caution when enabling your IIS logging.

To enable logging, with the Logging feature open (as in Figure 11-7), review the settings and browse to the IIS Logs Directory. The default directory is %SystemDrive%\inetpub\logs\LogFiles; and, as shown in Figure 11-8, you will notice that when you browse to your log file directory, you will see one folder per IIS site (web application). Depending on which site's information you are trying to gather, find the appropriate log file under the ID of the folder.

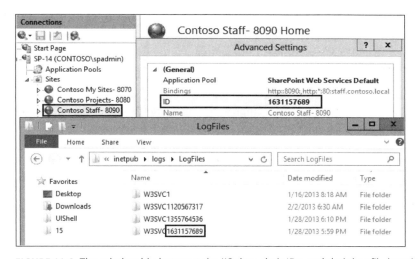

FIGURE 11-8 The relationship between the IIS sites, their IDs, and their log file location.

By adjusting your log files to be multiplexed into one log file per server, IIS log setup is another area of potential server resource savings. For example, if your IIS is hosting 20 web applications, the server is processing a lot of formatted information and writing it into 20 separate IIS site logs. By creating a centralized, server-based, unformatted binary log file, you will save on server resources because the service will have to write to only one file.

Microsoft Log Parser

Now that you have figured out where your logs are located and have seen that you actually have log files to review, what is an efficient way to comb through the data? Microsoft has created a program called Log Parser to help you solve that problem. At the time of writing this chapter, Log Parser is at version 2.2, and was published in April 2005. You can download Log Parser 2.2 from *http://tinyurl.com/PCfromDC-LP22*.

Log Parser is a powerful tool that can handle several types of input file formats, including:

- Log files generated by IIS.

- Text files such as XML, CSV, TSV, NCSA, and W3C.

- Windows Event Logs.

- NetMon capture files (.*cap*).

- Custom objects. If you find that Log Parser cannot parse the information that you want to go through, you can create a custom input file format plug-in.

Running queries against log files that might have millions of records is a daunting task, and not something that you want your web server to manage along with the web traffic. So just like you did previously in the "Setting up ULS Viewer" section, you are going to share the IIS LogFiles folder with read-only permissions for the SharePoint administrator so that you can run Log Parser from your client desktop and not from the server.

While Log Parser is an invaluable tool, there are a couple of problems with using Log Parser. One problem is that Log Parser is a command-line executable, so there is no GUI. The second problem is that you need to be able to write SQL queries to return the data that you are interested in finding. For those of you who do not want to spend the day looking up queries on Bing and are tired of command-line operations, there is an add-on from the Exchange Gallery of Microsoft TechNet called Log Parser Studio (LPS). You can download LPS from *http://tinyurl.com/PCfromDC-LPS*. Once you have set up your folder share and you have installed Log Parser, you can install LPS.

Setting up LPS

With your LogFiles folder permissions set for only the SharePoint Administrator, Shift+ right-click the LPS icon and run LPS as the SP Admin. Once LPS opens up, familiarize yourself with the program layout (see Figure 11-9). Notice that there are 117 queries already created for you, along with descriptions and the actual query as well. This should be enough to help you create your own queries and add them to the library.

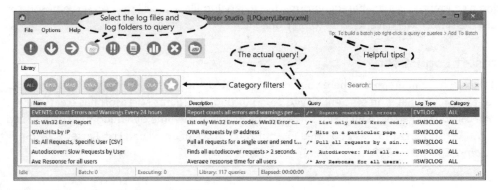

FIGURE 11-9 An introduction to the LPS layout.

To start getting back information, assign a log file or folder to have LPS query against. Press Log Folder to open up the Log File Manager window. Next, add the folder and the files that you want to query. When you go to select a folder, you will actually have to select a file to open, but once you click Open, notice that the saved file is marked like all the files within the folder (see Figure 11-10).

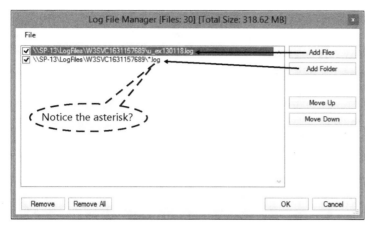

FIGURE 11-10 Addition of the log files and folders.

Out of the box, LPS does not give you the ability to query how many requests are made per second, but there is an out-of-the-box query to return the number of requests per hour. Look for the IIS:Request Per Hour query, and double-click the row to open up the query window, as shown in Figure 11-11.

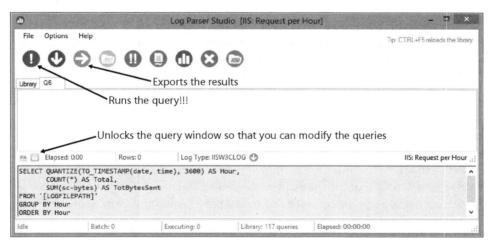

FIGURE 11-11 How to run a query to return the requests per hour from IIS.

After you run the query, the number of requests per hour for that site will be displayed. Click the green arrow to export the .csv file so that you can work with the numbers in Microsoft Excel. To get the number of requests per second (RPS), you take your total amount of requests for the hour and divide by 3,600. Another important thing to keep in mind is that if you have a network load balancer (NLB), and your total requests per hour are dramatically different for each web server, then you have some research to do into why your NLB is not distributing calls evenly.

Performance-testing your environment

Performance testing is used to help make the user experience better. Performance testing is done to reduce bottlenecks and establish your baseline numbers for future testing. Without performance testing and recording baseline values, how do you know if your site is running slow or if the page load times have degraded over time or degraded after the last branding enhancement? Running performance tests, and then finding and fixing any bottlenecks prior to going live, will help reduce the chance of accidentally tarnishing your corporation's web presence. Not having your bottlenecks addressed in the performance testing stage will become evident as you go through load testing and stress testing.

Performance-testing your environment is not an activity that should be taken lightly. You should put as much time as required into preparing for your testing, and not just rush ahead to get to the pretty graphs at the end. To create a valid performance test for your environment, you must know how your organization uses SharePoint. You will probably create several performance tests based on your user utilization (also known as a *Transactional Mix*) to help with finding bottlenecks and pain points for the users.

Creating your test plan

There are lots of questions that will need to be answered and a lot of work that will need to be done before moving on to load testing. As with any plan, you should know ahead of time what your goal for testing is going to be. You should understand the objectives and how to reach them consistently and reliably. If you create a test plan and cannot re-create the results, then you do not have a valid test plan. Your tests need to be reliable, consistent, and repeatable.

What is your objective? If your objective is to measure throughput capacity, then pay close attention to the RPS and page latency. If you are testing search performance, you might be looking at your crawl times and indexing rates. If you want to measure hardware performance, you might look at % Processor Time and RAM utilization. If you are testing pages that have custom code, conduct your performance testing of the code in isolation before bringing it into SharePoint for testing. After your isolation testing, compare the performance of how well your custom code worked in isolation compared to how your code ran within SharePoint. You really need to know and understand your objective so that you can create a valid test model before starting your performance testing, especially if you are planning on conducting load testing as well.

After you have determined the metrics that will tell you if your performance is acceptable, and you have completed a metrics table that also tells you what is marginal and what is not acceptable, it is time to start doing performance tests.

The odds are good that you are interested in creating an environment that loads a webpage quickly, uploads documents quickly, and allows you and your users to view documents quickly. To help with determining the baseline numbers, there is a tool created by Microsoft called Visual Round Trip Analyzer (VRTA). This is another tool that was built upon Netmon (previously discussed in the "Microsoft Network Monitor" section) and is downloadable from *http://tinyurl.com/PCfromDC-MSVRTA*.

The VRTA helps you visualize the download of webpages and identify best practices, and it will even recommend changes to your environment that will help improve web performance. VRTA examines the communications protocol, identifies the causes of excessive round trips, and recommends solutions.

Test your environment over a variety of scenarios. For example, you might test the following:

- Cold page load (uncached, first page load of the day), as shown in Figure 11-12

- Fresh page load (uncached, browser closed then opened), as shown in Figure 11-13

- Refreshed page load (cached), as shown in Figure 11-14

- Refreshed page load (browser cache cleared), as shown in Figure 11-15

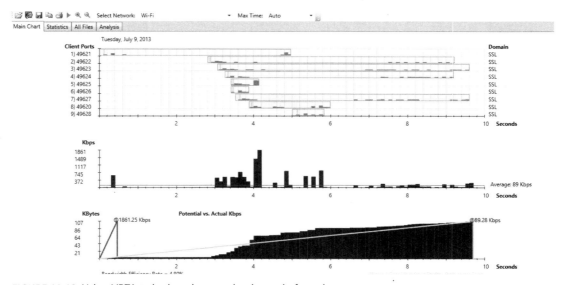

FIGURE 11-12 Using VRTA to look at the page load speed of a stale page.

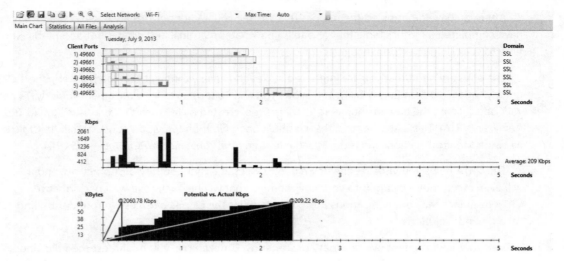

FIGURE 11-13 Using VRTA to look at the page load speed of a freshly opened browser.

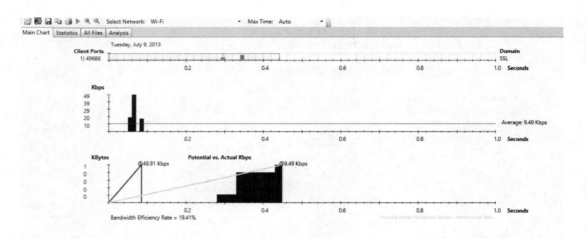

FIGURE 11-14 Using VRTA to look at the page load speed of a refreshed browser page.

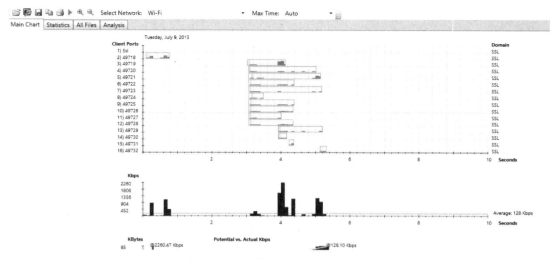

FIGURE 11-15 An example of returned page speed after the browser cache has been cleared and the page had been refreshed.

The things that you should notice are not just the load times, but also the bandwidth efficiency and how many different items and item types (different colors) are being loaded. After you have your data captured, you can click the Analysis tab and have VRTA tell you how to improve your performance.

One way to clean up your environment and increase the performance of your pages is to look at your network's bandwidth efficiency. Another way to improve your performance is to look at how you have your CSS files, JavaScript files, and image files loading. To track down your speed issues, you should consider using IE Dev Tools. You can use these tools to create a waterfall presentation of your network traffic and troubleshoot your performance issues. With IE Dev Tools, you are going to focus on page loads after your browser cache has been cleared and page loads when you refresh a page.

As shown in Figure 11-16, there are two ways to get to your IE Dev Tools: either by pressing F12 or selecting Tools (Alt + x) | Developer Tools.

FIGURE 11-16 Enabling IE Dev Tools.

Next, as shown in Figure 11-17, select Network | Start Capturing. Once you are capturing your network traffic, either go to one of your pages or refresh a page that you have open. When your page starts to load, the summary waterfall will start to appear.

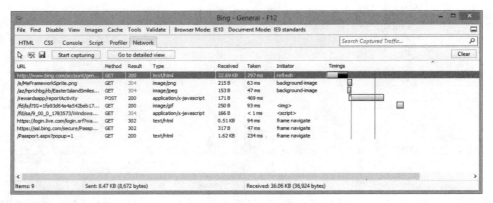

FIGURE 11-17 A waterfall summary of a page request and load.

There is a ton of information on this chart. You can see that this page load has 13 items downloaded, and that Bing.com was sent 9.8 KB of data and in return received 32.6 KB of information. For each item requested, you have the ability to look at the URL and view the method used for the request (*GET, POST, PUT*, and so on), the size of the item received, and how long the item took to download. Understanding the protocols for the results will help you improve your performance. Table 11-1 shows three result codes as defined by W3.org.

TABLE 11-1 Standard result codes

Code	Title	Meaning
200	OK	Request has succeeded
302	Found	The requested resource resides temporarily under a different Uniform Resource Identifier (URI). Because the redirection might be altered on occasion, the client should continue to use the Request-URI for future requests. This response is only cacheable if indicated by a Cache-Control or Expires header field.
304	Not Modified	If the client has performed a conditional *GET* request and access is allowed, but the document has not been modified, the server should respond with this status code.

You can read through all of the status code definitions by going to *http://tinyurl.com/PCfromDC-w3*.

It is important to understand the codes returned because you need to know how your requests are getting returned. If your branding team has decided to change your site's look and feel, and you get bombarded with complaints about how slow things have become, you should know why. You do not want your branding team to say that your environment cannot handle their modifications, when the problem is actually the 30 JavaScript calls that they added.

To drill down into the network information a bit further, double-click the top URL, which should be the URL of the page that you requested. If you click the Timings tab, as shown in Figure 11-18, you should see the detailed view of the page request for the URL.

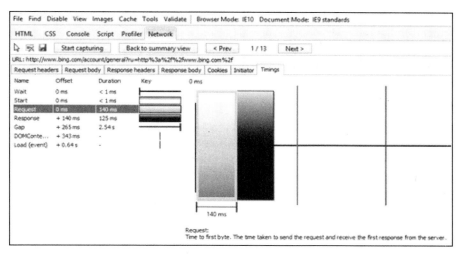

FIGURE 11-18 A detailed view of the page load timings.

Every request that you send has a standard set of processes that it goes through, as shown in Figure 11-19 and described in the following list. The Timings window will be a very useful tool when you are trying to fine-tune your page load performance.

- **Wait** This is the amount of time spent in a sending queue. There are only so many connections allowed by a browser into one domain at the same time.

- **Start** This is the amount of time it took to create the request and send it.

- **Request** Also known as *time to first byte,* this is the amount of time from when you send the request to when the first byte is returned by the web server.

- **Response** This is the time taken to receive the response data from the server. It would be the time from the first byte returned to the last byte of the web server response to your request.

- **Gap** This is a critical number. It is the amount of time between the response and when the page is finished loading.

- **DOMContentLoaded** This is represented by a green vertical line. The *DOMContentLoaded* event is the same as *document.interactive*, which means that JavaScript can now run on the page. DOM stands for *Document Object Model,* which w3 defines as follows:

  "...platform- and language-neutral interface that will allow programs and scripts to dynamically access and update the content, structure, and style of documents. The document can be further processed and the results of that processing can be incorporated back into the presented page."

- **Load** Represented by a red vertical line, load is the amount of time taken to finish your page load from start to finish.

It is possible to have items loaded, or deferred until after the page load, which means that the client can interact with the page while objects are still being loaded. If you want to see an excellent example of how Microsoft cleaned up their files on page load for their SharePoint.Microsoft.com site, read "How we did it: Speeding up SharePoint.Microsoft.com" at *http://tinyurl.com/PCfromDC-spPerformance*. This blog post was written by Tony Tai when he was the senior product manager for SharePoint Server.

Remember that performance testing is not just about your page layouts and design. You could have NLB issues, improperly set-up NIC teaming, or a bad switch that could impede page response time as well. Another way to increase performance would be to enable Kerberos authentication. This would help by reducing the amount of network traffic used for authentication and by reducing the number of times users get authenticated down to one.

Load-testing your environment

While performance testing affects your clients' experience, load testing is mostly done to see how your clients' experience will affect your server operations. Load testing is done to find the highest level of utilization that a system can handle and still function properly without error, while still maintaining the standards that you established in your acceptable response time matrix.

For example, if 1,000 users hit your home page at the same time, a page load time of 2.5 seconds or less is acceptable, while anything over 3.5 seconds is a failure. Another example would be when there are 200 requests per second, an average CPU percentage utilization of less than 75 percent is acceptable, while spikes over 90 percent utilization for more than 30 seconds are not acceptable. From a load-testing scenario, start your testing at a basic level and keep increasing the number of users and simultaneous requests until you have reached an acceptable threshold, and keep the load test running for a period of time to really hammer your servers. The top-level threshold should be for a given period of time. If you are not likely to be hit by 50,000 simultaneous requests per second for 48 hours straight, don't test for it. You should make your load test as close to real life as possible. Load- and stress-testing your environment beyond what your farm is designed to handle can do real damage to your environment, so do not test for 50,000 simultaneous users when your environment is not designed for it—especially if your environment will only ever see 1,000 simultaneous users.

Test environment options

When it comes to building out your test environment, the first thing to determine is the type of environment that you want to create. If you will be testing a brand-new SharePoint Server 2013 environment that has not been signed off and approved to go live, then you are probably only looking to build out a client test machine and a load agent. If you are trying to test the performance of your current live production farm, consider creating a duplicate farm to run your tests against. You will not get good baseline numbers from a live production farm if there are fluctuations in simultaneous requests to the server that you are testing, and if you do take down your farm or destroy a server, you do not want to do it to your live production environment.

There are three common types of environments used in on-premises testing web servers. One environment runs everything off one client, as illustrated in Figure 11-19.

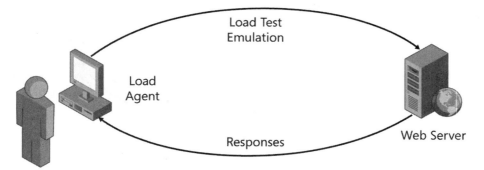

FIGURE 11-19 The most basic of load test scenarios.

The other two environments separate the load agent from the client. This is done because you might have more than one load tester or because you have only one server with enough RAM and CPU processing power to handle load testing. It may also be the case that your client does not have the hardware required to run the load test scenario successfully, as shown in Figure 11-20.

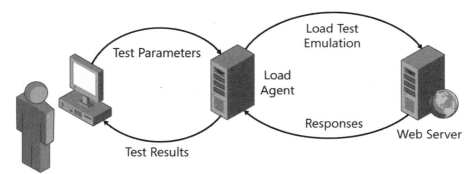

FIGURE 11-20 Load testing using a remote load agent.

By separating the load agent from the client, it also affords you the opportunity to run multiple load agents to help load-test your environment, as shown in Figure 11-21. Eventually, after you scale out your load test, you will run into a simulated user threshold for each load agent, and you will need to add another load agent to help with your simulation. You do not want your load agent to become a bottleneck for your testing environment. Your load agent should not exceed 75 percent CPU utilization, and you should not go below 10 percent availability of your physical RAM.

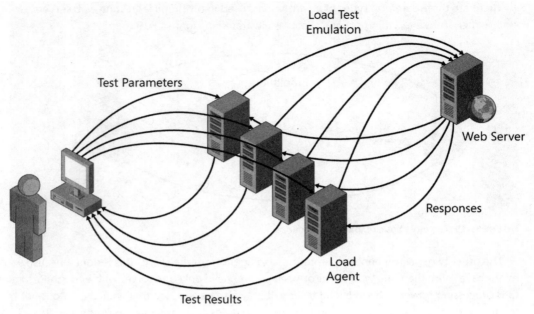

FIGURE 11-21 Load test utilizing multiple load agents.

Setting your load test standards

The first steps for creating your load test are to understand what you are trying to accomplish and how you are going to accomplish it, and know what results are acceptable or not. The goal for a load test is to find out the number of users that your environment can handle while they perform everyday normal activities, with enough headroom for service applications of SharePoint to do their job without causing errors within the farm. To help accomplish this goal, you will need to understand the following terms:

- **RPS**   The number of requests received by a farm or web server in 1 second. RPS is an industry standard used for determining server and farm utilization and load.

- **Total user count**   The maximum number of people who are accessing your site. This number could be the total number of unique users in AD.

- **Peak concurrent user percentage**   What the highest percentage of total users actively surfing your site at any given time. This could be when everyone gets in on Monday, after having coffee....

- **Green zone**   The performance envelope that your servers should be within while load tests are underway, or during normal business utilization.

  - Server Latency (Avg. Response Time): < 0.5 second.

- CPU Utilization (% Processor Time): 50 percent or less. This will allow for spikes in the farm caused by services such as Search Crawls and User Profile Synchronization and leave you enough headroom in CPU utilization before you enter the red zone.

- Available Memory (Available Mbytes): > 4 GB.

- **Red zone**   The acceptable peak for system performance. This is an area that your server can spike into momentarily, as to not create an adverse experience for the user or do permanent damage to the server itself. (Yes, this is a bit overly dramatic, but consider yourself warned.)

  - Server Latency (Avg. Response Time): > 1.0 second.

  - CPU Utilization (% Processor Time): 75 percent or less.

  - Available Memory (Available Mbytes): < 2 GB.

  - Average Page Load Time (Avg. Page Time): > 3.0 seconds

Next, you need to take a look at real numbers for how you are going to load-test your environment. If you already have an environment, pull out real numbers by using Log Parser, as discussed in the "Inspecting your IIS logs" section earlier in this chapter. If you do not have an established environment, there are some best-guess ratios that you can use so long as you know the number of users that will be using your SharePoint farm.

Determining your farm's capacity

By now, you should have a farm deployed and be ready to test to see if your theory and reality for farm load are anywhere close to being equal. SharePoint is a powerful tool, and the improvements within SharePoint Server 2013 to handle requests make SharePoint a resourceful tool that can handle more than you would expect. The question is, "How much can my farm really handle?" Figure 11-22 is an example of user utilization profiles. The chart shows how you can determine a rough estimate of the minimum RPS that your environment will need to be able to handle while staying within the green zone.

Total User Count	25,000			
Concurrent User Percentage	30%			
Peak Concurrent User Percentage	60%			
User Type	% of Type	Avg RPH / User	Avg RPH @ Peak Load	Avg RPS
Light Users	10.00%	20	30000	8.33
Typical Users	60.00%	40	360000	100.00
Heavy Users	20.00%	60	180000	50.00
Extere Users	10.00%	120	180000	50.00
Total	100.00%		750000	208.33
Avg RPH @ Peak Load = Total User Count * Peak Concurrent User % * User Type % * Avg RPH per User				
Avg RPS = Avg RPH @ Peak Load / 3600				

FIGURE 11-22 A table showing the Contoso SharePoint farm utilization.

Knowing your estimated user count and peak percentage will allow you to determine how many users will be making requests, while knowing the estimated requests per hour for each user will help you determine an estimated RPS at your farm's maximum load. It is very important to know your minimum RPS figure so that you will know if you pass or fail your load test. Odds are good that you will not hit your average RPS number during your load testing, so it will be important to be able to figure out exactly how many users your farm can actually support. As shown in Figure 11-23, your farm not only needs to be able to handle your users, but also handle the SharePoint requests as well.

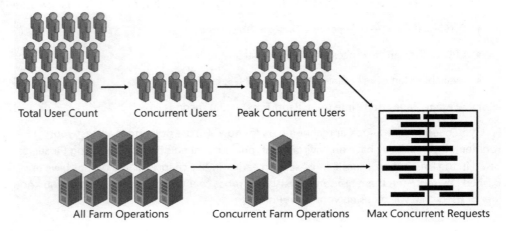

Total User Count   Concurrent Users   Peak Concurrent Users

All Farm Operations   Concurrent Farm Operations   Max Concurrent Requests

FIGURE 11-23 A representation of how the maximum number of concurrent requests is determined.

After you run your load test, you will be shown the average RPS that actually occurred. This number will never be the same as the one from the RPS worksheet because SharePoint makes its own requests to web services, such as the farm topology service, to get information about the rest of the farm before displaying content. So your RPS will not only vary depending on what you are trying to accomplish with your load test, but also depending on your distributed cache and your request management service.

You can download the RPS worksheet from *http://tinyurl.com/PCfromDC-RPSWS*.

Setting up Visual Studio Ultimate 2012

There are several tools available to conduct load tests, including web-based companies that you can use to hit your external sites. Most of these tests will work to provide your RPS and page load times but will not be able to tell you if your servers are running in the green zone or how close you are to exceeding your farm's capacity to even respond to requests. Microsoft Visual Studio Ultimate 2012 is built with presets to inspect your servers based on the server functionality in your farm. Not enough organizations have Visual Studio Ultimate as a resource, so to show your bosses a demonstration of how amazing the product is, you can download a test version from *http://tinyurl.com/PCfromDC-VS2012*. Also, be sure to install any updates associated with Visual Studio 2012. If you are not notified automatically about available updates, you can download update 1 (KB2707250) from *http://tinyurl.com/PCfromDC-SP1*, and don't be surprised if there is a second update available by the time you read this paragraph.

The first step after downloading Visual Studio is to install the program. For most administrators and/or architects who have never touched a bit of code in Visual Studio, installation might be a bit intimidating. Don't worry, you will click Next a bunch of times, clear a bunch of check boxes, go get a cup of coffee, and you will be done (probably after you are done with your coffee). In this installation walkthrough, Visual Studio was installed from the downloaded *.iso* file.

After starting your installation, you will be greeted by a warm contractual warning and a couple of check boxes. If you are using the free download trial version, consider sending the Customer Experience Improvement Program a bit of usage information. If you are doing a demonstration on a client's environment, that is their choice, and it is safer for you to not check this option and simply click Next when you are ready to continue. In the next window, if you are only going to be doing testing on your environment and not any coding, you can clear all of the optional feature boxes, or clear the Select All check box, and then click Install.

After you have completed the installation of Visual Studio and the installation of the updates, it will be time to start VS and begin creating a Visual Studio load test project.

From the Visual Studio Start Page, create a New Project, as shown in Figure 11-24.

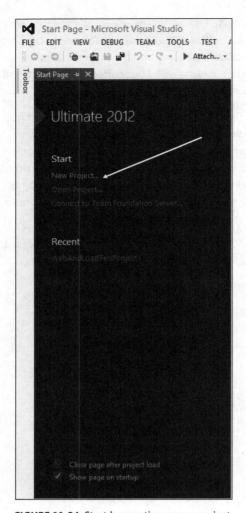

FIGURE 11-24 Start by creating a new project.

Once you click the New Project link, a New Project window will open, as shown in Figure 11-25. You are going to create a Web Performance project.

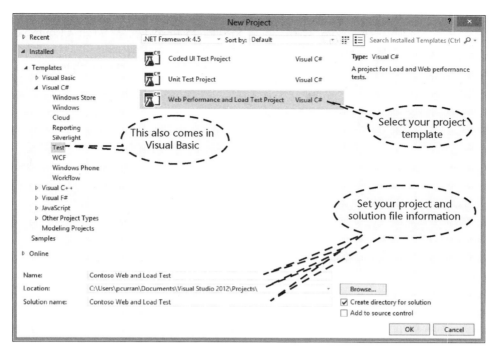

FIGURE 11-25 Create a new Visual Studio 2012 project window.

Creating your Performance Web Test

Your load test will encompass many moving parts. The first thing you are going to create is a Performance Web Test (.webtest file). This file is the actual script that Visual Studio will use when it runs the load test. It is usually very easy to create a .webtest file, as all you have to do is click around within your website using Internet Explorer, and perform the functions that you want to test. By default, when you create your Visual Studio Project, a WebTest1.webtest file will be created and opened for you to start your script. For example, you might want to test Search by actually doing a search, or clicking around within your top-level site to test site functionality and response, upload a document that starts a workflow, or view a Microsoft Word document with your WAC server. You can create test sections that will not just test your farm, but are created to test different parts within SharePoint itself. Another test that should be tried, especially before you consider yourself finished with testing, is that you should start a full crawl and user profile synchronization while you are load-testing, and eventually, while you are stress-testing, your environment.

Before starting the creation of your Performance Web Test script, think about what you actually want to test. Once you think you know what you want to do, type your ideas into a spreadsheet and adjust as necessary. If you are going to be testing the upload of files, especially large files such as videos, create a script to back up your content databases and a script to restore your content databases after you have completed your test. You always want to have your test bed be exactly the same for each run of your testing; otherwise, you will never get valid results.

After you have documented your test, open up your Visual Studio solution and open your *.webtest* file. After opening the file, press Record, which should open Internet Explorer, as shown in Figure 11-26. You are now going to create the web test that the load test will use to see how many RPS your farm can handle. To keep the math simple, to help determine the number of RPS, this test is going to create a web test that is going to make only one page request.

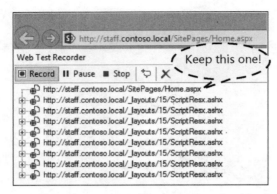

FIGURE 11-26 An image of the pages that Visual Studio will use for its load test.

When you have completed recording your Performance Web Test, Visual Studio will run a test to make sure that your Performance Web Test parameters are actually valid. When Visual Studio has compiled your performance test, delete everything that is not a request to a URL. That means, for this example, keep only the requests to *.aspx* pages. For other testing scenarios, there may be a need to keep other requests, like client object model calls.

If your web test is failing, double-clicking within the Error Message cell will open a new WebTest tab and Visual Studio will execute your *.webtest* solution. This will show you where your web test has failed so that you can go back into your *.webtest* solution and fix the outstanding problems. After you have fixed all the failing issues, your test results should show Passed, similar to Figure 11-27. Save your web test and rename the WebTest1 to something more useful.

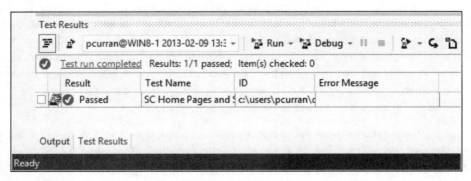

FIGURE 11-27 The Test Results show the successful completion of a Passed Performance Web Test.

Once all the issues have been verified as resolved and you have changed the Performance Web Test name, it is a good idea to give your performance test one last run because you will be using your performance test in your load test. As shown in Figure 11-28, after you select the properties of the Performance Web Test, you can add a specific user to impersonate while running the web test.

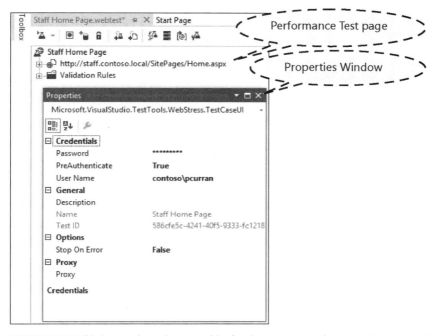

FIGURE 11-28 This image shows how to add a fixed user name and password to your web test.

Creating a valid performance test is the foundation for your load testing and stress testing. If you do not create a performance test that matches how your organization or clients will be using their farm, then you are not testing for a valid scenario and your load and stress testing will not be accurate representations of the real load. You must know how the farm will be used and what people will be doing to access their information to help you build out successful performance-, load-, and stress-testing plans. There is more on this topic in the "Putting it all together" section at the end of this chapter.

Creating your load test

After completing the build of your performance test, you can now build your load test. The load test solution will allow you to set various parameters to test in your environment, such as the number of simultaneous users and what servers to monitor. Remember that the purpose of the load test is to determine the RPS that your environment can handle while staying within the green zone, of how many RPS your environment can handle before entering the red zone.

Based off the RPS requirements from the RPS worksheet, you are going to copy and paste the Performance Web Test that you created three times and rename each one based on the nomenclature in the Excel document. Your Solution Explorer should look similar to Figure 11-29.

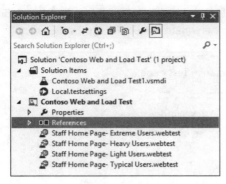

FIGURE 11-29 An example of the Solution Explorer.

Next, add a new load test solution to the project. To create an empty load test, choose Add Load Test from the Project menu, as shown in Figure 11-30.

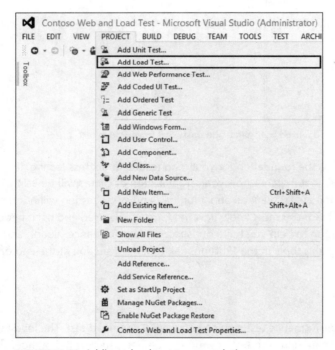

FIGURE 11-30 Adding a load test to your solution.

From here, the New Load Test Wizard opens to help you with creating your load test. Click Next to start the fun!

In the second screen (shown in Figure 11-31), the wizard will ask you for a load test scenario name and to select the Think Time Profile. This test is going to use the Do Not Use Think Times option. The *think time* is the amount of time the Visual Studio will use to pause between requests; for example, after your home page loads, this is the amount of time you spend thinking about where to click next.

A zero think time maximizes the RPS for your performance test; think of it as a potential self-inflicted denial of service attack. This is another reason why you do not want to do load testing on a live production environment.

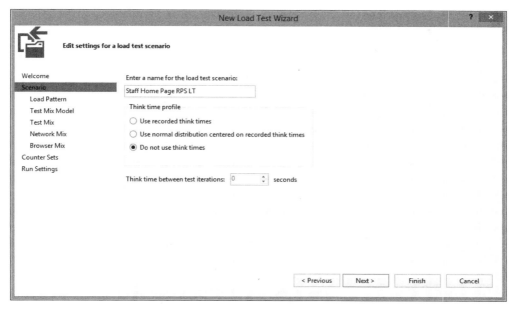

FIGURE 11-31 Setting the think times for the load test.

In the next window, where you determine the Load Pattern, this test is going to use a Constant Load of 1 concurrent user (see Figure 11-32). As you will see shortly, your one virtual user is going to be a very busy person. This is a workaround to the limits of using the demo version of Visual Studio 2012 Ultimate, which can have only up to 25 concurrent users. There is a demonstration of how to do a load test for more than 25 concurrent users in the "Putting it all together" section at the end of this chapter.

The next window (shown in Figure 11-33) allows you to select the Test Mix Model, meaning how you want your performance test to run. The first test mix model is a test mix based on the total number of tests for each virtual user. For example, you could create performance tests based on specific job functions and then assign a utilization percentage for that test. If the project management team spends 20 percent of their time uploading documents, 50 percent of their time updating lists, and 30 percent of their time reviewing dashboards, then you would create three separate performance tests (one test for uploading documents, one test for updating lists, and a final test for going between dashboard pages). This test model would be used when you are basing your test mix on transaction percentages from IIS logs. The second test mix model, based on the number of virtual users, would be used when you are basing the load test on the percentage of users running a specific test. The third type of test mix model is the Based On User Pace test mix model. This model will allow you to perform specific tests for a specific number of requests per hour until the load test is complete. The final test mix allows you to have the users conduct their performance tests in a specific order.

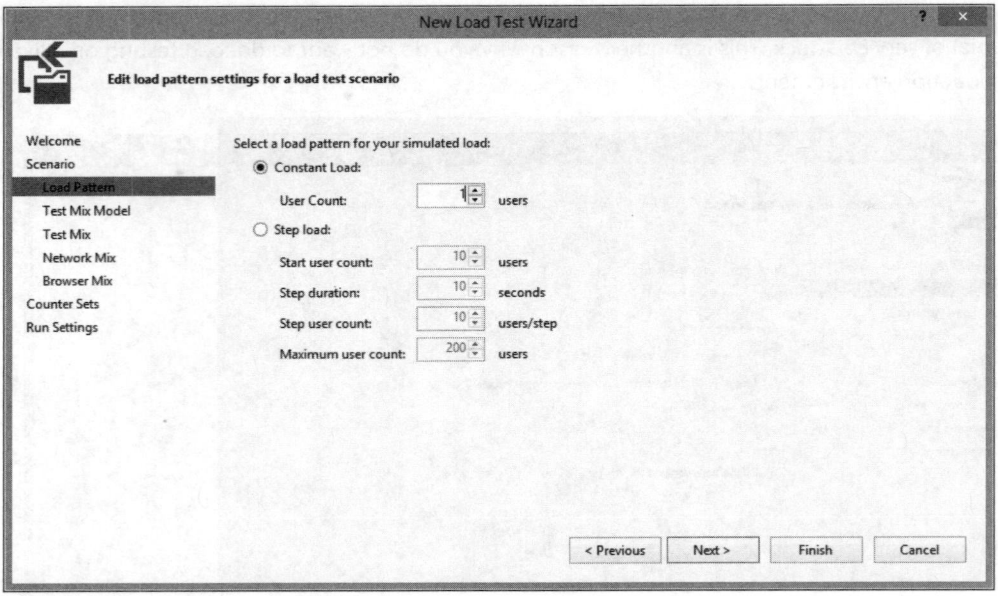

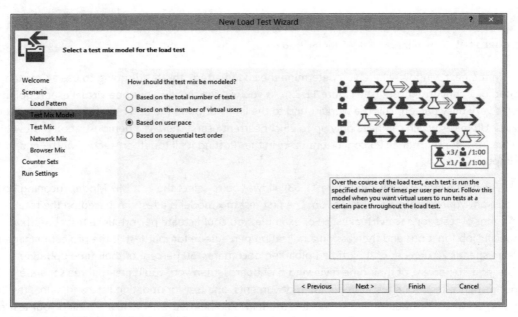

FIGURE 11-32 The Load Pattern window.

FIGURE 11-33 The Test Mix Model wizard page.

The next page is the Test Mix page. The test mix allows you to select the performance tests that you have already created for your load test. This demonstration will be using the tests created in the previous section, "Creating your Performance Web Test." Refer to your RPS worksheet once again to determine the numbers that you will need to enter.

Click Add, select your test from the Available Tests section, and move it to the Selected Tests section, as shown in Figure 11-34.

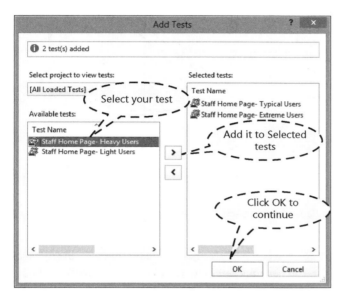

FIGURE 11-34 The Load Test Wizard's Add Test window.

After you have added your tests to the Test Mix, enter how many requests per hour each type of user will require. As shown in Figure 11-35, take the values from the RPS worksheet and enter them into Visual Studio.

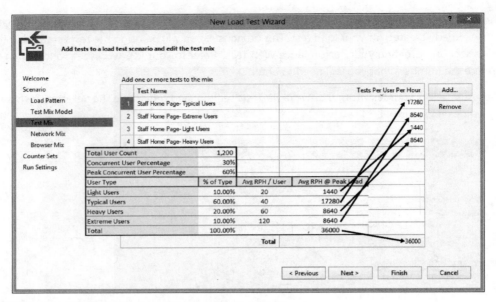

FIGURE 11-35 The distribution of the load based on user type.

Basically, this test consists of having one virtual user make a request to the Staff home page 36,000 times an hour.

For the Network Mix (see Figure 11-36), select the appropriate network that your users will be employing to surf to your web server(s). You have the option to distribute the network load between different types of networks, in case your environment is used by remote offices on a T1 line and mobile users along with your local network users. If you are going to do any testing outside of LAN network testing, Network Emulation will have to be configured. You can read about how to set up Network Emulation in the article "How to: Configure Network Emulation Using Test Settings in Visual Studio," at *http://tinyurl.com/PCfromDC-Emulation*.

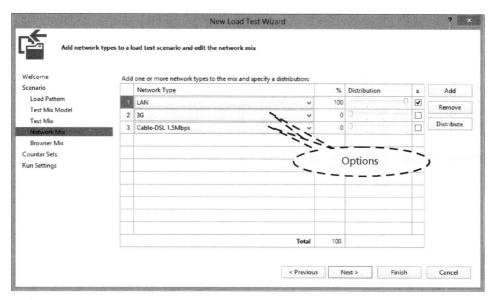

FIGURE 11-36 Available options for load testing on different network types.

The next window for setting your Browser Mix (shown in Figure 11-37) should be pretty self-explanatory, especially after filling out your Network Mix. However, setting up the Counter Sets window is a bit trickier. The Counter Sets window is where you add all the servers that you want to monitor during the load test. If you do not have all of the Visual Studio updates installed, you will not have the same options available to you as presented here. By default, you will see only the local machine groupings of Controllers and Agents in the Preview section. For this example, you want to monitor the effects of the load on the servers in your SharePoint farm, and if you were doing a simulation that passed actual user names and passwords, you would want to monitor your authentication servers as well. To start, you will need the server names of the servers in your farm. Click the Add Computer button on the bottom of the monitor window to add a computer, and then add a SQL Server server name. There are predefined counter sets to monitor your servers. Select SQL, and because SQL is an application server, select Application as well. Continue to add all your SQL servers in the same manner. After you have added your SQL Server servers, add all your SharePoint servers. For the SharePoint servers, select the SharePoint 2010 WFE counter set because the counter set contains prebuilt filters to monitor specific criteria within SharePoint. Also, select IIS and Application counter sets because SharePoint servers use both of those server roles. Click Next to continue.

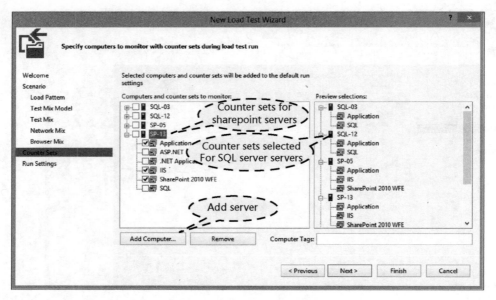

FIGURE 11-37 This window shows the counter set options for the servers in the farm.

This test is going to be timed. If you have not run through your site(s) using your performance test multiple times, and you are worried that your pages might return slowly, you would set the warm-up test duration to something that would allow your script to hit all of your webpages so that everything is ready for the load test. A warm-up test would also be a good idea if you want to bring up your CPU temperature slowly for the load test so that you do not shock the system too much, but primarily you add a warm-up test to load components into cache and memory before the actual test starts. A 5-minute warm-up time is usually a good starting point for most load tests.

In the Run Settings window (shown in Figure 11-38), set your Run Duration to 20 minutes. A 20-minute run time gives Visual Studio enough sampling data points of your environment, and running tests over 20 minutes will not provide any worthwhile changes to your test data. So don't waste your time—keep your load tests to 20 minutes.

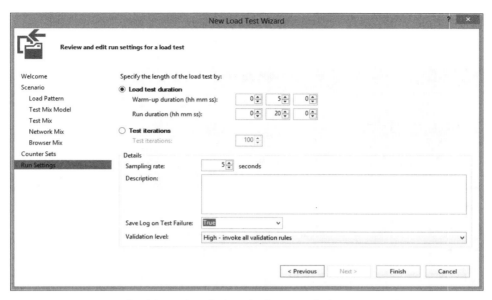

FIGURE 11-38 An example of the options for length of time used when creating the run settings.

After you have finished filling out your time parameters, click Finish to complete your load test solution. After clicking Finish, the Load Test tab should open. Now it is a good idea to go into your Solution Explorer and rename the *LoadTest1.loadtest* file to something a bit more practical and descriptive.

At this point, you can go ahead and click Start Test to begin your new load test, but you have not set your green and red zone thresholds. You should have your green and red zone limits already documented, so take your thresholds and put them into the Counter Sets so that you will receive a notification when you have breached a threshold.

The first threshold to set up will be the availability of RAM. Since you have added the Application type counter set to all the servers, modifying only the Available MBytes within the Memory counter category of the Application counter set (as shown in Figure 11-39) will set a rule that will be monitored for all the servers. Expand the tree to get to the Compare Constant that has already been created. Right-click Compare Constant and select Properties to set the Threshold Values. Set the alert so that you will be notified when the data point goes under your available memory threshold numbers, so keep the value of the Alert If Over set to False, and set your Critical Threshold Value to your red zone threshold value. Set the Warning Threshold Value to the upper end of your green zone threshold value.

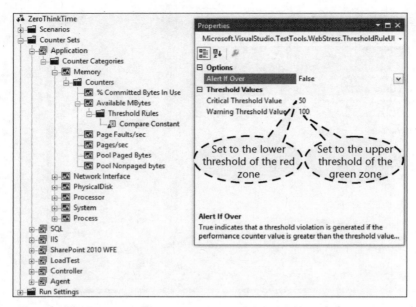

FIGURE 11-39 Setting the Threshold Values of the Available MBytes.

After setting up your memory thresholds and warning, follow the same procedures for the Server Latency (Avg. Response Time), CPU Utilization (% Processor Time, as shown in see Figure 11-40), and Average Page Load Time (Avg. Page Time).

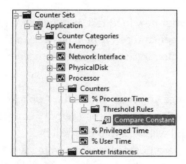

FIGURE 11-40 Location of the % Processor Time category.

The settings for % Processor Time and Available MBytes have threshold rules by default. To create the threshold rules for Avg. Response Time and Avg. Page Time, right-click the appropriate counter, as shown in Figure 11-41, and select Add Threshold Rule. Set the Compare Constant values to the appropriate threshold value. The option to use Compare Counters is used when you want to compare the current counter against other performance counter values.

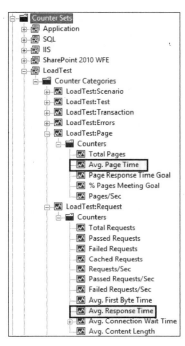

FIGURE 11-41 Location of the Avg. Page Time and Avg. Response Time.

Now that you have set up parameters for your test, it is time to run your load test. While the load test is running, remember that eventually you will want to kick off a search crawl and start a User Profile Service (UPS) synchronization. While you are load-testing your farm, open an Internet browser and take a look at the sites for yourself. Open Developer Dashboard (this will take up CPU utilization), and the other tools mentioned earlier in the chapter and see for yourself what your load test does to the performance of your farm. Once your load test is complete, address the errors that were found and then run the test again. If you are running the test with an NLB, make sure that there is actually a balanced load between all your web servers. As you review the test results of this demonstration, notice that the farm had an RPS of approximately 25.5 (see Figure 11-42).

Overall Results	
Max User Load	1
Tests/Sec	3.65
Tests Failed	0
Avg. Test Time (sec)	0.27
Transactions/Sec	0
Avg. Transaction Time (sec)	0
Pages/Sec	3.65
Avg. Page Time (sec)	0.27
Requests/Sec	25.5
Requests Failed	0
Requests Cached Percentage	75.9
Avg. Response Time (sec)	0.046
Avg. Content Length (bytes)	11,092

FIGURE 11-42 Results of the load test.

Taking a look at the results, the RPS is equal to 25.5, while according to the RPS worksheet, there should have only been 10. As previously depicted in Figure 11-23, while the load test is going on, SharePoint is making its own requests as well, and over the period, SharePoint increased the RPS by 150 percent.

After completing the load test, it will be time to draw up the plans for how to attack the reallocation of your server resources. In a physical world, you will not be able to do too much when it comes to adding processors, but there is always the option of adding web servers or an NLB to help distribute the workload. One thing to be aware of while testing with multiple web servers that are load balanced is that depending on how you have the Affinity of the NLB cluster set up, your load test might hit only one of your web servers. To get around this, you can either change the settings of your NLB or create a Performance Web Test that uses server names instead of URLs. There is more information on load testing in the "Putting it all together" section at the end of this chapter.

Stress-testing your environment

At this point, you have maximized your throughput and reduced your bottlenecks with performance testing. You have established green zone threshold values and know what utilization your farm can sustain without error by doing load testing. Now here comes the fun part! It's time to determine where things break. Remember that this is not dealing with your ordinary .NET IIS website. You are required to run with at least 12 GB of RAM and at least 4 CPU cores for a reason, and it is because SharePoint is so much more than an ordinary IIS website. Having such high hardware requirements makes for a very robust farm and makes it very difficult to break.

The purpose of stress testing is to try to overwhelm the server farm resources (or even the network or NLB). This type of stress testing is also known as *negative testing*. The major point to understand about stress-testing your environment is that is not just about knowing where things break, but how they will break and how they will recover. Having the knowledge that if you exceed your farm's threshold, that the NLB will need to be physically unplugged and reset to get it to start working properly again is very important. Will exceeding the threshold of your farm create a nice message window, or will you have a catastrophic failure? Knowing what will happen on the negative or destructive side is necessary, but also knowing how your farm will recover is just as important—especially if your farm does not recover and requires a reboot to start functioning again. It is better to have an understanding of your farm's nuances and document the solutions on how to recover from issues before going live, then after everything has shut down.

Through stress testing, think about where you want your environment to fail first. During stress testing, as different parts of your environment fail—such as your web server's lack of ability to re-spond to web requests or your SQL Server's inability to handle the input/output (IOPs) requirements from your web servers—then you will have to address different solutions. If you are having issues with recovery, attack this area of testing first.

Creating your stress test

You have already determined your red and green zone envelopes, so you know where your farm is happiest. Now slowly increase the load on your environment until parts of your environment start to fail (see the example in Figure 11-43).

FIGURE 11-43 This error happens when the server resources are low and the web server cannot keep up with demand.

In the "Creating your Performance Web Test" section earlier in this chapter, you created a web test for conducting your load test. For the sake of consistency, you are going to use the same Performance Web Test for your stress test as well, but instead of using one concurrent user, you are going to add users to the test until your environment is stressed beyond capacity.

Just like before, you are going to create a new Load Test Project (Project | Add Load Test). Once the New Load Test Wizard has opened, click Next. Give your scenario a useful name, and select Do Not Use Think Times.

Now this is where things will start to differ from the creation of your load test in the previous section. Because this demonstration is using the demo version of Visual Studio 2012 Ultimate, you can have a maximum of only 25 concurrent users. This is fine because you did your stress test using only one, very busy, concurrent user. The problem with this method is that you are doubling your RPS for every user added, so adjust the requests per hour accordingly in the Test Mix window. As shown in Figure 11-44, this example will increase the load on the servers by 10 percent every 2 minutes to a maximum of 25 users or a 250 percent increase in RPS.

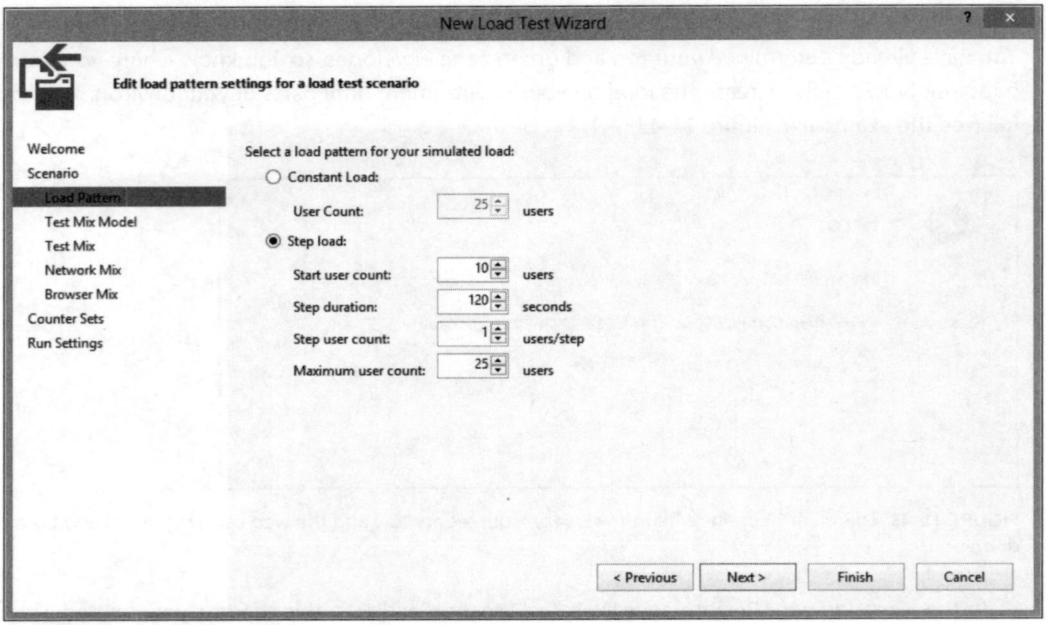

FIGURE 11-44 Step Load test settings.

In the next window (shown in Figure 11-45), create a Test Mix Model based on user pace. For the test mix, break down your numbers from the "Creating your load test" section earlier in this chapter and only use 10 percent because you are starting the stress test with 10 concurrent users.

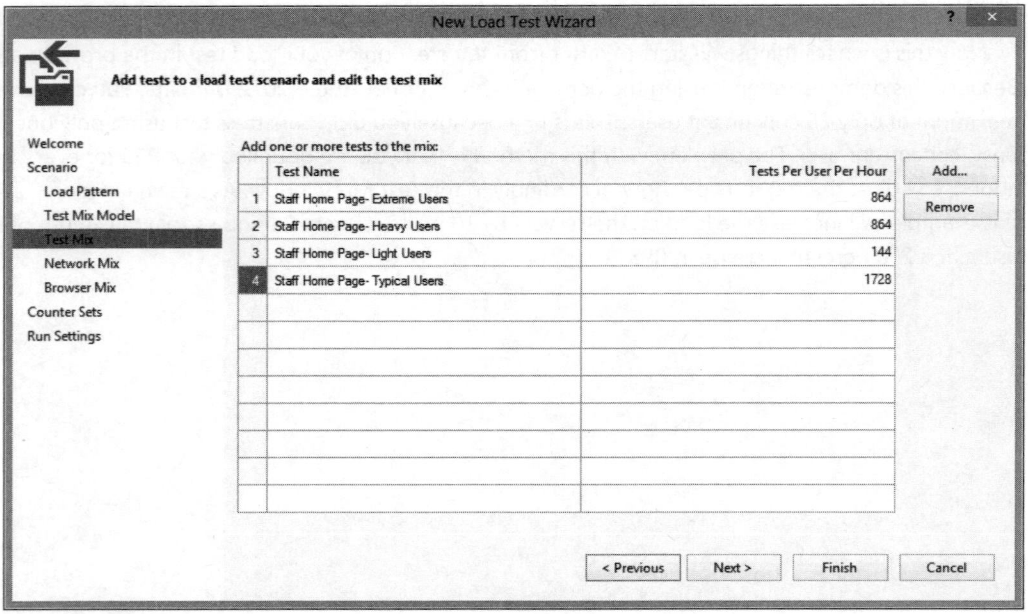

FIGURE 11-45 Requests per user per hour.

Finish up the rest of the settings the same as in the "Creating your load test" section, except increase your Test Run Time from 20 minutes to 32 minutes to test all the increases in concurrent users.

Other load test options

Visual Studio 2012 Ultimate is a great tool for load testing, but the ability to handle only 25 concurrent users with the trial version is a bit limiting. Hopefully, you will be able to show your boss the benefits of having Visual Studio 2012 Ultimate for running tests on your environment, and your boss will purchase a copy of it for you. If you are not that lucky and need to show your boss options, Microsoft still has older versions available for testing as well. Maybe your boss will like one of these products.

Visual Studio 2010 Ultimate

If the requirement for demonstrating a load test for your boss is below 250 concurrent users, then you should try using Visual Studio 2010 Ultimate. The maximum number of concurrent users for the Visual Studio 2010 trial version is 250.

Download the *.iso* file from *http://tinyurl.com/PCfromDC-VS2010iso*, and install the service pack from *http://tinyurl.com/PCfromDC-VS2010-SPiso*. If you are going to run this setup on a Windows 8 or Windows 7 environment, install the Forward Compatibility Update from *http://tinyurl.com/PCfromDC-VS2010CU*. To export documentation from your test sessions, you should have Office Professional Plus 2010 installed (*http://tinyurl.com/PCfromDC-Office*) as well as the service pack for Office 2010, which you can get through Windows Update.

Visual Studio Team System 2008 Team Suite

If your oss wants you to demo a load test for more than 250 concurrent users, you can download a 90-day trial version of the Visual Studio Team System 2008 Team Suite from Microsoft to run your load tests. You can download the Visual Studio Team System *.iso* file from *http://tinyurl.com/PCfromDC-VS2008*. Download and install the service pack after you install Visual Studio Team System 2008. You can download the *.iso* file from *http://tinyurl.com/PCfromDC-VSTSsp1*.

The installation of Visual Studio 2010 and Visual Studio Team System 2008 is very similar to the installation performed for Visual Studio 2012 Ultimate in the "Setting up Visual Studio 2012 Ultimate" section earlier in this chapter, except that you just want to install the product using the default settings.

After you create a web test, Internet Explorer should open and allow you to start recording your web session. If you are using Visual Studio Team System 2008 and the recording window does not pop up as it did for Visual Studio 2012, some troubleshooting will be required. To use Visual Studio Team System 2008 with Windows 8, close all instances of Internet Explorer, and then go into the registry and delete following entries located at

- HKEY_CURRENT_USER\Software\Microsoft\Windows\CurrentVersion\Explorer\Discardable\ PostSetup\Component Categories\{00021493-0000-0000-C000-000000000046}

- HKEY_CURRENT_USER\Software\Microsoft\Windows\CurrentVersion\Explorer\Discardable\ PostSetup\Component Categories\{00021494-0000-0000-C000-000000000046}

For more Visual Studio Team System 2008 troubleshooting help, visit *http://tinyurl.com/PCfromDC-Recorder* and read "Diagnosing and Fixing Web Test Recorder Bar Issues" by Michael Taute.

If you decide to run Visual Studio Team System 2008, there is one more modification that might be helpful to avoid a *System.OutOfMemoryException* error. Try modifying the *VSTestHost.exe.config* file, which by default is located in the C:\Program Files (x86)\Microsoft Visual Studio 9.0\Common7\ IDE folder. Remember to make a backup of the file prior to modifying the *.config* file. Within the *<runtime>* tag, add *<gcServer enabled="true" />*.

Putting it all together

You have been given the tools to go out and start testing websites and their environments to help you validate your SharePoint architecture. It is now time to take that knowledge and run through a very common scenario.

Scenario

Another consulting firm has implemented SharePoint Server 2013 at Contoso, but it did not supply Contoso with any farm documentation. You have been called in by Contoso to do a review of its environment and verify that its farm can handle the estimated user load and that Kerberos has been implemented correctly on the staff site.

As a guest in the Contoso environment, you will not be able to use the existing software on your laptop because you will not be allowed to plug in to its network. You have received the only paperwork that Contoso had on file, along with its current user web utilization. You have received a copy of the farm layout (Figure 11-46), and a spreadsheet of the server hardware layout (Figure 11-47). (Remember that this is a demonstration on load testing and troubleshooting the Contoso environment, and you should deploy your farm based on your infrastructure and planning design documentation, not the Contoso farm in this section.)

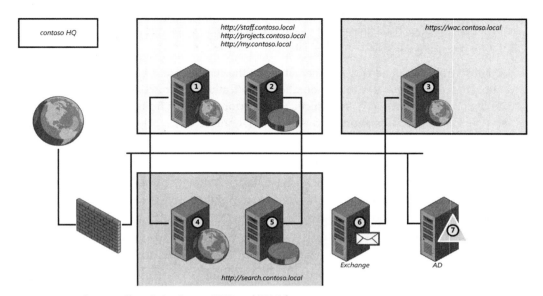

FIGURE 11-46 Contoso SharePoint Server 2013 and WAC farm.

Server #1	SharePoint 2013 Server- Content			Server #2	SQL 2012 for Content Farm		
Contoso.SP-13	Processor Cores	4		Contoso.SQL-12	Processor Cores	4	
	RAM (GB)	4			RAM (GB)	6	
	C:	80 GB			C:	80 GB	
	D:	250 GB			D:	500 GB	
	E:	DVD			E:	DVD	
	Server OS	2012 Enterprise			Server OS	2012 Enterprise	
	Product	SharePoint 2013 Enterprise			Product	SharePoint 2013 Enterprise	
Server #3	WAC Server 2013						
Contoso.SP-04	Processor Cores	4					
	RAM (GB)	4					
	C:	80 GB					
	D:	250 GB					
	E:	DVD					
	Server OS	2012 Enterprise					
	Product	SharePoint 2013 Enterprise					
Server #4	SharePoint 2013 Search Farm			Server #5	SQL 2012 for Search Farm		
Contoso.SP-05	Processor Cores	4		Contoso.SQL-03	Processor Cores	4	
	RAM (GB)	4			RAM (GB)	6	
	C:	80 GB			C:	80 GB	
	D:	250 GB			D:	500 GB	
	E:	DVD			E:	DVD	
	Server OS	2012 Enterprise			Server OS	2012 Enterprise	
	Product	SharePoint 2013 Enterprise			Product	SharePoint 2013 Enterprise	

FIGURE 11-47 Contoso server purpose and hardware list.

Read through Figure 11-47 and notice that the original consulting group had put the farm into an unsupported state by installing only 4–6 GB of RAM, and when questioned, Contoso said that the structure was designed based on the ability to handle the current user load.

Contoso would like load test documentation for the current farm state, as well as additional load test documentation for any farm configuration modifications. Contoso would also like the load test to hit the home page of every site collection and perform a search from the Search Center using the Everything, People, Conversations, and Videos tabs. Contoso would like to load-test the WAC server as well.

Contoso has given you a Windows 8 desktop with 6 GB of RAM and a single four-core processor. The Contoso utilization profiles are shown in Figure 11-48. Contoso does not have Visual Studio installed and does not have a full-blown license to any of the Visual Studio Ultimate products.

Total User Count	1,200						
Concurrent User Percentage	30%						
Peak Concurrent User Percentage	20%						
User Type	% of Type	Avg RPH / User	Concurrent Users	Avg RPH @ Peak Load	Avg RPS	Think Times
Light Users	10.00%	20	24	480	0.1333	180.0000
Typical Users	60.00%	40	144	5760	1.6000	90.0000
Heavy Users	20.00%	60	48	2880	0.8000	60.0000
Extere Users	10.00%	120	24	2880	0.8000	30.0000
Total	100.00%		240	12000	3.3333	

FIGURE 11-48 Table of Contoso SharePoint farm utilization.

Verifying sites

The first thing, and hopefully the easiest thing, to do is to click through the sites that Contoso wishes to have load-tested. Starting with the Staff site, go to the rest of the company's sites, such as Projects, Search, and My Sites. While you are surfing around, verify the functionality of the WAC server. To get started, open up Internet Explorer, enable the Developer Tools, and start capturing your network traffic for the page loads. Because Contoso has asked for before- and after-modification documentation, it would be a good idea to save the page data as a *.csv* file as you go through the different sites (see Figure 11-49).

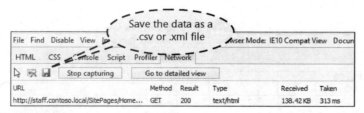

FIGURE 11-49 Location of the Save button.

As you go through your sites and record your findings with IE Dev Tools, also verify the functionality of the WAC server, as shown in Figure 11-50.

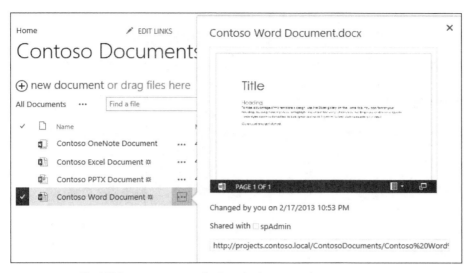

FIGURE 11-50 The WAC server seems to be functioning correctly.

It is great news that the WAC server is rendering the Word file, but when you go to review the page load network capture, you notice that the WAC server is being called over HTTP (see Figure 11-51). The WAC server should be used over HTTPS, and even Contoso has asked for it to be over HTTPS, but things do not appear to be that way. Make sure you save this page's output!

/_vti_bin/client.svc/ProcessQuery	POST	200	application/json	1.45 KB	172 ms	XMLHttpRequest
/_layouts/15/WopiFrame.aspx?sourcedoc...	GET	200	text/html	4.16 KB	109 ms	innerHtml <fra...
http://wac.contoso.local/wv/wordviewerfr...	POST	200	text/html	22.97 KB	422 ms	click
http://wac.contoso.local/wv/resources/10...	GET	304	text/css	506 B	< 1 ms	<link rel="style...
http://wac.contoso.local/wv/App_Scripts/...	GET	304	application/javascript	0.51 KB	< 1 ms	<script>
http://wac.contoso.local/wv/App_Scripts/...	GET	304	application/javascript	0.51 KB	< 1 ms	<script>
http://wac.contoso.local/wv/App_Scripts/...	GET	304	application/javascript	0.51 KB	< 1 ms	<script>
http://wac.contoso.local/wv/App_Scripts/...	GET	304	application/javascript	0.51 KB	< 1 ms	<script>
http://wac.contoso.local/wv/App_Scripts/...	GET	304	application/javascript	0.51 KB	< 1 ms	<script>
http://wac.contoso.local/wv/ResReader.a...	GET	200	image/png	7.59 KB	16 ms	<img>
http://wac.contoso.local/wv/resources/10...	GET	304	image/png	507 B	< 1 ms	<img>
http://wac.contoso.local/wv/docdatahand...	GET	200	text/xml	1.00 KB	109 ms	XMLHttpRequest
http://wac.contoso.local/wv/ResReader.a...	GET	200	image/png	7.59 KB	15 ms	<img>
http://wac.contoso.local/wv/ResReader.a...	GET	200	text/xml	3.78 KB	16 ms	XMLHttpRequest

FIGURE 11-51 Contoso's capture of the WAC service *GET* calls over HTTP.

Verifying Kerberos

One of the great things about Windows 8 is that it has the ability to run Klist out of the box. To verify that Kerberos is functioning correctly for Contoso, open a command prompt window, type **klist,** and press Enter. You should see a Kerberos ticket similar to the one shown in Figure 11-52.

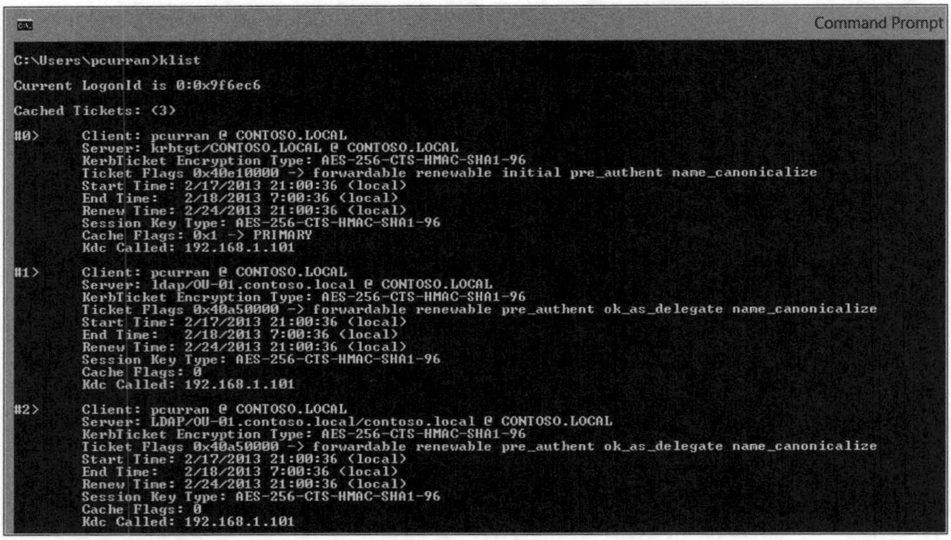

FIGURE 11-52 List of tickets using *Klist.exe*.

As you can see, ticket #0 has the Kerberos ticket information, but if that is not good enough, you can always go to the SharePoint server itself and open the Security Logs in the Windows Event Viewer and check the logons, as shown in Figure 11-53. You should be able to find an Event Property that shows the logon process as Kerberos.

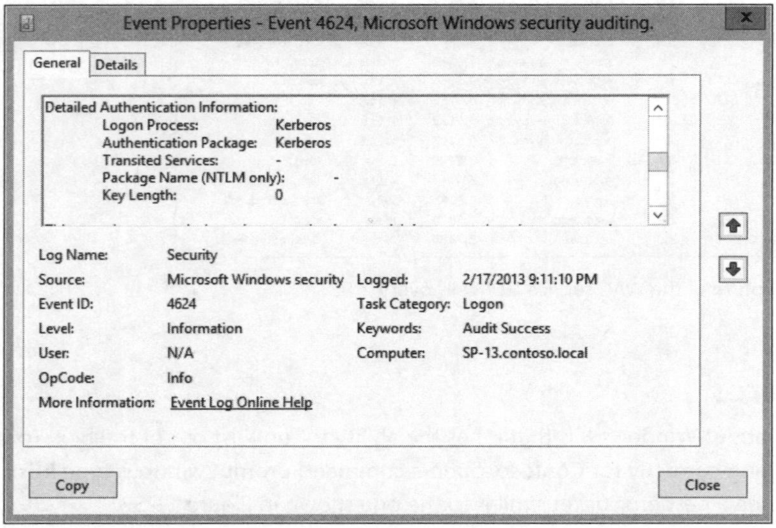

FIGURE 11-53 The Event Viewer Event Property.

Setting up Visual Studio Ultimate 2010

Contoso has asked that all changes be documented, which means that before anything is done to set the farm back into a supported state, a load test should be done on the before side so that Contoso can see how the changes affected their environment. As you know, the big problem with the Visual Studio 2012 Ultimate trial version is that you are able to test for only up to 25 concurrent users. As previously shown in Figure 11-48, the requirements for Contoso put this test at just below the 250 concurrent user maximum for the Visual Studio 2010 Ultimate trial.

Create the performance test

The next step is to create your performance test by creating a web test, and then going to the sites that Contoso has specified in its instructions. By surfing through the company's sites and recording the URLs, you will be able to not only grab the URLs to test but also the parameters passed through the URLs. Once again, when you are done with creating your web test, delete all the extra posts so you are only sending requests to the *.aspx* pages, as shown in Figure 11-54.

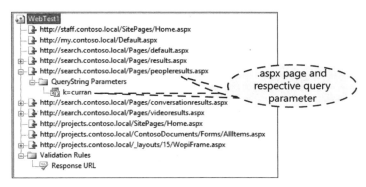

FIGURE 11-54 The Performance Web Test sites and parameters.

One thing to be aware of is the number of requests that the performance test is making. It is not a coincidence that there are 10 requests for this; when it comes time to create the load test, it will be easier to do the math.

After you create your performance test, run it and have your test validated. The validation is useful because you do not want to run 20 minutes of invalid web testing, but it also allows you to look at the performance numbers returned from your test. After running the initial web test, Figure 11-55 shows that there is a huge discrepancy in total time between the search farm and the rest of the farm. After running the test 10 more times just to be safe, the issue still remained.

Request	HTTP Status	Total Time	Request Time
http://staff.contoso.local/SitePages/Home.aspx		0.513 sec	0.381 sec
http://my.contoso.local/Default.aspx	OK	0.646 sec	0.474 sec
http://search.contoso.local/Pages/default.aspx	200 OK	6.456 sec	6.369 sec
http://search.contoso.local/Pages/results.aspx?k=curran	200 OK	7.416 sec	6.573 sec
http://search.contoso.local/Pages/peopleresu		7.365 sec	6.393 sec
http://search.contoso.local/Pages/conversation	OK	0.582 sec	0.349 sec
http://search.contoso.local/Pages/videoresults.aspx?k=curran		1.035 sec	0.854 sec
http://projects.contoso.local/SitePages/Home.aspx	200 OK	0.290 sec	0.199 sec
http://projects.contoso.local/ContosoDocuments/Forms/AllItems.aspx	200 OK	0.258 sec	0.155 sec
http://projects.contoso.local/_layouts/15/WopiFrame.aspx?sourcedoc=%2FCo 200 OK		0.108 sec	0.108 sec

(Annotations: "Serach has issues!" and "WAC Server")

FIGURE 11-55 Metrics after running the Performance Web Test.

After going through the Search Farm event viewer, there were issues with the SharePoint server communicating with its SQL server. While running a ping test between the two servers, one of the NICs on the SQL server would turn off and on at random intervals. So after replacing the NIC and rerunning the performance test, our numbers improved to within expected times, as shown in Figure 11-56.

Request	HTTP Status	Total Time	Request Time
http://staff.contoso.local/SitePages/Home.aspx	200 OK	0.380 sec	0.277 sec
http://my.contoso.local/Default.aspx	200 OK	0.441 sec	0.307 sec
http://search.contoso.local/Pages/default.aspx	200 OK	0.476 sec	0.409 sec
http://search.contoso.local/Pages/results.aspx?k=curran	200 OK	0.755 sec	0.485 sec
http://search.contoso.local/Pages/peopleresults.aspx?k=curran	200 OK	0.531 sec	0.361 sec
http://search.contoso.local/Pages/conversationresults.aspx?k=curran	200 OK	0.593 sec	0.335 sec
http://search.contoso.local/Pages/videoresults.aspx?k=curran	200 OK	0.497 sec	0.322 sec
http://projects.contoso.local/SitePages/Home.aspx	200 OK	0.201 sec	0.148 sec
http://projects.contoso.local/ContosoDocuments/Forms/AllItems.aspx	200 OK	0.217 sec	0.147 sec
http://projects.contoso.local/_layouts/15/WopiFrame.aspx?sourcedoc=%2FCo 200 OK		0.090 sec	0.090 sec

FIGURE 11-56 Total time for all sites are within the expected time.

Create the load test

According to the statistics, Contoso has 1,200 total users, but only 20 percent of them are on at a given time. That means that you really only need to worry about the requests for 240 concurrent users. The good news is that those users are all doing different jobs and are sending requests at a different rate. That is why the users are broken into different utilization categories and assigned an estimated requests per hour (RPH) value. This test is going to use the same web test that was created in the last section. After creating a copy of the web test, create your load test by going to Project | Add Load Test.

After the wizard page opens, click Finish, as you will be creating your load test manually. Under Scenarios, delete the default Scenario1, then right-click the name of your load test and select Add Scenario, as shown in Figure 11-57.

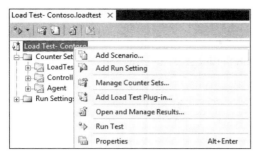

FIGURE 11-57 Adding a scenario to your load test.

Name your scenario based on the type of users that you are creating. For example, you might call the first group Light Users. Once again, you are going to want to work with zero think times, but this time, instead of working with only one very busy user, you are going to enter 24 for the User Count based on the RPS worksheet (1,200 x 20 percent x 10 percent). You are going to use the Based On User Pace, and then select the appropriate web test and enter the data off your RPS worksheet for the Tests Per User Per Hour (Avg RPH/User). Now remember that the web test is actually using 10 requests for its test, so you can either really tax your farm or adjust the numbers accordingly. This initial test will be testing the environment and not adjusting the numbers for the extra requests. If you wanted to adjust for the number, just drop off the trailing zero. So the Light Users would be two requests per user per hour. Setting up the rest of the test will involve using the default settings, except this test will be using Internet Explorer 8 for the test's browser compatibility. After adding the first set of users, add the rest of the other user groups. When you have finished adding your user groups, your Scenarios should look similar to Figure 11-58.

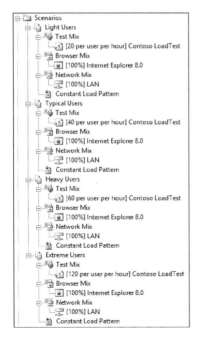

FIGURE 11-58 User Scenarios.

The next step is to set up the Counter Set Mappings by assigning the counter sets to the servers that are running within your SharePoint environment. Use the same procedures that were demonstrated in the "Creating your load test" section earlier in this chapter. To add the counter sets manually, expand the Run Setting and right-click Run Settings1 [Active], as shown in Figure 11-59.

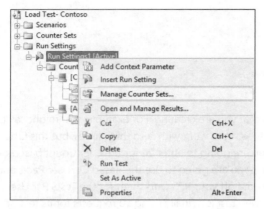

FIGURE 11-59 Adding counter sets manually.

As shown in Figure 11-60, configure your Counter Set Mappings to the Contoso farm layout from the Scenario section.

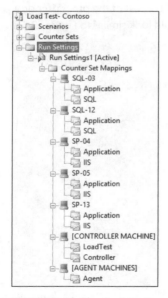

FIGURE 11-60 The Contoso Counter Set Mappings.

Under the properties of Run Settings1 [Active], adjust your Run Duration to 20 minutes and set your Warm-Up Duration to 5 minutes. Once you have completed all your adjustments, such as setting your Threshold Values and getting your load test parameters set, it will be time to run the first test.

Remember to surf through the pages of your test to verify how this type of load would be experienced by a user. Also, surf through the sites that were used in the load test after the test is finished. If there were errors/failures during your test, you will want to see how the farm bounces back.

Once your test is completed (see Figure 11-61), document and keep the baseline numbers to compare against the next load test after making changes to your farm.

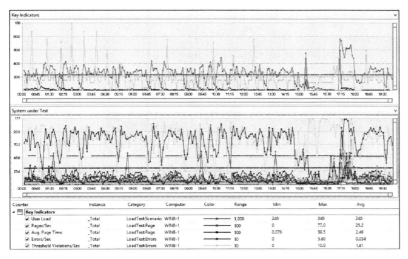

FIGURE 11-61 The results of the first load test of the Contoso environment.

It is now time to make all the appropriate changes to get the SharePoint farm back into a supported state, and then run the same load test again. Document the changes and results from the changes made (see Figure 11-62 to see the results).

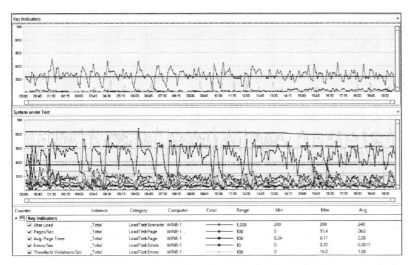

FIGURE 11-62 The load test results after the server hardware has been upgraded.

Documentation

Contoso's final requirement was to document the effectiveness of all changes. Luckily, Visual Studio gives you the ability to export reports and actually run comparison reports containing charts for comparing baseline numbers against other load tests that you have run.

This load test used Visual Studio 2010 with SP1 and Office Professional Plus with SP1. If you run into issues with the Create Excel Report button being dimmed, open Excel and make sure that all the COM add-ins are selected, especially the Load Test Report add-in.

After you have run more than one load test, the first thing to do, from either the Summary page or the Graphs page, is click Create Excel Report, as shown in Figure 11-63.

FIGURE 11-63 The location of the Create Excel Report button.

This should open Excel with a Generate A Load Test Report window. Select the Create A Report option and click Next to continue.

In the report type window, select Run Comparison, and then click Next. In the Load Test Report Details window (shown in Figure 11-64), add the Report Name.

FIGURE 11-64 The window to enter the load test report details.

In the next window (shown in Figure 11-65), select the load tests to compare.

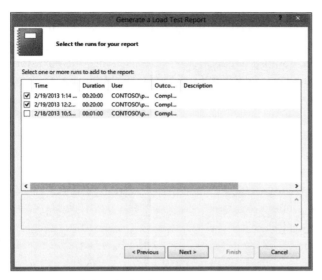

FIGURE 11-65 Select the load tests to compare.

If you wish to have more counter sets to add to the report, select them in the next window.

When you have finished making your selections, click Finish to generate the first report to give to Contoso. As you can see from Figure 11-66, by adjusting the hardware to bring the servers back into a supported state, there has been a fantastic improvement in speed for most of the users.

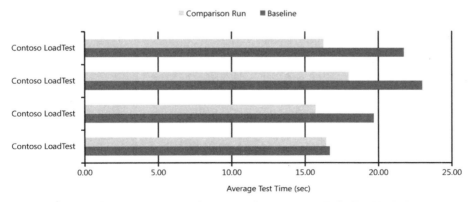

Top Performance Improvements

Scenario	Test Case	Baseline	Comparison Run	% Change from Baseline
Extreme Users	Contoso LoadTest	16.69	16.44	1%
Heavy Users	Contoso LoadTest	19.69	15.70	20%
Light Users	Contoso LoadTest	22.99	18.00	22%
Typical Users	Contoso LoadTest	21.73	16.25	25%

FIGURE 11-66 The automated comparison page generated by Excel.

Finally!

You have documented the issues found within the Contoso environment, you have created the performance tests, and you have executed the load tests. You have fixed the outstanding issues and were able to document the effect that your changes had on the Contoso environment. You have successfully met all the requirements that Contoso put upon you as a consultant. (The next step would be to convince your boss to purchase you a copy of Visual Studio 2012 Ultimate.)

Index

Symbols

$ (dollar sign) symbol, assigning objects to PowerShell
    variable using, 51
_app_bin folder, 21
| (pipe) symbol, piping output object to cmdlet, 51–52
_vti_pvt folder, 21

A

AAM (Alternate Access Mappings)
    path-based site collections utilizing, 10
    zones and, 198
Access
    adding databases to SharePoint, 100–101
    backward compatibility of imported databases, 105
    supported databases for, 248
Access Services web service application, 100–101, 105,
        144
ACS (Azure Access Control Service)
    authorization server for cloud-hosted apps, 191–193
    for SharePoint Online, 83
    SSS and, 202
Active Directory Federation Services (ADFS)
        2.0, configuring SAML token-based
        authentication environments using, 186
Add-PSSnapin Microsoft.Share-Point.PowerShell
        cmdlet, 52
AD DS (Active Directory Domain Services)
    Claims mode option allowing for implementation
        of, 198
    password management and, 238
    Windows authentication and, 184–185
Add-SPDiagnosticsPerformanceCounter cmdlet, 310
Add-SPServiceApplicationProxyGroupMember
        cmdlet, 94
Add-SPShellAdmin cmdlet, 43

ADFS (Active Directory Federation Services)
        2.0, configuring SAML token-based
        authentication environments using, 186
ADMIN folder, 23
administrator
    farm
        configuring anonymous policies, 206
        configuring user policies across zones, 204
        picking objects for web application
            policies, 206–207
    site collection
        granting user rights, 13–14
        HTML field security, 15
        picking objects for web application policies, 206
        recycle bin, 349
        search features for, 13
admin.sitemap file, 21
ADMISAPI folder, 22
aliases, SQL Server, 133–137
"All users, All hosts" profile type, creating Windows
        PowerShell ISE, 47
"All users, Windows PowerShell ISE" profile type,
        creating Windows PowerShell ISE, 47
Alternate Access Mappings (AAM)
    path-based site collections utilizing, 10
    zones and, 198
AlwaysOn Availability
    protecting databases using, 363–367
    using SQL Server aliases in configurations, 367
AlwaysOn Availability Groups
    about, 128
    SQL Server support for, 126
AlwaysOn Failover Cluster Instances
    about, 128
    SQL Server support for, 126
analytics processing component, of Search service
        application, 109

Y

Z

About the authors

SHANNON BRAY, MCM, MCT, MCSD, MCSE, MCDBA, MCITP, MCPD, is a Microsoft Certified Solution Master (MCSM) for Microsoft SharePoint. Shannon has been working with the SharePoint platform since 2006 and has presented SharePoint topics at Microsoft's TechED, TechReady, and SharePoint Conference. Professionally, Shannon serves his company as the chief SharePoint architect and has vast experience in both the infrastructure and development sides of the product. This is Shannon's second book; he coauthored *Automating SharePoint 2010 Administration with Windows PowerShell 2.0*. You can reach Shannon on Twitter: @noidentity29. Shannon is a former military diver, and when he is not working with SharePoint, he enjoys diving off the coast of North Carolina and exploring shipwrecks.

PATRICK CURRAN, MCT, MCTS, MCP, MCITP, MCPD, MCSA, is currently the director for the Federal Group at Planet Technologies, where he is also a senior SharePoint architect. Patrick has been working with SharePoint since 2003, doing everything from administration, branding, and development to upgrading and troubleshooting. Patrick works with clients from all over the world and has been designing and deploying farms of varying complexity over the years, especially within the Federal realm, where nothing is small or simple. Patrick has spoken at SharePoint Saturday events all over the country, and he can be reached through Twitter: @PCfromDC. Patrick still enjoys getting out onto the football (soccer) pitch and kicking the ball around with the wee-ones when possible.

MIGUEL WOOD, MCM, MCT, MCITP, MCPD, MCSE, MCSD, MCCDBA, is an MCSM for SharePoint and currently fills the roles of director, Central Region, and chief architect for Planet Technologies. Prior to his current roles, he served as president and CEO of TekFocus, a worldwide provider of specialized Microsoft training and services. With his technical and business experience, he provides enterprise expertise to clients of all sizes. Miguel is an active presenter, delivering keynotes to technical sessions at many Microsoft technology conferences, covering SharePoint, SQL, ASP.NET, and other topics. Miguel currently resides in Dallas, Texas, with his wife and two sons. Miguel is a U.S. Army Airborne Infantry veteran, studied electrical and computer engineering at LSU, and enjoys singing with live rock bands when not working or learning new technologies. Miguel can be reached on Twitter, @miguelwood, and other social media sites, including Facebook and LinkedIn.

Now that you've read the book...

Tell us what you think!

Was it useful?
Did it teach you what you wanted to learn?
Was there room for improvement?

Let us know at http://aka.ms/tellpress

Your feedback goes directly to the staff at Microsoft Press,
and we read every one of your responses. Thanks in advance!

 Microsoft